Dress in the Age of Jane Austen

Regency Fashion

Hilary Davidson

Yale University Press, New Haven and London

Hilary Davidson is a dress and textile historian and curator based between Britain and Australia, where she is an honorary associate at the University of Sydney. She has lectured, broadcast and published extensively across her field.

First published by Yale University Press 2019
302 Temple Street, P.O. Box 209040, New Haven CT
06520-9040
47 Bedford Square, London WC1B 3DP
yalebooks.com / yalebooks.co.uk

ISBN 978-0-300-218725 HB
Library of Congress Control Number: 2019939614

10 9 8 7 6 5 4 3 2 1
2023 2022 2021 2020 2019

Designer: Mitchell Onuorah
Copyeditor: Rosemary Roberts

Printed in Italy

Front cover: William Blake, Mrs. Q. (Mrs Harriet Quentin), 1820, coloured engraving on paper, after a portrait by François Huet Villiers, 1812. This is thought to be the portrait Austen described as: 'Mrs Bingley . . . is exactly herself – size, shaped face, features, & sweetness; there never was a greater likeness...' (Letter 85, 24 May 1813). National Gallery of Art, Washington, DC.

Spine: Unknown artist, 'Morning Walking Dresses', *Bell's New Weekly Magazine*, January 1807, hand coloured engraving on paper. Victoria and Albert Museum, London.

Back cover: J. Berryman, 'The Five Positions of Dancing', from Thomas Wilson, *An Analysis of Country Dancing* (1811), coloured engraving on paper. British Library, London.

Endpapers: Henry William Bunbury and William Heath, *Lumps of Pudding*, 1811, hand-coloured etching on paper. A delightful evocation of the effect of Regency fashions as worn on a range of different body types. The caricature figures are performing a country dance with enthusiasm, if not elegance. Lewis Walpole Library, Farmington, Conn.

Published with assistance from the Annie Burr Lewis Fund

To B. K. and A. L. C. Davidson
History is a child of arts and analysis.

Acknowledgements

First thanks go to Aileen Ribeiro, whose remark, one snowy day at Chawton House, that there was no good book on Regency dress and she thought I could write one got me thinking. The ground had been prepared years earlier by the opportunity Alison Carter Tai gave me to reconstruct Jane Austen's pelisse, when she was Senior Keeper of Art and Design at Hampshire County Museum Service and Archives. Alison's expertise, encouragement and intellectual generosity have continued to be invaluable. This interest in the dress culture of Austen's time and place sparked while I was living in her Hampshire heartland was the start of it all. The county's resources have naturally featured heavily in the research. Mary Guyatt and the staff and trustees of Jane Austen's House Museum have been sterling in their support. A Fellowship at Chawton House (then Library) provided foundational research. My thanks to Gillian Dow, Darren Bevin, Sarah Parry, and fellow fellows Leigh Wetherall Dickson, Marybeth Ihle and Yi-cheng Weng for their conversation and company. Hampshire Record Office provided further archival riches.

Further afield, the inaugural V&A/Pasold Research Fellowship from the Pasold Research Fund supported vital time exploring the dress and print collections of the Victoria and Albert Museum. Special thanks go to Susan North, Suzanne Smith, Jenny Lister, Sarah Westbury and Susanna Cordner at the Clothworkers' Centre for their kindness and collegiality. Sincere thanks to Elaine Uttley, Fleur Johnson, and Rosemary Harden at the Fashion Museum, Bath, for access to their wonderful collections and resources; as well as to Roger Leong at the Powerhouse Museum (MAAS), Sydney; the Kent History and Library Centre, Maidstone; Sarah Whale and the staff of Hatfield House, Hertfordshire; and the Medieval and Early Modern Centre at the University of Sydney. At the Museum of London, fond gratitude to Beatrice Behlen for allowing me to revisit the collections and bring more to publication; and thanks also to Sean Waterman, John Chase and Emily Austin for their assistance with images. At Yale University Press, Gillian Malpass's initial encouragement began the book on its journey. Mark Eastment and Sophie Neve have been an incredibly patient editorial team, while the marvellous Anjali Bulley, with Mitchell Onuorah and Clare Davis, worked visual miracles with humour and style. Rosemary Roberts's copyediting improved this book with tact, grace and an eagle eye.

The ideas have been honed, developed and challenged by conversations with Gina Barrett, Jenny Batchelor, Charles Bazalgette, Sarah Bendall, Stephanie Bishop, Clare Brown, Barbara Burman, Paula Byrne, Kimberly Chrisman-Campbell, Valerie Cummings, Christine Davies, Alice Dolan, Serena Dyer, Edwina Ehrman, Rebecca

Evans, Catriona Fisk, Caroline Hamilton, Laura Jocic, Alexandra Kim, Sheila Kindred, Katharine Kittredge, Beverly Lemire, Deirdre Lynch, Lorna Mackenzie, Jane Malcolm-Davies, Kylie Mirmohamadi, Alden O'Brien, Sandra Leigh Price, Rebecca Quinton, Amelia Rauser, Joan Ray, Harriette Richards, Margot Riley, Emily Rosenberg, Laura Rubin, Mary Schoeser, Elizabeth Semmelhack, Colin Sewell-Rutter, Chloe Wigston Smith, Kay Staniland, John Styles, Kathryn Sutherland, Jenny Tiramani, Sally Tuckett, Amanda Vickery, Susan Vincent, Lindie Ward, Kylie Winkworth, and Janet Wood, as well as my students, members of audiences and seminars, and the online Twitter community. My thanks to all. Deirdre Le Faye has been particularly generous with her references and expertise. Alison Matthews David is a sterling cheerleader, as a friend and colleague. Unfailingly incisive of mind and compassionate of heart, our brief encounters worldwide provide intellectual and emotional sustenance. Lesley Miller has nurtured and encouraged my research endeavours from the start, always accompanied by wise advice.

Support has come in innumerable ways – large and small, soulful and practical – from Kelsey Adams, Meg Andrews, Suzanne Chee, Penelope Crook, Paola Di Trocchio, Laurel Fox, Tony Harris, David Hunt, Colin Klein, Louis Levallier, Helene and Ted Markstein, Peter McNeil, Daniel Milford-Cottam, Timothy Murray, Fiona Reilly, Katie Somerville, Matthew Wallman, Corey Watts, Evelyn Welch, and generous private owners of objects. Family and friends who kindly opened their homes made it possible to write in many corners of the world. From London to Lyme Regis; Bondi, Bali and Bath; New South Wales and New York, I thank Sarah Allely and Miles Merrill; Cressida and Nathan Barron; the Bate family; Lucy Coles and Rhett Hill; Louey Hart; Anna Hodson and Adam Stofsky; Mary Maddocks, Archie Maddocks and Sophia Charalambous; Dalia Nassar and Luke Fischer; Sue and John Rado; Irene Rado-Vajda, Arlen Harris, and Daniyal Harris-Vajda; The Daniel Reece; Emelia Simcox and Russell Carey; Natalia and Simon Zagorscy-Thomas.

Especial thanks to Michelle Starr and Christian Read; and James Petersen and Donyale Harrison, who also loaned her professional eye with good cheer. I am deeply grateful to Emma Zappia for keeping me physically able to write; to Neil Swanson, for helping me avoid writing's lee shores; and Jakob Ziguras, for unflagging encouragement in the beginning (and the Jane Austen Action Figure). Like true Mr Darcys, Annunziata Asquith and Adam Batenin gave vital help during a crisis when the book could have vanished. Melanie Seymour and Sandra Clarke both sprinkled their own kind of fairy-godmother dust on the project. Equally magical was the help of Elizabeth Seymour and April McNee as diligent, wise and gracious research assistants.

Finally, love and thanks to Gilmore Davidson, Mek Zwart and Connor Davidson (not least for dubbing George III 'King Wackypants'); my father Lennox, who I wish could have read this, and, most importantly, my mother Barbara, who gave me a foundation of language, literature, ideas, history and love.

Notes for the Reader

In quoting from and citing Jane Austen's correspondence, I have used the fourth edition of *Jane Austen's Letters*, Deirdre Le Faye (ed.) (Oxford: Oxford University Press, 2011); all letter numbers and page references relate to this edition.

The editions of the novels referred to in the notes are those cited in the bibliography. In the case of the finished novels, the title (usually abbreviated) is followed by book, chapter and page numbers. In the case of juvenilia and unfinished works, the title is followed by a reference to the edition and a page number. For the abbreviations used in references to Austen's works, see the list at the head of the section 'Primary Sources and Editions' in the Bibliography (p. 308)

In transcriptions from manuscript and published works, long 's' has been converted to the modern short 's'.

Dimensions are given in imperial measure followed, where appropriate, by a metric equivalent in parentheses. For more general purposes: 1 inch = 2.54 cm and 1 yard (3 feet) = 91.44 cm.

The prices of British goods are expressed in pounds, shillings and pence (indicated by the abbreviations £, *s.* and *d.*). In that currency, there were 20*s.* to £1, and 12*d.* to 1*s.*; £1 was therefore worth 240*d.* A guinea was £1 1*s.*, or 252*d.* As an approximate indication of values during the Regency period, the average annual income for an English labourer in 1800 was around £15–20. £20 was a year's salary for a butler, exclusive of food, board and some clothing. In 1800, 21 per cent of families in England and Wales had an annual income over £100; 7 per cent had an income over £200; and those enjoying an income of £1,000 or more per annum comprised only 1.25 per cent of the population – about 28,000 families. Income over £150 per annum put a family roughly in the top 10 per cent of earners.[1]

In connection with chapter 7, it is important to note that I use the name 'East Indies' in the sense that was current during the Regency period. At the turn of the eighteenth to the nineteenth centuries, the 'East Indies' referred to the wide territory stretching from the Indian subcontinent, through south-East Asia and the islands to the south, as far as China.

The illustrations and descriptions in 'Changes in the Construction of Women's Gowns' are intended as a general guide only.

Introduction

A history of the ladies' dresses in England, for merely half a dozen years, would furnish matter for a bulky volume.[1]

'One likes to hear what is going on, to be au fait as to the newest modes of being trifling and silly[.]'[2]

'Civility', 'fancying', 'imprudence'. Jane Austen used these three words more in her writing than any other author.[3] They epitomise dress in the age when Austen lived and worked. A rising middle class sought ever greater *civility*, they consumed new *fancies* from other lands and times and manufacture that influenced fashions; and accusations of *imprudence* were flung against wealthy style leaders and their unsuccessful imitators.

Austen (16 December 1775–18 July 1817) is one of the world's most influential, studied and beloved authors. Her works are synonymous with the fashions of the 'Regency' period, awash with high waists, heaving bosoms and cutaway coats. Yet, what did people who lived during the times and places Austen knew really wear? She is foremost a social commentator, and dress is a nuanced social marker, so clothing and needlework pinpoint niceties of character in her novels. Austen's letters reveal a lively sartorial interest, beside concerns about how to dress well on a limited income. During the author's short life, unprecedented and accelerated change saw Britain's turbulent entry into the modern age. Clothing reflected these transitions. Over a period of twenty years, fashion moved from ornamented width to minimal, streamlined 'naturalism', then widened again with the advent of Romanticism. How did these changes correspond to national and global events? To what extent does the microcosm of dress in Austen's defined, middling-gentry world reflect larger concerns and trends? How did her contemporaries obtain clothing? What systems of local and commercial fashion exchange existed and how did technological progress affect those networks? How did fashion incorporate the burgeoning availability of consumer goods? This book attempts to paint a realistic picture of dress in Austen's era by addressing these questions.

❋ ❋

Throughout, the lodestone of the discussions is the references to dress and textiles in Austen's six completed novels and other fictional and epistolary writings, and what is known of her life and family. If Austen is how many people first encounter Regency fashion, she provides an excellent approach to understanding it, and 'for us to visualise Austen characters in all their qualities, we need to look at the clothing proper to them to be consistent with her precision'.[4] I approach Austen not as the monumental, singular author, but as an exceptionally observant woman, who was part of the best-biographised, non-elite, late Georgian family. What has emerged repeatedly is just how typical the Austens were as middle-class consumers. Their methods of acquiring, wearing and maintaining dress fall within the general patterns of their status and income. Austen's fictional spheres are modelled closely on her observations from this pattern of life. The family, with Jane at the centre, is both the point of origin for examination and the exemplar of wider phenomena. Her 'sharp, uncompromising gaze' is as accurate, wry and humorous when turned to clothing as it is on all other subjects. The textures of life, depicted fictionally with reticence, are more specific and unconstrained in her surviving letters, 'when Austen, like other women letter writers, is able to lose the "countenance" . . . she is expected to wear in public'.[5] These slippages let us into a more private world, where trivial domestic details that early editors dismissed are valuable records of dress practices. As in Austen's fiction, close study of the particular can reveal the universal world of clothing.

What prompted this book was its absence when I sought a single-volume survey of Regency dress. Besides fulfilling my selfish desire as a reader, the book's purpose is twofold. One is to provide others interested in Jane Austen's life and times with an understanding of dress as she, her acquaintance and her fictional characters would have understood it. The second is to create an introductory scholarly volume on Regency dress, to be built on, argued with, disagreed with, or used as a bibliographic guide by other scholars (some readers may be here only for the pictures, and you too are welcome). My aim is to synthesise current scholarship, adding a strong material understanding of the historical garments people wore, how they were produced and how they can be interpreted. Larger theoretical concerns are blended with an unfolding of aesthetic modes, and a survey of fashion, clothing and textile cultures interwoven with broader political, cultural and technological transformations.

History and Fiction

The early nineteenth century in Britain can be slippery to characterise. The eighteenth century springs into being in history books with robust Enlightenment vigour. After the Revolutionary period, 1775–93, the Western world changed. How do we define the particularity of this time, where the end of the 'long' eighteenth century blurs into the beginning of the 'long' nineteenth century? Regency people are Georgians, but are they also proto-Victorians? Might they be Romantics or Classicists? The temporal definition remains the Prince of Wales's Regency, 1811–20, which coincides with Austen's publication period of 1811–17. The Regency is a

✵ ✺   *Dress in the Age of Jane Austen*

flexible concept, a summary of the early nineteenth century sometimes starting at the French Revolution, sometimes finishing at Victoria's accession in 1837 – a transitional period that redefined clothing norms and shaped the nineteenth-century world. For clothing I define my 'long Regency' as 1795 to c.1825 – from when waistlines began to rise until soon after the Regent became George IV. Henceforth, 'Regency' refers to this rough quarter century unless otherwise specified.

The Regency is defined by strong clothing narratives. The French embraced Anglomania, waistlines rose and dresses turned white and flimsy, ornamented with fripperies borrowed from other times and cultures. Women's heads retreated into bonnets; their bosoms were newly defined and uplifted. Men transformed Classicism into a focus on the athletic body. Their muscular thighs sprang into pale, defined relief by contrast with their broad, wool-clad shoulders. Disrupted from the Continent by war and blockade, British fashion embraced French style, after Napoleon's final defeat in 1815, to succumb to a new tide of romantic influence, before George III obligingly departed and turned the Prince of Wales into George IV. Several long-lasting, major clothing changes emerged. Trousers replaced knee-breeches in the male wardrobe. Women's stays retreated into underwear, never seen again in respectable society. Front-opening gowns, established for a century, became back-opening gowns. Cotton overtook linen as the plain fabric of choice. Embellished display disappeared from male dress, replaced by sombre surfaces emphasising the lines of good tailoring. British-manufactured textiles finally started surpassing desirable imported Asian cloths, such as muslin, and made cheaper dress accessories more readily available to ordinary consumers.

Like many fashion histories, this work emphasises the clothing of the middling and upper classes, 'partly because the dress of the middle classes reflects one of the most influential elements of British society at the time', but also because Jane Austen's life and works sit so neatly there.[6] Upper-echelon clothing has received a disproportionate amount of attention as the Regency's aesthetic bastion and aspirational destination, although recent scholarship on dress of the lower sorts is changing this. While my discussion ranges from court to courtyard, its attention is closest at the genteel centre, the middling sorts and upper gentry, who owned land or were engaged in professional trades. It also concerns the people who lived and worked with them, the aristocracy they looked up to, and the labourers supporting their lifestyles. Austen gives us an excellent entrée into the complexity and social implications of gentry clothing systems of her time.

An 1824 review praised Austen's skill in envisioning 'the inmates of the cottage, the farm-house, the manse, the mansion-house, and the castle [and] my lady's saloon too', 'sketches of that sober, orderly, small-town parsonage, sort of society in which she herself had spent her life'.[7] She was born the seventh child and second daughter of Cassandra Austen (née Leigh, 1739–1827) in the parsonage at Steventon, Hampshire, in 1775, where her father, the Reverend George Austen (1731–1805), had the living. Her brothers were James (1765–1819), George (1766–1838), Edward (1767–1852), Henry (1771–1850), Francis ('Frank', 1774–1865), and Charles, who followed her (1779–1852).

Jane was devoted to her older sister Cassandra (1773–1845) from childhood, and the pair were unusually close, especially after Cassandra's fiancé died in 1797. Neither ever married. From her early teens, Austen entertained her literate, lively family with hilarious short fiction and boisterous histories, now collected as the *Juvenilia* (1787–93). She began drafts of some of her later published novels in the late 1790s.

In 1800 George Austen retired and moved his womenfolk to Bath, where they lived until his unexpected death in 1805. Austen began *The Watsons* there c.1804 but never completed it. Mrs Austen and the girls moved around, living in rented accommodation and then with Frank's family in Southampton until, in 1809, Edward – who had been adopted by wealthy childless cousins and took their surname Knight in 1812 – offered his relatives Chawton Cottage, part of his Hampshire estate. Austen lived the rest of her life there until her death from a long (and unidentified) illness in July 1817, aged 41. Four novels were published (anonymously) in her lifetime: *Sense and Sensibility* (1811), *Pride and Prejudice* (1813), *Mansfield Park* (1814) and *Emma* (1815). *Persuasion* was published posthumously in 1817, in a set with a revised version of her first completed novel, now called *Northanger Abbey*, and a note revealing her authorship.[8] Austen drafted the incomplete manuscript now called *Sanditon* before her death. Of the estimated 3,000 letters she wrote in her lifetime, 161 survive, mostly to Cassandra,[9] plus miscellaneous poems, plans and incidental writings.

The family was never wealthy. The Revd Austen did not save much of his annual income of about £600, and after his death the women relied on small inheritances and financial support from the brothers to survive, meaning that the sisters were always careful about money, and small sums mattered. Earnings from her writing eased Austen's worries somewhat – notably £140 from *Sense and Sensibility* – and totalled £684 13*s.* in her lifetime. She invested much of this to bring her an additional £30 per year. Being of genteel birth, Austen had social constraints on her money, such as charity and paying for letters received. Her budget for 1807 shows that, of her £50 15*s.* 6*d.* for the year, more than £4, or roughly a month's income, was spent on parcels and letters, though the principal expense was £13 19*s.* 3*d.* for 'Cloathes & Pocket', vital to maintaining the appearance of her gentility.[10] Of her actual dress, the only known survivals are a pelisse (fig. 1.15), a shawl (fig. 7.22), a topaz cross, a turquoise ring and a turquoise bracelet.[11]

In person, Austen was tall and slender to the point of thinness, with naturally curling brown hair, round pink cheeks and bright eyes. Written references to her appearance have a range of opinions about her attractiveness, but she appears not to have been thought plain. Cassandra painted the only two securely identified portraits of the author: a full-face watercolour the family did not consider a good likeness (fig. 0.1) and a full-length back view of her sitting outside (fig. 0.2). Other contenders for images of Austen are the Rice portrait in oils on canvas, the Byrne portrait by an anonymous artist (fig. 0.3),[12] the watercolour from the album of the Revd James Stanier Clarke (fig. 0.4), and a black paper silhouette. Discussion around these pictures is extensive and often contested.[13]

The traditional critiques applied to Austen's writing have been that she ignores big history, meaning the charged political situations and theatres of war unfolding all over Europe, summarised by the complaint that 'At the height of political and industrial revolution, Miss Austen composes novels almost extra-territorial to history', although scholars regularly challenge this view.[14] A twenty-first-century critic asserts that Austen 'keeps historical reference to a bare minimum', yet writes two sentences earlier about her descriptions of 'volatile social formation as the English landed gentry of the early nineteenth century interlocked with an acquisitive high bourgeois society' – history references equally important to the emergent nineteenth century and its dress.[15]

Ironically in an age of growing material consumerism, Austen's fictional references to dress generally decline as her publications advance. *The Watsons* (1804–5) and *Northanger Abbey* (1803) are replete with minutiae of clothing, and discussions of it – a 'striking preoccupation with the world of goods', where later she 'learns to pinpoint her characters' possessions more exactly'.[16] Conversely, the fewer details attract greater significance as Austen's skills improve. When the author mentions an article of clothing or a piece of textile, the reader must pay close attention, as it tells us something about the action or character, helping us to understand her works by exploring the cultural code underlying such specificity.[17] Behind the scenes in the letters, however, Austen despaired of and delighted in the niceties of getting and wearing dress as much as the next person.

Dress in fiction relies on readers' shared experience of normality, and understanding of social and sartorial conventions. The design of garments, and how they look when worn, is nearly always missing from the '"literary mirror" when held up to nature; it is a pre-existing image assumed by the author to be familiar to the reader'.[18] Therefore, if the text is scrupulously realised, as with Austen, fiction can become a medium for reconstructing clothing. While there is a caution in using fiction as evidence for historical research, Austen is a particularly alert historical writer. Indeed: 'Austen as an historian of her time . . . [is] an important but frequently overlooked feature of her practice as a novelist.' The same writer continues:

> the novelist's status as an historical agent is ultimately indivisible from the history in her writing . . . Partly in consequence of the extended interval during which . . . Austen's narratives gradually became history, reality and temporality are admixed so that Austen's status as an historian of the everyday turns out to be an unusually precise description of her achievement.[19]

Austen's contemporary readers recognised this. During her life and immediately afterwards, the reality of her created worlds impressed others who had lived through the same time. 'Most Novellists fail & betray themselves in attempting to describe familiar scenes in high Life . . . here it is quite different. Everything is natural, & the situations & incidents are told in a manner which clearly evinces the Writer to belong to the Society whose manners she so ably delineates', wrote one Austen acquaintance about *Mansfield Park*.[20] In the year after the novelist's death, an unknown critic wrote that

> Her characters, her incidents, her sentiments are obviously all drawn exclusively from experience . . . she seems to have no other object in view, than simply to paint some of the scenes which she has herself seen, and which every one, indeed, may witness daily . . . She seems to be describing such people as meet together every night, in every respectable house in London . . . Her merit consists altogether in her remarkable talent for observation. . . in recording the customs and manners of commonplace people in the commonplace intercourse of life.[21]

Fig. 0.3

Unknown artist, *Miss Jane Austin*, 1814–16, pencil and ink on vellum. The sitter wears a white-worked muslin morning gown with long sleeves and a lace frill around the low neck. A high-collared habit-shirt underneath reaches the ties of the decorative satin cap at the chin. A shawl is draped over the right arm. Private collection.

People who read Austen and knew the times she wrote in considered her true to life, natural, accurate and observant – an excellent ground for studying 'commonplace', albeit respectable, dress of her time.

Juliette Wells emphasises that the more nearly people's important qualities in representational fiction approach the universal, the better the fiction is judged to be, so clothing, their historically determined appearance, is less relevant.[22] But clothing, perceived by its wearers and observers as part of characters' identity, creates half the physical self.[23] In fiction as in life, 'the dressed body is a fleshy, phenomenological entity that is so much a part of our experience of the social world, so thoroughly embedded within the micro-dynamics of social order, as to be entirely taken for granted'.[24] Presenting how and why people took what for granted in their clothing is the work of dress history, especially as historical bodies are so bound up in our perceptions of their dressed bodies. How Austen's contemporaries saw people wearing clothes is not

Fig. 0.4

James Stanier Clarke, portrait of a woman, identified as Jane Austen (R. J. Wheeler, 1998), 1810s, watercolour on paper. The subject of the portrait wears a very stylish ensemble, comprising a carnation- or coquelicot-coloured silk tippet, edged with deep falls of black lace. The matching black velvet cap is festooned with ribbons and ostrich feathers, and the woman holds a fur muff. Private collection.

the same as how we see them retrospectively. To the Regency observer in London's streets a Frenchman stood out immediately, as did an English miss strolling in the Tuileries to Parisians. The dandy seeking perfect fit found it in a tighter jacket than any gentleman now would tolerate, while visible shoulder blades and upper arms could constitute scandalous female nakedness. Throughout, I have sought what was 'entirely taken for granted' in dress during Austen's lifetime and re-read her writings in the context of how she and her audience would have understood the clothed Regency body.

Observations of 'the long and continuing battles for the posthumous body of Jane Austen', played out among her biographers, 'continually being torn into parts and put back together again', are apt for this work.[25] If 'whatever had most to do with [Austen's] bodily life is hardest to track down', then the clothing of her age's various imaginary and real bodies has not been paid enough attention in its own context. Even before the spate of 1990s screen adaptations, a 1970 article regretted that 'For the public at large, and even . . . for some serious historians . . . the past seems to remain a Never-Never Land in which . . . the heroines of even Jane Austen's novels are scantily draped in damped muslin.'[26] I question such Regency dress mythologies wherever possible.

The 'heritage' Austen relies on presenting Regency fashions as part of the display of period objects authenticating the narrative space.[27] This book is *Dress in the Age of Jane Austen* because I recognise that in popular culture 'Regency England becomes a timeless, mythological place called Austenshire', dominated by the flickering light of cinema bedazzling audiences with all its 'bonnets and carriages and parks and starched pinnies, and Colin Firth and Alan Rickman striding about in ruffled shirts and shiny boots'.[28] The modern bodies of actresses portraying Austen heroines 'evoke, through carriage, gestures and attitude, a late twentieth-century Western female corporeality' enacting 'history as the present in costume' and an assertive physicality appealing to modern viewers.[29] No actor will ever wear his tight jacket and breeches with the unthinking ease of the Regency gentleman, who knew no other clothed experience. The weather requirements of filming costume dramas bias screen audiences towards an endless-summer view of Regency dress, according well with muslins and parasols. 'In any search for Jane Austen,' as Emily Auerbach cautions, 'we must break free of dear Aunt Jane . . . We must strip off those ruffles and ringlets added to her portrait, restore the deleted fleas and bad breath to her letters, and meet Jane Austen's sharp, uncompromising gaze head on.'[30] In dress terms the 'ruffles and ringlets' are the fashion-plate, screen idealisations of Regency dress, and the 'fleas and bad breath' are prosaic flannel underwear, stockings darned into lumps, and muddy, manure-coated streets. However, filmed Austen can suggest the lived effect of clothes in her lifetime, 'of interest . . . as objects of desire in their own right'.[31] If readers, re-enactors, curators, collectors, writers and designers now desire Regency clothing, the screen has shaped their vision.[32] This book takes its approach between these polarities of history and heritage.

Structure

The structure moves away from straight chronology and reflects instead Britain's social spheres as Austen would have experienced them. I focus most on England, but consider the British Isles and the British nation in the wider world, to create maps of Regency 'clothing communities', which can be understood as 'a group of friends or family, a village, a village in relation to an urban centre, a geographical region, a main road . . . positioned within their locality, and within a wider ideological and social context'.[33] I take my cue from Austen for subjects and discussions covering a surprisingly large area, from the midst of 'rural' Hampshire to New South Wales. Like many histories of clothing, the book therefore leans towards the feminine sphere – Austen's realm of knowledge and one through which her male relatives and characters are seen.

The seven chapters move from the most inward to the furthest geographical reaches of the experience of Regency dress, in concentric circles. Each expands a little further from the experience of 'Self' (chapter 1), the physical and imaginary Regency body, and the role of fashion. The next chapter, 'Home', concerns dress in the domestic spheres. The third social area – 'Village' – is where the shared experience of dress between friends, neighbours and local communities occurred. Chapter 4, 'Country', travels outwards to the populous countryside, where most people still lived, and considers how rural life and cross-country transportation contributed to dress. By contrast with provincial areas, the 'City' (chapter 5) and other urban centres were important to constructing fashioned public images. 'Nation' then considers the larger relationships of British dress with its neighbours, including the effect on dress of years of continental wars. The final chapter, 'World', locates Regency dress within its global contexts and complicated cultural trade networks, with surprising connections back to Austen. Even her modest local sphere was connected to global dress production, consumption and practices. Although she never left England, the experience of Austen's extended family and the currents of influence among the dressed world in which she moved shape broader discussions. Her attitudes to global events are not necessarily pertinent; what is relevant here is how the same 'true Indian muslin' could and did grace British women in Antigua, London, Calcutta and Sydney simultaneously.

Many areas of clothing are not addressed owing to lack of space. Academic, judicial and legal dress are specialised clothing, less respondent to fashionable change.[34] Ceremonial dress is confined to clothing worn for court presentations, not for events such as coronations.[35] Uniforms worn in charity and public schools, and clothing of religious orders are likewise excluded. Dress of the poor has a new, recent bibliography,[36] and children's dress is beginning to be covered in other publications, though still needing more detailed scholarship; neither is covered here. Masquerade and fancy dress is a subject ranging across too many non-quotidian times and places to explore. Jewellery, spectacles, watches, canes and other Regency accessories are considered only in relation to ensembles.

I touch on the greater social ramifications of social, political and economic changes across the turn of the nineteenth century where they affect discussion of clothing. There is a significantly greater literature on these subjects than on dress, easy for interested readers to access. Many recent works on clothing and textile history address these bigger pictures in micro-studies of external factors that influenced consumers. As Austen's writing is the focus here, attention to her work and milieu stands in place of other histories, and I ask the reader's indulgence for any gaps. I have mined the wider Austen family where possible to look at clothing as they experienced it; in this area I am grateful to previous Austen scholars, especially Deirdre Le Faye, whose dedicated archival study has created a strong foundation for family research.

I have tried to keep to the period usage of terms for discussing the items of apparel people wore, and the practices of adorning and altering the body. In Regency parlance, 'fashion' means the current style, the modish manner of being (chapter 1). 'Dress' or 'dresses' generally refers to the ensemble of male or female clothing, the entire effect, not individual female main garments, which are called 'gowns'. It also means the state of full dress, formal clothing for evenings. 'Costume' I avoid as a term, except where it appears in a contemporary text, as it is used in current scholarship for performance wear.

The subject is dress in the British Regency world; other cultures are considered only in relation to the central theme (the relationship between North American and British dress is beyond this book's scope, and has its own scholarship). Where there is published research only from non-British sources, I use this wider knowledge. In some ways, the research has been easy, as few authors are more written about than Austen. But wading through the vigorous and ever growing bibliography is quite an undertaking, as the clothing of her lifetime touches obliquely on every conceivable area of life and study. Being a twenty-first-century historian has meant keeping abreast of prolific new digital resources, giving access to otherwise inaccessible sources, while becoming anxious about sources untapped. Proof of the centrality of dress is its appearance everywhere in the archives, when least expected.

Among the flood of Austen publications, it is curious that Regency clothing has not yet had a dedicated academic monograph. One of the difficulties when writing about the period is that it straddles a change of century. Key dress histories present excellent Regency-era research as part of wider narratives on the long eighteenth century or fashion's development.[37] Others study one aspect of the period closely, or lose continuity across the 1799/1800 divide through century-specific models.[38] All this information is difficult for researchers seeking Regency-specific dress to extract from larger works, although a number of good shorter books exist on the subject.[39] The earliest of these, and a volume to which I am indebted, is Penelope Byrde's *A Frivolous Distinction: Fashion and Needlework in the Works of Jane Austen*, for many years the only work centralising Austen and dress.[40] Short articles in magazines and journals, and book chapters investigate a variety of aspects of dress and textiles in Austen's work. Muslins, fashion and shopping are popular topics, along with needlework.[41] Publications from museum exhibitions offer good illustrated information.[42]

Looking at Austen's object-strewn world from other disciplines offers some broader perspectives. Georgian and Austen studies often consider dress in passing, and new approaches in Austen biography and exhibition show the insights that material-culture-inclusive research creates.[43] Issues around bodies and embodiment in Austen's writing generate a more theoretical standpoint.[44] The previous lack of a single volume on Regency dress is, I hope, remedied here, providing a resource for readers of these secondary texts, and of the vast biographical and critical literature on Austen.

Materiality

Fashion is always about bodies – is produced, promoted and worn by bodies – and the body must be dressed in almost all social encounters. If fashion concerns the imaginary body, an ideal to be aspired to, dress balances clothing and adornment on the lived, experiential body. Dress in the age of Jane Austen also overlaps and interconnects with many different spheres; from relaxing at home to visiting friends, dressing for dinner, walking in damp fields, sea-bathing, watching royalty in St James, staving off heat in Bermuda, or serving on military campaign on the Continent. This book embraces the overlaps by looking at how clothing in everyday life for Austen's network acted upon their bodies, real and social, and how fashion is inextricable from its production, distribution and consumption.

Dress was, for Jane Austen, her family, her milieu and by extension her fictional characters, a negotiation based upon personal networks of taste and consumption possibilities, and it is in the eighteenth century that 'the consumer' appears for the first time as a social character. Consumption studies have made an impact upon dress histories, and underlie my research. I use these data where I can, though restricted by limited space for in-depth discussion. What people consumed came to communicate their identity, furthering the argument that 'fashion should never be decontextualised from the wider web of actions, choices, consumer behaviours and relationships in which individuals are enmeshed'.[45] To aspire was to buy, trade, make and imitate in new ways, with increasingly cheap goods sold in more complex distribution networks. The world of spending on novel and exotic paraphernalia became accessible to a new range of potential buyers during the consumer revolution of the long eighteenth century, when people, no longer content with using the same old things until they fell apart, increasingly aimed at 'the latest fashion' or something 'fashionable'.[46] More and more, dress could be replaced or updated before it wore out to reflect changes in desirable details.

Austen lived in a world increasingly reliant on its material things as markers of social connection. An object in her text has a keen relationship with a material object; this physical world of things is an essential part of my study. Although traditional history has seen a 'material turn' in the last decade or so, it is sometimes not as material as those who customarily work with things might wish. Dress historians have long called for historical narratives to incorporate material clothing. Giorgio Riello champions this approach:

Historians must integrate the findings derived from the study of material culture into their archive-based and theory-led research. Objects or artefacts (what historians call goods and commodities) need to be used as primary sources. Ignorance about object-based analyses is as dangerous as lack of attention to costs, profits, markets' dynamics, and the organisation of production.[47]

Barbara Burman urges 'scholars of material culture [to] deploy the full range of social historical techniques: the skills of the curator, the social historian and the analysts of literary and visual records must somehow be combined'.[48] My background as a museum curator and dress artisan informs an approach inherently founded in what surviving historical clothes and their accessories reveal. I have looked, for example, at both the contemporary images showing perceptions of clothing's role in identity, and the real things that can subvert fashionable rhetoric.

When a non-dress historian suggested recently that 'historians can study the lived, embodied experience of gender . . . by adopting an interdisciplinary approach to material culture that combines the materiality of men's clothing with the representational', she was advocating a fundamental practice in dress history.[49] This field is necessarily multi-disciplinary with a basic technique of combining images, objects and text to analyse meaning. Close attention to historical clothing is effective in revealing larger social and economic concerns, from cotton linings marking out the fibre's new global dominance to gaiters telling us a gentleman is a successful farmer. This approach can be misunderstood. Even twenty-first-century publications have made assumptions about the taxonomic tendencies of 'costume historians' (the phrase itself is outdated), who get so lost in the trees of listing frills and ruffles that they cannot explore the forest of meaning. Other disciplines can 'discover' clothing history without engaging with the historiography. Having read works containing inaccurate dress history that the existing literature could have remedied, I am aware that this book could leave me hoist by the petard of my own ignorance in reverse. Besides literature on textiles and dress, women's work, domestic production and consumption, written clothing and fashion cultures in the long eighteenth and nineteenth centuries, I have delved into histories of literature, society, royalty and aristocracy, maritime and military fields, domesticity, consumption, gender, economy and colonialism for contextual understandings. Many of these areas have had stimulating new attention paid to them recently. Any misunderstandings I cheerfully own, and hope experts will (kindly) alert me to.

It is possible to synthesise theoretical and practical information. Curators are no longer seen as obsessed only with details, and historians only with documentary facts. Researchers of all sorts want to know what people were wearing, as well as why and how and what it meant when they did. An account book detailing the cost of stays and the frequency of their purchasing is less useful if the reader does not know what stays look like and how they shape the body. Conversely, there is no point cataloguing and categorising stays without setting them in a broader social context. There is a need to integrate and write new histories on the foundation of methodologies encompassing fashion theory, economic history, gender, the body, domesticity and the material turn. How does someone with no prior knowledge start to get accurate information about Regency period clothing and the contexts in which it was produced, consumed and worn, the social roles it played? For these readers, and those who need to date garments, it is still helpful to have stylistic changes delineated and types of garments named and quantified (see pp. 290–91).

Therefore, this book starts from 'the recognition of the essentially inseparable relationship between things, ideas and experiences, between material and mental worlds', and uses this entanglement of objects, words and actions as a method to examine dress in the age of Austen.[50] There is a balance between text and images, theory and practice, specific pieces of surviving clothing and the ideas they embody. I also acknowledge the ways an ever increasing number of people engage with Austen through 'non-textual practices', including replica clothing and Regency dance events, creating different knowledge and perspectives.[51] Jane Austen festivals around the world steadily increase as more women feel what it is like to dance wearing stays, and men learn to negotiate the inertia caused by top hats. To this can be added the experience of sewing Regency clothing or engaging in other period reconstruction, such as embroidery, millinery and shoemaking. A re-creation of Austen's silk pelisse was my way into dress of this period, and gave valuable insight into sewing practices, the relationships between makers and wearers, and Austen's own physical body.[52]

This book presents Regency dress in the wake of histories reconsidering the interconnected global world and the materiality of the past. Recent Austen scholarship also recasts 'Aunt Jane' as a realistic, unromantic, professional author, whose incisive pen and extensive family connections participated in a huge range of dress practices, or uses things 'to map the threads connecting her . . . to those on the international stage'.[53] Applying the analytical techniques, traditional to literature studies, of reading between the lines, extrapolating, and tracing connections with contextual material, a whole world of British clothing is conjured up from Austen's 'little bit (two Inches wide) of Ivory [worked] with so fine a Brush', the ground for portrait miniatures rendered as exquisitely as her own satin-stitch.[54] Austen's life is the pebble I drop into the global pond to follow the ripples of early nineteenth-century British dress as far as they go, lapping against shores of the outposts of empire.

❀ ❀

Chapter 1

Self

Dress was her passion. She had a most harmless delight in being fine; and our heroine's entree into life could not take place till after three or four days had been spent in learning what was mostly worn, and her chaperone was provided with a dress of the newest fashion.[1]

Human bodies are clothed in culture. Haircuts, sun exposure, marks left by work and leisure, the shaping by clothing and by mental images construct a socio-cultural 'body' identifiable in time. 'Dress lies at the margins of the body', Joanne Entwistle reminds us, 'and marks the boundary between self and other, individual and society. The boundary is intimate and personal, since our dress forms the visible envelope of the self.'[2] Everyone in the Regency got up in the morning and put on garments that reflected their different physical and cultural environments, balancing material garments and conceptual aesthetic imaginings to dress both their real and their social bodies. The resulting dress underwent sophisticated and constant observation by their communities, as Austen's fiction so precisely captures.

This chapter presents the fundamental bodily and imaginary selves that characterised Regency experiences of clothing, first through an overview of Regency aesthetics, encompassing the prevailing styles and construction of dress, and the influence of Classicism, and various romantic nostalgias suffusing fashion. It moves into the contemporary understanding of fashion's forces and moral qualities. In relation to dress, signalling 'fashion' was less relevant to ordinary people than what clothing revealed about its wearers. Fashion imagery contributed to ideals of beautiful, elegant figures, often relying on the health and beauty, or manipulation of the 'natural' body to create Regency silhouettes.

❋ ❋

Garments

Austen's lifetime encompassed a profound period of change for the self's boundary envelope. She was born in 1775, when French sartorial abundance ruled fashion. Stiffly boned stays gave women straight waists, underneath a front-opening gown wide at skirt and cuffs. Hooped underskirts increased formal dress to extraordinary widths. Ornate silks covered fashionable men, powder or wigs hiding their natural hair. Full-skirted coats had tight shoulders, and thigh-length waistcoats hid the breeches fastenings. Both sexes wore heeled, buckled shoes, and frills, furbelows and embroideries festooned their garments.[3] But by 1800 fashion had transformed into its opposite – slim, plain and proportioned to the body, as the confrontation between old and new French fashion shows (fig. 1.1).

As Austen reached her 20s, the waistline of women's gowns rose from near its natural placement to underneath the bust. The change created the essential look of the period, christened the 'empire line' in the twentieth century, after the period of the French First Empire (1804–15).[4] While the neo-classical trend partly explains such a rapid rise, the illusion of a raised waistline was formed as early as 1785 by wide sashes tied around the waist of chemise-style dresses.[5] The crucial change happened around 1795. A tailor complained of the 'quick transition of fashion in these particulars in 1793, when we were wont to cut waists full nine inches long from under the arm down to the hip . . . and in the year 1796 we have been obliged to cut them but three inches in the same place'.[6] Austen drafted *First Impressions* (reworked later into *Pride and Prejudice*) and *Elinor and Marianne* (*Sense and Sensibility*) in the late 1790s. The Regency's defining silhouette emerged as its defining author blossomed in skill.

AH! QUELLE ANTIQUITE !!!   A Paris, chez Depeuille, rue des Mathurins S.t Jacques N.o 174.   OH! QUELLE FOLIE QUE LA NOUVEAUTÉ.....

Different construction techniques accompanied the changing form. Skirts were
raised higher on the existing gown bodice, leaving the original longer waist inside,
in case the line dropped again. But it soon became clear that the change was
permanent. The linen bodice lining became unattached from the outer fabric
at the front, creating two separate overlapping flaps fitting over the bust (fig.
1.2). The gown's front skirt was attached to the front bodice panel, which was
then pinned or buttoned at the shoulders. This stomacher-, bib-, apron- or 'fall-
front' opening became usual, and the whole style came to be called the 'round
gown', as it closed in front. From 1795 to around 1800 gowns retained the pleated

Self   ❀ ❀   25 back bodice, inherited from 1780s fashions, in round gowns and in 'open gowns' with long trains and matching petticoats. By the turn of the century, fashion's slimmest lines took the bulk out of the bodice leaving only the low-set shoulder seam to create a distinctive 'kite'-shaped back. Austen drew this in 1799 as part of sketches of a new dress she was having made. From around 1804 bodices began to be fastened at the centre back with tapes or buttons, as seen on the back of Austen's blue dress (fig. 0.2). A gown made with this new type of construction was a 'frock'. The cut dominated from c.1810, and by 1820 front-opening gowns were finally superseded, as most gowns opened at the back. Specific details of the rapid changes over the twenty-five year period are outlined in the timeline 'Changes in the Construction of Women's Gowns' (pp. 288–9).

The high waistline fluctuated in position. From being directly under the bosom at around the turn of the century and through the first decade of the 1800s, it started lowering through the early teens. After 1814–15, waistlines varied widely. Day gowns show them returning almost to the natural waist by the early 1820s. At the same time many 1815–20 evening gowns have front bodice depths of as little as two and a half inches, narrower even than the first shortening. The fall-front opening was disappearing by 1810, though daywear retained it longer. The new integrated bodice allowed for unified decorative treatments at the front, and a new smoothness achieved over the bust by using bias cutting and darts. 1790s sleeves became tighter, fitting to the arm with no gathering at the sleeve head, and increasingly shorter until they reached the height of simplicity as tubes around 1800–05. Thereafter, they gradually became fuller at the sleeve head, starting at the back, and increasing steadily in size to become a true puff by the late 1810s.

A rapid sophistication of cut affected gown skirts. The economical eighteenth-century method of using uncut fabric widths for skirts, joined at their straight, selvedge sides, translated well to the columnar styles of the late 1790s. Gowns from this date have abundant straight skirts pleated at the back (fig. 1.3). They used up to five widths of fabric in one skirt, creating bulk around the torso, and ending in long trains following the wearer for a good yard or two. Classical formality rapidly narrowed skirts after 1800. Now gowns lost at least one fabric width. Gathering attached the skirt to the bodice all the way round, moving further to the back year by year. By the late 1800s dressmakers started cutting gores – long triangular side pieces – which took bulk from the waistline and added it to the hem. At the same time, trains mainly disappeared and skirts shortened. 1820 saw women wearing distinctly triangular, bell-shaped gowns, gathered at the back (though Austen did not live to see this change, as she died in 1817). Older costume typologies identify a change from classical aesthetics, exploiting the shape of the body, to romantic or Gothic style, exploiting the shape of the dress. Although these classifications are art historical, it is true that from severe, linear, austere simplicity, a soft, curving femininity was established by the 1820s, one featuring stiffer surfaces with increased decoration. In just over two decades the cut and conception of women's dress had changed completely.

Fig. 1.3

William Redmore Bigg, *Christening of the Heir*,
c.1799, oil on canvas. The women of the family
wear white cotton morning gowns with the full
skirt, rising waistline, pleated back and long train
of the late 1790s. At this date, the gentlemen's
swallowtail coats are not cut into the front; their
natural hair is still powdered. Yale Center for British
Art, Paul Mellon Collection, New Haven, Conn.

Fig. 1.4 Above Left

John Smart, portrait of Colonel Reynolds, 1810, watercolour on ivory. The colonel's coat has lapels cut in a crisp M-shape, with raw edges, and a separately attached, turned-back collar. His natural hair is curled at the temples in antique style. Victoria and Albert Museum, London.

Fig. 1.5 Above Right

Waistcoat, double-breasted, 1800–10, re-used embroidered green silk satin. Many Regency garments in museum collections are made of re-used fabrics, particularly decorative silks. Makers were often unconcerned by seams left from the previous garment's construction, seen here at the top left shoulder. Metropolitan Museum of Art, New York.

For men, the basic ensemble comprised coat, waistcoat (pronounced 'wesket') and knee-length breeches ('britches'), often held up with braces. Stylistic change came through adjustments of cut and material, though less marked than in women's clothing. In the 1790s men's coats had front openings in a tapered 'swallowtail' style and waistcoats with angled 'skirts' covering the groin. Through the 1790s waistcoat skirts rose and then were cut straight, across the top of the breeches. By about 1800, double- or single-breasted coats were open below the waist with two 'tails' at the back, cut in at the waist in a square or an inverted U shape. The large turned-back collar, emphasising the shoulders, could be finished with velvet. 'Surtout' or frock-coat styles, usually double-breasted, saw coats regain their skirts, which edged back into fashion around 1815. Tightly fulled cloth (felted after weaving) allowed edges to be cut without the textile fraying, creating a crisp edge round the coat, and knife-sharp M- and then V-notched lapels (fig. 1.4). Sleeve-head volume kept pace with women's – tight around 1800, then slowly expanding to become pleated and puffy by 1820. Ankle-length tight pantaloons or

Dress in the Age of Jane Austen

loose trousers added choice to legwear (see chapters 6 and 7). The greatest change was in fabrics. Nearly all the decorative possibilities of bright colours, silks and cotton prints withdrew into the space of the waistcoat (fig. 1.5), and plain wool reigned as the outer fabric of choice (fig. 1.6).[7]

Aesthetics

These changes in material garments occurred alongside significant aesthetic influences. Sir William Wraxall, looking back from 1815, saw classically inspired styles as 'finally levelling or obliterating almost all external distinction of costume between the highest and the lowest of the sex in the country'.[8] His observation exaggerates, but over a thirty-year period the world began modernising, and the rapid style changes are emblematic of larger conceptual concerns. Historians distinguish between the early modern (c.1500–1800) and modern periods (c.1800 onwards), and the Regency is the tidal space where these two great washes of history meet, mingle and change. Part of the hysteria of contemporary fashion coverage in the Regency period was alarm over the epoch's swift transformations and innovations. Magazines abound with 'shocked old ladies and snorting old gentlemen, bewailing modern tendencies, the total lack of respect, the boldness of behaviour of the girl of to-day, and in particular the extreme indelicacy of her clothing'.[9] Exposing nipples or leaving off petticoats were the extreme waves of fashion upon a stormy tide. Among Austen's gentry acquaintance, though the current moved inexorably under the cultural waters, the pace of sartorial change was sedate and less confronting.

Austen's work also covers transitions from eighteenth-century frankness to nineteenth-century gentility. Euphemistic language began to replace Regency coarseness, as people lamented, even at the time: 'nobody ever *sweats* . . . they only *perspire* . . . No lazy over-fed gentlewoman is at present *fat* – the lady is only *jolly* . . . There is [*sic*] now no *fops* or *beaus*, they are either *dandies* or *swells*.'[10] Correspondingly, the pressure of gentility morphed discussion of clothing along with the garments themselves. The revealing dress of their forebears retrospectively shocked Victorians.

Increased gender differentiation shifted Regency clothing. Previously, male and female clothing could share excessive colours, cloths and embellishment. Increasing divisions between gender expressions in dress contrasted with pre-Revolutionary shared aesthetics. A growing 'separate spheres' ideology could be seen, defining men as productive citizens against a 'purportedly unproductive, feminised sphere of consumption'.[11] While stays shaped women from underneath, men's clothing idealised bodies through external tailored structures. Women were the fair sex, arbiters of fashion. Masculinity was thus defined in opposition to affectation and appearance, and concern for the external aspects of dress – rather than its character – marked a gentleman as frivolous and suspiciously feminised.[12] The contradiction was that much attention was needed to avoid the appearance of desiring to attract attention. Respectability, situated in not worrying one's mind with trifles of dress, required some degree of mind to maintain the said dress with care. Foreign observers noted that, in the determined simplicity of their dress, Englishmen 'showed the tyranny of their fashions. [They] submit to it with the greatest reverence.'[13] The tyranny now was of simplicity instead of splendour, in an inverted fashion system. 'The dichotomy is observed if not explained', Barbara Gelpi suggests, 'in the wry comment from the *Lady's Magazine* in 1803 that "with the ladies, it is the object to shew how little will do for a dress; with the gentlemen, how much they can carry without fatigue. Hence the total disuse of silk, linen and cambric, and the substitution of broadcloth and leather."'[14] By the 1820s, women had become the keepers of ornamented dress, pale and pretty against dark and serious men in a convention that still operates in evening dress (fig. 1.7).

Aesthetic modes during the Regency shucked off the immediate past in clothing, yet sought to revive much older fashions, swapping stiff formality for studied informal nonchalance. The prevailing taste made Classicism the major aesthetic influence of the age of Austen. Historians acknowledge the strong influence on fashion from the 1780s of a new appreciation of the classical world, Greek and Roman, promulgated through archaeological excavations of Herculaneum (1738) and Pompeii (1738–1804), and the tradition of the Grand Tour, which circulated first-hand knowledge of antiquity. Less attention has been paid to *how* these influences became embodied in worn ensembles. Amelia Rauser argues that 1790s neo-classical fashions emerged in Naples and were transmitted through elite women travellers like Lady Charlotte Campbell (1775–1861) on their return to Britain and France.[15] She traces how wall paintings were models for women such as Emma Hamilton (1765–1815), famous, particularly, for her striking classical 'attitudes' or *tableaux vivants* based on ancient

Fig. 1.7

Benjamin West, *The Hope Family of Sydenham, Kent*, 1802, oil on canvas. The family group, displaying a rich variety of clothing details, contrasts women clad in white cotton with men wearing black wool, the dress foundation that would define the new century. The older widow's dignified black satin completes the ensemble's aesthetics. Museum of Fine Arts, Boston.

Roman pantomimes (fig. 1.8).[16] Although Hamilton's greatest fame rests on her subsequent relationship with Vice-Admiral Horatio Lord Nelson (1758–1805), she studied classical culture, while her husband, Sir William Hamilton, British envoy to the Kingdom of Naples, supplied Greek artefacts to the new British Museum. Emma performed draped in simple, straight white muslin tunics, caught under the bust like a statue, with her abundant hair free or bound in a scarf, embodying classical aesthetics. To have seen Lady Hamilton perform was a mark of the cultured traveller, and she embodied Hegel's later call for artistic clothing showing the 'fine, free, living contours of the body' covered in unstructured textiles.[17]

A great Regency fashion legend is that many women dampened their muslin gowns to make them cling 'more inseparably to . . . elastic limbs', in the words of one thinly veiled critique of Lady Charlotte Campbell.[18] That lady is famous for an odd fashion from 1793–4 of adding a belly-pad under the gown to create a plump abdomen in imitation of pregnancy, or classical statuary.[19] *Ne plus ultra* gowns in that season required a higher waistline to accommodate the swell, and probably contributed to the rising waistline. Such was the fashion the *Lady's Magazine* recounted as a novel anecdote in 1794: 'I met a young woman dressed in an elegant white muslin gown, who to all appearance had no stays on, was far gone with child and with her breasts fully exposed to view. I supposed from her dress that she was an easy lady and accosted her as such.'[20]

Self

But Campbell sought deliberately to imitate antique drapery and was an infamous fashion-setter, used to shocking onlookers. The behaviour of a handful of aristocratic *élégantes* was not the everyday experience of the majority. Campbell might have dampened; Austen certainly did not. Nor did the average Englishwoman indulge in the post-Revolutionary Parisian practice of wearing a pink knitted silk body-stocking to imitate naked flesh. In 1798 Austen's cousin Eliza de Feuillide (1761–1813) recorded the kind of 'uproar' a beautiful army wife caused in a country town by wearing

> only one thick muslin Petticoat and a thin muslin Robe over that, of which the sleeves come only three inches below her shoulders. Her Ears throat & bosom are entirely bare for She never wears Earrings, necklace, tucker, Handkerchief or Stays, and on her Head She generally has no other ornament or covering than a little curled black wig . . . the height of the present fashion.[21]

Even the 1794 correspondent to the *Lady's Magazine* admits that the lady had the *appearance* of wearing no stays. Illusion has always been a fashion essential, and clothing had recently been a dense and structured thing. The idea of fashion expressing 'the rights of nature and of grace', contrasting with the opacity of previous dress through 'easy shape and flowing drapery', conjured imaginings of antique nudity.[22] Countless writers extolled the virtues of the elegant Greek loose, 'natural' dress.

Not only the bodies of Grand Tourists, but also print media – increasingly popular – disseminated ideas about classical form across Britain. Academic and general interest in the classical world underpinned the pre-eminence of pale, floating textiles, and the new emphasis on the body (fig. 1.9). The study of antiquities was regarded as a means of divining eternal truths underlying visual diversity. Ancient sculptors, said Sir Joshua Reynolds, left behind them 'models of that perfect form', or, in Thomas Baxter and William Miller's words, 'nearly all that is elegant or dignified in Art'.[23] The latter authors produced *An Illustration of the Egyptian, Grecian, and Roman Costume* (1810), an influential publication presenting line drawings of costume and figures copied from classical artefacts. Such studies introduced technical historical terms for clothing – peplos, chiton, chlamys from the Greeks; the Roman toga, tunica, pallium, stola.[24] Here was the pinnacle of visual interest in 'dress of the ancient world', which had been growing from the 1780s.

The best-known publications merging clothing and Classicism were *Costume of the Ancients* (1809) by the influential collector Thomas Hope, illustrated by Henry Moses, followed by their *Designs of Modern Costume* (1812; fig. 1.10).[25] Hope's designs were influential enough to make Elizabeth Grant Smith (1797–1885) misremember their power in her *Memoirs of a Highland Lady*. She recalled helping her mother with her classically inspired toilette in 1804: 'Her gown was of white satin trimmed with velvet, cut in a formal pattern, then quite the rage, a copy of some Grecian borders in Mr. Hope's book; . . . the gown was short-waisted and narrow skirted, but we thought it beautiful.'[26] Hope did not publish until 1809. His introduction detailed costumes based on thorough antiquarian knowledge. Besides the obvious connections with Regency style in columnar clothing, muscular physiques and elegant draping, the capes of driving coats appear in the folds and circularity of togas. The forms ran deep into dress. Austen never needs to mention classical influence directly in her work, because its absorbed elements are pervasive – especially muslin gowns (fig. 1.11; see chapter 7). Countless museum survivals, portraits, fashion plates and other media show how ubiquitous the 'little white dress' was. All women of gentry class and above would have had at least one. These gowns recur throughout the Regency, like seams in the marble they mimicked.

Austen's prose emulates the neo-classical qualities of beauty through truth, pared down to essential refinements, and refusing artificiality. Her characters' avoidance of descriptions of clothing matches the simplicity that fashion strove for, an artful artlessness echoed in Austen's restrained, sparkling prose, letting character rather than form shine through. 'Neo-classical' was applied to Regency decorative and

Fig. 1.9 Opposite

Adam Buck, *The Artist and his Family*, 1813, watercolour and pen and ink on cardboard. The artist's portrait of his family is modelled on classical poses and accented with antique sculptures and vases. Buck's Hessian boots, pantaloons and cutaway coat are perfectly in fashion. His wife's dress is carefully arranged so as to appear as draped Grecian clothing. Yale Center for British Art, Paul Mellon Collection, New Haven, Conn.

Fig. 1.10 Below

Henry Moses, 'Le Beau Monde', from Thomas Hope and Henry Moses, *Designs of Modern Costume* (1812), engraving on paper. Moses' work depicting ancient sculpture and vase art as line drawings resonates through his vision of high society. The figures' poses, drapery, shawls and curled hair are carefully classical in style. The outline style emphasises the antique lines.

visual arts only in the 1880s, as a term of opprobrium. The style at the time was simply the 'true' or 'correct' taste, a resurgence of the arts with a revolutionary and serious character, reacting against Rococo frivolity.[27] Vases and sculpture were held up as forms of art with clear aesthetic and ideological intentions, speaking truth, and providing evidence of the 'simple laws of just taste'.[28] The principles of a somehow self-evidently right taste dovetailed smugly with Britain's self-image as the new democratic leader in shaping European fashion. Nikolaus von Heideloff's introduction to his second *Gallery of Fashion* volume (1795; fig. 1.12) considers that:

> In former times Greece was considered the first country in the world where the Fair Sex had acquired a superior taste in their vestments and every person of taste has admired the elegant simplicity of their dresses. In our memory France has given her dresses to other nations; but it was reserved for the Graces of Great Britain to take the lead in Fashion and to show that if they do not surpass, they certainly equal the elegance of the most celebrated Grecian dresses. In short, beauty, shape and taste are nowhere more general nor anywhere better united than in England.[29]

United they might have been, but Britain's wet, cold winter was no climate in which to imitate the antique. In another fashion contradiction, material sheerness lessened the idealistic appeal of transparent draperies. Balancing real-world propriety, warmth and neatness with antique affectations made for uneasy dress trade-offs. Austen played on these ambivalences in a juvenile piece. When she speaks of a character as an affecting object, lying 'wrapped in a book muslin bedgown, a chambray gauze shift, and a French net nightcap', the contemporary reader would recognize these fabrics as transparent.[30] The bed-bound lady is clad in immodesty. Note Austen's later epistolary amusement at observing Mrs Powlett, who 'was at once expensively & nakedly dress'd'.[31] So was Lady Hannah Ellice, 'an affected lisping, chalk-faced flimsily dressed dawdle', in the eyes of Anglo-Irish novelist Maria Edgeworth (1768–1849). Fellow bestselling author Fanny Burney (1752–1840) described the 'flimsy,

Fig. 1.11

Peter Edward Stroehling, portrait of Princess Mary, 1807, oil on copper. One of a series of portraits of the daughters of George III, showing that filmy, revealing muslin dress had become an acceptable artistic convention, even for royalty. The princess's gown clings to her body, and there is a suggestion of the nipples of her unsupported breasts. The shawl arrangement is fanciful. The Royal Collection.

falling drapery of the present day'.[32] Women more usually incorporated a sedate Classicism in curled and filleted hairstyles, draped themselves in long rectangular shawls, and added tunics, ribbons and embellishment in historically inspired styles, rather than seeking sensational naked-seeming dress.

Similarly, the Arcadianism central to Rococo taste sustained an idyllic, peaceful vision of a golden age of wild nature in fashionable consciousness, especially beside the tide of urban, industrial change that was altering people's relationship with their environment. It did not abate during the long Regency.[33] The Enlightenment calls of Voltaire and Rousseau, especially in the latter's *Emile* (1762), to return to nature had begun to influence dress with pronouncements such as 'Everything that hinders and constrains nature is in bad taste,' and 'We are not our clothes. Often they detract from us by their elaborateness.'[34]

Fig. 1.12

Nikolaus von Heideloff, 'Afternoon Dress', *Gallery of Fashion*, vol. 6, November 1796, hand-coloured engraving on paper. Heideloff's publication responded to the French *Galerie des modes* but promoted English taste. He claimed the plates depicted ensembles actually worn by fashionable ladies, like this round gown with coquelicot-coloured ribbon accents.

Besides goddesses and warriors, classical antiquity was peopled with artless, innocent, rustic nymphs to imitate. A taste for simple 'ribbons, gauze, muslin and flowers' in 'a young girl who despises fashion' would, in Rousseau's opinion, 'create an outfit a hundred times more charming' than brilliant ensembles, as Marie-Antionette and her ladies attempted in their 1780s faux-pastoralism.[35] Their (loosely) peasant-inspired hats, cotton gowns and large fichus emerged more strongly in European fashion after the Revolution, translating easily into the dress of gentry British women, but perhaps more genuinely connected to the working rural environment through landed estates. By the early Regency, descriptions of fashion plates include frequent references to more homely Arcadias in 'gypsy', 'cottage' and 'woodland' bonnets and hats, with a wide flat brim of the kind Mrs Elton (*Emma*) is eager to adopt to demonstrate her rural simplicity: "'I shall wear a large bonnet, and bring one of my little baskets hanging on my arm . . . Nothing can be more simple, you see . . . There is to be no form or parade – a sort of gipsy party.'"[36] Her eagerness to *seem* natural can be constructed only through thoughtful artifice and the adoption of romanticised accessories – an inherent contradiction in all fashionable seeking for unconscious grace.

Classicism was not the only historical echo resonating through fashion. Dressing like an antique maiden was essentially a romantic impulse and had little to do with an appreciation of the underlying geometric order and austere formality of ancient cultures.[37] The growth of interest in the distant past simultaneously included the Middle Ages, recently characterised as 'Gothic' by enthusiasts such as Horace Walpole. Penelope Byrde suggests that medieval dress may have inspired the common fashion of long sleeves with curved cuffs reaching over the knuckles, though descriptions refer to these as 'Spanish sleeves'.[38] A fantasy nostalgia for the sixteenth and seventeenth centuries heralded the romantic nostalgia of the 1820s and the new philosophical ideals of Romanticism in continental philosophy, and incorporated Gothic taste's sensationalist reflection of history through a mirror, darkly. Austen's youthful *History of England*, which defends Mary Queen of Scots, anticipates the Regency popularity of the sixteenth-century monarch.[39] By 1808 the Mary Queen of Scots or Marie Stuart cap was very fashionable, dipping to a peak at the centre front, as were full Marie sleeves (sometimes identified as 'mameluke') caught at regular intervals down the arm. Further elements of Tudor and Stuart dress conjured a romantic historicism through other details such as ruff collars, imitating Elizabethan fashion, pointed stomachers and Medici collars of lace opening at the front. Sleeves with 'panes' (vertical bands) and puffed epaulettes evoked Renaissance slashed clothing (fig. 1.13); 'Spanish' cloaks referred to the dashing shoulder capes of the country's Golden Age. The 'vandyke' style of pointed trimmings evoked both the beauties Anthony van Dyck painted at the court of Charles I, and the arches of medieval churches. Vandyking increased from the late 1810s as dress decoration proliferated. English society started looking back on itself and responding to its own history, considering the past from the future, and romanticising its stability, from the transitional Regency perspective.[40] Art and culture embraced the historical epic, notably through the romantic writings of Sir Walter Scott, a mutual appreciator of Austen's work, and inventor of the historical novel. Austen's work, by contrast, looked at what people were in the precise present, reflecting modernity.

The fourth major aesthetic influence on dress was Orientalism. A fascination with – and fabrication of – eastern ideas and styles, an amalgam of Asian, African and Middle Eastern cultures, had influenced fashion for centuries.[41] The Mediterranean ancient world was simultaneously part of the 'East' for contemporary Britain. As war cast spotlights on these areas, military campaigns inspired new styles to recharge the cultural power of Orientalism. According to Adam Geczy, the Orient, as a concept, was 'understood as a shapeless yet conveniently identifiable set of signs and values', a vague place of otherness, 'marker of the outwardly exotic and the globally connected'.[42] 'The mass appeal of oriental allusion', Geczy continues, 'was of a piece with the appeal . . . to naturalness.' Fantastical dreams of the East provided a rich banquet of exotic difference that the fashion hungry eagerly consumed. Garments such as the male banyan (see chapter 2) were kinds of orientalist 'clothing sympathetic to the body . . . informal, liberating', which suited new relaxed structures of dress.[43]

Turbans, in particular, entered the lexicon of female Regency dress, especially for women of an intellectual or literary bent, suiting the orientalist fantasies blowing through fashion. *La Belle Assemblée* reported in January 1825 that 'the sash and headdress of costumes were both imitative of the Asiatic Turk, but the turban was improved by the disposal of the plumage' in English style.[44] Asia still needed to be tempered via Western taste to be consumable in everyday fashion. One evening in 1799 Austen chose to wear a 'Mamalouc' cap borrowed from a friend instead of her white satin cap, as 'it is all the fashion now'.[45] The name was popularised after Napoleon Bonaparte (1769–1821) invaded and occupied north Africa from 1798, ending centuries of Mameluke dynasty rule and bringing mameluke ('mameluk', 'Mamlouc', 'memeluke') caps, sleeves and other parts of dress into British fashion in support. The merging of historical, romantic, orientalist and military references in one garment epitomises Regency style's ability to absorb fantasies about other times and places.

The combination of aesthetic influences meant that:

> in our days, an English woman has the extensive privilege of arraying herself in whatever garb may best suit her figure or her fancy. The fashions of every nation and of every era are open to her choice. One day she may appear as the Egyptian Cleopatra, then a Grecian Helen; next morning the Roman Cornelia; or, if these styles be too august for her taste, there are Sylphs, Goddesses, Nymphs of every region, in earth or air, ready to

lend her their wardrobe. In short, no land or age is permitted to withhold its costume from the adoption of an English woman of fashion.[46]

As Romanticism emerged from reflections on Britain's past, tensions between ideas of 'nature' and the artifice required to achieve something like those ideas on the daily body underlay much of Regency aesthetics. The constructed 'natural' further contrasted with fashion's embrace of clothing details from foreign times and places 'unnatural' to the comfortable British gentry consumer. As Daniel Purdy interprets it, 'To be modern is to be permanently cut off from the idyllic past', though 'modern' Regency dressers understood 'themselves as representatives of a particular historical moment'.[47] Romantic nostalgia for the unexperienceable past in clothing, simultaneous with culturally arbitrated naturalism, was therefore a condition of the emergent modern century.

Fashion

Dress and the bodies wearing it help us to analyse the social spheres Austen represented in her writing, which have been so formative in contemporary understanding of Regency dress. Fashion histories sometimes present ideals of period styles without addressing what people actually wore and how individuals negotiated their own relationship with fashion in the clothing they put onto their bodies every day. Joanne Entwistle reiterates that dress is a means by which bodies are made social and given meaning and identity: 'The individual and very personal act of getting dressed is an act of preparing the body for the social world . . . the way individuals learn to live in their bodies and feel at home in them.'[48] Real clothing from the past has a complicated relationship with the fashion of its time, articulated in this unusually thoughtful period consideration of dress:

> It is the tailor who fashions the man: . . . forms him, licks him, makes him, fashions him, endows him with a shape and a character, and he becomes fashioned; and if the tailor be Stultz, he becomes a man of fashion – a fashionable man . . . What, indeed, is human nature but a bundle of clothes. What are all the distinctions of society but distinct suits of clothing? . . . In short, from the coal-heaver to the chancellor, from Drury to Almack's, human nature is a Monmouth-street, a collection of suits – black, white, and grey – silk, gauze, and frivolity – leather and prunella, goats hair and gold lace . . . Thus is fashion all, and all in all. And, according to the fashion of the clothes, are the fashion of the man and the fashion of the woman.[49]

Untangling what fashion is and what is in fashion has taxed commentators for centuries:

> Is it the economist's sense of regular changes in visual appearance of any type of good intended to stimulate sales? dress historians' sense of annual or seasonal manipulation of normative appearance through clothing? or is it fashion in the fashion pundit's sense of those forms of self-conscious, avant-garde innovation in dress pursued by an exclusive social or cultural elite?[50]

Clothes carry meaning, and what can be 'read' from them is 'the manifestation of economic achievements and limits, of cultural affiliations and exclusions, of social practice and structures and personal choices'.[51] Clothing helps 'to explain the difficult relationship between change and stability, between a modern notion of society that finds its fluidity in time and the many manifestations of the preservation of social rules'.[52] In Austen's day the same points held true, although fashion had broader application to taste and its expression across the range of socialised material goods.

Regency critics of fashion – 'that magical term, the sound of which conveys, in itself, beauty, grace, taste, every thing' – continued their predecessors' characterisation of fashion as a tyrant, an enchantress, or an abstract yet irresistible force of agency swooping down to entrap the unwary, helpless to resist its overweening dictates.[53] To be a servant or slave to fashion's whims was monstrous. And yet, as is repeatedly seen in the history of fashion, the gentry could not be entirely out of fashion. The old paradox is that women must know about fashion to eschew its excesses; men to assess the degree to which the woman they admire keeps up with but is not overtaken by it. If Henry Crawford in *Mansfield Park* had been alert to nuances of dress, he would not have committed the faux pas of speaking to a girl not 'out' (formally debuted into society).[54] The 'relationship between innovation and preservation, between the changing material, social and cultural world and the way in which material culture is either shaped or is, by contrast, a factor shaping such change' was often a conundrum for Regency dressers.[55] Their attitude to reconciling tensions between custom and fashion is summarised in a moral novel:

> 'You very much mistake me if you suppose I reprobate every conciliation to the fashions of the times we live in. On the contrary, I think we are positively bound by the laws of civil society, to accommodate our plans of life, to those of our fellow creatures, in whose age and country we live.'[56]

Fanny Burney encapsulated what dress ought to do for its wearer: suit the style of their beauty and 'assimilate with the character of her mind, gender and class'.[57] Many agreed it was important to be well and respectably dressed for one's station, standing out neither in excessive originality nor ostentatious neglect of garments. 'A degree of conformity . . . to preclude the appearance of particularity, is reasonable and becoming', and defined the appropriate sartorial middle ground for the gentry Austen immortalised.[58] Below the aristocratic upper elite, more genteel than the labouring peoples comprising the majority of Britons, the gentry and professional classes sought to balance prosperity and respectability, taste and appropriate display in their social bodies. Taste was the polite, mannered key to negotiating fashion with reason and feeling to achieve the elusive moral and physical quality of elegance. The plea 'In your . . . dress, and in all other things, aim at propriety and neatness, avoiding all extravagances' matches Austen's personal attitude to dress emerging from her letters – namely, that one should follow 'the principles of decency . . . the rules of reasonable frugality and Christian simplicity'.[59]

'Elegant' conveys Austen's highest approbation in life as in her art. She rarely uses 'fashion', but, when she does, the word is imbued with the correct faint disapproval of men or women of fashion. *Frederic Latimer: Or, the History of a Young Man of Fashion* (1799), concerns the reformation of a thoughtless young buck into a true gentleman. Part of his maturing is learning to identify 'the very criterion of female perfection' as being 'exactly the reverse of those who are called "Women of Fashion"'.[60] Latimer-like reform 'is plain and easy, if we have courage enough to shake off the tyranny of fashion, and to consult our reason and our feelings', maintained a doctor around the same time, emphasising the importance of a moral compass and right thinking against being swayed by whim or novelty.[61] Other authors make this explicit: it is not seemly for genteel persons to be too concerned with dress, a party line Austen upholds by implication in her fiction. When the Misses Steele first arrive in *Sense and Sensibility*, therefore, and Austen describes their appearance as 'by no means ungenteel or unfashionable. Their dress was very smart, their manners very civil', she is warning against their character by attributing to the sisters a shell of fashionable display. Lucy Steele's eventual partner in duplicity, Robert Ferrars, is similarly dismissed as having 'a person and face of strong, natural, sterling insignificance, though adorned in the first stile of fashion'.[62] Others warned 'A dress indeed may be made in the first style of fashion and yet may infringe on every rule of good taste and altogether disfigure the lady for whom it has been made.'[63] *Emma*'s Augusta Elton comes irresistibly to mind. Taste in dress was determined by a discrimination of mind and a realistic self-knowledge, which adapted the dress to the wearer; by consulting 'imagination . . . guided by taste, and an attention to the figure, not by caprice and fashion', she 'cannot fail to appear handsome and elegant'.[64]

Cynosure of fashion reigned when people aped style without elegance or the subtler qualities of gentility, to which even the aristocracy aspired. Maria Edgeworth mused on 'what a comfortable thing it is to see our dearest relations *look* and act like gentlemen and gentlewomen',[65] proving Lord Chesterfield's point that 'taste requires a congruity between the internal character and the external appearance', an idea with deep social implications.[66] Dress ought to proclaim the inward person in an 'ideal conjunction of clothing, rank and moral status' despite the vagaries and dictates of abstract fashion.[67] The horror of a woman of fashion was 'a modern belle', with assured, 'almost masculine', ease, loud conversation and 'the scarcely clothed colours of her fashionable form', unfeminine, immodest and brash.[68] Writers of the period shared a disgust for enthusiasm and originality – the 'love of singularity and ambition for notoriety . . . [in] the pretensions of fashion' in dress.[69]

Contemporary writers on clothing further articulated their concerns in two areas. First, expenditure on fashionable clothing diverted spare money from charitable concerns, and time for its construction from poor work (see chapter 3) and household labour. Second, fashion occupied the thoughts unnecessarily and diverted people from attending to higher activities, interfering with learning, education and religion. The charge of mental distraction levelled at fashionable women suffuses an anecdote recounted to Edgeworth:

> 'How many times a day' [said one lady friend] 'do you think of your dress?'
>
> 'Why three times – Morning, evening and night besides *casualties*.'
>
> 'But this won't do you must *think* of it seriously – at other times and when you go to the country always dress to keep the habit.'[70]

According to *The Female Instructor* (1817), fashion interfered with charity and destroyed feminine amity. Yet the construction of clothing gifts for female acquaintances strengthened bonds of friendship, as chapter 3 explores. Commentators were concerned with the moral implications of attention to appearance at the expense of character. Austen agreed: none of her characters directly discussing dress or fashion are notable for their quality of mind or heart. 'A woman cannot be educated against the "dangerous Diversions in Fashion . . . by being removed from temptation, for once of age and living in the world she has been guarded from, she will be ill-equipped to deny their force. Immunity to such seductive pleasure can be achieved only through the wisdom gained by Reading and Philosophy."'[71] Elizabeth Bennet (*P&P*), as judged by the Bingley sisters wafting their 'air of decided fashion', is not fashionable. Her manners are very bad and she has '"no conversation, no style, no taste, no beauty"'.[72] However, she reads, and therefore might deny fashion's force.

The discussion in the library at Netherfield Park about feminine accomplishment and improving the mind by reading rehearses the dynamics of false or artificial appearance against true virtue and wit, of fashion versus elegance. A contemporary female author could be describing Lizzy in advocating 'the delightful art of saying the most ingenious things with a graceful simplicity', and declaring 'it is [these women] who call forth the powers of wit in men, and communicate to them that easy elegance which is never to be acquired in the closet', a distinction well-dressed Miss Bingley unfortunately demonstrates.[73] Wit and vivacity untempered by a pious moral core could not establish true beauty. Contrast the urban dazzle of *Mansfield Park*'s Mary Crawford, ultimately dismissed as a superficial belle, and Fanny Price, whose beauty grows in others' perceptions as the rightness of her principles and humility is revealed. But Fanny's progress is also measured by the transition from a deficient to a well-supplied wardrobe, from lack to possession of gowns. Thus, dress objects, inevitably shaped by fashion, could never be completely excluded from a person's moral dimension.[74]

Opposing the fashion-as-tyrant idea is recent scholarship demonstrating how active individuals below the gentry rank engaged their working, practical body with the social body. John Styles's work, in particular, examines how plebeian consumers could partake of 'fashion' across a spectrum of dress practices, exercising fashionability through choosing wearable accessories to compose an ensemble, rather than cobbling one together through necessity.[75] The act of choice is the expression of individuality and a token of participating in established social categories. Fashion in this sense represents cleanliness, agency, improvement, decoration, novelty and ephemerality. Plebeian fashionability worried people of Lord Chesterfield's mind, because well-dressed lower classes threatened social order by blurring the lines between seeming and being. One's appearance was supposed to reflect one's place in the world, 'first ideas [being] of considerable consequence' to onlookers in understanding their own relationship to other people.[76]

Similarly, wealthy men were ridiculed for wishing to dress like their grooms, old women for dressing too young and merchants for imitating the court.[77] Fashion, then, was deceitful, an imposture on the viewer that distorted their correct social relationship with the wearer. 'In character should every man be clad' was the theme of the age, as *Dress and Address* (1819) protested: 'A noble like a nobleman should go / The militaire in warlike pomp and show', and 'a proper dress suits every class in life'.[78] Lancashire governess Ellen (Nellie) Weeton (1776–1849), who kept a meticulous diary and copies of her letters, chided herself for feeling ashamed of a fellow coach traveller she had identified as a gentleman when she discovered, after seven hours in his company, that 'his hat and coat were old, his shoes dusty, and his stockings of old grey yarn'. 'Had he had a good coat on,' she admits, 'I should have probably been proud of his company.'[79] Clothing has 'always been a primary trope for the deceitfulness of the material world'.[80]

People did (and could) not universally adopt new styles. One effect of the rapid Regency changes was a greater distinction between old- and new-fashioned dress, as is seen across contemporary images (fig. 1.14). Mother Goose in late eighteenth-century garb, for example, stands out as a quaint, countrified, homely figure among her listeners in modern attire in Regency children's book illustrations, reflecting a spectrum of social clothing. Old Mrs Bates's clothing is probably archaic (*Emma*). Roughly, the older one was, the more one was supposed to cover up.[81]

For all the public consensus operating, private records tell another story. When Mrs Mary Topham (1756–1825), genteel London-based widow of barrister and antiquarian John Topham (1746–1803), received £15 extra to her normal income, aged 62 in April 1818, she spent it immediately and completely on clothes. The cost of 'A work'd muslin gown' at £2 10s. and 'Long Shawl' at £5 15s. are nearly equal to the magnificent cost of £8 8s. for a 'Silk Pellisse', the most expensive item she purchased in the fifteen years (1810–25) of personal spending, detailed in her account book.[82]

Austen herself splurged part of a £5 windfall on a poplin gown from London for her sister Cassandra.[83] Because Austen is a master ironist, alert to both sides of any position, she puts her finger on this emotional, pleasurable dimension of clothing. 'Woman is fine for her own satisfaction alone,' says *Northanger Abbey*'s narrator. 'No man will admire her the more, no woman will like her the better for it. Neatness and fashion are enough for the former, and a something of shabbiness or impropriety will be most endearing to the latter.'[84] The official line of social judgement has always been tempered by the individual relationship to material clothing.

If Austen's approbation is 'elegant', her delight is 'pretty'. She describes clothing as 'pretty' eighteen times in the letters – her commonest taste description. Although Austen's tongue is near her cheek when she talks of 'my hat, on which you know my principal hopes of happiness depend', a measure of her felicity *did* rest on being arrayed to her own satisfaction.[85] Sometimes pleasure in dress shines from her pen: 'My Cloak came on Tuesday, and, tho' I expected a good deal, the beauty of the lace astonished me. – It is too handsome to be worn – almost too handsome to be looked at.'[86] Austen is typical of the 'careful discrimination and tempered engagement' Amanda Vickery ascribes to the sober Georgian middling ranks – 'not slavish followers of every fashion'.[87] The rise and fall of fashion's tides allowed for genteel bobbing as well as exhilaration.

If 'reconciling an appropriate attachment to dress to conceptions of virtuous femininity' was, as Jennie Batchelor argues, one of eighteenth-century literature's most difficult tasks, Austen manages it by not concerning her heroines with dress.[88] We only ever know

Fig. 1.14

Henry Raeburn, portrait of John Johnstone, his niece Betty Johnstone, and her aunt Miss Wedderburn, 1794–5, oil on canvas. Johnstone was an official of the British East India Company. Betty's fashionable white muslin wrap-front gown and antique-style hair contrast with her aunt's straight-fronted gown, the colour of which is just visible under her muslin apron. National Gallery of Art, Washington, DC.

obliquely what an Austen heroine wears. When Edmund Bertram (*MP*) is complimenting
Fanny Price – "'I see no finery about you; nothing but what is perfectly proper. Your
gown seems very pretty. I like these glossy spots'" – his thoughts are also running
on Mary Crawford, who he thinks has a gown something the same.[89] Again, dress
is a vehicle for materialised thought. Heroines only refer to the article of clothing
they wear, a gown or a habit, or say that they are dressing, or adjust their dress in
a moment of distress – they do not describe it.[90] Catherine Morland (*NA*) worries
about her *future* clothing choices, 'debating between her spotted and her tamboured
muslin'.[91] The clothing functions; its fashion does not. It is only the absurd, vulgar and
empty-headed who talk of their own clothing and care about others'. Isabella Thorpe
remembers wearing her yellow gown, Mrs Allen's passion is dress (*NA*); vacuous
Miss Steele (*S&S*) evaluates the price of clothing; in *Emma*, Miss Bates enumerates
her clothes as part of her prattle, Harriet Smith compares her colour to her gown's
whiteness, and Mrs Elton makes sure everyone attends to her dress by speaking of it;
while Lydia Bennet (*P&P*) is profligate with her garments.

The rule applies also to male characters. They are described by others or the narrator, but by themselves only if they are coxcombs, like Robert Ferrars (*S&S*), or pedantically concerned with minutiae, like Mr Collins (*P&P*). Frank Churchill (*Emma*) makes much business about his gloves and his hair, and is thereby suspect in Austen's moral regime. Mr Darcy's high-minded '"Her dirty petticoat quite escaped my notice"' (*P&P*) sums up the effect clothing was supposed to create: 'The best chosen dress is that which so harmonizes with the figure as to make the raiment pass unobserved. The result of the finest toilet should be an elegant woman, not an elegantly-dressed woman.'[92] In a micro way this conveys the macro trend that 'in the eighteenth century, bodies were more like mannequins, while in the subsequent era the body asserted its independence. It did this through simplicity, concentrating on the person not the thing,' though of course with mixed real-world success.[93]

Joanne Entwistle emphasises the tension between the physical body and the forces pressing against it to create socially processed, fashioned bodies, while arguing for the importance of individual experience, where fashion's abstractions are 'translated into actual bodily presentation'.[94] I too champion the role of the body in studying historic dress, agreeing that 'worn garments are never generic artefacts. They retain a "footprint" of the wearer as their unique "memory": they reveal signs of use, and they often show cut and construction choices made for specific consumers'.[95] Worn clothing in collections is one way of re-materialising fashion, as is seeking out how people experienced dressing in the past. Austen's voice as observer of appearance allows us to contrast idealised fashion-plate figures from magazines with the unflattering reality of a Mrs Blount appearing at a ball 'exactly as she did in September, with the same broad face, diamond bandeau, white shoes, pink husband, and fat neck'.[96] Fashion, another source decided, 'is the kind of dress which sometimes is admirably suited to certain figures and hence all are anxious to have it under the vain hope that it will become them equally well'.[97]

Regency people had fewer clothes and so their individual garments became part of their identity. One could recognise the person by their worn-in coat hung on a hook, retaining their shape and physical characteristics. Everyone wears garments individually. Their person contributes to the silhouette, as Austen's niece Anna Lefroy (1793–1872) found when she tried to distinguish between her two aunts seen from behind and wearing identical bonnets. Everything in a person's ensemble revealed something about them to the Regency observer. Cut, fit and style of garments were important in conveying the message, but equally important were textile and workmanship. Sources constantly reiterate how observers instantly recognised fabric quality in dress. 'The materials used and the craftsmanship employed in the construction of a garment can yield precious information about the cost, market, and final user of such an artefact,' says Giorgio Riello from his experience of studying objects.[98] Surviving clothing is one way of examining how Regency people negotiated prevailing fashion with their individual embodiment. This was the reason for re-creating the only garment known to have belonged to Austen – a brown silk pelisse (fig. 1.15).[99] The analysis revealed that the woman who wore the pelisse was very slender and tall for her time, around 5 feet 7 inches, matching eyewitness descriptions of Austen exactly. Combined with other qualities, including the brown colour she is known to have liked, and the modest yet fashionable style, close material study of an object backs up the assertion that the pelisse was Austen's, as well as telling us things about her physical self unknowable in other ways.

Images

To turn from the real to the ideal, it is clear that the new aesthetic influences on dress increased the experience of 'the actual woman being virtually replaced by a satisfactory image of the Dressed Woman' by substituting for the plain facts 'satisfying mythic and fictional varieties', available in a range as never before for the Regency consumer.[100] Engraved plates of fashionable dress included in monthly magazines and pocket-books disseminated visual representations of the idealised styles to a wider audience, and have provided a route into Regency fashion ever since. The plates detailed novelties in cut, trim, colours and style, and showed viewers attitudes and modes of wearing dress. Henry Moses' sketches for fashion plates perfectly illustrate the links between the classical aesthetic and its translation into fashion rhetoric. Moses produced the engravings for Hope's *Costume of the Ancients* (1809). In his working drawings (fig. 1.16), we see how he overlaid the year's styles directly onto the kind of naked figures posed in classical arrangements that he studied for Hope, as realised in *Designs of Modern Costume* (1812).[101] The ancient world literally provides the structure for patterning didactic elegance in the contemporary world through attitude and composition of ensemble. The two mediums of artistic line and clothing influenced each other through the visual rhetoric of classical sculpture's muscularity and drapery.

Fashion plates show fashion, harmony, beauty and novelty in a perfect state. The equally prolific satirical caricatures by the Cruikshanks (father and son), James Gillray, Thomas Rowlandson and their ilk depict those ideals realised on human bodies (fig. 1.17). The real effect, seen walking down the street, must have been somewhere between the fashion plate and the caricature. Plates delighted in quirk, invention and exaggeration as aspirational fashion – the very qualities detractors of fashion railed against. They are often taken at face value as accurate representations of Regency styles, but need to be understood in context. The accompanying text, explaining the materials and colours, was at least as important as the pictures for readers used to understanding clothing through haptic qualities of fabric, weave, weight and fibre. Plates can be considered diagrammatic, requiring the text for full comprehension. Looking at surviving garments emphasises the difference between fashion's vision and its lived reality, where slow changes in construction alter the prevailing mode, and gowns could be refashioned from eighteenth-century silks. Not all fashion plates were created equal. Comparing them with real clothing reveals different relationships in each periodical's visuals. The cut and accessorising of surviving garments finds better reflection in plates from the *Lady's Monthly Museum* and the *Lady's Magazine* (figs. 1.18–1.19) than in those from *La Belle Assemblée*, which, by contrast, featured notably imaginative, overdressed confections every month,

Fig. 1.16

Henry Moses, sketches for a fashion plate, 1818–19, pencil and pen and ink on paper. Moses has overlaid fashionable dress onto foundation bodies in classical style. Their naked forms alone are the basis for fashionable dress, with neither stays nor petticoats. Victoria and Albert Museum, London.

Fig. 1.17

George Cruikshank, *Monstrosities of 1818*, hand-coloured etching on paper. Caricaturists revelled in depicting the absurdity, extravagance and vulgarity of human bodies struggling into the fashions of the moment. The female figures show the forward-leaning stance known as the 'Grecian bend', and an arc behind the waist mocks the effect of bustle pads. Library of Congress, Washington, DC.

MONSTROSITIES of 1818

Self

MORNING DRESS.   FULL DRESS.

Publish'd Oct.r 1st 1804 by Vernor & Hood, Poultry.

R. Sands

Fig 1.18

Robert Sands, 'Morning Dress [left]. Full Dress [right]', Lady's Monthly Museum, October 1804, etching on paper. The morning dress ensemble includes a net tippet with black trimming, and a folding or fan parasol. The evening gown's skirt is cut high at the front, revealing the petticoat. Rijksmuseum, Amsterdam.

Fig 1.19

Unknown artist, 'London Morning Walking [right] and Evening [left] Dress', Lady's Magazine, November 1811, etching on paper. Dress in fashion plates from the Lady's Magazine reflects surviving historical clothing in its lines, shapes, colour and adornment. The morning dress comprises a silk fur-trimmed pelisse; the evening dress is of gold satin trimmed with swansdown, and a lace cap. Chawton House Library.

Engraved for the Lady's Magazine.

London Morning Walking & Evening Dress.
No II 1811.

courtesy of dressmaker and milliner Mrs Bell (fig. 1.20).[102] There was a difference, too,
between plates drawn from life, those depicting gowns worn by fashion innovators,
and those that showed a look in the hope of promoting it. Fashion plates convey
stance and attitude, important in their own way for disseminating fashionable
ensemble arrangements, and modes of aspirational bodies. Images often appeared
in several publications, copied or redrawn with mixed success and no attribution, to
provide content for the journals.

Historians have often suggested that women took plates to their dressmakers to
copy, a practice common in the later nineteenth century but for which I have yet
found no primary evidence in the Regency. Austen's entire works contain no mention of two-dimensional representations of a dressed body involved in creating dress.
More commonly re-used were fashion engravings in pocket-books. These compact
memoranda books, diaries and repositories of useful information were printed in the
autumn for the following year, usually containing engravings of two or three fashion

Self

Fashionable Dresses of 1803.

—Peregrine having rescued Mary from Robbers, supports her to the Inn of Dennis Brielgrudder.

CANTERBURY.

Fig. 1.21

In her pocket-book for 1804, Austen's young niece Fanny Knight experimented with bringing the monochrome fashion engravings (found in all such publications) to life, cutting out parts of the figures and adding scraps of silk, muslin and ribbon (though their original positions have been lost). Kent Family History Centre, Diaries of Fanny C. Knatchbull.

figures.[103] These appear consistently among fashion images that women cut out and re-used. The albums of clergyman's daughter Barbara Johnson (1738–1825) and an otherwise unknown Mary White contain not one fashion-plate picture; they are all from cheaper, more widely available pocket-books.[104] The teenage diaries of Austen's niece Fanny Knight (1793–1882) show how she cut away parts of the figures and backed them with fabric scraps – a delightful material engagement with fashion dreaming (fig. 1.21).[105] We know Fanny Knight also read *La Belle Assemblée* because her 1814 yearly edition survives.

Physicality

In a unique visualisation of her imagination, Austen found a watercolour she considered the exact likeness of Jane Bingley (née Bennet; *P&P*), the most beautiful of the heroines (fig. 1.22). The painted woman embodies Regency female pulchritude: blonde, plump, high-busted, soft-featured and round-eyed. No wonder observers could never quite decide whether Austen herself was pretty, as her long, thin body (by her own and many observers' estimation) did not fit current notions of attractiveness. Tall, womanly, full-formed and fair, like the fictional Bertram sisters (*MP*), fits the mould better.[106] Austen applies 'beauty' and 'handsome' to characters of both sexes, and, unlike dress, physical appeal is discussed at length throughout the novels.

The ideal male Regency figure was 'lean and muscled. Wide shoulders, slim hips and a flat stomach make him an inverted triangle. He is classical statuary made flesh, or rather, fabric.'[107] The image of the heroic male carved into antique marbles provided a pattern for modern masculinity, which has never disappeared. Tailors brought to life the 'perfection of cold marble' on warmer, less perfect bodies as 'the male dress changed almost insensibly from formality to ease', as contemporaries saw it.[108]

Bathing and grooming polished up Regency attractiveness. As Catherine Morland (*NA*) grows, her 'love of dirt [gave] way to an inclination for finery, and she grew clean as she grew smart', meaning well turned out.[109] Cleanliness, in the words of a more didactic author, 'constitutes a woman's most pleasing charm . . . that regular comfortable nicety which renders . . . her person pleasing to behold, at all hours of day'.[110] Here again is the neatness Austen prized, the emergent nineteenth-century focus on cleanliness as a quality to notice and value in others' dress, in white gowns and snowy cravats. In Bath one morning, the gowns of a Mrs and Miss Holder 'looked so white and so nice' they went some way to gaining Austen's positive opinion.[111]

Being away from urban crowding probably helped the gentry's and upper classes' nutritional advantages. Health is underestimated as a factor in historical beauty. When Emma is described as '"the complete picture of grown-up health"', Mrs Weston means there is '"health, not merely in her bloom, but in her air, her head, her glance"', making her '"loveliness itself"' in the eyes of her fond teacher.[112] A person with a good complexion, regular features, and figure undistorted by malnutrition, illness or labour, having no skin disfigurements, plump enough from regular feeding and possessing a full set of teeth was well on the way to being handsome merely through physical fitness, by comparison with much of British society. The microscopically faithful portraits of street people that John Dempsey (1802/3–1877) painted from the 1820s show how rare physical regularity must have been, and how hard lives told on the body (fig. 1.23).

Once basic attractiveness was established, its viewers dissected the comprising elements minutely. It was not enough to have the lineaments; one must have spirit, moving the form with '"a certain something in her air and manner of walking, the tone of her voice, her address and expressions"', as Caroline Bingley (*P&P*) decrees.[113] Austen's characters spend lengthy passages scrutinising various kinds of physical appearance, from Sir Walter Elliot's harsh assessment of women on the street in Bath (*Pers.*), to Emma Woodhouse's consideration of Jane Fairfax's outstanding elegance and distinction.[114] Elegance was strong enough to compensate for plainness in Austen's world. She is remarkable for observing the difference emotions make to people's beauty: Anne Elliot regains the bloom she is often described as having lost as the possibility of happiness with Captain Wentworth unfolds. Respectable society disapproved of the use of cosmetics to disguise irregularities.[115] In general, powder and rouge were the only acceptable additions, with lotions such as Gowlands (endorsed by Sir Walter Elliot) to improve the complexion.

Hair is the easiest part of the bodily self to mould into a social, dressed body, and new techniques and styles of hair were as much a part of achieving Regency fashion as

clothing and a good figure. Women's clean, natural, unpowdered hair was divided into 'front' hair (from the ears forward), usually cut shorter than the long 'back' hair. Ideals of antique beauty reigned equally here, with periodicals evoking hair in the Grecian style, Roman style, à la Madonna and a host of other fanciful inspirations, all centred on curls.[116] Jane Austen was the lucky possessor of hair naturally curly enough to 'want no papering' (see fig. 0.1) to create the desirable ringlets.[117] Her niece Louisa Hill (née Knight; 1804–1889) remembered Austen's long hair reaching her knees, although by the age of 23 she always wore it 'plaited up out of sight' under caps, saving her 'a world of torment as to hair-dressing'.[118] Figure 1.24 shows a woman believed to be Maria Edgeworth: she wears a simple knot bun, and her naturally straight front hair is struggling to hold the curls universally popular 'in all their diversities'.[119]

Female hairdressing involved transforming part of the body daily into a social marker of style. When Miss Bates asks Emma '"how do you like Jane [Fairfax]'s hair? You are a judge. She did it all herself. Quite wonderful how she does her hair! No hairdresser from London I think could,"' the lady's pride reveals their poverty.[120] Jane has the taste and skill to manage her hair without a lady's maid, and she is long used to doing her own coiffure. Emma, of course, has a maid to curl her hair. Before the advent of reliable mirrors, and with style focusing on the back of women's heads, the eyes and hands of another were essential to creating Regency hairstyles. Austen once did her hair with a friend's help, 'which I fancy looked very indifferent, nobody abused it, however, and I retired delighted with my success'.[121] Help with coiffures was a valued skill in employees. Various servants assisted Austen's follicular efforts. In

Fig. 1.24

1798 Nanny Littlewart was dressing Austen's hair; and in 1804 a Jenny in Lyme Regis 'fasten'd up my hair to day in the same manner that she used to do up Miss Lloyd's'.[122] Haircutting was a separate business, conducted by a professional, usually male, who either came to the house or saw clients on his own premises. In Godmersham, Kent, Mr Hall charged Elizabeth Austen (1773–1808); wife of Edward Austen/Knight '5s. for every time of dressing her hair', but charged her sister-in-law Austen only half as much – 2s. 6d. – the same as he did Cassandra – which Austen attributed to his respecting either their youth or their poverty. The kindly man included hairstyling fit for an assembly ball in the bargain price.[123] It was, indeed, cheap compared with the 10s. Monsieur Trichot charged Maria Edgeworth's relatives before a London ball.[124] Another Mr Hall in London eight years later cut and curled Austen's hair, which she thought looked hideous.[125]

Female elegance frequently exploited false hair and wigs. As *The Book of English Trades* (1818) described the situation:

> Wigs and other ornamental decorations made of hair, are now become so common, that there are few ladies, notwithstanding they possess the most beautiful hair, who will not wear a manufactured article in preference to their own hair, under the impression that they can improve nature, and add to their charms.[126]

These additions ranged from a 'front', a row of ringlets sewn to a tape and tied around the head, to a full wig made from one's own hair (or a daughter's), perhaps left over from cutting the radical short 'crop' of the kind Austen's niece Anna and the governess Ellen Weeton sported in the 1800s, in a congruence of bodily and fashionable selves. Deficiencies in the abundance or quality of tresses could thus be discreetly rectified in private. Hats and caps were expedient covers for inadequate hair, requiring only a front to peep out, which could be any colour the wearer chose, a substitute greying ladies embraced readily to disguise their age. Mary Elizabeth Lucy of Charlecote Park, Warwickshire (1803–1889), wrote in her childhood memoirs of 'a very pretty little old lady always dressed in . . . a black satin hat turned up over a wig of brown curls', and Austen's own aunt Mrs Jane Leigh Perrot (1744–1836) appeared in her sixties with 'hair of dark brown, curled on her forehead'.[127] Mrs Topham bought new fronts in 1815, 1817, 1822 and 1824 for between 9 and 18s., and a full 'tete' – a head of hair or larger wig – cost her 9s. in 1817 and 1821. 'Curls for behind', showing on the nape, cost 5s. in 1817; 'drop curls' (single ringlets) 4s. in 1820. Natural hair was made up unnaturally, to imitate naturalness.[128]

Men's hair fashions underwent a similar conceptual change with the disappearance of obviously false powdered hair

and horsehair wigs. Economics had a hand in encouraging naturalesque hair. In 1795 'an annual tax of one guinea was laid upon all persons who should in future wear hair powder' to raise money for the government; 'this very much injured the trade; [1796] and 1799, were seasons of uncommon scarcity with regard to wheat [for hair-powder]: these circumstances produced a revolution in the trade, the wearing of hair-powder was nearly abandoned, and still continues out of fashion'.[129] So Classicism and finance together encouraged fashions from the late 1790s for cropped, curled, artfully dishevelled men's hairstyles modelled after antique sculpture, with names to match. In 1799 Austen playfully worried that her brother Edward 'would not approve of Charles being a crop' as the new fashion might imply sympathy with the Revolutionary French.[130] Men groomed themselves à la Titus, or in the Brutus fashion, and kept their faces clean shaven, with side-whiskers appearing into the 1810s. Grey horsehair wigs soon marked out old, fusty gentlemen, and were acceptable only for professional or occupational reasons.

Older men also adopted 'natural' wigs to compensate for time's attack on their locks (fig. 1.25). By 1822 the ageing George IV's flaxen wig appeared in 'bad taste' beside a visitor's natural grey hair.[131] Wigs also kept out the cold, like a fur hat. Actress Dorothea Jordan (1761–1816), the Duke of Clarence's mistress and mother of his ten children, bought herself one in 1809 from the 'idea that it prevented cold'.[132] In a world used to heating on demand and waterproof fabrics it is harder now to appreciate the value of being warm and dry.[133] A brown, curled wig is part of the repertoire of cosy clothing from the wardrobe of elderly banker Thomas Coutts (1725–1822), founder of the establishment still bearing his name.[134] The constant expenses of washing, repairing and curling false hair, and using it to maintain a respectable appearance, made wigs a marker of genteel rank.

Gentility in the age of Austen was full of such bodily markers, showing how the wearer absorbed and delineated the tides of fashion and new stylistic modes, tempering novelty with taste and culturally appropriate sensibility. Creating a self involved dressing the physical body in mental robes expressed through material ones. New fashion images helped to inculcate these ideals and the aesthetic concepts that shaped fashion's forms, either by defining what was 'natural' and then faking it, or by indulging in exotic romantic nostalgias. Yet self-regulation was primarily achieved by and for the eyes of others, as constant external assessment determined the success and attractiveness of the gentry social body. Immersed in the cultural waters of their time, Regency people absorbed or resisted the tides of fashion, or let themselves be carried a little way, refreshed by old ideas made new again, washing off the encrustations of eighteenth-century style, as Austen did in her fiction.

Fig. 1.25

Walter Stephens Lethbridge, portrait of John Wolcot, c.1817, watercolour and bodycolour on ivory. Aged 79, the elderly satirist wears a wig that does not match what is left of the natural colour in his eyebrows. He is clad in a banyan or nightgown. National Portrait Gallery, London.

Chapter 2

Home

I thought of you . . . in the Draw'g room & in your China Crape; – therefore, you were in the Breakfast parlour in your Brown Bombasin; if I thought of you so, you would have been in the Kitchen in your Morning stuff.[1]

Jane Austen lived in an intensely domestic environment. For years biographers focused on a supposed cloistered rural existence, a spinster bound to her parents and unmarried sister, visiting various brothers and their children as kindly Aunt Jane. To an extent this is true. Had Austen married and run her own household, her life would have been more strenuously managerial. But regardless of marital status, home was always where clothing was created and maintained, and these occupations made up a large proportion of quotidian living. This chapter is concerned with the intimate activities of making and mending clothing worn closest to the body. It examines underwear, the first trappings of creating a social body, and how people appeared to one another at home. Where the gentry dressed, how they cleaned and cared for their clothes, and the role of household servants in aiding these tasks are likewise considered. When Austen and her contemporaries first arose from bed and put themselves together for a quiet day at home, this is where they started.

Undergarments

Washable white garments were dressing's foundation. Women wore a shift or smock, a long tunic of linen, or occasionally cotton (fig 2.1), with a wide, round or rectangular neckline as the gown demanded; they wore no underpants. The shift reached the knees, having long side gussets, and had short, straight sleeves no longer than the elbow. A gathered muslin frill could be sewn around the neckline and removed during laundering. 'Chemise', a French import, overtook the older English 'shift' in one of the period's language gentrifications. Much criticism of Regency high fashion centred on an idea that women discarded their chemises to give the illusion of nudity and reduced bulk, or wore gowns that looked like chemises, in 'the nakedness of the mode'.[2] Wearing no shift was probably an extremely rare practice, enabled by using a thicker textile for the gown to hide the body. In respectable wear, a woman's chemise was essential as the invisible first layer. If it was abandoned, there should have been no way to tell.

Men's linen shirts comprised a skilful union of rectangles and squares, and were almost without exception white (fig. 2.2).[3] The long sleeves ended in single or double (folded-back) cuffs, and could be finely pleated through ironing to get their bulk to fit neatly into tight coat sleeves. Shirts opened about a foot (30 cm) down the front and fastened only at the neck and cuffs, with thread or fabric-covered buttons. They reached mid-thigh. If drawers were not worn, the shirt's tails could be tucked between the legs. Although cotton was on the rise during the long Regency, linen firmly held its place for body-wear, lasting longer and wicking moisture from the body better than cotton. Not until the mid-1820s did consumers start accepting cotton shirting.[4]

Shirts were underwear: private, intimate and potentially vulgar. Austen's only
fictional mention of a shirt is the famous washing list in *Northanger Abbey*, which
the heroine hopes is a Gothic missive. Their presence is stronger in the letters,
as Austen and her female relatives sewed shirts for their menfolk. Finer muslin,
gathered in narrow frills down the front opening, covered any gaps from the
slit and provided a snowy fall through the waistcoat, delicately hemmed and
contrasting with the denser main fabric of the shirt. The collar was universally
square at the edges. Starching gave a crispness exploited in the fashion for collars
so high they caressed the jawline, with the collar points called 'ears' (fig. 2.3). Lady
Stanley asked in 1800 'is it the fashion for the shirt collar to stand as high as the
corners of the eyes? It is of consequence I should be informed before the new set I
am making is finished.'[5]

Collars were doubled over and were tied closed with a cravat, stock or (especially further down the social scale) kerchief. Pre-sewn stocks, made from a yard width of muslin or cambric gathered into two plain ends a couple of inches wide, fastening at the back, made arranging graceful folds easier. Plain white cravats, made from a length of fabric, or a rectangle or square of linen or lawn folded into a triangle, were correct for day and evening, but patterned and coloured neckcloths were informal choices, 'admitted only as undress costume'.[6] The accounts for 1797 of Parson James Woodforde (1740–1803), of Weston Longville, Norfolk (a living worth £400 a year), document the extra fabrics needed to complete men's shirt ensembles: '3 yards of Jaconnett Muslin' made him six cravats each a yard wide; 1¼ yards of cambric muslin supplied four stocks, and an extra yard of the same made twelve frills.[7] Tying a neckcloth with crisp precision was a mark of style and taste; according to an author surveying changes in fashion in 1810, 'The modern neckcloth . . . has undergone more ridicule than the rest of the dress in the aggregate.'[8] Many guides to the art of neckwear demonstrated how to achieve individual ties, culminating in the publication *Neckclothitania*, celebrating neckwear's diverse shapes.[9]

Stays

Women wore stays as bust support over their shifts. The garment determined the woman's dressed shape, and underwent significant transformation in the long Regency. In the 1790s stays changed from being heavily boned constructions, creating a solid, mono-bosomed cone, stopping at the waist, to light garments that followed the body's contours, with high, rounded, individual breasts, imitating instead of reshaping the natural female body. The change in shape may have related to the rise of female staymakers, who were more aware than their male counterparts of the relationship of stays to the female body, though they were also responding to fashion.[10]

As waistlines rose, waist-length stays kept pace with the outer gown, creating hybrid forms, while 'short stays' finished at the ribs (fig. 2.4). Tabs at the waist – no longer required to support the weight of petticoats – began to disappear, and eventually became gussets for the hips in 'long' stays (fig. 2.5).[11] Boning was reduced, and the construction fabric changed from leathers and sturdy linen twills to lighter, tightly woven cottons. Gussets under the bust lifted and separated the breasts. Looser stays met with medical approval:

> Among many improvements in the modern fashions of female dress, equally favourable to health, to graceful ease and elegance, the

Dress in the Age of Jane Austen

discontinuance of stays is entitled to peculiar approbation. It is, indeed, impossible to think of the old straight waistcoat of whalebone, and of tight lacing, without astonishment and some degree of horror.[12]

One of Austen's obscure dress references is to the 'pattern of a stomacher' that Jane Fairfax sends to her aunt, Miss Bates (*Emma*).[13] A stomacher was a triangular piece of cloth that filled a gap at the front of an earlier design of stays. By the date of *Emma*, stomachers were not in fashionable use. The possibilities for Austen's meaning are, first, a smaller woollen protective garment: 'After the age of 40 one may use either a flannel pectoral or stomacher until the flannel age arrives.'[14] Or, secondly, either Miss Bates or her elderly mother might wear jumps (also known as 'waistcoats'), softer, unboned upper-body garments consisting of a pair of stomacher-fronted stays or 'bodies', long common as informal domestic wear.[15]

The Victoria and Albert Museum collection contains a cotton bust bodice dating to the first quarter of the nineteenth century. It looks like a cropped midriff top, with short sleeves, adjusted by means of sash-like lengths behind, and demonstrates the variety of bust supports available to Regency women.[16] At the height of classical simplicity around 1800, some women apparently really did go

Fig. 2.4

Short stays, 1790s, cotton with silk embroidery and boning, lined with linen. In transitional style, these stays retain the earlier conical shape and tabs, but are made of a lighter fabric with reduced boning; the gathered gussets allow the breasts a more natural form. Victoria and Albert Museum, London.

without stays. Frenchwomen were infamous for it, and elite women's nipples are detectable in portraits from both sides of the Channel. The extreme fashion was not universal. Although near-natural breasts were clearly acceptable enough to be shown in a portrait of a British royal princess (see fig. 1.11), the mode was unlikely to have been seen at evening parties in deepest Hampshire. The practice of dressing without stays was ridiculed in caricature and satire, though women referred to the practice. Princess Caroline's maid noted Her Highness taking off her stays on regular occasions.[17]

However, 'stays', at the time, meant stiff, boned garments. During the Regency, the French term 'corset' or 'corsette' gained fashionability, eventually eclipsing the older 'stays', though authors interchanged the terms in the same work. Fanny Burney wrote home about Paris fashions in 1802: 'Stays? everybody has left off even corsets!', differentiating between types of garment.[18] 'Corset' properly denotes a softer, lightly boned or unboned garment. The flexible bust supports emerging in such variety in the first decade of the century did not necessarily fit Regency conceptions of 'stays'. A single staymaker like Marston in London could advertise his 'French, Spanish, improved Grecian, Italian, a-la-Circassian, and every other stay . . . in the greatest variety of shapes'.[19] In the same issue of *La Belle Assemblée*, Marston's competitor went one better with the 'Armenian divorce corset', heralded as giving the bust grace, elegance and ease, and intriguingly 'divested of the trouble of lacing'. Surviving garments give only suggestions of the plethora of innovations. If a woman was modestly endowed, the close-fitting short gown bodice alone could support her breasts. The whole of their roundness was fashionable and 'natural' for the first time.

As waistlines dropped – which happened earlier for day than for evening wear – it became more difficult to leave the bust unsupported, and long stays dominated by about 1820. Long stays had a smoothing effect over the waist and hips, suited to the tubular skirts of the 1800s, 'to give the true Grecian form' and 'compass into form the chaos of flesh'.[20] The change from stays that covered the body from shoulder to waist, to those running from bust to hip, set the foundation for the hourglass shape of the Victorian age. A female staymaker identified one of the subtler fashion shifts during the long Regency, when around 1810 the 'commendable elegance of the Grecian costume . . . is now about to give place to the unnatural tapering of the waist', an effect created by long stays.[21] They were made from cotton sateen, jean and coutil, with minimal stiffening of baleen, or cotton cording quilted into channels. The style retained the central busk of wood inserted in a wide channel down the front, as implied in portraits where women have pinned their gown neckline to the centre support, so that it follows the line of the breasts (see fig. 7.19).

Some men wore stays. Figures of 'irksome dandies, circled in their stays' in caricature make much of the small-waisted man, and he appears in fiction as a man of fashion, 'of high ton, dressed in a tightly-buttoned coat, apparently supported by stays' (fig. 2.6).[22] The Prince Regent, growing ever fatter, turned to stays to streamline his bulk. The surviving pattern for his waist-shaper shows that it could have reduced

Fig. 2.5

Long stays, 1810s, hand-woven linen. These
stays have no boning apart from the central
busk. By c.1820 long stays of this style, covering
the torso from the bust to the natural waistline
or the hips, had almost entirely superseded the
variety of shorter bust supports with which
women experimented during the Regency. Kent
State University, Ohio.

his girth to a lissom 52 inches (132 cm).[23] His brother the Duke of Cumberland
was so associated with the wearing of stays that the male garment was dubbed
'Cumberland stays'.[24] Masculine waist shaping was not well regarded – one text
judges men who went in for it as 'Episcene non-naturals', 'clipp'd in the middle like
an hour-glass'.[25] However, there is evidence of its regular use. A London tailor, for
example, advertised a staymaker on his staff, 'who designs and fashions the most
approved stays for Gentlemen, from the Glasgow Stiffener to the Bath Corset'.[26] The
Workwoman's Guide (1838) gives instructions for making heavy-duty men's stays in
the form of a belt of material, 'worn by gentlemen in the army, hunters, or by those
using violent exercise', probably to support the abdominal muscles.[27]

Austen decorously never mentions stays or corsets in fiction, but one of her best-
known personal fashion comments concerns her learning

> from Mrs. Tickars's young lady [maid], to my high amusement, that the
> stays now are not made to force the bosom up at all; that was a very

Home

unbecoming, unnatural fashion. I was really glad to hear that they are not to be so much off the shoulders as they were.[28]

Another writer complained of 'The bosom shoved up to the chin, making a sort of fleshy shelf'.[29] Freed from conical shapes, staymakers apparently explored the ways they could mould malleable flesh.

A distinctive feature of late Regency silhouettes was a rounded back, seen in caricatures and known as the 'Grecian bend' (see fig. 1.17); it was thought to be caused by 'ungraceful' short waists, which 'rendered the women . . . all humpbacked'.[30] A contrasting opinion was that 'Stays, corsets, and bands of every description . . . must infallibly produce mischief . . . [giving] place to contraction, shrivelling and emaciation. This has the effect of . . . throwing the shoulders out of their natural position, contracting the chest, and causing an ungraceful stoop in walking.'[31] A small bustle pad, inside or outside the petticoat, rounded the skirt at the back to increase its curves and the contrast of the bend. The padding had been popular before 1800, and by about 1810 it returned. By 1815 it was a detached roll tied round the waist.

Like lack of stays, contemporary and modern fashion commentators identify the putting off of petticoats as a scandalous Regency novelty. But for all the cries that 'Some of our fair dames appear . . . with no other shelter from sun or frost than one single garment of muslin or silk over their chemise – if they wear one!', petticoats were an essential feminine undergarment.[32] Petticoats – meaning any skirt(s) worn under the main gown – were made of serviceable cambric, linen, lawn, or eventually cotton; they could be functional, warm or durable underwear, or a finer-quality underskirt that might be seen. Miss Bates's pleasure that her mother's old petticoat 'would last a great while – and, indeed, she must thankfully say that their petticoats were all very strong' (*Emma*), evokes how women wore their petticoats more or less visibly according to shabbiness.[33] To have sturdy petticoats was an economic consideration supporting one's conspicuous respectability. Mentioning mundane undergarments in conversations, though, smacks of the Bates's descent in gentility. 'Coat' was common shorthand for a petticoat, as on a washing bill of 1800 that lists '2 Callicoe Coats', '1 Dimity under Coat' and '1 Flannel D[itt]o'.[34]

Surviving petticoats made of the same decorative fabric as the matching outer gown show the persistence of the eighteenth-century underskirt. Gowns from 1795 to the early 1800s could still be open at the front and require a matching petticoat. Less fashionable printed cotton day gowns with petticoats appear in collections into the early 1820s. Any skirt without a bodice could be a petticoat, of the kind Austen meant when she observed 'coloured petticoats with braces' in 1814.[35] The comfortable domestic wear of such petticoats can be seen in figure 2.7. Rising waistlines saw the development of the bodiced petticoat, the upper part sometimes made of coarser material; this provided an undergarment up to the right level under the bust, without the need for bulky waist ties. Some surviving petticoats and petticoat skirts, especially in the later 1810s and 1820s, have merely two

Dress in the Age of Jane Austen

straps or tapes running over the shoulders to hold them up. Petticoat construction matched that of outer skirts, gaining gores just as gowns did into the 1810s.

Petticoats could be made of gown-quality material, or from worn-out gowns, in the way that Austen contemplated using one of her many old muslin gowns, of which she was 'tired and ashamed'.[36] The hems of petticoats could be visible below a much shorter overdress, and were often decorated especially to be revealed. This fashion increased as hems grew broad again after 1815, and petticoats with frills and flounces added bulk and visual interest to lower skirts. Under one of the popular thigh-length tunic over-gowns or 'robes', the petticoat formed the skirt. At the height of the narrow-skirted phase in the 1800s, advertisements for 'patent elastic Spanish lamb's wool, invisible petticoats, drawers, waistcoats, all in one' reflected attempts at *trompe l'oeil* nudity in undergarments.[37] 'Elastic' petticoats of stretch materials such as stockinette suggest further attempts at creating figure-hugging underskirts. Perhaps fashion triumphed when women *appeared* to wear no petticoat, whatever sleight of hand was required to achieve it.

Women's knee-length drawers first came into fashion around 1805, made with a joined crotch, or with two separate legs on a waistband. The article was distinct from calf- or ankle-length pantaloons, also borrowed from the masculine wardrobe. Like the petticoat, pantaloons or pantalet(te)s had decorative pin tucks and lace on their visible hems (see fig. 2.6). Knitted undergarments with legs were advertised as 'Ladies' Hunting and Opera drawers in elastic India cotton', in 1811; and 'drawers with attached feet' in 1813.[38]

THE HEN-PECKED DANDY.   320

The Demon of Fashion SIR FOPLING bewitches —   For as she is resolved upon wearing the Breeches,
The reason his Lady betrays —————   In revenge he has taken the Stays!.

Contemporary comment called pantelets 'trowsers'. Aristocratic women as high in status as Caroline of Brunswick (1768–1821), wife of the Prince of Wales, wore the new 'tight trowsers', a fact specifically commented upon in her divorce trial.[39] Six years earlier her fashion-forward daughter Princess Charlotte (1796–1817) had adopted drawers, 'which, it seems, she and most young women now wear'. Charlotte's governess objected that the drawers were too long, and showed. Young Charlotte retorted that 'The Duchess of Bedford's are much longer, and they with Brussels lace.'[40] Drawers partook of well-established anxieties about blurring gender boundaries in clothing. Bifurcated garments were the preserve of masculinity. It was admitted that drawers might have their utility, 'but when they appear below the jupe [skirt] they are masculine and disgusting'.[41] It was risqué for women to acknowledge that they had two legs, but by about 1820 drawers – now the favoured term – were established in female wardrobes.[42]

Men's drawers had a longer, more respectable history. Euphemistically called 'small clothes' or 'unmentionables', they acted as washable, removable linings to breeches (fig. 2.8). Underneath tight buckskin or chamois they protected the leather and the wearer from each other. Masculine drawers were made of linen, fine knits, or wool flannel for warmth, joined at the crotch except at the front, on a broad waistband, and with the same diagonal cut as breeches, and similar extra fabric and room to move over the buttocks. Drawers tied about the knee with tapes at the cuff, and stretch materials, or wool flannel added warmth.[43]

In fact, fluffy unbleached wool flannel was surprisingly common underneath Regency clothing. For romantic Marianne Dashwood (S&S), "'a flannel waistcoat is invariably

connected with the aches, cramps, rheumatisms, and every species of ailment
that can afflict the old and the feeble'".[44] The offending article was a prophylactic
undergarment. Flannel underwear supported flimsy muslins and robust tailoring
alike to protect both sexes from maladies. For men, the underwear comprised
drawers, like Thomas Coutts's surviving pairs.[45] The 'waistcoat' (in the old sense
of an undershirt) had long or elbow-length sleeves and buttoned down the front
(fig. 2.9). Because wool flannel was washable it could be worn next to the skin. Mrs
Longsdon of Derbyshire, wife of local fustian manufacturer James, wrote to her son
John in the winters of 1811 and 1812, imploring him to wear a flannel waistcoat
in the cold weather.[46] His brother William had been sending flannel shirts home
for washing since 1803, and other washing bills distinguish between waistcoats and
flannel dressing waistcoats.[47] Flannel underwear was recommended as treatment for
gout and flannel was, indeed, the fabric of illness. When Austen reported 'my uncle
is still in his flannels, but is getting better again', it conjures being enveloped in the
soft, comfortable warmth desirable when sick.[48] Men could have their stockings or
breeches lined with flannel, or use a 'slip' waistcoat with a flannel body, and a cloth
collar to appear at the chest.

Flannel petticoats were protection against cold and damp, but distinctly prosaic,
with all the appeal of wearing thermal underwear under evening dress. Marianne's

Home

repulsion, echoing Austen's own opinion of flannel as a 'disgraceful and contemptible' article, is visualised in figure 2.10.[49] The proffered solid skirt is the kind with which an imperious lady at a Lyme Regis ball girded herself against the night air, in a satire on the popular resort. She advises a cold man to get a flannel undergarment, wearing six herself, and he is unsurprised, given 'the load of flannel which under / The rest of your numerous garments you've got, / That you find these apartments a little too hot.'[50] Women also wore flannel upper-body garments, a simple wraparound bodice, buttoning down the front, with gores for hips and bust. The 'waistcoat' Fanny (Palmer) Austen (1789–1814) bought for 12*s.* 6*d.* in 1814 is probably this type of underwear.[51]

Elizabeth ('Eliza') Jervoise (1770–1821) was the wife of George Purefoy Jervoise (1770–1847), MP for Salisbury in 1813–18 and Hampshire in 1820–26. The couple moved regularly between their Hampshire estate, Herriard Park near Alton, and The Moat in Wiltshire, and their meticulously preserved bills and account books are mines of information about Regency gentry dress. Mrs Jervoise regularly sent a flannel waistcoat for washing among her personal linen, and her housekeeper wore 'night waistcoats' in 1811.[52] The latter were probably flannel, for warmth, but might have been made of the calico Mrs Topham bought in lengths for 'waistcoats' in 1822–3.[53] Staymaker Mrs Gibbon considered warmth around the torso the real purpose of stays, while doctors recommended calico waistcoats for summer wear to replace winter's flannels.[54] The regular presence of advertisements for Welch [*sic*] flannel houses in periodicals bespeaks the ubiquity of the unglamorous fabric underlying Regency clothing.

Everybody wore stockings, or socks, made of silk, cotton, linen ('thread'), and wool or worsted, usually reaching above the knee.[55] For men wearing breeches, stockings were essential to cover the lower leg, and they drew on to above the knee, held up by the knee band of his breeches or the strings of his drawers. In winter, for warmth, or all year round to prevent leg hairs from poking through thin knit, men wore understockings – a waistcoat for the legs.[56] Women's stockings were the same length and held up by garters tied around the thigh or under the knee. The shaping for the ankle, running from heel to calf, is called the clock, often a different colour or beautifully embroidered (see fig. 2.6). Cotton stockings bought in bulk were most common for the gentry. Prices varied between around tuppence per pair, bought by the dozen, to at least the 5*s.* per pair that Mrs Topham paid in 1815.[57] Clearly, the difference is in quality, of which Austen said she 'greatly prefer[red] having two pair only of that quality [of stocking] to three of an inferior sort'. As stockings wore out quickly and needed constant darning to remain wearable they were purchased often.

Stockings were essential to keeping dry and providing warmth when walking and going out in the weather. John Souter attested that their 'principal use [was] to defend these parts of the body from cold'.[58] Medical experts agreed. Improper covering of feet and legs 'pre-dispos[ed] those parts for the gout, rheumatism, dropsy, and a variety of other complaints'.[59] Unlike men, women wore no leg-protecting boots. Changing damp stockings immediately after walking, as Mr

❊ ❊   *Dress in the Age of Jane Austen*

Fig. 2.10

George Moutard Woodward and Isaac Cruikshank, *A Hint to the Ladies, or A Visit from Dr Flannel* (1807?), hand-coloured etching on paper. The unromantic, unglamorous nature of flannel garments is conveyed by the lady's expression upon being offered a thick flannel petticoat. Wellcome Collection, London.

Woodhouse is concerned Jane Fairfax should do (*Emma*), staved off the kinds of cold Marianne Dashwood (*S&S*) contracts by sitting in wet shoes and stockings. Elizabeth Bennet's dirty stockings from walking across fields are the equivalent of mud-splashed boots, taking the brunt instead of her less washable gown (*P&P*).

Worsted stockings provided warmth and durability. The toughness of this yarn, made of the harder hair of sheep, is found in Thomas Coutts's stockings (fig. 2.11). When he complained of pain in walking, his future mother-in-law found his worsted stockings twisted with hard lumps of darning. She quickly supplied him with new ones.[60] Likewise, Ellen Weeton advised her brother to 'have the feet of your silk stockings lined with something soft . . . or the darning will hurt your feet'.[61] Worsted stockings were popular charitable donations because of their long-lasting healthful properties. In 1798 Austen gave a pair of worsted stockings to each of four village women of the parish, and in 1800 bought another ten pairs at Oakley, possibly for donation.[62] The price varied with quality but was higher than cotton: one worsted pair, at 2s. 6d., cost Mrs Topham the same as a dozen cheap cotton pairs.[63]

Stockings came in a wide variety of colours: brown, grey, olive and purple for walking; dark blue, black and natural wool; silk in a range of vivid hues to match fashionable colours of the moment, or to set off a coloured pair of shoes. The finest quality stockings were knitted silk, desired for their fit and sheen; Austen had at least

Home

four pairs, some of which Cassandra marked for washing by sewing initials into the tops. Their niece Fanny Knight thought the stockings she bought from a travelling salesman were great bargains, at 12s. for silk and 4s. 3d. for cotton.[64] Reports from fashion pages reveal that fashionable silk versions were ribbed or made of fine gauze, and had lace or embroidered clocks.

Nightwear

Diana Sperling's amateur watercolour sketchbooks of 1812–23 provide a rare look at Regency women's innermost dress.[65] Sperling (1791–1862), the daughter of a middle-gentry landowning family near the Essex–Suffolk border, painted sprightly vignettes of family life and the dress worn living it. *Mrs Van Murdering a Spider* shows two women in their nightdresses (fig. 2.12). These long linen or calico versions of shifts covered women to the ankle and wrists, with a high, buttoned collar like a shirt but finished with a frill.[66] Men's nightshirts were longer versions of their daily shirts, as an 1811 letter attests: John Longsdon wrote to his mother in Derbyshire from London requesting that she send an old shirt as a pattern for nightshirts.[67] Although most night garments were serviceable, frivolous and seductive options for sleepwear existed. A Miss Brownlow of Bath, known to Maria Edgeworth, ordered 'transparent night chemises of the thinnest muslin and *gauze* – some striped some spotted – with bows of white satin and other absurdities' for her honeymoon attire.[68]

The long back hair seen in Sperling's sketch required a nightcap or night bonnet to prevent tangling while sleeping, preferably in hardy check or calico, as they were 'in constant wear', as Austen said.[69] Caps kept the head warm and the hair untangled, and prevented oils from less frequently washed hair transferring to pillowcases. One woman's collection of underclothes, dated 1818–36, at the Gallery of Costume in Manchester includes nightdresses, a chemise, a morning gown, neck frills and pockets, all with laundry numbers that show the lady owned at least eighteen nightdresses, nine chemises and six plain striped cotton nightcaps.[70]

Men warmed their heads in draughty bedchambers with round knitted nightcaps (see fig. 2.11). Confusingly, nightcaps were not only for night: 'nightcap' could mean any soft cap worn at any time – as opposed to structured hats – especially by poorer or older men (fig. 2.13). One old Scots farmer wore a striped nightcap 'which had long served for hat and cap; except on Sunday', while Dorothy Wordsworth (1771–1855, the poet's sister) met an old man wearing an apron and nightcap on a Lake District road.[71] Nightcaps were an accepted part of male 'undress'. For either sex, 'undress' meant informal, looser clothing suitable for wearing around the house, and receiving some visitors before one was formally dressed.[72] The mode was also called 'morning wear'. When Mr Bennet (*P&P*) wishes to 'sit in my library, in my nightcap and powdering gown, and give as much trouble as I can', he is sartorially matching Mrs Bennet's 'undressed' hysterics.[73] His 'powdering gown' is a kind of long, loose open robe, variously called 'dressing-gown', 'morning gown', 'banyan' or the old-fashioned 'nightgown', worn with a soft cap or turban, and slippers (fig. 2.13).[74] Men's morning gowns were often made of imported printed cottons, hence the name 'India gowns'. Portrait traditions dressed men of letters in cap or turban, gown and slippers, invoking an oriental air.[75]

From 1781 to 1802, Parson Woodforde bought the material for a morning gown each year, always patterned cotton. The 'contemptible article' made an appearance when Woodforde 'Had a thin flannel lining put to the Arms and Shoulders of my Cotton Gowns for the Morning . . . very comfortable wearing this time of the year', another tactic for keeping cold at bay, in addition to fur linings in winter banyans and gowns.[76] Dressing-gowns could also be made of flannel. By the early nineteenth century, men's morning gowns had moved from the looser oriental-style robe to a fitted garment, with lapels and set-in sleeves, quilted for warmth or made of woollen fabrics (fig. 2.14). They still provided more comfort and ease of movement than heavier day coats. Woodforde puttered around gardening in his cotton morning gowns, with an 'old shabby hat', and was happy for visitors to catch him in this state.[77] Perhaps less happy would have been the Mr Rose extolled by Miss Steele (*S&S*) as 'a prodigious smart young man, quite a beau' when fully dressed, but 'if you do but meet him of a morning, he is not fit to be seen', implying that his daily donning of his smart appearance represents a falsity of character.[78]

Women's dressing-gowns were more intimate than men's, and were worn over nightgowns. Maria Edgeworth wrote letters standing in her dressing-gown, before dressing for breakfast with Lord Byron (1788–1824).[79] In her final illness, Austen received family visitors in her dressing-gown, and her heroine Marianne Dashwood's dressing-gowned state of distress in London prevents her from receiving non-relatives.[80]

Home   ✳ ✳

Fig. 2.15 Opposite

Fanny Burney, exhausted from visits in 1802, 'rested upon a bed for the remainder of the day . . . in a close cap, my feet in their native, undraperied state, hidden by a large, long, wrapping morning gown'.[81]

The way Mrs Bennet calls for her housekeeper to 'put on my things in a moment' after languishing in her dressing-room for days suggests she is doing so in her dressing- or morning gown or other unstructured robe, perhaps a bedgown.[82] Like nightcaps, bedgowns were not necessarily worn to bed but were a convenient, short, skirted gown. The Wordsworth siblings' servant Sally went to visit in a new bedgown her cousin had given her.[83] Sufficient affection could overwhelm formality. When staying with Lady Lansdowne, Edgeworth received hugs during the dressing hour from a hostess 'only half dressed with a shawl thrown around her', while the author was herself 'without shoes and half dressed'.[84]

If nightwear is relatively poorly represented in the archives, clothing for maternity and nursing is even more discreet, usually mentioned only in connection with confining the torso when pregnant. It is true that 'most written sources from the eighteenth and early nineteenth centuries are strangely – even maddeningly – silent on the facts of women's pregnancies, how they managed their daily challenges, or what they wore', even though reproduction was a central part of women's lives.[85] The high waistlines of Austen's age were arguably better suited to accommodating an expanding belly (fig. 2.15) than any previous style. Women generally adapted their usual clothing around pregnancy.[86] The drawstrings, tapes and pins that fastened clothing made garments convenient and adaptable for shifting body shapes, which makes it harder to identify possible Regency maternity gowns in collections. Austen is pragmatic about reproduction in letters, while not mentioning dress worn during pregnancy. Her sister-in-law Mary, for example, 'seldom either looks or appears quite well. Little Embryo is troublesome, I suppose.'[87] Mrs Jennings's enquiry 'How does Charlotte do? I warrant you she is a fine size by this time' (S&S) emphasises the communal nature of visual communication of pregnancy, as well as her cheerful vulgarity.[88] Everyone in Emma's Highbury knows that Mrs Weston is pregnant without being 'told', making Mr Elton's asking her to dance at seven months' gestation a greater faux pas than merely snubbing Harriet Smith, while at the same time emphasising that maternity was not necessarily a barrier to activity.[89] On the day her baby was due, for example, the Duchess of Hamilton travelled by coach from Hamilton to Edinburgh.[90]

Austen was discursive about the material conditions after birth:

> Mary does not manage matters in such a way as to make me want to lay in myself. She is not tidy enough in her appearance; she has no dressing-gown to sit up in; . . . and things are not in that comfort and style about her which are necessary to make such a situation an enviable one. Elizabeth [Austen] was really a pretty object with her nice clean cap put on so tidily and her dress so uniformly white and orderly.[91]

Her personal preference for neatness and tidiness shines through.

Doctors and midwives were stern about the use of whaleboned stays during pregnancy and 'the aggravated mischief of such a pressure on the breasts and womb in a state of pregnancy'.[92] Softer jumps, worn with a stomacher, had been used for a long time pre- and post-partum to accommodate 'natural expansions' and access to nursing breasts.[93] A dictionary of 1808 alludes to this function when defining jumps as 'a kind of easy stays open before and worn by nurses'.[94] Nursing gowns are perhaps more easily identifiable when gown openings shifted from front to back: a plain cotton front-opening gown of the late 1810s could be for nursing. Fashion plates of women in morning dress with infants beside them may be subtle depictions of nursing dress.[95] As more women entered the staymaking profession, maternity stays, combining firmer support with expanding qualities, began to be advertised.[96] Pregnant re-enactors have experimented with replica side-lacing soft corsets from the early nineteenth century and found them easily adaptable to thickening bellies.[97]

How early-nineteenth century women dealt with menstruation is nearly undiscoverable. After extensive searching, the only documentary reference I found may be the 'napkins' that Eliza Jervoise regularly sent for washing among her own and her female servants' personal body linen. Medical treatises go into detail about the monthly process but never mention women's textile strategies for managing it. Later nineteenth-century references suggest women may have pinned absorbent diapered or linen cloths to their shifts or to tapes tied around the waist.[98]

Undress

'Undress' described the informal ensemble into which one changed from night attire for breakfast (taken some hours after rising – nine o'clock in the Austen household), working at home or paying morning visits. Part of the line between formal and informal dress was its tightness. To be loosely dressed was for the home, in private comfort, before drawing oneself together to face the outer world. Distracted by an emerging poem, William Wordsworth (1770–1850) sat at breakfast in 1802, stockingless, his shirt neck unbuttoned and his waistcoat open.[99] The heroine of the novel *The World* is teased by her cousins, who

> were perpetually finding fault with the looseness of my morning dress. I really pitied their ignorance, but could hardly forbear laughing when I saw them come down as prim to breakfast, as if they were dressed for visitors. It was in vain for me to tell them that women of fashion were above such regards; I was again forced to comply, and to stick pins into my cloaths.[100]

Ellen Weeton is more explicit, and says that when, in 1812, crossing to the Isle of Man at night, she had herself loosened her clothing; but of her landing she writes, 'in a totally unlaced and unpinned state, I was obliged to crawl through the streets, to the Inn, being perfectly unable to dress myself tight again.[101]

Morning and day dress was everyday clothing. Jane and Cassandra Austen both had stuff gowns for morning and daywear from at least 1798 to 1813,[102] though the *Repository of Arts* pronounced stuff gowns 'completely vulgar' in 1809. Their suggested substitute of 'round dresses of brown or deep purple muslin, ornamented with vandyke borders' suited the sisters' tastes.[103] Austen commissioned 'a plain brown cambric muslin, for morning wear' from Bath, and Cassandra could wear a 'brown bombasin' in the breakfast parlour at Godmersham.[104] Austen had a matching gown of the same fabric. Some time later, in 1813, she wrote to Cassandra debating cutting the trains of their bombazine gowns to 'give them up as morning gowns', though Austen would rather have sacrificed her blue gown for that purpose.[105] Just as old gowns could be turned into petticoats, good garments could be downgraded when grown shabby. Day dress often used tightly woven, crisp, printed cottons with dark grounds, or detailed patterns on undyed backgrounds in less sophisticated styles (fig. 2.16). They contrast strongly with delicate muslins, and shine with domestic practicality – gowns to withstand the assault of the laundry tub, of smoking stoves, runaway chickens, the mud and muck of daily life. Washable aprons around the waist or pinafores over the shoulders, as the Sperling ladies wore to put up wallpaper, further protected fabric and hid dirt.[106]

White was the overwhelmingly popular colour for morning undress among the gentry, and for receiving and making visits, a step up from a common print gown. Her niece Fanny received Austen's approbation for 'looking as neat & white this morn'g as possible', a style Cassandra illustrated (fig. 2.17).[107] Fashion plates show elaborately worked white morning dress throughout the Regency, in popular fabrics such as cambric or jaconet muslins. The white-work lace gowns, and embroidered muslin pelisses in collections are mostly morning wear (fig. 2.18). Austen teased Cassandra in 1813 that she needed to add the newly fashionable flounces to her clothing, asking satirically 'Are not some of your large stock of white morning gowns just in a happy state for a flounce?', after being visited by a Miss Chapman revelling in a double flounce.[108] For some women a 'large stock' was a reality. 'Lady Lansdowne's taste – brilliant in cleanliness – finest materials muslin or lace and work white as the driven snow', observed Maria Edgeworth, before adding 'But I am sure there must be a warehouse of morning gowns to supply her for I never saw her in the same twice.'[109]

A series of small things completed the undress Regency wardrobe. Caps, pockets and a huge variety of handkerchiefs and other covering clothes accessorised the respectable social body to create an appearance suitable for public consumption. 'Home costume' had longer sleeves and higher necklines than dress for later in the day. Where a neckline was low, it could be filled in with a neck-handkerchief, tucker, fichu, tippet, or later a chemisette – a fancier word for structured neck-handkerchiefs with collars. Chemisettes became false fronts, with no sleeves, tying like a tabard around the upper body to give the impression of an elaborate undergarment or decorative shirt. All these chest-covering garments were sewn from finer lawns, linens and muslins than shifts, and had elaborate collars and embroidery to keep pace with fashion. Small false fronts were easier to clean and iron than voluminous body-linens.

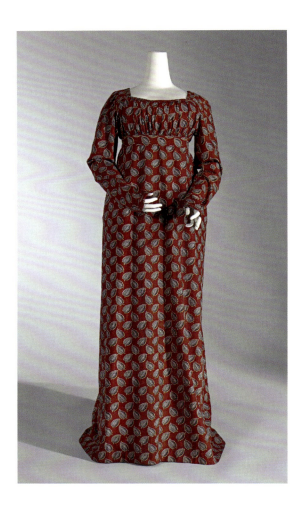

Fig. 2.16

Round gown, c.1802, cotton (with detail of the bodice). Another example of the long-sleeved, darker gowns worn during the day. The colour and print meant that the marks and dirt of daily living were disguised, and the cotton fabric allowed them to be washed out easily. National Gallery of Victoria, Melbourne.

Separate collars of muslin, lawn and lace were part of, or attached to, chemisettes in fashionable styles, including the ruffs historicism made popular (fig. 2.19). Austen's portrait from behind features her blue cotton morning dress worn outside, accessorised by a neck-handkerchief with a high collar finished with a ribbon, and a matching soft bonnet (see fig. 0.2). Diana Sperling recorded her kinswomen wearing sleeveless gowns or petticoats, with long-sleeved 'habit-shirts' underneath (from riding-habits; see chapter 4 and fig. 2.7). Habit-shirts were cut like their masculine equivalent, with high collar and full sleeves, and were noted as popular with the 'female whose matured years ask the aid of more covering than the French tippet or lace pelerine [a light indoor shoulder cape]'.[110]

The getting of caps and their style permeate Austen's letters more than any other garment, conjuring their usefulness and affordability as sites of novel fashion response: 'my old [cap] looked so smart yesterday that I was asked two or three times before I set off whether it was not my new one'.[111] 'It was the fashion for girls to wear caps in the morning when you were in your teens', wrote Mary Elizabeth Lucy. 'I was the family milliner for I often made caps for dear Mamma', who paid her. For herself, Mary made a cap of blonde net with a ruche of tulle round it, and

Fig. 2.17

Cassandra Austen, portrait of Fanny Knight, 3 September 1805, watercolour on paper. The girl is painted in a white morning gown with long sleeves, full, short oversleeves and a sash. Her front hair is cropped short to behind the ears, and her back hair caught up simply with a comb. Jane Austen's House Museum, Chawton.

a fresh pink rose pinned on one side.[112] Mary's making evokes the infinite variety of caps bedecking the heads of Regency women. Periodicals give caps of satin and lace, or lace and muslin as suitable for morning dress, and ladies' heads tended to be covered even in domestic privacy – men could uncover the head indoors during the day. Pity the poor girl on the verge of leaving the house, harassed by her mother

> to take off her beau-cap and put on her other cap 'for under your bonnet you know. I always put my beau cap in my bag and keep a bonnet cap which I just put on my head after breakfast when I am going, but young people never think of these things . . . and the consequence is Isabella always tells me when we are going anywhere "Mamma my caps are all dirty. I have not one I declare fit to be seen."'[113]

Austen made 'two or three caps to wear of evenings' for herself in 1798.[114] They kept the head warmer too, as Austen 'longed for a snug cap' instead of a fashionable velvet ribbon, one evening in 1813. Happily, she did not catch cold with her head exposed.[115]

Fig. 2.18

Morning gown, c.1810, self-striped cambric muslin (with detail of the sleeve). Morning gowns were often made of plain white cotton, yet could be elaborately decorated with pintucks, needle lace and white-work embroidery. This gown's built-in fichu, with a high collar, creates the illusion of a shirt worn underneath. Los Angeles County Museum of Art.

If morning caps were universal for post-adolescent women, the habitual wearing of evening caps denoted middle age. The Austen sisters notably adopted these earlier than usual, in their mid-twenties, which their nieces regarded as dowdy. 'There was little public recognition of [women's] "middle age" at all', Amanda Vickery explains. 'Rather, there was an alarming haemorrhage of youth from the late twenties with absolute "old age" in women appearing to arrive at least a decade earlier than today, around fifty'.[116] Caps were one of the ways women managed the transition sartorially, and they hid many sins: greying, unwashed or undressed hair, and locks cropped during illness. Austen's complained of her sister-in-law Eliza, recovering in January from an illness in December, 'She cuts her hair too short over her forehead, and does not wear her cap far enough upon her head', either to keep the heat in or to hide her shorn hair.[117] Mrs Topham's account book (1810–25) shows a 'comfortable widow' spending frequently on caps and their trimmings.[118] She buys a muslin cap (4s. 6d.; paying 1s. 6d. for an extra muslin frill), dressed caps (£1 4s.), silk caps (12s.), gauze caps (12s.) and Persian caps (a soft silk; two for 2s. 8½d.), often two at a time. In 1824 Mrs Topham's cap cost more, at a guinea, than a turban she bought at the same time (18s.). Between entries for ready-made caps, she records costs such as 'bobbin net for 2 Caps', and 'Making Caps [14s.] and adding 2 yds lace'.[119]

Men's clothing had incorporated pockets since the sixteenth century, tucked into multiple corners of coats, waistcoats and breeches. As short-fronted coats came into fashion, pockets appeared in the long tails at the back, sometimes taking up their whole length. Women's pockets through the eighteenth century were detached bags with a slit opening, tied around the waist under the skirt, a secure method of concealing objects required often to hand (fig. 2.20).[120] Many authors have asserted that these pockets disappeared with the reduction in the volume of dresses, and were replaced from the late 1790s with a small handbag sometimes called an 'indispensible', but usually a 'reticule' or 'ridicule'.[121] However, both appear to have been used during the Regency, depending on circumstances. While an observer in 1805 remarked that it was out of the question for ladies to wear pockets, *La Belle Assemblée* reported the

pocket's 'return' in March 1806.[122] Surviving gowns throughout the early nineteenth century have the characteristic slits in their side seams used to access pockets underneath. As late as 1815, there were complaints about reticules: 'no possible reason can be given for this strange metamorphosis of a *pocket* to a *ridicule*, and its contingent change of residence from the side to the arm'.[123] The bag was another marker of increasing gentility. 'To what churchwarden's lady the abolition of pockets is owing, and the ridicule owes its celebrity, I know not', grumbled an anonymous author in a periodical. 'In the company of a fan, a vinegaret, or a pocket-hand-kerchief scented with attar of roses, vulgar copper halfpence can hope for no place.'[124] The private, practical space of pockets contrasted with the public performance of respectability that reticules aspired to. Reticules were 'valued for delicacy and ornamental charm with a fraction of the capacity of a pair of tie-pockets', but pockets were thought to distort the columnar silhouette.[125] Hidden pockets were more secure (though Lucy Locket lost hers in the nursery rhyme). By the end of the Regency the old pockets were seen as dowdy and countrified. But they never quite disappeared, hidden beneath petticoats instead of immediately under the gown.

Handkerchiefs were a universally useful piece of clothing. The prefix 'hand' deceptively encompasses a huge range of sizes and purposes of these square cloths: the genteel young lady's decorative linen pocket handkerchief, like the one Austen embroidered for Cassandra (fig. 2.21); the mature matron's worked muslin neck-handkerchief, folded into a triangle and covering her décolletage; bright twilled silk Barcelona handkerchiefs, bedecking the collars of young working men. In fact, kerchiefs of all sorts, shapes, sizes and textiles are so ubiquitous that they appear in at least two-thirds of depictions of Regency dress. The handy pieces of fabric stopped gaps, hid skin from sun and wind, and could be adapted to many purposes, from covering the hair to mopping sweat.

Fig. 2.21

Cassandra Austen's handkerchief, 1800–17, embroidered linen. Jane Austen embroidered the handkerchief for her sister in satin stitch, in which she 'was considered especially great' (J. E. Austen-Leigh, 2008, pp. 78–9). The exquisite precision and regular, smooth texture of the stitching back up Austen's own boasts of being an excellent needlewoman. Jane Austen's House Museum, Chawton.

Handkerchiefs came in many different kinds, including small shawls or the large squares used to fill in the necks of the dresses, called variously 'handkerchiefs', 'double handkerchiefs' or 'neck-handkerchiefs'. Male handkerchiefs were white, of cambric and muslin, unless the word refers to some form of neck-cloth, when colours were commonly worn. Parson Woodforde owned night handkerchiefs of coarse long-lawn, 27 inches (c.70 cm) square. Besides those made of calico or 'Coloured Handkerchiefs, red and white', he also bought 'East Indian Silk Handkerchiefs' (see fig. 7.14), large grey silk 'Barcelona Handkerchiefs' for female relatives, and '2 Silk Handkerchiefs from Spittal Fields, Chocolate Ground and Yellow Spots' for servants.[126] Mrs Topham's accounts reveal a similar range of handkerchief expenditure. Among the muslin handkerchiefs for everyday use, bought in half-dozens at 2s.–3s., she also bought cambric handkerchiefs of better quality, costing £2 8s. for ten, and Scotch handkerchiefs at a guinea the dozen. Among decorative items listed in the accounts are a figured gauze handkerchief (half a guinea), a bobbinet handkerchief (1s. 9d.), which may have been trimmed with lace or was perhaps a kerchief for the bosom, and a flashy purple and amber silk handkerchief for 5s. A 'pocket handkerchief' was the smallest size.[127]

Domesticity and Dress

Dressing was a lengthy business. The complication of putting on or changing gowns and shirts, then arranging, tying, pinning and accessorising one's gown, and doing one's hair required time. Where did Regency people do this dressing? The 'dressing-room' was a private, less formal drawing-room, not necessarily where people dressed.[128] Dressing-rooms in Austen's life and fiction present cosy, intimate spaces. Mrs Bennet (*P&P*) retreats to hers with nervous prostration or for private chats. Marianne Dashwood (*S&S*) recovers from her illness in Mrs Palmer's, the dressing-room being a halfway point in returning to public sociability; an Austen relative did the same thing in 1809.[129]

Architectural plans show that the 'Ladies Dressing Room' could be the same size as the drawing-room, an arrangement Jane Austen found in their Bath house in 1801, where 'the apartment over the drawing-room pleased me particularly, because it is divided into two, the smaller one a very nice-sized dressing-room, which upon occasion might admit a bed'.[130] When she refers to the place where the body is clothed, Austen seems to use the term 'dressing-closet', while 'dressing-room' implies the sitting-room sense. At the house of her brother Henry in Henrietta Street, London, Austen and her niece Fanny had a 'little adjoining Dressing-room' to their apartment, and felt 'most commodiously disposed of'.[131] The smaller space echoes Maria Edgeworth's 'little room over the boudoir and within Harriets bedchamber', which 'serves for a gownery. I have had cloak pegs put all round it and it has an ample deal wardrobe, so that we can *hang up* instead of folding up in a hurry.'[132] Before coathangers, hanging was a luxurious use of space compared to shelves (see fig. 2.12).

Bedrooms often housed the actual dressing-tables or dressing-boxes that furnished the necessities of appearance. In a letter describing the appointments of a house she stayed in, Edgeworth described a Regency dressing-box:

> in each bed chamber [was] a dressing table so completely stored with things necessary for the toilette that a beau or belle who had the misfortune to lose his or her dressing box would have felt no inconvenience from that loss – brushes soft and hard for coat and hat – hair-brush – powder pomatum – ivory comb – tortoise shell combs of different sorts – pincushions and even papers ready cut in abundance for curling the hair – and such an abundance of drawers little and large and wardrobes![133]

The masculine dressing-room could be on the ground floor off the library, suggesting that it resembled a study. Dressing-rooms might contain 'a writing desk and table with everything that could be wanted for writing'.[134] The dressing-room is where John Dashwood (*S&S*) contemplates letter-writing, but Sir Walter Elliot's also holds 'Such a number of looking-glasses!', which Admiral Croft sends away, leaving only 'my little shaving glass in one corner, and another great thing that I never go near' (*Pers.*)[135] Access to a full-length mirror (pier-glass) to check one's entire appearance was not universal (fig. 2.22). Smaller dressing or hand-mirrors were more common (the modern silvered-glass, tin-mercury technique made mirrors cheaper only after 1835).[136] The accurate, full-length mirror was a vehicle of modernity and a means of regulating appearance, making visible 'previously unfamiliar images (one's back and profile), and stir[ring] up sensations of modesty and self-consciousness'.[137] The last result worried fashion critics: the 'oracle' of a mirror might be useful 'did not the medium of self-love, through which you consult it, blind your perception and obscure your views'.[138] Family and servants were trustier assessors of elegance.

Rooms were never entirely private owing to the presence of servants. The majority of domestic servants were employed in modest establishments, or in single- or two-servant households, rather than large estates.[139] These housekeepers, housemaids or chambermaids, ladies' maids, laundry maids, valets and gentlemen's men all had a vital hand in the upkeep of gentry clothing. They lived closely with the family, and assured their respectable appearance through washing, ironing, brushing, making and mending clothes, packing trunks and organising bedrooms, as well as arranging hair and assisting with dressing.[140] 'A very good servant', whom Emma gets in to do needlework, is, for fastidious Mr Woodhouse, 'a civil, pretty-spoken girl', who 'always curtseys and asks me how I do, in a very pretty manner'.[141] Austen's letters convey a more relaxed, friendly relationship between employer and employees living in such proximity. Sackree (or Caky), the Knights' nurse at their estate in Godmersham, Kent, is a beloved family member, appearing throughout the letters, and fictionalised in *Persuasion* as 'the old nursery-maid of the family', who was 'now living in her deserted nursery to mend stockings'.[142] Jolly Mrs Jennings (*S&S*) also values the comfort of gossip with her maids.[143]

Servants' role in dressing started as early as lighting a warming fire in bedrooms before their occupants awoke – the kind of housemaids that Mrs Whitaker, the Sotherton housekeeper, dismissed for wearing white gowns in *Mansfield Park* (contradicting Edmund Bertram's later opinion that '"a woman can never be too fine while she is all in white"').[144] How to balance fashion and function in servants' dress was a vexing question, not least for the servants themselves. Poor Anne Elliot (*Pers.*) must hear complaints from her family on servants' comportment. Her sister Mary Musgrove thinks her mother-in-law's '"upper house-maid and laundry-maid, instead of being in their business, are gadding about the village all day long"', while the mother-in-law believes Mary's nursemaid Jemima to be '"always upon the gad; and from my own knowledge, I can declare, she is such a fine-dressing lady, that she is enough to ruin any servants she comes near"' (fig. 2.23).[145] White was an aspirational impracticality for housemaids mired in charcoal and dust, but young women in service had their own leisure time and their own taste to satisfy.

In smaller houses, housemaids performed the duties of ladies' maids by helping women dress and arrange their hair. It is unclear whether Sarah at Longbourn (*P&P*) is such a maid of all trades. When Mr Bingley appears too early one morning, Mrs Bennet directs the woman to stop doing Lizzy's hair and help

Jane on with her gown instead. The mother's own hair is only half-dressed, suggesting either that there are two maids in the household who can assist in the toilette, or that Mrs Bennet is doing her own, which seems uncharacteristically competent.[146] At Mansfield Park, the Bertram girls have Ellis as their personal maid, but Mrs Norris, campaigning to belittle Fanny Price's household position, considers housemaids able and sufficient to help that niece dress and take care of her clothes.[147] The maidservants of this well-to-do establishment are sufficiently aware of fashionability and good taste to sneer at Fanny's Portsmouth clothes. As 'she had but two sashes, and had never learned French', her ignorance encompasses fashion as well as education.[148] In general, employers were as concerned about quashing fashionable impulses in their employees as the servants were about fulfilling them. Edgeworth found herself 'beginning to fall in love with' a friend's maid only after the girl flattened her fashionably arranged cap and 'quite laid aside her conceit'.[149]

Dress in the Age of Jane Austen

Conversely, women employed solely as ladies' maids were valued for their taste and skill in dressing, such as the two 'elegant ladies' who wait upon Charles Bingley's sisters (*P&P*).[150] Lady Bertram attributes all the success of Fanny Price's appearance at her first Mansfield Park ball to the loan of her own maid Chapman to help with the girl's toilette and hair, though the happy thought occurs to her aunt too late, and in fact Fanny has managed by herself. *Northanger Abbey* and *The Watsons* also feature the loan of maids.[151] *The Duties of a Lady's Maid* is explicit on the roles and responsibilities of these women, not least in hints about their own dress: 'The first thing you ought to consider on this subject is never to dress out of your station nor attempt to rival the ladies of the family.'[152] The author goes on to warn that gentle manners cannot be put on 'as you would do a bit of trimming or a bouquet of artificial flowers'. Too much fashion when applying for a place could make the lady of the house 'suspect that you will spend more time in dressing yourself than in attending to her'; and girls are warned 'never [to] succeed in procuring a good husband by vain show and misplaced finery'. Ironically, the guide's description of 'a dashing dressy girl [who] has much more chance of attracting the attention of those who will squire her about for mere show and fun, or will spend her time in joking and bantering, or still worse, who may be of loose character and libertine principles' fits Lydia Bennet, a gentleman's daughter.[153]

Female domestic servants in larger houses might be provided with uniform dress. Usually, they wore normal clothing in durable printed or plain fabrics, with accessories to protect clothing from the depredations of work: aprons, neck-handkerchiefs, removable sleeve covers, mob caps. Many employers bought servants clothing as personal presents. Austen herself delighted in the happiness a 'new red Cloak' added to the life of the Chawton Cottage housemaid, Sally.[154] Some of the status hierarchy of servants' gift clothes is seen in Fanny Austen's pocket-book. In 1814 Fanny acquired a cap costing £1 4s. for her sister, while a whole gown for her servant Betsy cost only 12s.

Hand-me-downs from employers were a job perquisite. Such garments not only provided wearable clothing but were valuable assets for realising money in second hand markets. However, servants wearing the same clothes as their employers, or seeking fashionability, caused uneasy social murmurs. The only thing that discomposes poor, lazy Mrs Price (*MP*) during her Sunday walks in Portsmouth is seeing her housemaid Rebecca out wearing a flower in her hat – possibly because Mrs Price herself is a pretty woman with an appearance worn down through drudgery.[155]

The cautions to servants are variations on the advice doled out to gentry women about the desirability of respectable economy in dress. To be a good woman was to regulate the self through clothing, at every social level. Mistress and maid were each

Fig. 2.22

Robert Cruikshank, 'A Short Set-to at Long's Hotel', from *The English Spy* (1825), hand-coloured aquatint. The servant or valet, in his distinctive short striped coat, brings in the day's clean shirt, and will also shave the gentleman. The freestanding mirror had become established by the mid-1820s.

responsible for monitoring the other's appropriate appearance. Men found themselves reflected in their valets, or upper male servants who attended to dressing (fig. 2.22), although Austen's nephew James-Edward Austen-Leigh (1798–1874), remembered:

> Well-dressed young men of my acquaintance, who had their coat from a London tailor, would always brush their evening suit themselves, rather than entrust it to the carelessness of a rough servant, and to the risks of dirt and grease in the kitchen; for in those days servants' halls were not common in the houses of the clergy and the smaller country gentry.[156]

When Austen writes of affording 'the comfort of a servant', she evokes how daily life required significant physical work.[157] Shared, though hierarchical, domestic labour was essential to get things done. Although gentry women's leisure time increased with the household's affluence, all females laboured together on the endless household sewing.

Plain Sewing

Needlework filled women's lives in the age of Austen. Sewing clothing and trifles for themselves, their friends and relations, or supervising employees' work, occupied a large part of gentry women's time. Austen differentiates between 'work' and 'employment'. 'Work' always means needlework; 'employment' covers other activities, such as drawing, playing music or studying. Even 10-year-old, under-educated Fanny Price could 'read, work, and write', after growing up in an impoverished, once-genteel household.[158] Work was thought to provide moral and material benefits:

> A knowledge of what is termed plain work [including making and mending], and which our modern belles affect to despise, is, I am persuaded, very necessary to every woman, be her rank in life what it may; and I cannot but think there is something very quiescent and modest, very consonant with the female character, and very favourable to reflective habits, in needle-work. It inculcates economy, checks wandering and idle habits, and induces quiet and steady manners.[159]

Mrs Bennet, who bundles up her work and leaves the room to allow Mr Collins to propose to Lizzy (*P&P*), is hardly the epitome of this description.[160]

A knowledge of plain work was essential to supervising servants and hired seamstresses. To judge their success, a gentry mistress must know what good work was, and how to do it. Skill with a needle was a valuable asset in any female servant. Housemaids did the tedious hemming of household linens and sometimes long shirt and shift seams. Larger houses engaged seamstresses for a week or two to work on batches of clothing, as Emma Woodhouse does. For less affluent employers, such as Jane Austen's father, staff needed to have a variety of skills. The Austens' new maid in 1798 'seems to cook very well, is uncommonly stout, and says she can work well at her needle'.[161] The constant mending alone provided plentiful domestic work for women and servants. Learning to work was seen as an advantage for young girls and a way of raising their circumstances. A prudent young bride in didactic fiction planned 'to have a girl in the house . . . to assist me with needle-work, for the benefit of *learning*; this will save *my time* and *her money*, and may be easily managed by a person who has all the fore part of the day at command', with the emphasis on 'command', as it was servants who undertook the bulk of the house work of shopping, cooking, cleaning, tidying and washing.[162] It is pertinent that diarist Mrs Anna Larpent (1758–1832) began doing 'useful work' only in 1794 after the departure of her housekeeper, who previously had undertaken the more skilled work in making up shirts and other garments after housemaids had done the straight stitching, 'leaving Mrs Larpent at leisure to choose what she might like to do herself'.[163] A bill from illiterate seamstress Elizabeth Hall to Eliza Jervoise's housekeeper illustrates this division of work: Hall made an X to sign her receipt of money 'for making a part of 7 shirts . . . Collars, Wristbands and all the work of Seven Shirts (except the Hemming the Selvedges and making the plain Hemming, and Sewing the Seams of the Bodies), 12s. 3d.'[164] Possibly the same woman made twenty-three pairs of 'ristes', which Mrs Jervoise annotated as 'Wristbands made, entirely stitched twice and two Button:holes / Collars stitched twice with Button Holes / 3 /at 2d each'.[165]

Austen brings nice distinctions to her fictional needlework. Her fine or flighty ladies do not undertake domestic sewing, contenting themselves instead with decorative efforts (see chapter 3). Heroines engage in practical useful 'work', as Austen and her circle did. Catherine Morland (*NA*) is expected to contribute a good share of linen sewing for her large family. Her mother upbraids her for 'growing quite a fine lady. I do not know when poor Richard's cravats would be done, if he had no friend but you.'[166] In real life, Austen's niece Fanny Knight spent one wet autumn afternoon in 1805 doing a 'good deal of work, vis, marked [embroidered his initials] for William a shirt', marked stockings for Sackree, and finished half her collar and half the collar of her mother's neck-handkerchief. Six days later, she had finished the tail of her blue frock.[167]

Female family members provided male relatives' body-linen, as the Austen women did. In 1796 Jane prided herself on 'being the neatest worker of the group' at home making her brother Edward a batch of shirts.[168] Making body-linens six or a dozen at a time was an economy of material and construction, and made washing easier. 'Irish', Holland and shirting linens bought by the 'piece', a length of around 25 or 26 yards, allowed shirts to be made in bulk. Planning plain sewing involved geometrically dividing fabric along straight lines. Early instruction books on making clothes stress economical ways to lay out and cut linen in arrangements of squares and rectangles, leaving almost no scraps (fig. 2.24). Young girls and servants could assemble straight pieces with little supervision, while adult women's sewing became mechanical through long practice, as Larpent's diaries record.[169] The level of technical skill in plain work could be extraordinary. The finest Regency linen shirts contain external back-stitching of 50 stitches per inch (20 stitches per cm). Modern machines can barely produce the same quality. James Austen-Leigh, writing after the spread of sewing-machines, remembered his aunt's needlework, both plain and ornamental, as 'excellent', and claimed that it 'might almost have put a sewing machine to shame. She was considered especially great in satin stitch,' as figure 2.21 demonstrates.[170]

Needlework fulfilled the moral need for female activity and the avoidance of 'absolute idleness, inexcusable in woman', which 'rendered her contemptible. The needle is, or ought to be at hand for those intervals in which she cannot be otherwise employed.'[171] Women used workbags, rectangular fabric pouches with drawstring tops, to contain their needlework in progress. Workbags turn up in Regency carriages, on visits, in dressing-rooms, and drawing-rooms at all social levels.[172] They were an extension of women's personal space, a constant companion, providing ready material for the hands. Austen's heroines work steadily throughout the novels. Even Elizabeth Bennet (*P&P*) wields her needle – notably at Netherfield Park, when the regularity of her task keeps her mind free to watch interchanges between Mr Darcy and Caroline Bingley that are key to the later plot. Austen's language emphasises the chore that such work could be. Lizzy has 'great delight' and is 'sufficiently amused' by what she watches –

Fig. 2.24

Cutting diagram for a man's shirt, from *The Lady's Economical Assistant* (1808). Lengths of linen were cut for multiple shirts at once, to use the fabric most economically. Geometric cutting allowed any small, even scraps to be used in other garments. British Library, London.

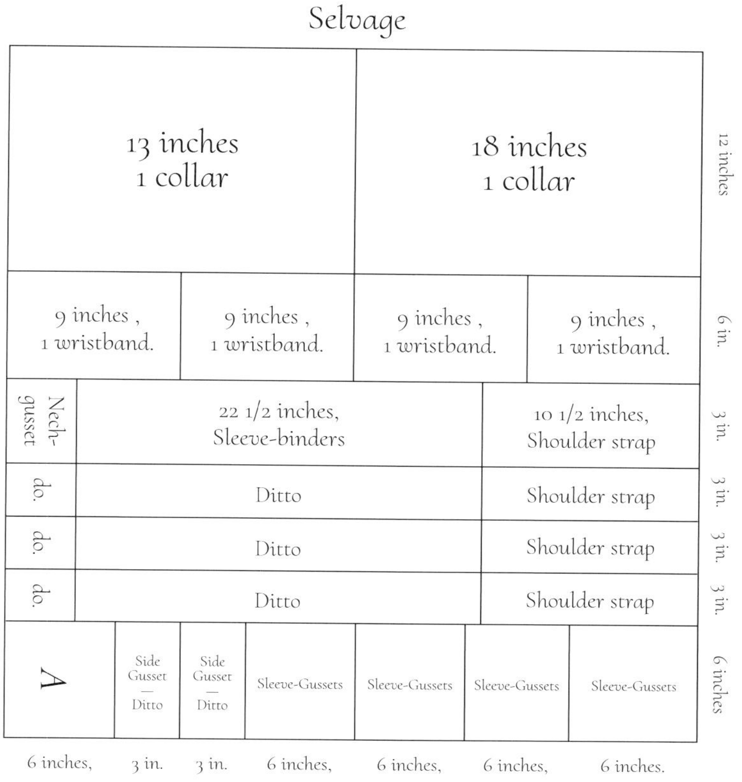

			12 inches
13 inches 1 collar	18 inches 1 collar		

9 inches , 1 wristband.	9 inches , 1 wristband.	9 inches , 1 wristband.	9 inches , 1 wristband.	6 in.
Neck-gusset	22 1/2 inches, Sleeve-binders		10 1/2 inches, Shoulder strap	3 in.
do.	Ditto		Shoulder strap	3 in.
do.	Ditto		Shoulder strap	3 in.
do.	Ditto		Shoulder strap	3 in.
A	Side Gusset — Ditto	Side Gusset — Ditto	Sleeve-Gussets	Sleeve-Gussets	Sleeve-Gussets	Sleeve-Gussets	6 inches

6 inches,   3 in.   3 in.   6 inches,   6 inches,   6 inches,   6 inches.

not by what she is making. Later, she attends to her work 'with an eagerness which it did not often command'.[173] The tedium of sewing is also expressed in *Northanger Abbey*: 'Catherine said no more, and, with an endeavour to do right, applied to her work; but, after a few minutes, sunk again, without knowing it herself, into languor and listlessness, moving herself in her chair, from the irritation of weariness, much oftener than she moved her needle.'[174]

But working at home also provided women with opportunities for sociability, reflection and distraction. Home was the place where both companionable and solitary sewing provided a source of emotional support.[175] Sewing communally was a pleasant activity for women and a socially acceptable pastime in mixed company – something productive to do while maintaining those networks of feminine information that kept society running. The Elliot sisters (*Pers.*) sit quietly at work of a morning; the Dashwood women (*S&S*) have a shared working table.[176] Portable workbags complemented static work-boxes and -baskets (fig. 2.25). Jane and Cassandra's dressing room had a small table supporting '2 Tonbridge-ware work boxes of oval shape, fitted up with ivory barrels containing reels for silk, yard measures, etc.'.[177] Downstairs, the Austen drawing-room layout had 'A small writing-desk, with a smaller work box, or netting-case . . . all that each young lady contributed to occupy the table; for the large family work-basket, though often produced in the parlour, lived in the closet.'[178] It was Austen's habit to sit in the drawing-room until luncheon, working – which she liked – if visitors were there.

The plain work undertaken varied with the company: making and mending under-clothing was not appropriate outside the family circle. Although Austen-Leigh thought 'It may be that useful articles, which would not now be produced in drawing-rooms, were hemmed, and marked, and darned in the old-fashioned parlour', Austen herself was careful to keep from her mother the ungenteel behaviour of a Mrs Armstrong, who 'sat darning a pair of stockings the whole of my visit', 'lest a warning should act as an example'.[179] Anna Larpent distinguished between working with company present in the country, but putting work away when in London, even for family visits.[180]

Among family, sewing could be bonding. 'Good cheer and merriment may have been as important as intellectual discussion', Bridget Long suggests.[181] Dorothy Wordsworth had William read new poems while she made petticoats. Austen's niece Anna Lefroy recalled the gaiety occasioned among the female family members by reading cheap novels and amusing trivia out loud as Austen 'sat busily stitching away at a work of charity'.[182] 'She spent much time in these occupations', said Austen-Leigh, 'and some of her merriest talk was over clothes which she and her companions were making, sometimes for themselves, and sometimes for the poor.'[183] These clothes were probably the caps, baby clothes and body-linens mentioned, together with mending and alterations, throughout the letters.

Solitary sewing gave time for reflection and consolation, a private mental space to mull things over.[184] Anna Larpent found sewing could exercise her thoughts:

> I always Employ 4 hours a week in plain work &c. both to know how to do it, to keep my mind Active in these duties of Economy – & during that time I reflect and digest much of what I study & observe at other times the mechanism of such work not preventing the action of my Mind.[185]

Working gave her time to consider her reading. She came to learn that needlework could be a powerful comfort in times of anxiety. When distressed once, Larpent wrote:

> I can smile, I mended two shirts and two shifts . . . and had it not been a duty how much rather would I have studied history or poetry, but I protest . . . fulfilling my female duties warms my heart as much as Mental pursuits delights it.[186]

Fictionally, the young ladies in Caroline Fry's educational novel are "glad the bustle of . . . planning our dresses is over; . . . we have nothing more to contrive, and therefore need not talk or think about our work; I really shall be glad to give my mind to better thoughts'".[187] The long hours Austen spent over her needlework appear to have fuelled rather than hampered her writing. Her niece Marianne Knight (1801–1895) recalled:

> Aunt Jane would sit quietly working beside the fire in the library saying nothing for a good while, and then would suddenly burst out laughing, jump up and run across the room to a table where pens and paper were lying, write something down, and then come back to the fire and go on quietly working as before.[188]

Perhaps she used her time stitching to hone sentences mentally before committing them to paper, sewing becoming an aid, not an obstacle, to creative thinking.

Austen exploits needlework as a dissembling plot device for heroines who use the work of their hands to distract from agitations in their souls. When Elinor Dashwood (S&S) discovers that her love, Edward Ferrars, is unmarried she 'sat with her head leaning over her work, in a state of such agitation as made her hardly know where she was'; in a similar situation, Emma Woodhouse adopts the same attitude, 'having recourse to her workbasket, in excuse for leaning down her face, and concealing all the exquisite feelings of delight and entertainment which she knew she must be expressing'.[189] Gentlemen use the props too: Edward Ferrars 'apparently from not knowing what to do' on an awkward social visit, 'took up a pair of scissors that lay there, and . . . spoiling both them and their sheath by cutting the latter to pieces as he spoke'; Mr. Darcy gains a private whisper by adopting the pretext of admiring Lizzy's work.[190] Regular stitching could conceal irregular beatings of the heart.

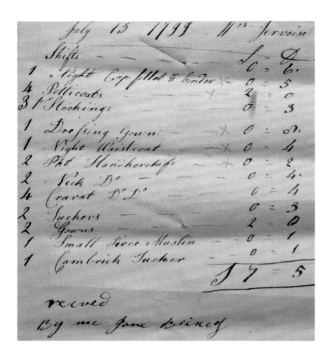

Besides constant mending, laundry was the other great domestic women's business related to clothing – a physical, strenuous task that they organised and executed. Washing was done in bulk either at home by servants, or sent out to professional washerwomen. Gentry women did not often do their own laundry, and John Styles notes that even some plebeian women paid for the service, indicating how exhausting it was.[191] Body-linens were dated, monogrammed, numbered, or had other markings on them to record their owners, and to facilitate keeping track of what had been washed when; it was for this purpose that Frank Austen's shirts were marked by a number of friends and relations. To stay clean, it was necessary to have a quantity of linen, as it all had to be washed in one go, weekly, monthly or quarterly, depending on the household's size. Keeping linens in recorded circulation ensured that no one garment was over-washed. In larger households, the linen-marking system extended to all domestic washable textiles, such as sheets, towels and the rest.

A washing list, of the kind that so deflates Catherine's Gothic hopes in *Northanger Abbey*, was a receipt, recording the items sent for laundering, and the cost; the list was a check for owner and laundress to ensure that nothing went astray (fig. 2.26).

Besides the labour-intensive nature of washing, the facilities might not be available to gentry women. Domestic washing required a large copper, plenty of hot water, a mangle, quantities of harsh soap, and a good deal of beating, scrubbing and wringing. Indeed, one of the complaints against cotton was its lack of durability compared with linen or worsteds, as aggressive washing techniques and soaps shortened textiles' lifespan; in 1796 Austen's 'new coloured gown is very much washed out, though I charged everybody to take great care of it'.[192] Various external laundresses did her family's laundry, including a Widow Kennet. Women paid for washing out of their private purses, making it a considerable proportion of the ongoing cost of dressing, as Ellen Weeton complains. At a point when rent and board would take nearly all her money, her first concern was 'what I must do for clothes, washing &c.?' She later breaks down the difference between cheap and expensive ('near 8 shillings a fortnight') washing costs.[193] Washing during 1807 cost Austen £9 5s. 11½d., 21 per cent of her yearly expenses.[194] Even when staying in a London house with acquaintance, washing was a separate cost, and may have required engaging a local washerwoman rather than the house servants. As cleanliness and neatness denoted genteel respectability it was essential to maintain these qualities in clothing.

Regency household receipt books are crammed with techniques for the proper cleaning of clothes: the differences between normal and clear starching, cleaning cotton and silk stockings, how to wash and set a lace collar, and many dry-cleaning

Fig. 2.27

John Lewis Krimmel, *Woman Pressing and Folding Laundry*, 1819–20, watercolour on paper. Laundering was time-consuming and labour intensive: behind every white dress and shirt was a huge amount of work to keep it clean and whole. Joseph Downs Collection of Manuscripts and Printed Ephemera, Winterthur Library, Delaware.

techniques for removing spots with French chalk or turpentine all show why a skilled washerwoman or laundress was an economic aid to preserving clothes. Once the washing was done and dried (two days), it had to be carefully ironed and starched (another day). Ironing was done on an ironing blanket, using flatirons, warmed over a fire, and tested manually for heat (fig. 2.27). It was a skilled job to crisp fine lawns or pleat shirt sleeves without scorching the fabrics or getting charcoal on them.

The realms of unglamorous and unfashionable underwear, sewing and washing, and the small ways and practical strategies for creating domestic bodily comfort are subjects sometimes downplayed in fashion histories. However, they were vital in keeping the Regency gentry warm and respectable. This chapter is the book's longest in an effort to give the subject the same importance and focus Austen and her peers experienced in their daily collaborative labour. Carried out overwhelmingly by women, this labour provided the clean, decent clothing hiding under images, among accounts and in surviving quotidian articles. Private home dress wrapped Regency bodies for at least half of every day and underpins all the public performances of clothed selves required in the social spheres presented in the following chapters.

❊ ❊

Chapter 3

Village

Such pictures of Life in Country Villages as I deal with . . .[1]

Just outside the home was the village. If Jane Austen is a novelist of '*discrimination* within a knowable community, . . . of narrowly drawn, closely dissected, . . . spheres, castes, classes, and circles, in which every detail . . . is delved for social meaning', the village was where clothing communities truly began.[2] This local neighbourhood, the setting for daily lives and dramas, for clothing provision from shops and makers, for networks of fashion dissemination and charity, is the famous '3 or 4 families in a village', which Austen told her niece Anna while she was writing *Emma* – her most village-centred fiction – was just the thing to work on.[3]

For all fashion's rapid pace, the people one lived and worked among were more important to forming dress cultures in the age of Austen. Her fictional village world was one that contemporary readers recognised: 'The picture of the younger Miss Bennets, their perpetual visits to the market town where officers are quartered, and the result, is perhaps exemplified in every provincial town in the kingdom', wrote a critic at the time.[4] Austen's 'ordinary business of life' happened in a close network of hamlets, villages and provincial town centres strung across England in a way that meant few were truly isolated. Her family lived in Steventon and Chawton villages, and the town of Southampton, and she spent time in Godmersham, Kent, and various south coast towns (for Bath and London, see chapter 5). As Laurie Kaplan realised, the acquaintance connection could form an 'urban village', even in the midst of London, part of a clothing community held together through shared relationship and knowledge, local fashions, making, and shops.[5] The social spaces of these 'villages' are this chapter's subject.

❀ ❀

Local Fashions

Fashioning the self was inextricable from participating in the local community, and a shopping trip into the nearby commercial centre gathered news as well as sundries. Constant rain from the day of their invitation to the Netherfield ball until the ball itself prevents the Bennet girls in *Pride and Prejudice* 'walking to Meryton once. No aunt, no officers, no news could be sought after – the very shoe-roses for Netherfield were got by proxy'.[6] The immediate 'village' represented communal dress transmission. In a small town, everyone saw everyone else regularly, and knew what was bought. Constant mutual observation by neighbours was a way to enforce a class-based dress code, one based in shared situations (fig. 3.1).[7]

The Austen family network expected consumption to be shared and discussed collectively. When Austen bought bargain gloves, she knew everybody at home would 'be hoping & predicting that they cannot be good for anything'. In the same vein, she disapproved of her niece Anna's purple pelisse, not so much for its surprising colour but for suspecting 'its being got in secret, & not owned to anybody'.[8] Anna trespassed against family etiquette of discussion. Contrast this with Austen's new gown in 1801, where everyone had an opinion: 'I get more and more pleased with it. – Charles does not like it, but my father and Mary do; my Mother is very much resigned to it, and as for James, he gives it the preference over everything of the kind he ever saw.'[9] These are tangled webs of 'social judgement', in Sutherland's phrase, the gamut of familial dress approval, social and cultural ties constraining new clothing.[10]

Austen documents the importance of dress transmission through people's bodies, or through constructed garments – fabric 'bodies'. Austen's 'neighbourhood of voluntary spies' used their eyes as physical dress transmitters, removed from the intimacy of acquaintance.[11] Mrs Smith (*Pers.*) links into the network of Bath servants' gossip through her nurse, to relish reports of lace and finery passed on about '"pretty, silly, expensive, fashionable"' Mrs Wallis.[12] Too ill to see for herself, Mrs Smith can participate in communal dress through her proxy eyes. People watching dress applied economic as well as style evaluations. In *Emma*, the wonderful monster Mrs Elton assumes that her dress will be assessed through public scrutiny at the Highbury ball, while assessing others, and happily allocating herself first place in the village style stakes. In *Sense and Sensibility*, Miss Steele transgresses the normal politely silent visual inspection to ask Marianne Dashwood about her dress with breathtaking impertinence. She did not

> bestow half the consideration on [her dress], during the whole of her toilette, which it received from Miss Steele in the first five minutes of their being together, when it was finished. Nothing escaped her minute observation and general curiosity; she saw everything, and asked everything; was never easy till she knew the price of every part of Marianne's dress; could have guessed the number of her gowns altogether with better judgment than Marianne herself, and was not without hopes

Fig. 3.1

James Pollard, *The Greengrocer*, c.1819, watercolour and pen and ink on paper. The difference in social status between the shopper and the proprietor is clear from their clothing: the customer's is more elaborate and of finer fabrics, while the greengrocer wears three aprons, to protect her clothes and to hold money and the tools of her trade. Yale Center for British Art, Paul Mellon Collection, New Haven, Conn.

of finding out before they parted, how much her washing cost per week, and how much she had every year to spend upon herself.[13]

The exchange in London is scarcely different from that in a village or country town as it takes place among a group of people socialising with their small county circle. As Sutherland observes, 'The sense of being watched, hedged in and discussed by a whole community informs all Austen's novels'; it is a society that closely restricts mental and physical space, particularly for women, who were allowed little solitude or independence.[14]

Styles explains the power of local custom as a mediating influence on fashion, mutually influencing consumption. It was 'not a force to be found everywhere . . . in equal intensity, but strongly depends on specific – sometimes local or even familial – conditions.'[15] Austen's village environments epitomise these spaces of fashion-making. 'It is not very unusual', opined an 1817 ladies' manual, 'to see neighbouring

Fig. 3.2

Unknown artist, 'Morning Walking Dresses', *Bell's New Weekly Magazine*, January 1807, hand-coloured engraving on paper. Indoor morning dress has been adapted for outdoors, in the lady's case, by adding a pelisse and stylish hat. Her companion wears fashionable pantaloons, riding-boots and a top hat in his version of casual daytime clothing. Victoria and Albert Museum, London.

young women engaged in a constant state of petty warfare with each other, to vie in ostentatiousness, in costliness or in elegance of apparel.'[16] Whatever the Duchess of D—e was wearing, outshining the girl next door was of real importance, as it was 'to gain the earliest intelligence respecting changes in the metropolis; to detect in the attire of a luckless competitor, traces of a mode which for six weeks has been obsolete in high life'.[17] Personal connection was crucial for this knowledge. When Mrs Gardiner (*P&P*) arrives at Longbourn she immediately describes the newest London fashions. Later, when Jane Bennet returns from London she too informs her family of the latest styles.[18] If fashion was subject to constant surveillance, it is fashion as seen that was absorbed and passed on at a personal level.

Stepping out to purchase some pins at the haberdasher, to return a call or to see a man about a horse required a degree of formality in clothing above domestic morning dress. Regency fashion journalism is replete with descriptions of visiting, walking, morning, promenade, curricle, carriage and 'half-dress' – and every combination of these styles (fig. 3.2). The reality appears to have been simpler, 'all reducible to two heads, viz. the undress and the half-dress' or 'the intermediate order of dress', as reflected in people's discussion of their own clothing, and often by silent contrast with 'full' dress (see chapter 5).[19] Undress was for home, and half-dress – rarely called such by its wearers – was suitable for daywear outside the house, or activities before dinner or evening. A call paid at home before the early afternoon saw the receivers clad in morning dress and their visitors wearing walking or visiting dress, distinguished by better fabrics, darker colours and extra embellishment. A Miss Kitty known to Fanny Burney was surprised one morning 'in her round dress, night-cap, and without her roll and curls' by a captain come calling early, though she had worn silk for days in anticipation of his visiting at noon. Although Kitty bolted to get dressed, the gentleman followed too quickly and she 'was seen in her linen gown and mob [cap]' of morning undress.[20] The morning 'curricle' dress that Susan Sibbald (1783–1866) recorded in her memoirs takes its name from being a 'short, open garment', just as curricles were open carriages. She vividly remembered the dress, worn in 1801, as 'showing the petticoat in front, which was trimmed in the same way as the dress with short sleeves, the body [bodice] open and low, showing an embroidered "French habit shirt," now called a chemisette and a small white chip hat, gipsy shape, around which was a wreath of small pink roses'.[21] Informality was not necessarily simplicity.

Female walking-dress required a bonnet or other hat. Fanny Knight got a cap 'fit for morning carriage wear', of white sarsenet and lace 'exceedingly like [Jane and Cassandra's] own satin and lace of last winter [1812]; shaped round the face exactly like it, with pipes and more fulness, and a round crown inserted behind'.[22] 'A line of white-robed ladies; mothers, aunts, and sisters [who] had just come out of their

Dress in the Age of Jane Austen

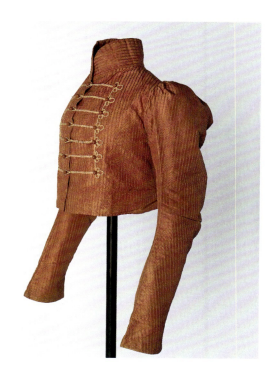

house without hat or bonnet' to see a small male relation on a horse, are in their morning dress, too excited to bother with adding the externals.[23] These ladies are also missing a spencer or pelisse over their morning dress to convert it for outdoors.

Pelisses were common Regency outerwear and appear in infinite variety. The imported French word originally meant a man's coat or mantle with a fur lining, but during the Regency, when applied to men's garments, it almost exclusively refers to a military context (see chapter 6). For women it denoted a style of coat-dress, made in any kind and weight of fabric, from sheer cotton muslins to fur-lined luxury, worn indoors and out, in all seasons, and reaching anywhere from the wearer's knees to her ankles. Fashion's new columnar form allowed for a coat-dress in a way impossible with wider pre-Regency styles. It could be cut with a separate skirt piece, like a gown, or flow uninterrupted from shoulder to hem, as Austen's own silk version does (see fig. 1.15). Some pelisses had cutaway fronts revealing the skirt below; some enveloped the neck in high ermined rolls. The garment was a staple for women in Austen's world; Captain Wentworth (*Pers.*) refers to it as an analogy for his ageing ship:

> 'I had no more discoveries to make than you would have as to the fashion and strength of any old pelisse, which you had seen lent about among half your acquaintance ever since you could remember, and which at last, on some very wet day, is lent to yourself.'[24]

Maria Edgeworth distinguished between her 'sage-coloured French pelisse' for carriage visits, and her grey cloth pelisse for walking visits.[25] Her half-sisters Fanny (1799–1848) and Harriet (1801–1889) had purple French and blue cloth pelisses for the same respective purposes, demonstrating that walking-dress needed some weather protection in its textile, while a carriage protected the wearer and kept her warmer.

The spencer was another masculine loan into female wardrobes, and the man who invented one of the iconic styles of Regency dress was friends with the brother of the iconic Regency author. Fashion histories often attribute the short half-coat's invention to George Spencer, 4th Duke of Marlborough (1739–1817); however, the earliest references in periodicals of around 1795 name the originator as his brother Charles (1740–1820) who 'betted some friends, that he could sport a fashion, the most useless and ridiculous that could be conceived, and that it should . . . be universally adopted'.[26] Coincidentally, Charles was Henry Austen's colonel in the Oxfordshire militia and a great friend of his. By cutting off his coat-tails, Spencer created a garment that perfectly complemented women's newly risen waistlines. Men wore spencers over other coats for warmth, but women wore them only with gowns, and under outer coats and cloaks. Austen reported on fashions from Bath, that 'black silk spencer[s], with a trimming round the armholes instead of sleeves' were much worn, 'some are long before, and some long all round', making them tunic-like.[27] Fashion images show the cropped jacket in endless adaptations, a convenient way to keep arms and chest warm while lending an outfit colour and fashion (fig. 3.3).

Church and Mourning Dress

The entire community regularly came together in church, dressed in their good clothes, and affording the curious excellent views of their neighbours (fig. 3.4). Mary Musgrove (*Pers.*) certainly feels that having 'a great many more people to look at' in the church at Lyme than at Uppercross contributes to her 'really agreeable fortnight' there.[28] Anglican orthodoxy was not immune from fashion. Ellen Weeton railed against the present age, 'so little scrupulous, that Fashion, whatever garb she wears is permitted; indeed, every pain is taken to allure her to take her seat in Christ-Church. That Church is altogether *fashionable.*'[29] Fashion meddling with piety attracted especial disapproval. 'The time bestowed on the toilette accounts for the empty churches and chapels on a Sunday – at least empty, as far as rank and fashion go', thundered the author of *Dress and Address*, complaining that 'self-adoration engrosses that which ought to be of a higher nature'.[30] How much worse was criticism of clergymen who attempted to be 'high in . . . fashion'. Weeton would have agreed with Edmund Bertram that '"A clergyman cannot be high in state or fashion. He must not head mobs, or set the ton in dress."'[31] The trope shadows *Emma*'s Mr Elton, a young, handsome clergyman who thinks well of himself and whose eventual marriage to a desperately fashionable woman reveals weak character.

Village gaze encompassed the clergyman as well as the congregation, social judgement applied doubly to the appearance of a leading community figure, '"where the parish and neighbourhood are of a size capable of knowing his private character, and observing his general conduct"'.[32] At one end was the old and dowdy 'prunella' – the dark wool fabric of parsons' gowns.[33] In the middle, respectable clergy attire was a suit of black clothes and a small neckcloth. At the other end, even men of God could succumb to the tyrannous claws of fashion. A clergyman might be a 'pulpit-puppy', a Dandy-parson, an Exquisite-clergyman, Buck-curate or Bottle-preacher, 'ultra-exquisite in dress . . . snow-white his linen, lily-white his hand'.[34] Schooled at Oxford among well-off young men, and often with no vocation, parsons and curates – like Austen's brothers James, and handsome, flirtatious Henry – were as prone to foibles in dress as the next man, and might be looking back at their parishioners and angling for a wife among the nicely turned out. Mary Crawford (*MP*) mocks young women in church '"starched up into seeming piety, but with heads full of something very different – especially if the poor chaplain were not worth looking at"'.[35] Dressing for church served other purposes besides honouring the Sabbath.

The church occasion requiring maximum attention to dress was getting married.
Canon law decreed marriages could be solemnised only between eight o'clock in the
morning and noon; therefore, wedding dress often adhered to day-clothing conventions. Wedding dress had not yet codified into an exceptional gown for the day, though
pale colours were popular.[36] Austen never describes wedding dress. Emma's is conjured
by omission at third hand: 'The wedding was very much like other weddings, where
the parties have no taste for finery or parade; and Mrs Elton thought it all extremely
shabby, and very inferior to her own. "Very little white satin, very few lace veils; a
most pitiful business."'[37] Maria Bertram (*MP*) is 'elegantly dressed; the two bridesmaids
were duly inferior'.[38] In her letters Austen only mentioned 'What an alarming Bride
Mrs Col'n Tilson must have been; such a parade is one of the most immodest pieces of
Modesty that one can imagine. To attract notice could have been her only wish.'[39] Real
brides more often matched fictional Emma's modest approach. Mrs Elton would have
been likewise disappointed by the simple wedding ensemble of Lady Byron (Annabella
Milbanke, 1792–1860): 'a muslin gown trimmed with lace at the bottom, with a white
muslin curricle jacket, very plain indeed, with nothing on her head', under a cream silk
pelisse (see fig. 3.5) not much fancier than Austen's.[40] Mary Elizabeth Lucy married in
what would become traditional wedding dress: snow-white silk with a wreath of orange
blossoms, a 'lace veil of texture fine as a spider's web', accompanied by bridesmaids in
white cashmere wearing bonnets lined in pink silk.[41] Eugenia Wynne (1780–1853), one
of the three (of five) sisters whose journals comprise *The Wynne Diaries*, was married in a

similar ensemble, her 'bridal array' consisting of 'a white satin under dress and a patent net [gown] over it, with a long veil'.[42] It is interesting that in her daydreaming Isabella Thorpe (NA) resolves upon the quality, not the design or colour, of her wedding gown, reflecting Regency dressers' haptic concerns, and how viewers could identify cost by looking.[43] Austen shows us in Mansfield Park how a gown like Fanny Price's white muslin with glossy spots was suitable for wearing both to attend her cousin's wedding, and her own first ball, though she is anxious that it might be too fine for dancing.[44]

Mrs Elton could have satisfied her aspirational tastes with the fanciful confections in magazines. An issue of the Repository of Arts in 1816 offered 'A Frock of striped French gauze over a white satin slip: . . . superbly trimmed with a deep flounce of Brussels lace . . . surmounted by . . . white satin and a wreath of roses', supposedly made by Mrs Gill of Cork Street, Burlington Gardens, 'for a young lady of high distinction'.[45] Papers regaled readers with details of royal wedding dresses and trousseaux. In 1818 Princess Elizabeth (1770–1840) wore a gown of rich silver tissue lavished with lace, and two years earlier Princess Charlotte's wedding gown, which survives in the Royal Collection, was also of silver and lace.[46] At the other end of the scale, one half of an

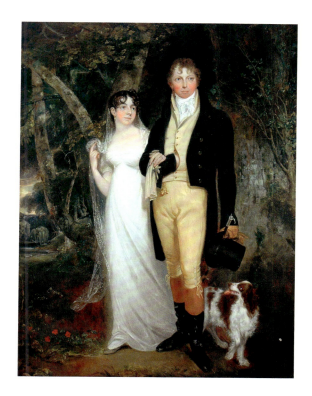

Fig. 3.6

William Armfield Hobday, *Captain and Mrs Edmund Burnham Pateshall*, 1810, oil on canvas. The newly married captain wears morning dress with a dark blue coat, cream waistcoat and leather breeches, the epitome of English masculine style. Scarborough Museums and Gallery.

eloping 'fashionable couple' found herself journeying through Stourbridge 'having no covering but a flannel petticoat and a great coat' in her haste to join with her intended. Presumably, suitable attire awaited her in Gretna Green just over the Scottish border.[47]

The gown itself was only part of the important set of new wedding clothes the bride took to married life. Here Austen offers better perspective. For Mrs Bennet, Lydia's wedding clothes from London, are 'a privilege without which her marriage would scarcely seem valid', and her misplaced priority for the girl: 'She was more alive to the disgrace which the want of new clothes must reflect on her daughter's nuptials, than to any sense of shame at her eloping and living with Wickham a fortnight before they took place.'[48] Maternal calculations for Jane's potential wedding to Bingley allow three or four months for the preparations, including obtaining wedding clothes.[49] These comprised all aspects of outfits, including the homely 'petticoats, Pockets and dressing Gowns for any *Bride expectant*' that Austen was unable to make for her niece Anna Austen in 1814, owing to illness.[50] Before the tragic death of Cassandra's fiancé, she was supposed by a visitor in 1796 to be working on her own wedding clothes.[51] And it is wedding clothes that Austen's characters expressly purchase in towns. Marianne Dashwood (*S&S*) is accused of being in London for the purpose, while in *Persuasion* Henrietta and Louisa Musgrove go (more modestly) to Bath to fit themselves out with wedding clothes.[52] The £500 Henry Tilney's mother had to buy wedding clothes in *Northanger Abbey* is a huge investment in a wardrobe, when a gown cost between 1 and 8 guineas. People such as Lucy Steele (*S&S*), who borrows all her sister's money to 'make a shew with' for her elopement, made do with a smaller outlay.[53] Austen shows men's wedding clothing in just one instance, when Lydia Bennet (*P&P*) is longing to know whether Wickham would be married in his blue coat, which tells us that he has not bespoke new wedding clothes (we can assume because of his extensive debts).[54] Other sources are just as reticent about male marriage attire. As for women, good, respectable morning dress would have sufficed for nearly every man at his wedding (fig. 3.6).

Mourning dress was a longer public display of formal emotion. Mourning etiquette required dressing in black clothing (fig. 3.7), or adopting black accessories for a certain amount of time, depending on the degree of connection with the deceased. The community demonstrated the bereavements of their acquaintance in clothing, and, given the Regency's large families and high mortality, there would have been a regular need for mourning dress.[55] On 23 January 1805 Fanny Knight wrote in her pocket memorandum 'We heard from Bath that Grand Papa Austen was dead.' Four days later the family 'went into deeper mourning', perhaps having obtained clothes suited to the degree of loss in the intervening time.[56] Frank Churchill

(*Emma*) is expected to undergo at least three months of deep mourning after the loss of his aunt.[57] His new stepmother Mrs Weston's 'broad hems' are the deep bands of crape she is attaching to a gown as her acknowledgement of the death in the family.[58] If a death was on the horizon, a family could prepare their clothing at home, digging out black gowns and armbands, or dyeing older garments black. 'William was mistaken when he told your Mama we did not mean to mourn for Mrs Motley Austen', wrote Austen in 1817. 'Living here we thought it necessary to array ourselves in our old Black Gowns, because there is a line of Connection with the family through the Prowtings & Harrisons of Southampton.'[59] The degree of relation guided the degree of outward respect through dress.

Austen described dress worn to a funeral in March 1817, only months before her own death on 17 July, indicating perhaps what her relatives wore to her funeral: 'Mrs Philmore attended as cheif Mourner, in Bombasin, made very short, and flounced with Crape.'[60] Bombazine (spellings vary), a textile of wool woven with silk or cotton, was the traditional fabric for mourning. With silk crape, the main textile signifier of grief, it presented a dull, decorous surface, although for evening it could be set off by 'bugle [beads] and black' accessories in the hair.[61] Mrs Austen considered a 'mourning Calico' in 1801, suggesting the use of one of the increasingly cheaper cotton fabrics.[62] In *Persuasion*, Elizabeth Elliot wore black ribbons for the death of her cousin's wife in 1814, and the widower Mr Elliot wears crape round his hat as his mark of mourning. It is his groom's accompanying him in mourning (with which employers furnished their servants), rather than being in the Elliot livery, that prevents Mary Musgrove from recognising him.[63] The conventions were a visible codification of grief that could be taken to extremes, as Austen observed of one Dr Hall of Bath, who in 1799 was 'in such very deep mourning that either his mother, his wife, or himself must be dead.'[64]

Many of Austen's letters of 1808 from their home in Southampton discussed mourning-dress plans with Cassandra, who was with their bereaved brother's family in Godmersham after the death of their sister-in-law Elizabeth Austen. They reveal the managing and altering required to darken one's wardrobe. In a letter of 7–9 October, Mrs Austen 'has picked her old silk pelisse to pieces, and means to have it dyed black for a gown'; on 13 October Jane asks Cassandra for some directions about mourning.[65] By 16 October she was sending her sister 'such of your Mourning as I think most likely to be useful, reserving for myself your Stockings & half the velvet'. Austen then described her own arrangements:

> *I* am to be in Bombazeen and Crape, according to what we are told is universal *here*; and which agrees with Martha's previous observation. My Mourning, however, will not impoverish me, for by having my velvet Pelisse fresh lined and made up, I am sure I shall have no occasion *this winter* for anything new of that sort. – I take my Cloak for the Lining – and shall send yours on the chance of its doing something of the same for you – tho' I beleive your Pelisse is in better repair than mine. – *One* Miss Baker makes my gown, & the other my Bonnet, which is to be silk covered with Crape.[66]

Dress in the Age of Jane Austen

Fig. 3.7

Mourning dress, 1820, silk. The requisite colour
and dull fabric for mourning did not preclude
fashionable cut, as this gown demonstrates. Its
puffed sleeve tops, bias satin trimmings and
gauzy sleeves and skirt make this grief à la
mode. Metropolitan Museum of Art, New York.

We see here one of Austen's many strategic reworkings of dress to improve her
existing wardrobe. Her black velvet pelisse was doing double duty as mourning,
and her main winter coat. The mourning dress was being made up new in the town.
Her nephews Edward (1794–1879) and George Knight (1795–1867) capitalised on
new purchases of mourning dress for their mother by insisting that an old black
coat be complemented with pantaloons – the latest style in 1808.[67] Grief need not
impair fashion, even for adolescent boys.

Many references to mourning clothes occur in letters sent by a writer who was away
from home when a death occurred, requesting items to be sent for the emergency. If in
doubt as to the degree of mourning required, the sable tide could creep inwards from
the accessories. 'Weepers' (black armbands) for men, black gloves, black crape sashes
tied around hats or bonnets all sufficed to signify mourning, even with a coloured outer
garment, 'as one cannot be expected to make up such ruinous articles' as gowns, pelisses
and coats 'for every mourning'.[68] Men had the advantage in cost, as so much of their
wardrobe was already black, or at least sombre. The important thing was that the
community recognised the mourner's adherence to the social rituals of public dressing.

Village

Local Merchants

Neighbourhood dress required neighbourhood shops. Mrs Topham's account book is a paean to the stock of local haberdashers, milliners and drapers, and a window on how consumers patronised them (fig. 3.8).[69] Although she lived in Cavendish Square in London, her shopping reflects everyday consumption in the local area, instead of the larger-scale metropolitan buying of the kind the Austens did when in town. It is the same pattern of regular spending that Austen suggests of Kitty and Lydia Bennet (*P&P*), 'who were usually tempted . . . three or four times a week' into their nearest market town, Meryton, a mile from home, 'to pay their duty to their aunt and to a milliner's shop just over the way'.[70] Women shopped regularly and in small quantities for dress-related items. The size of the town or village determined how many separate specialist shops it possessed. Every place larger than a hamlet had at least a shoemaker, and a village store combining a grocery, draper and haberdasher. An evocation of the rich retail dress jumble is found in a description of a colonial shop's

> dimities, Irish linen, . . . check, fine English calico, nankeens; prints, corduroy, cambrick, table cloths, fancy waistcoats, trowsers, shirts ready made, superfine blue and bottle green broad cloths; men, women, and children's shoes, gentlemen's dress ditto; fancy coloured and black Barcelona silk handkerchiefs, pasteboards for bonnets, ladies' white kid gloves, gentlemen's fancy York ditto; gilt and plated buttons small and large, small shot, small tooth combs, ribbands of colours, pins and needles, threads, tapes, sewing silks of all kinds.[71]

Although the list is from the other side of the world, these items appear regularly in Englishwomen's accounts. The contents tally with the vision of fictional retailing that Austen presents best in *Emma*. Ford's was 'the principal woollen-draper, linen-draper, and haberdasher's shop united' in the village of Highbury. For the residents, this is the central dispensary of new dress, 'the shop first in size and fashion in the place'. The village is large enough to support a dedicated dress and textile retailer, a place where local demand shapes, yet is informed by, the dress taste, knowledge and discrimination of the proprietors. The store sells figured and plain muslins, ribbons 'from town', and all manner of things to tempt young women like Harriet Smith.[72] Village lending libraries contained more than books, being retail centres that afforded patrons other opportunities to shop (fig. 3.9): Austen's heroine Charlotte in *Sanditon*, having chosen 'new parasols, new gloves and new brooches for her sisters and herself' in the library, then 'turned from the drawers of rings and brooches, repressed further solicitation and paid for what she had bought'.[73] These smaller retailers were one of the main ways that people in provincial and rural communities kept abreast of fashion and maintained their appearance by regular spending on the repair, accessorising and other intricacies of clothing.

Austen touches on dress supplies within smaller towns and rural areas, keeping in mind the tyranny of distance highlighted in *Northanger Abbey* by Mrs Allen's lament that '"We are sadly off in the country; not but what we have very good shops in

Fig. 3.8

Mrs Mary Topham carefully recorded small personal purchases in her account book. A large proportion were clothing and haberdashery. Skeins of silk, ribbons, a velvet bonnet, black shoe binding, a piece of bobbin lace, papers of pins, a pair of gloves and lengths of calico were among the items she shopped for over the new-year period in 1816. Chawton House Library.

Salisbury, but it is so far to go – eight miles is a long way." [74] In Basingstoke, for example, Austen popped into a Mrs Ryder's, and 'bought what [she] intended to buy, but not in much perfection . . . Miss Wood as usual is going to Town very soon, and will lay in a fresh stock.' [75] Local retailers relied on London as a source of fashion wares. Austen's tart 'as usual' suggests a reliance on quick turnovers, not investing in regular stock. Larger provincial towns such as Basingstoke or Southampton had drapers, haberdashers, hosiers, tailors, shoemakers and milliners, as well as market stalls selling fabrics and haberdashery. Austen considered her nearest urban centre poor in some dress provision: 'Though I do not believe Southampton is famous for tailoring, I hope it will prove itself better than Basingstoke' – a complaint belied by the landed gentry Jervoise family living 5 miles from Basingstoke at Herriard, whose bills demonstrate their regular patronage of Basingstoke tailors. [76] Provincial tailors could be the source of ready-made clothing, a new addition to the middle-class retail sartorial world. Some regional English urban tailors at this date began keeping a small stock of made-up garments to satisfy immediate, transient demand: 'A client might fail to collect a finished garment; a customer might offer a used garment in part-exchange; a tailor might produce ready-made items in the inevitable slack periods. Indeed, tailors could choose to sell bespoke commissions as ready-made to secure an immediate sale.' [77] Men's ready-made clothing was more easily available than women's. However, although Austen had complained in 1798, 'I cannot determine what to do about my new Gown;

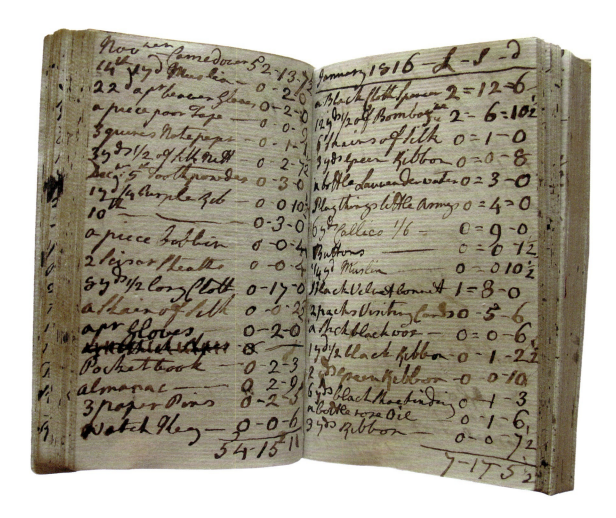

Fig. 3.9

James Green and Thomas Rowlandson, 'Lending Library, Scarborough', from *Poetical Sketches of Scarborough* (1813), coloured engraving on paper. A range of people patronise the lending and shopping possibilities of the Scarborough Library; their age and status show in their clothing, from the older woman, accompanied by her footman carrying her parcels, to the local men conversing by the window.

Fig. 3.10 Opposite

John Dempsey, *Black Charley, Shoemaker at Norwich*, 1823, watercolour on paper. The footwear proprietor is the best-dressed of all Dempsey's subjects, wearing a good-quality embroidered satin waistcoat, fine cloth coat and radiantly white linen, though a few years behind 1820s fashion. Gaiters hide his own shoes, while an array of his wares is displayed around him. Tasmanian Museum and Art Gallery, Hobart.

I wish such things were to be bought ready-made', other references confirm the availability of pre-made garments.[78] In 1812 Austen's mention that 'There was no ready-made Cloak at Alton that would do, but Coleby has undertaken to supply one in a few days; it is to be Grey Woollen & cost ten shillings' tells us that the Hampshire town nearest to her home at Chawton offered ready-made as well as bespoke female clothing, although it may have been limited to items like cloaks requiring little fitting.[79]

A portrait of 'Black Charley' provides a rare vision of one such local dress merchant (fig. 3.10). The Norwich proprietor stands in his doorway, fashionably dressed, with his range of footwear seen behind him in the shop and around the door. Charley may have manufactured on site or ordered shoes in from London, where materials could be got more cheaply. The major Regency change in shoes was the rapid shrinking of the heel that had defined eighteenth-century footwear, expressing class rather than gender differentiation. The reduction started in the 1790s, and heels disappeared by the mid-1800s. Shoes ended in pointed toes for women, which became rounder through the 1800s to 1810s, evolving into a squarer toe for both sexes by the 1820s. The basic shape for men and women was a pump, with latchets and buckles, or laces for men; more genteel or evening shoes had a round, low throat. Based on shoemakers' trade cards and bills, between 1790 and 1820 women's shoes cost between 1s. 8d. and 8s. 4d. Men's shoes and boots started at around 5s. and could cost as much as £2 1s. 8d.[80] In 1800 Austen thanked Cassandra for purchasing some 'not particularly beautiful' but well-fitting pink

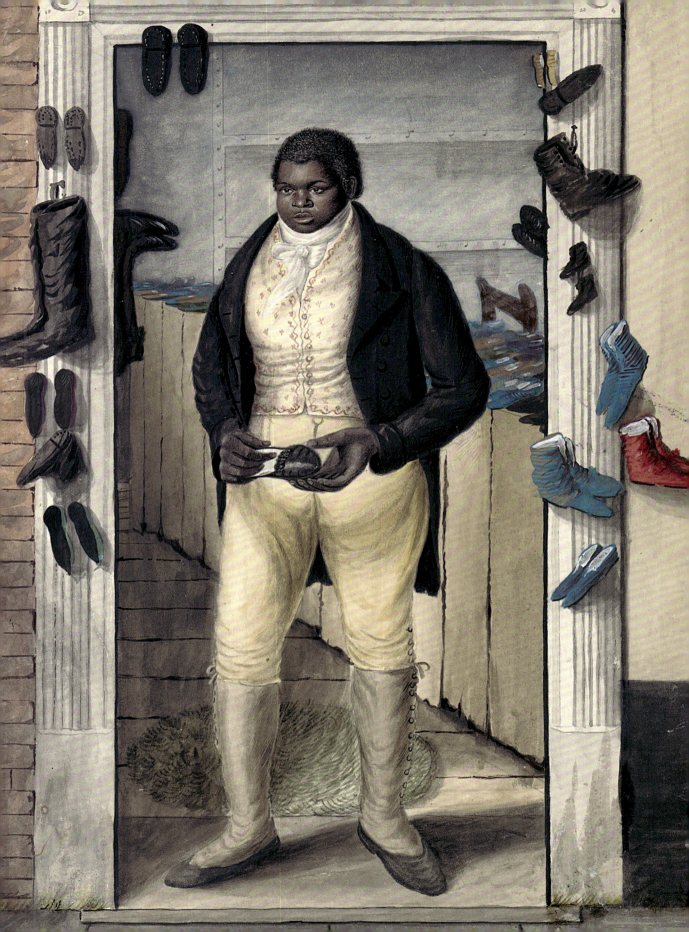

shoes and another 'faultless' pair her sister bought for her, ready-made in a London warehouse.[81] Because shoes were made on 'straight' lasts (the wooden form), with no left and right, it was easier to achieve a proxy fit. Wearers created left and right, if desired, through use.

For the genteel, gloves were essential for weather protection and style (fig. 3.11).[82] The finest leather was thin, bright yellow suede from unborn calves, made into 'chicken skin' or Limerick gloves that hugged the arm like a second skin. The 'sleek, well-tied parcels of "Men's Beavers" and "York Tan"' at Ford's in Highbury (*Emma*) are gloves – a fictional appearance matching the styles' real-life popularity, judging by accounts and advertisements.[83] Both sexes prized soft, smooth leather gloves that fitted the hand comfortably – 'light and pretty', as the Austen sisters preferred.[84] Novel colours such as 'Isabel', 'frangipane' and 'wainscot' abounded, but magazines assured their readers 'white kid, York tan and Limerick gloves are considered far more genteel than those of kid the colour of bonnets'.[85] Cotton, linen (thread), jean, nankeen, worsted and silk gloves were also popular. Women's accounts confirm a preference for plain, white kid gloves, worn wrist length for daytime, and above the elbow for evening. A coloured ribbon to hold up evening gloves around the arm was more versatile than buying to match a gown. At home, netted, lace or muslin mittens, like a white pair Cassandra lost, left the fingers free to work while keeping the hand warm.[86] Gloves were easily lost or torn. Twice Austen has male characters use the pretext of looking for gloves as a way to approach the woman they wish to speak with privately.[87] Accounts show gloves bought in multiple pairs that allowed substitution for missing halves.

One of Austen's most extended scenes of consumer consideration occurs in *Pride and Prejudice*. Lydia Bennet, meeting her elder sisters on their return from a long absence, exclaims:

> 'Look here, I have bought this bonnet. I do not think it is very pretty; but I thought I might as well buy it as not. I shall pull it to pieces as soon as I get home, and see if I can make it up any better.' And when her sisters abused it as ugly, she added, with perfect unconcern, 'Oh! but there were two or three much uglier in the shop.'[88]

Lydia's bonnet had deeper ramifications for contemporary readers. Headwear was an article of no small cost. Bought either whole, or in parts, a bonnet comprised a front, a solid or fabric back, and a riot of trimmings of the kind proffered at milliners' shops: ribbons of all sorts and colours, flowers, edgings, cord, gimp, galloon. Whole bonnets often cost a pound or a guinea in contemporary accounts. A finished gown could be acquired for the same amount, so a bonnet was quite an outlay for a girl on a limited allowance. Purchasing a hat of little taste, requiring the further efforts of 'some prettier-coloured satin to trim it with fresh' to make it tolerable, plus the extra expense (6*d.*) of the bandbox, spells clearly the financial profligacy and thoughtlessness Lydia will extend to her future matrimonial choice and income.[89] In both cases, haste negates taste.

Bonnets evolved from the eighteenth-century habit of pulling down a flat hat brim to hold it about the face; the back of the brim was soon lost. The deep front provided weather protection, though exquisites lengthened them for effect, as in the poke bonnets that satirists delighted in represented as two feet long. Regency bonnet styles were innumerable, reflecting every battle, celebrity, visiting member of the aristocracy or other passing fancy. Partaking of the latest headdress novelty was a way to engage with fashionable variety for less expense. Fashion magazines often displayed pages of caps, hats and bonnets (fig. 3.12), and these mutable accessories anchored changes of taste into genteel consumers' wardrobes more quickly than body garments. Headwear circulated among communities as the bearers of fashion and – as gifts – markers of esteem.

Two days after her birthday in 1798, Austen wrote to Cassandra telling her:

> I took the liberty a few days ago of asking your Black velvet Bonnet to lend me its cawl, which it very readily did, and by which I have been enabled to give a considerable improvement of dignity to my Cap, which was before too nidgetty to please me. I shall wear it on Thursday, but I hope you will not be offended with me for following your advice as to its ornaments only in part. I still venture to retain the narrow silver round it, put twice round without any bow, and instead of the black military feather shall put in the Coquelicot [poppy-coloured] one as being smarter, & besides Coquelicot is to be all the fashion this winter. After the ball I shall probably make it entirely black.[90]

Fig. 3.12

Unknown artist, 'London Head Dresses',
Magazine of Female Fashion of London and Paris,
February 1800, hand-coloured engraving on
paper (with detail). The plate shows a selection
of caps and soft fabric hats, typical of the focus
on headwear in Regency fashion periodicals.
Rijksmuseum, Amsterdam.

A bonnet 'cawl' was the soft fabric back, or the fabric covering of a solid back,
and was connected to the brim or 'front' of card or pasteboard (see fig. 0.2). When
Austen removed the cawl from her sister's hat, the bonnet itself would remain. In
one paragraph, she documented four different headwear treatments for two women
using the same piece of black velvet. Trimmings and ribbons were usually pinned
onto the bonnet base for ease of altering the decoration quickly to match a gown
or a new style, or to refresh an old bonnet, something Lizzy Bennet may be doing
when she is found trimming a hat.[91]

Getting and Altering Clothes

Clothing had a high net value for Regency wearers. It was a considerable, infrequent
investment for consumers of the middling and upper ranks, who planned, discussed
and collaborated upon new dress with relatives, acquaintances and professionals.
Garments were generally made for people individually. Every town and village had
multiple tailors to satisfy the local yeomanry's need for coats, waistcoats, breeches
and other garments, usually bespoke but, increasingly, ready-made (fig. 3.13).
For men who had no woman to sew their linens, ready-made shirts and assorted
undergarments, or those ordered from professional (male) gentlemen's shirtmakers
filled the gap. A substantial Preston tailor, declared bankrupt in 1821, owned a
large stock of ready-made clothes. Of 645 garments and accessories, 219 were men's

shirts.[92] Women very rarely undertook the sewing of men's outer clothing, as it required a specific set of skills in handling wools, stiffening and shaping, which sewing linens did not prepare for. Mary Wordsworth (1770–1859), making her husband's 'woollen waistcoat', may have been knitting or working on a flannel-type garment.[93] The poet's womenfolk likewise spent a day taking apart his old coats for the tailor, to make patterns for new garments.[94]

The yearly account of George Purefoy Jervoise of Herriard with Stephen Blake of Bentworth, Hampshire, details local tailoring prices (he employed Joseph Vickery of the same village to do mending and alterations).[95] Jervoise had his main clothes made in London (see chapter 5), but in 1802 Blake made him a coat. The bill of £2 4s. 9d. breaks down as follows:

> making . . . 6s.
> for Cloth, £1.9s.3d.
> for 1¼ yd Dimity, 1s.9d.
> for 16 Gilt buttons & 4 Small D[itto], 3s.
> for Buckram pockets tape canvas, 1s.3d.
> for mowhare [mohair] silk thread, 1s.2d.
> for a Velvet collar, 2s.4d.[96]

A superfine black cloth coat from London had cost Jervoise £3 13s. 6d. the year before. Although some of the price would come from the quality of the wool, the country tailor is around 40 per cent cheaper. What is relevant to village life is the identification of clothes with person created by this infrequent changing of men's dress. A yeoman farmer who bought a new coat every five years would have been known by the familiar shape and colour of his coat, his habitual movements creased into the wool the way old shoes reveal their wearer's feet.

Within a local community, sources suggest a somewhat haphazard approach to employing the skills of a professional mantua- or dressmaker. Servants and working women were frequently tasked with constructing clothes. 'There is a striking similarity', observes Serena Dyer, 'between the role of the mantua-maker, and the role of the lady's maid . . . local seamstresses were often called in as day servants in some households in order to construct smaller items of clothing.'[97] 'A most excellent servant' came Maria Edgeworth's way, who had 'lived as a lady's maid . . . can mantua-make and do all sorts of work.'[98] Even Harriet Smith, of uncertain status, little occupation, and possessed of a feminine education, does not do her own dressmaking, employing instead a young woman in Highbury to make up a gown for her.[99] A neighbour advises the heroines of a 1794 novel, on seeing the mantua-maker has not finished their gowns, that she could have recommended a farmer's daughter of the parish, 'who would have stitched them up presently, and all in the fashion too, for she is come home from Brittlesworth, our market town, to stay a few days with her brother'.[100] The bodies of young mobile women carried fashion with them, as they moved between employments, where they could observe new ideas in dress.

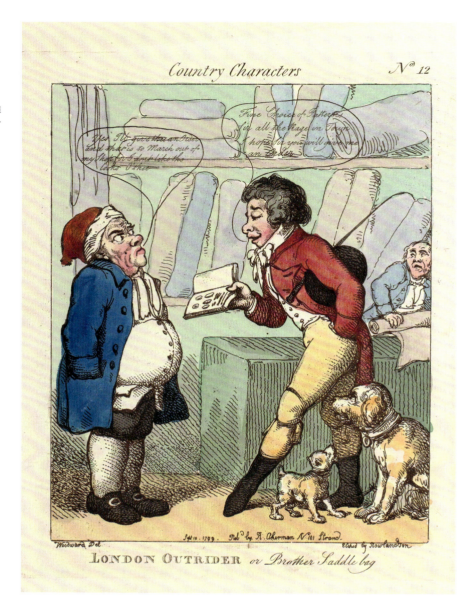

Mantua-makers and tailors visited clients at home, taking measurements, doing
fittings and showing new accessories for approval and purchase. Two entries
in Fanny Knight's diaries give an idea of the collaboration needed to produce
garments. On 6 November 1804, she went into Canterbury with her father from
their estate at Godmersham, Kent. There she had her ears 'bored' (pierced),
bought 'a bear [fur] long tippet[,] ordered a black beaver hat . . . & a Pelisse
of Lady's cloth trimmed with bear' for the coming winter. Five days later the
pelisse was finished, delivered (on a Sunday), and found to be too small. It
was returned to the mantua-maker, possibly after pinned alterations had been
made at home, and by 5 December, a month after ordering, had arrived 'and
just fitted me'.[101]

The degree to which gentry women made their own clothes is debatable, and there is 'a silence in women's correspondence in regard to the making of these more complex items'.[102] 'It must have been a temptation for the amateur to run up a dress when they were as simple as those of the early 1800s', Janet Arnold adduced. 'However they did need fitting – and probably a lot of muslin dresses made at home were worn for mornings, while the dressmaker, or mantua-maker . . . would have been called in to tackle the ones worn on more public occasions' (fig. 3.14).[103] Women making clothes at social levels above Austen's appear to do so for amusement. Much of the 'making' was decorative, like painting flowers on satin, rather than constructional. The move towards cheaper cotton textiles encouraged domestic production, as more fabric could be bought, and therefore might be treated less carefully. 'With less expensive fabric more readily available the cutting necessary when using plain seams in clothing construction was more acceptable' as, for the first time, plain sewing techniques practised on linen seamstressing could be used on outer garments.[104]

Did Jane and Cassandra Austen sew their own gowns and other non-linen garments? How much actual dressmaking the sisters did is unclear. Passages like the following shed no light on who is doing the making: 'I cannot possibly oblige you by not wearing my gown, because I have it made up on purpose to wear it a great deal . . . You must learn to like it yourself & make it up at Godmersham.'[105] Further confusion comes from the habit of referring to both an uncut length of fabric intended for a garment and the finished dress itself as a 'gown', as Austen makes explicit in a letter of 1813: 'I shall take the opportunity of getting my Mother's gown –; so, by 3 o'clock in the afternoon she may consider herself the owner of 7 yds of B[lac]k Sarsenet.'[106]

A 1799 letter suggests that the sisters did construct clothing, though 'making' could mean embroidering a length of fabric. Austen's impatience at the fate of her best gown accompanies her 'many thanks' to Cassandra 'for your trouble in making it, as well as marking my silk stockings'.[107] Once again, the phrasing could mean that, instead of sewing a new gown, Cassandra has turned, remade or altered something Austen owned already. Jane would be unlikely to identify a new dress she had not yet seen as her 'best gown'. Their niece Fanny Knight wrote a diary entry about a '<u>working</u> week with frocks and spencers', though again it is unclear whether she was making or altering.[108] The main issues for making clothing domestically were cutting the fabric economically and achieving a good fit. As contemporary advice pointed out, those who could afford it 'have their best dresses invariably made by a mantua-maker, as those which are cut out at home seldom fit so comfortably, or look so well, as when made by persons in constant practice',[109] which did not deter Elizabeth 'Betsey' (Wynne) Fremantle (1778–1857), naval wife and dedicated diarist. She spent many days in her cabin on her new husband's ship in 1797 'making a gown what [*sic*] will not fit very well, unluckily'.[110] She may have resembled 'Industrious Jenny' at her labours (fig. 3.15), a rare vision of women's domestic clothes-making.

Caroline Fry fictionalised the kind of dressmaking gentry women may have undertaken, suggesting it was common:

> It would be quite superfluous to describe the whole process of dress-making – every lady who has made her entré into the gay world, without a long purse at her command, knows what ensues upon wanting a ball-dress in a hurry, and can picture to herself the state of the apartment, during the first stage of the proceeding – the various articles of apparel consigned to the backs of the chairs – the piano converted into a measuring board – the attendance of all the females in the house, except the cook, with thimbles on their middle finger – the trying on, and cutting out, and fitting in.[111]

The vision of dressmaking colonising drawing-rooms illuminates why such domestic productivity could be impractical. This shared, semi-public room facilitated the family's sociability and could be spared at only limited times. The small garments and decorative work that predominate in records of gentry women's needle labour all fitted into a lap and therefore a workbag, or could be whisked into a work-basket at short notice (see fig. 2.25). A long gown is unwieldy to tidy away. On the other hand, the immateriality of women's slippers prompted a vogue for shoemaking, which meant embroidering or stitching the uppers of Grecian-style sandals and soft pumps, and sometimes attaching the sole (fig. 3.16). Mrs Austen made a pair –

Fig. 3.14 Opposite

Muslin gown, 1795–1805 (with detail of the
bodice, seen from the back). The transparent
fabric reveals the construction of this transitional
dress, which retains the back pleating of late
eighteenth-century gowns, while the waistline is
rising. Metropolitan Museum of Art, New York.

Fig. 3.15 Right

George Walker, *Industrious Jenny*, c.1810–15,
watercolour and pen and ink on paper. Jenny's
uncurled front hair and practical sewing are an
insight into everyday Regency life. Her straight
posture as she works suggests the stays worn
under her morning dress. Yale Center for British
Art, Paul Mellon Collection, New Haven, Conn.

probably embroidered – for her granddaughter Anna.[112] Dorothy Wordsworth sat
outside one hot summer morning and finished her shoes.[113] Ladies of the first rank
and fashion, not excluding the royal princesses, tried their hands at cordwaining.

Once their garments existed, Austen and her contemporaries sallied forth with
confidence into amending, turning, and renewing them, refashioning clothes for as
long as the fabric endured. Many surviving garments were remade from silks that
were already twenty or thirty years old. Older articles could be refreshed at the
modest cost of new haberdashery and some labour. Austen's letters frequently mention alterations, matching surviving garments that show evidence of amendments.
On limited incomes, the sisters adjusted their wardrobes to conform to their own

INDUSTRIOUS JENNY EVER USEFUL MISS!!
EMPLOYS HER TIME IN MAKING A PELISSE

sense of neatness and propriety. They swapped details of new modes and discussed plans for updating dresses, noting where flounces were coming in or when waists needed lowering. Their correspondence demonstrates practical knowledge of dress construction: how many skirt breadths can be got from a length of muslin; where angled side gores need to be added.[114] The practice of turning, taking a garment apart and remaking it with the other side uppermost, does not appear much in the material record, probably because the kinds of gowns that were turned wore into oblivion or were cut up for other purposes.

Professional changes carried out by local tradespeople appear in the letters. The Austen family had mixed successes with dyers changing the colours of existing gowns. Sometimes the chemicals caused the garments to 'divid[e] with a Touch', as happened to a blue gown in 1808; another instance found Austen asked to pay a bill for dyeing some silks, when her muslin gown had not yet been dyed, despite being promised several times.[115]

The point of alterations was not only to extend the life of a garment and prevent boredom with a limited wardrobe, but also to remain current, and to pass community scrutiny. The art-history perspective on Regency dress has focused on the stylistic increase of decoration through the 1810s, not how that was achieved. Haberdashery applied in inventive, novel ways was a quick, cheap means of achieving freshness and fashion, a significant vehicle for Regency women's expression of individual taste when investment in a new garment was a large financial outlay. The importance of trimmings cannot be overestimated (fig. 3.17).

Fig. 3.16

Grecian sandal, wool, silk, linen and leather, 1795–1805. The difficulty of reconciling an illusion of classical nudity with the practicalities of real clothing is seen in this *faux* Grecian sandal. A pink silk taffeta lacing panel mimics naked skin while holding the shoe onto the foot. Collection of the Bata Shoe Museum, Toronto.

Dress in the Age of Jane Austen

Mrs Topham's accounts show that extras such as lace, flowers, ribbons, pins, fringing, shoe binding and roses, gimp and galloon (types of braid), cord, tape, wadding and buttons formed 47 per cent of the quantity of textiles and clothing-related items bought by her between 1810 and 1825, though fabrics constitute the greater cost.[116] At 42 per cent of the haberdashery, ribbons made up the majority of purchases, acquired in every colour, width and quality on a weekly basis throughout the accounting period. Austen shows us how women might utilise these frequent ribbon purchases to renew their look: 'I have determined to trim my lilac sarsenet with black sattin ribbon . . . 6d. width at the bottom, 3d. or 4d., at top. – Ribbon trimmings are all the fashion at Bath.'[117] She specifies ribbons by their cost, a price gradation related to their width and quality, testifying to nuanced consumer understanding of textile qualities, which is hard to reconstruct from surviving gowns.

Ribbons were important for negotiating Georgian fashionability, and they appear often in Austen's letters as a central dress item bought from every near shop.[118]

Fictionally, Harriet Smith (*Emma*) declares she will want her new ribbons from Ford's directly after purchase – she has bought enough to make a large parcel requiring delivery; and Catherine Morland (*NA*) finds 'occasion for some indispensable yard of ribbon which must be bought without a moment's delay'.[119] Even meagre budgets could run to ribbons of sarsenet or taffeta, which might be embossed or of the type with a 'perl edge' that Austen tried 'to draw up into kind of Roses, instead of putting [the ribbon] in plain double plaits [pleats]'.[120] Her inventive needle skills wielded ribbons and other trimmings as changeable demonstrations of taste. Mrs Topham bought ribbons in small, specific lengths, often after larger purchases such as caps, bonnets or gowns, suggesting that she had definite end-purposes in mind for trimmings to complete the garment (fig. 3.18). Ribbon colour could also convey fashionability. Austen's letter of 1798 on hat alterations was probably written while she was working on what became *Northanger Abbey*; the popular 'Coquelicot' colour appears in the novel on Isabella Thorpe's bonnet, and throughout the 1790s fashions presented in the *Gallery of Fashion* (see fig. 1.12).[121]

Sources distinguish between gown and trimmings as separate aspects of fashionable dress. Henry Tilney (*NA*) catalogues Catherine's '"sprigged muslin robe with blue trimmings"'; Mrs Elton (*Emma*) professes to have '"the greatest dislike to the idea of being over-trimmed"', and demands to be complimented on her gown and its trimming individually.[122] But it can be difficult to quantify what 'trimming' meant. Mrs Topham, for example, records 'gymp trimming', as well as 'trimming for Bonnet', yellow, blue and green 'trimming', muslin, crape, stuff and bugle trimming, besides the endless ribbons and braids.[123] Trimming is both noun and verb, like 'dress', so its meaning can refer to the stuff itself or the action of attaching a trim.

All this production was not only for oneself. Exchanging small dress items helped to maintain personal communities, and transmitted novelties and techniques. One of the delights of Austen's letters is their view into networks of needlework and clothing gift exchange, labours of love reinforcing ties of family and wider acquaintance –'objects which will maintain the essential web of family connections and the flow of interest, as well as . . . support the claim to genteel status'.[124] The Austen network made caps, handkerchiefs, cloaks, purses and veils for friends and relations, or passed on others' efforts. Jane and Cassandra frequently embodied thought and care in little material objects for their relatives – a handkerchief for Mrs James Austen (née Mary Lloyd; 1771–1843), for example, a long strip of work for Fanny Knight from her Aunt Jane.[125] Gift exchange culture appears in the novels, as when Emma witnesses Jane Fairfax's emotional and physical labour in making new caps and workbags for Mrs and Miss Bates.[126] Sometimes the connection could be one-sided. Austen once spent a long paragraph of a letter trying to establish which 'kind lady' might have been so insistent on conveying 'some work or trimming which she has been doing' to some sisters, possibly themselves (though 'I dare say we shall not like the work').[127]

Knitting was a useful gift-making skill. Once Anna Larpent learned to knit in 1798, she made gaiters, mittens and stockings, and later tippets, muffetees, bedcovers and bedside rugs, often distributed among her family and friends.[128] Mrs Austen found

'great amusement in . . . glove-knitting; when this pair is finished, she means to knit another, & at present wants no other work'.[129] Knitting benefited impoverished Mrs Smith too (*Pers.*). After Nurse Rooke teaches her to knit, it occupies her invalid hours. Rooke also puts Mrs Smith '"in the way of making these little thread-cases, pincushions and card-racks, which you always find me so busy about . . . She has a large acquaintance, of course professionally, among those who can afford to buy, and she disposes of my merchandise."'[130]

Mrs Smith's productions would include the kind of huswife (hussive, housewife or hussif), thread-case or small needle-book that Mrs Dashwood gives to the Misses Steele (*S&S*). Hers, however, are 'made by some emigrant', a jab at Mrs Dashwood's thoughtless charity and lack of useful occupation.[131] Had she cared, she would have produced them herself, like the needle-case that Jane Austen made (fig. 3.19).

Fig. 3.19

Jane Austen, needle-case, 1800–17, paper,
silk, paint and pen and ink. Austen's delicate
handwork skills are shown off equally by her
painting, her embroidery and her handwriting.
The yellow ribbon adorning this little book
for holding needles is of coarse quality and is
probably the kind bought for 1d. or 2d. a yard.
Jane Austen's House Museum, Chawton.

The production of thread-cases 'places' Mrs Smith socially for contemporary readers: her items fall 'into the category of products that a woman of the gentility might make, but ordinarily only for family members and singular friends'.[132] Exchanges were acceptable as long as they remained entirely unmercantile. Mrs Smith's remunerated labour reinforces her genteel status because it supplies her '"with the means of doing a little good to one or two very poor families in this neighbourhood"' instead of enlarging her income, which would make her a worker.[133] There is a fine social line here regarding paid female labour. Women's needles were to be plied for acquaintance or charity without recompense. Contemporary discourse about milliners and their morals reveals how the more women's work publicly employed her body, especially in selling directly to male customers, the nearer came a shadow of whoreishness.[134]

The reciprocity of favours could be of mutual benefit. A Mrs Dickson was delighted with a netted purse Mary Austen (1790–1823; wife of Francis Austen) sent her, and in return, as Austen reported, desired Mary 'not to provide herself with a christening dress, which is exactly what her young correspondent wanted; and [Mary] means to defer making any of the caps as long as she can, in hope of having Mrs. D.'s present in time to be serviceable as a pattern.'[135] One of Austen's youthful stories was dedicated to her friend Martha Lloyd, 'As a small testimony of the gratitude I feel for your late generosity to me in finishing my muslin Cloak'.[136] The example of the Austens was common among their contemporaries. 'This day we have been all sitting together in the drawing room going on with our various little employments', recounted Maria Edgeworth; '– Mrs. Sneyd by turns making net for one of the Miss Leicesters'.[137]

Decorative Needlework

Decorative needlework went a step beyond dutiful plain sewing. Netting, knitting, embroidery and other non-constructional needle techniques hover somewhere between practicality and pointlessness. On one hand, such work created dress accessories essential to rapid fashion culture: reticules, purses, mittens, handkerchiefs, caps and other items. On the other, decorative needlework or 'fancy work', Vickery notes, 'could be a pretty amusement . . . but monster projects that could not be completed without assistance were a hypocritical extravagance'.[138] Austen warns us against those engaged in merely decorative work. This useless usefulness can indicate indolence (Lady Bertram, *MP*), vanity (Mrs John Dashwood), frivolity (Mrs Palmer) or superficiality (Mrs Jennings; all *S&S*). Lady Bertram is so helpless she is unable to complete even her 'long piece of needlework, of little use and no beauty', without Fanny Price's constant assistance in helping her through the hard parts.[139] These women embody conspicuous leisure in Austen's gentry classes.

Decorative sewing and embroidery were acceptable for working in company and public spaces, including the home when visitors were present. The third of the Wynne sisters, Harriet (1786–1860), wrote of embroidering a linen gown in a group, drawing on the pattern together, and spending 'a social morning working and writing'.[140] Mrs Larpent's projects included cross-stitch and tent-stitch items, and delicately embroidered dress borders and petticoats. However, decorative work could occupy the mind too much, to the detriment of character, as Austen consistently implies. Clothes-obsessed Mrs Allen (*NA*) has such 'incapacity for thinking' that 'she could never be entirely silent; and, therefore, while she sat at her work, if she lost her needle or broke her thread, . . . or saw a speck upon her gown, she must observe it aloud'.[141] Perhaps all that separates her from loquacious Miss Bates in *Emma* is the comfort of wealth, obviating worry about more pressing concerns.

As this chapter is quite feminine, it is pleasing to find men creating textile handworks. Naval Francis and Charles Austen had nimble fingers, trained in rope and netting skills. Frank used his skills to make a 'very nice fringe for the Drawingroom Curtains' when he and his family were living with Mrs and the Miss Austens in Southampton.[142] The next generation continued the tradition. Austen's two nephews amused themselves 'very comfortably in the Evening by netting; they are each about a rabbit net, and sit as deedily to it, side by side, as any two Uncle Franks could do'.[143] Frank inspired Austen's creation of handy Captain Harville in *Persuasion*.[144]

Fig. 3.20 Right

Netted reticule, early nineteenth century, silk, cotton and metal. The reticule or ridicule, made in every possible fabric and textile technique, was a very popular Regency accessory. Netting, used in this example, was easily achievable by ladies at home, and conformed with the taste for transparency. Metropolitan Museum of Art, New York.

Fig. 3.21 Far Right and Below

Selection of netted and beaded miser's purses, early nineteenth century, silk, metal and glass. A miser's purse was a long tube with one or more metal sliders that held the contents in a closed section and released them for access via a central slit. Although decorative examples were popular with women, men also used the convenient container for coins and other small items. Private collection.

Fig. 3.22 Opposite

Robert Home, *Portrait of a Lady*, c.1805–10, oil on canvas. The sitter is depicted in morning dress, worn with a chemisette of embroidered muslin and with her shawl draped behind. On the table are sewing accoutrements, including her work-box and tools, and tasks in progress, including a half-finished knitted purse. Home painted this portrait in India. Private collection.

Netting was a popular pastime, involving a mesh foundation with embroidery worked over the finished net, often to make reticules and slim miser's purses (figs 3.20 and 3.21). Although both could be knitted (fig. 3.22), netting was quicker and easier. A friend of Isabella Thorpe's '"is netting herself the sweetest cloak you can conceive"' and her friend Catherine also has a netting-box.[145] Fanny Austen listed at the back of her 1814 pocket-book the materials required to make the netted purses she made and gave, including 24 yards of thread.[146] The Austen sisters netted; Jane recorded a fruitless search for netting silk in 1798.[147] The skill appears in *Pride and Prejudice*, admired by Bingley and censured by Darcy. The latter's view that the word 'accomplished' '"is applied to many a woman who deserves it no otherwise than by netting a purse or covering a screen"' lumps the technique in with useless fancy-work.[148] Edgeworth concurs with him when she writes of Lady Bathurst: 'very well bred, well dressed [sitting] all evening . . . net[ting] and spangl[ing] with great delicacy and diligence a purse which will never be *used* by any mortal'.[149] Mrs Topham was an indefatigable purse-maker. She constantly bought skeins of purse thread and twist, gilt snaps, sliders, tassels, ribbons and netting needles to make purses for many acquaintances.[150]

Patterns and Periodicals

Dress moving between friends carried both affection and fashion. Using garments as patterns by copying them was a way to obtain new shapes and modes. The construction of a pretty tucker could be imitated easily, and a gown that fitted its wearer perfectly was a model for the next. Harriet Smith (*Emma*) dithers in Ford's about her 'pattern gown' – the template garment she needs to make her new one from the fabric she buys – being at Emma's house rather than her own.[151] Before commercial paper patterns, the use of an existing garment ensured fit and consistency in patterning, as *The Duties of a Lady's Maid* instructed: 'When you have once procured a pattern . . . which fits a lady's figure, and this you ought to make of soft paper or cloth, you will not require to measure a fresh one for every new dress' (fig. 3.23).[152] It is always easier to make something for the second time. Copying existing objects transmitted new fashions in material form, and built on what was already successful. Mary Austen sent via Jane to ask Cassandra in Godmersham to 'bring her the pattern of the Jacket and Trowsers, or whatever it is that [their sister-in-law] Elizabeth's boys wear when they are first put into breeches –; so if you could bring her an old suit itself, she would be very glad'.[153]

Fig. 3.23

Unknown artist, 'Ladies Dress Maker', from John Souter, *The Book of Trades* (1804), engraving on paper. The accompanying text reads: 'The plate represents the Dress-Maker taking the pattern off from a lady, by means of a piece of paper or cloth: the pattern, if taken in cloth, becomes afterwards the lining of the dress' (p. 225). This engraving, and a variant from the book's 1809 edition, are very rare depictions of the process of making Regency clothing for women. Rijksmuseum, Amsterdam.

Not all loans increased amiability in the social village. Austen once wrote tersely to Cassandra that she was quite pleased with their friends 'for wanting the pattern of our Caps, but I am not so well pleased with Your giving it to them'.[154] Delicious new headwear copied widely reduced its stylish effect. As a fictional correspondent complained, '"That malicious little S— sent to borrow my new polonese robe, or if I would have the goodness to send her the name of my dressmaker."'[155] Copying secured current modes at a fraction of the price. The sly Steele sisters (S&S) wheedle Lady Middleton's gowns – newly made in the latest London taste – out of her to use as patterns. The impoverished sisters thereby reinforce a beneficial social intimacy by flattering Lady Middleton, and acquire a stylish dress template, uniting 'smart appearance with the utmost frugality', that they could not otherwise afford.[156]

Anna Maria 'Nancy' Woodforde (1757–1830), the parson's niece, recorded two kinds of pattern in circulation. 'Mrs. Bodham lent me a Tucker and Ruff all in one by which I intend to make myself one like it.' A few days later, 'Lady Bacon brought me a Pattern to work my Muslin Petticoat by . . . from Lady Ca. Hobart who has worked one like it. I drew of the Pattern and returned it to Lady B this Evening.'[157] This pattern is a design for embellishment, which usually meant embroidery. An otherwise unknown Letitia Louisa Kerr kept an album of hand-drawn designs of stylised natural motifs and geometric figures for doing various kinds of needlework, including handkerchief corners, collarettes, corners for muslin aprons, tambour work, muslin over various nets, crowns for caps, flounces and silk or chenille embroidery.[158] Such patterns reinforce the importance of trimmings as a separate application of style to gowns. Borrowing and lending fashion periodicals through friends and circulating libraries must have been common, if they were to stimulate new fashions. The influence attributed to Nikolaus von Heideloff's *Gallery of Fashion* (1794–1803; see fig. 1.12) is hard to reconcile with its price. The publication cost 3 guineas for a yearly subscription – the cost of three muslin gowns. Separate monthly copies sold for 7*s.* 6*d.* per issue, or the price of a yard or two of good quality silk, and it seems that the number of copies printed of each issue never exceeded 450.[159] Periodicals provided monthly embroidery design patterns for small dress elements such as fichus, handkerchiefs and aprons, as well as fashion plates. Whether or not the images influenced ensemble styles, the patterns definitely saw robust use. Figures 3.24 and 3.25 show an embroidery pattern from a magazine and a nearly

Fig. 3.26

Fabric samples in the *Repository of Arts*, May 1812. Publisher Rudolph Ackermann promoted British textile manufacture on the frontispiece of each monthly issue. The fabric samples are a useful guide to how contemporary audiences named and understood qualities of weave. Private collection.

identical pattern realised by the needlewoman on a muslin gown. One testament to the popularity of periodicals is that the majority of surviving bound editions lack these fold-out additions. Ellen Weeton sent home for patterns for fancy-work when she was on a visit elsewhere, not sure 'whether they are in a work bag in the bottom, or middle drawer, or bound up with the last new Lady's Magazine in the top drawer'.[160] Since Weeton constantly complained about her poverty, her reference suggests that this periodical, at least, was affordable.[161]

People understood clothing through its material qualities, by touching it, feeling the quality, assessing the textile. Publisher Rudolph Ackermann took advantage of this as a marketing strategy. 'Patterns' of four new dress fabrics, combining 'Novelty, Fashion and Elegance', graced the frontispiece of each issue of the *Repository of Arts*, so that readers could feel new materials for themselves (fig. 3.26). In this sense a 'pattern' could be a textile sample, sent by manufacturers and retailers to prospective customers, or passed around via personal connections.

Charity and Old Clothes

The third regular place for dress construction in Regency women's lives was poor work – sewing clothes to improve the welfare of the impoverished of the parish. As Sutherland writes, 'Austen never suggests that our choices in life include freedom to act independently of wider obligations. If we are fortunate, . . . we have a duty of kindness and protection to those who are not; society, in the form of public opinion or the judgement of other individuals . . . provides a check on conduct.'[162] The village community tried to look after its own. Individual charity and provision for the poor was a part of everyday experience for Austen and her gentry peers, expected in an age with no welfare system as a moral duty to those less fortunate.[163]

The first books explaining how to make non-tailored clothing, such as *Instructions for Cutting Out Apparel for the Poor* and *The Lady's Economical Assistant*, aimed to aid women in the efficient construction of charity clothing.[164] The commodity investment required to sew meant that 'a woman of a humble class, and servants, would probably not be able to afford scissors or shears to cut out, let alone have the table space to spread the material'.[165] Genteel generosity made up the difference. The Wynne sisters worked the whole of 14 July 1803 for the poor, and made a frock in a day.[166] Households could keep a work-box filled with the requisites for charitable making, to be taken up among other needlework. Mrs Norris (*MP*), always ready to find Fanny Price idle, tells her "'If you have no work of your own, I can supply you from the poor basket. There is all the new calico, that was bought last week, not touched yet. I am sure I almost broke my back by cutting it out.'"[167] Calico features in the instruction books for items including nightgowns, drawers, pantaloons and shifts. Anne Streatfield, who wrote the *Economical Assistant*, expanded on the poor basket in her anecdote about an amiable woman,

Fig. 3.27

George Engelheart, portrait miniature of Mrs Boulton, 1812, watercolour on ivory. Mrs Boulton's clothing bespeaks comfort over fashion, though her cap is heavily beribboned and her gown is velvet. She wears spectacles like those of Mrs Bates in *Emma*. Victoria and Albert Museum, London.

who constantly kept a closet filled with articles of wearing apparel for the poor. Her method was to buy whole pieces of cheap, strong, printed linen; coarse calico &c. and then to cut out a number of each article at once; these were put into a large work-box, and were delivered to the servants when time permitted, to be made up. It was also her custom to employ her children in the work; . . . thus the children acquired a taste for employment – a knowledge of needlework . . . and an early habit of active benevolence.[168]

Mrs Norris's comment perhaps points out Fanny's uncertain household place between child and woman; family member and servant-like companion.

What is stressed repeatedly is doing one's duty by the (deserving) poor, even if one's own income was limited. Ellen Weeton never ceased lamenting her finances, yet cheerfully bundled off '2 pair of cotton stockings – a bed gown – a pair of flannel petticoats – a brown chip bonnet – a pair of scissors – a pair of shoes – and a pair of stays' to her aunt for distribution among 'the abodes of age and poverty'. She suggested the stays be given to a Miss Billington to serve as a pattern for making others.[169] Charity was vital to even the genteel poor. Jane Fairfax's small presents are more than amiability: she is extending her little income to her aunt and grandmother in material form (*Emma*). All the garments Miss Bates mentions are unfashionable, bespeaking a poor woman's obsession with warmth and limited resources (fig. 3.27). Charity clothing was usually the kind of foundational domestic essentials discussed in chapter 1.

A real Chawton inhabitant appears to have occupied a similar status to the fictional Bateses: acceptable as a social companion but lacking material resources. In November 1812 Austen suggested to Martha Lloyd, who had 'sometimes expressed a wish of making Miss Benn some present', that 'Cassandra & I think that something of the Shawl kind to wear over her Shoulders within doors in very cold weather might be useful, but it must not be very handsome or she would not use it. Her long Fur tippet is almost worn out.'[170] By January the next year she told Cassandra 'Miss Benn wore her new shawl last night, sat in it the whole even'g & seemed to enjoy it very much.' The same letter recounts donating an old shift to Dame Garnet in Chawton, and promising her 'a set of their Linen'.[171] Fifteen years earlier Austen documented other clothing gifts of the kind that were a regular part of gentry life. One Christmas Eve she relayed to Cassandra 'a faithful account' of her charities to the poor: 'I have given a pair of worsted stockings to Mary Hutchins, Dame Kew, Mary Stevens, and Dame Staples; a shift to Hannah Staples, and a shawl to Betty Dawkins; amounting in all to about half a guinea.'[172] Two years later Betty received a shift bought for her at Oakley, and was 'one of the most grateful of all whom Edward [Knight]'s charity has reached'.[173]

The threads of these stockings, purses and caps and other gifts bound together clothing communities across small towns and villages. Decorative forms of esteem – or trying to elicit esteem for one's decoration – created, reinforced and shared gentry ideas of dress. Every visit to a haberdasher or communally discussed alteration to an old gown was a stitch in the local social fabric, circulating new ideas through cloth, and extending love, duty and respect to acquaintance networks. In the village, discrimination in small matters of dress was essential to performing gentility among the people who mattered the most, one's immediate neighbours. The precision of Austen's observation of these processes, and how important they were to people of her class, show that at heart the Regency village used clothing consumption to convey values that could not be bought.

Chapter 4

Country

'. . . a country like this, where social and literary intercourse is on such a footing, where every man is surrounded by a neighbourhood of voluntary spies, and where roads and newspapers lay everything open.'[1]

Jane Austen was a gentlewoman. Her father was an Oxford-educated clergyman, her mother descended from minor nobility and the family welcome at great houses across south-west England. Her brother Edward's adoption by their wealthy, childless Knight cousins put him firmly among the greater landed gentry, 'a class that was neither gentry nor nobility [in the traditional sense], yet one that was clearly a leisured class, and . . . can only be called a middle-class aristocracy', owning estates and country houses like the fictional Darcys, Knightleys, Elliots, and Bertrams.[2] Aristocratic and bourgeois, landed and landless gentry families, were in transition during the age of Austen, and mobility was both upwards and downwards.[3] Her novels are not about the stable entity and 'single tradition of the cultivated rural Gentry' but about 'the continual making and remaking of these houses and their families'.[4]

Their stronghold was the countryside. Gilded urban lifestyles were impossible without prosperity trickling in from the estates, acres, farms, hamlets and villages comprising the greatest part of Britain, and home to about 80 per cent of its population in 1800; about 45 per cent were directly engaged in agriculture.[5] This chapter explores what clothes people living energetic country lives wore, especially how closely men's dress related to the countryside, how fashion penetrated provincial places and how improvements in travel and post facilitated new systems of fashion exchange.

❀ ❀

Country Style

Fig. 4.1 Opposite

William Owen, portrait of a man, c.1815, oil on canvas. Dark green wool, accentuated with a velvet collar, provides a foil to brass buttons on the coat and pure white linen. The subject's buff breeches stop above well-worn riding-boots, country dress emphasised by the whip, the dog and the setting of the picture. Yale Center for British Art, Paul Mellon Collection, New Haven, Conn.

Fig. 4.2 Below

George and Isaac Robert Cruikshank, 'The Honble. Tom Dashall [left], & his Cousin Bob [Tallyho, right], in the Lobby at Drury Lane Theatre', from Pierce Egan, Real Life in London (1821), hand-coloured engraving on paper. One of a series of prints 'drawn from life' illustrating Egan's book, which recounts realistic adventures of Regency bucks in the metropolis. Private collection.

If the village in the age of Austen was connected by women who lived within walking distance of one another's houses, the country was the realm of gentry men riding over the land, and much of their clothing has a relationship to this dynamic. Anne Hollander evokes how English country dress 'came to suggest the comfortable coat of horse and dog, the smooth fit and dun colour of the stag's hide. Wool and leather and linen came to give the gentleman's body a poetic harmony with his natural domain.'[6] The English country squire in unaffected, unadorned clothing became an exemplar of rational man across the Continent through the later eighteenth century. French fashion leaders wore silk, but the English esquire was seen to ride, hunt and shoot in his plain woollen tailored riding attire, affecting an easy naturalness, devoid of embroidery and symbolising patrician duty (fig. 4.1).

Hollander's paean to the fashionisation of country style goes on:

> The cravat, which might have been worn soiled and sloppily knitted by rough-living country gentlemen, was laundered into incandescent whiteness, lightly starched, and then folded with a sculptor's care around the neck and jaw . . . The thick and muddy country boots were refined, fitted and polished to perfection, and the whole ensemble was ready for transfer from the hedgerows to Pall Mall.[7]

We see this in illustrations to Pierce Egan's *Real Life in London* (fig. 4.2), showing Bob Tallyho, a Corinthian London buck, in full country dress styled for city life, accompanying his modish cousin Tom Dashall.

Fig. 4.3

Benjamin Marshall, *John Hilton, Judge of the Course at Newmarket, John Fuller, Clerk of the Course, and John Stevens, a Trainer*, c.1804 , oil on canvas. Three men who work constantly with horses show the way practical details of clothing for equine occupations merged into fashionable men's dress. Yale Center for British Art, Paul Mellon Collection, New Haven, Conn.

Riding-dress was one of the greatest inspirations for menswear from the late eighteenth century onwards, the core of the country-squire Anglomania that Europeans embraced. Elements of riding clothing traditionally worn on country estates became normal metropolitan style. Boots (rather than shoes), the split coat-tails designed for sitting on a horse, chamois leather breeches and waistcoats made of lighter fabric conveyed sporting insouciance everywhere (fig. 4.3). Riding-coats had skirts sloping away at the centre front, unlike the tail-coat with its horizontal straight cut at the front. Those actually intended for riding were in dull colours but not black – green, buff or blue, or red for hunting (fig. 4.4). The buff leather breeches so evocative of Regency masculinity originated from riding clothes able to withstand a long day in the saddle.

Riding style, focused in 'the almost universal prevalence of boots and *lower garments* [breeches]', meant that by 1806 all men 'would seem just to have come from the *manage* [riding arena]; though nine-tenths of those *jockeys* may be fairly classed with the *dismounted cavalry*'.[8] Previously, it was only on horseback that gentry British men wore boots, which had heels to keep the foot in place in the stirrups and legs to protect against rubbing and the weather. Boots were country footwear, associated with rural values; for a long time they were considered 'alien to the notion of "gentility"', and then they were 'both legitimised and fostered by war'.[9] After the French Revolution, boots signified democracy and participation in public life,

Fig. 4.4

Henry Alken, 'Mounted Sportsmen', from *Sporting Sketches* (1817), hand-coloured engraving on paper. Alken's sketches from life show the vivid visual impact of red hunting-coats, worn with jockey caps. The effect of the wearers' movements and actions on the fit of the coats is also conveyed in detail. George Arents Collection, New York Public Library.

and later the martial mobilisation of the nation (see chapter 6). Soon boots were acceptable even in the city, worn over pantaloons or under trousers by riders and walkers alike. Boots also conveyed status because they cost twice as much as shoes, both to buy and to maintain. Their fashionability continued after the 1815 peace, and though boots as a style item declined with the dominance of trousers in the 1820s, they were fixed in the male wardrobe (fig. 4.5).[10]

The problem was that the groom and his master could 'with equal ease assume the cast of habits of both'; groom-style clothing and behaviour affected by gentry men further blurred class distinctions in a society in transition.[11] In a lampoon of the fashion for male dress in 'stable' style, a fictional 'young man of the very highest ton' had 'dress as well as conversation [that] proved his humility, since both were evident imitations of his groom'.[12] In real life, Lady Lyttleton complained to her mother:

> A set of hopeless young men, who think of no earthly thing but how to make themselves like coachmen, and in order to improve each other, have formed themselves into a club, where they spend their time inventing new slang words, adding new capes to their great-coats, and learning to suck a quid of tobacco and chew a wisp of straw in the most vulgar style; for it is not only on the box, but off it, in all society, that these ornaments of the present age chuse to be mistaken for their coachmen [fig. 4.6].[13]

London Published April 1 1817, by S Knight 34 Rathbone Place.

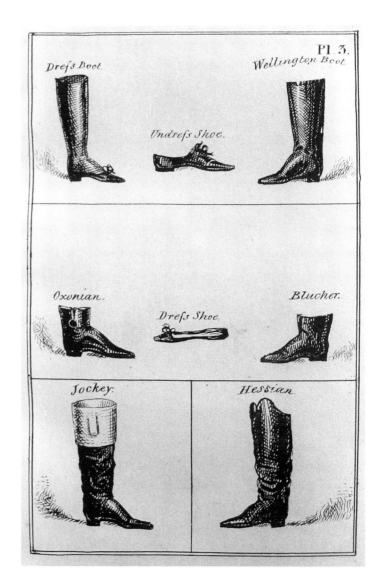

Complaints of the country in dress encompassed members in the House of Commons, who had 'lost all sense of decorum in their appearance' by wearing 'Dirty boots, spurs, close great coats, hunting-frocks' or 'a coachee's bang-up coat'.[14] There were limits to rural enthusiasm. Beau Brummell (see chapter 5), though usually dressed in a perfected esquire fashion, when visiting country houses never concealed his distaste for exercise, stables, coaching, hunting, shooting and anything involving actual dirt and dishevelment.[15]

Tallyho's ostentatious gaiters are a fashionable version of the rural accessory (see fig. 4.2). The Austen gentleman most invested in working the land is Mr Knightley (*Emma*), and the only garment mentioned in relation to him is a pair of 'thick leather gaiters'.[16] These leg coverings embody his English rural gentry masculinity, a practical solution to keeping stockings under breeches clean and whole when riding

Fig. 4.6

G. M. Woodward, *The Effects of Truth*, October 1794, tinted engraving on paper (detail). The fashionable young man repudiating the debt collector wears a caped spencer over his greatcoat, and carries a whip, in the height of fashionable style inspired by the dress of grooms and coachmen. Victoria and Albert Museum, London.

or working. Sketches of country workers repeatedly show farmers in gaiters, and they recur in images of comfortable country gentlemen.[17] Tailors and shoemakers could provide the utilitarian legwear in leather (6s.), serge, kerseymere (more expensive at 12s.), drill, leather and fustian, along with their variants, 'knee-caps', boot-tops and 'spatterdashes'.[18] The reference to his gaiters establishes Mr Knightley firmly on his estate's land, not too far from yeoman farmer Robert Martin in pragmatic dressing.

Women's fashion took less direct inspiration from country clothing. Mrs Elton (*Emma*) adopts her informal, pastoral style only when playing at farming, and Austen's masterly monologue delivered while Mrs Elton is strawberry-picking shows how soon the lady tires of the real effort involved.[19] Women were less eager than men to emulate rural style, because of its dowdy, unfashionable implications (except for naturally rosy complexions). Conversely, over-attentiveness to fashion might signal country unsophistication, such as the 'dashing' wife of one Mr Briscoe 'an honest country gentleman', 'very dressy, very fashionable, very huffish and passionate', but droll, in the opinion of author Dorothea Herbert (c.1767–1829).[20] Urbanite Mary Crawford is relieved to find her brother-in-law, the Mansfield Park parson, looking the gentleman, and her sister 'without preciseness or rusticity', instead of having become countrified.[21]

Fig. 4.7

Alexander Carse, *The Arrival of the Country Relations*, c.1812, oil on canvas. An elegant urban Edinburgh family welcomes relatives from the country. The differences in their styles of dress are subtle, but distinctly realised, the rural visitors favouring simpler, more covered clothing. Duke of Buccleuch's Collection.

Country informality could be a matter of nuance. For men, a false shirt front or 'dickey' was 'a thing permissible in the country when fine dressing was impossible'.[22] If country dress was worn in the city, it might be the quality of cloth, or the colour of boots that distinguished the two to the contemporary eye. Alexander Carse's painting *The Arrival of the Country Relations* (fig. 4.7) contrasts two family groups, of urban and rural origins, through subtle clothing cues.[23] The didactic novel *Caroline Lismore* uses this contrast to show simple country style in a positive light against London fashions. The heroine's cousins, 'far from appearing like country bumpkins, were elegant in their manners; and their dress, far from bearing that antiquated appearance, she had hoped to have the pleasure of comparing with her own attire, was modern, though of the simplest and plainest make'. The hour in the morning and two before dinner that Caroline takes composing her attire is shown as wasted in comparison to her industrious cousins' efforts at self-improvement.[24]

Working Dress

The experience of agricultural and related labour comprised the norm for the majority of Britons. Farmers, ploughmen, carters, milkmaids, blacksmiths, beggars, ragmen, tinkers, pedlars, fishermen, thatchers, drovers, field hands, harvesters, millers, stone-cutters and -crushers, miners, coopers, masons, carpenters, chair-menders, joiners, fencers, cottagers, washerwomen and all the multitude of tradespeople had their own relationship with clothing. Indeed, the subject of Regency working dress could fill its own book.[25] The bodies of such working people composed the background to daily life for Austen's milieu, and her works quietly include the labouring people who made the country run.[26] It is as decorative background in vistas of everyday life that rustic working people and (incidentally) their clothing are depicted by artists such as William Pyne (fig. 4.8). In a similar way, country travellers glancing from the windows of coaches trundling through Derbyshire or Kent noticed 'women in their blue bodices and black flat hats and men . . . in carters frocks', looking 'as if they were picturesque decoration'.[27]

Durability and practicality were priorities for country dress, though it is important to reiterate that ordinary people had access to and participated in fashionable attire, and that clothing was the area in which they enjoyed the greatest transformation in their material lives during the long eighteenth century.[28] Fashion still influenced 'non'-fashion. Pyne summarised his rural subjects' clothing as having 'such colours as are usually exhibited in great variety by persons whose attire is regulated by no rules of taste', a statement rooted in class differences.[29] Dorothy Wordsworth's gentry taste assumptions infuse similar comments on a widow who came to the door to beg, 'dressed somewhat in a tawdry style, with a long checked muslin apron, a beaver hat, and throughout what are called good clothes'.[30] Here is the rustication that the fashion-minded dreaded, unless it was filtered though quaintness, as, for example, in details like 'waggoner's cuffs' – deep shirred or smocked muslin cuffs – and other romanticised facets of tradespeople's clothing.

Fig. 4.8

W. H. Pyne, *Etchings of Rustic Figures: For the Embellishment of Landscape* (1815), etching on paper. Pyne sketched from life prolifically, recording hundreds of labouring men, women and children around Britain. The figures convey individual blends of practicality tempered by fashion that characterised country working people's dress. Chawton House Library.

Clothing that prioritised movement also embodied town and country distinctions. Sketches of rural women display the outer gown rolled up, leaving the lower petticoat visible, which would bear the brunt of wear, tear and dirt better than decorative gown fabric. When Caroline Bingley (*P&P*) notices Elizabeth Bennet's petticoat "'six inches deep in mud'" after the girl's 3-mile tramp across fields, her implication is of Lizzy's being a country rustic as much as a walker.[31]

The street characters John Dempsey painted in detail from 1820 (see fig. 1.23) show the durable clothing popular among those working outdoors, including fustian breeches, made of a fawn-coloured corduroy or uncut velveteen (as seen in collections of dress), which fabrics were excellent at repelling water.[32] Fustian was a popular choice among more professional staff on country estates that provided clothing during employment. Research into one tailor's shop in 1820s Epsom, Surrey, showed that its customers were:

the local folk . . . landowners, parsons, attorneys, surgeons, shopkeepers, and lodging house keepers . . . besides all the Butlers, Footmen, Stewards, Grooms, Coachmen, Postillions, Gamekeepers, Gardeners [fig.4.9], and one Cowman for whom clothing was purchased, and who sometimes bought items for themselves. Occasionally a footman or butler would pay a small sum for a better quality garment than his employer had authorized.[33]

The Jervoise accounts include many such suits made by Stephen Blake, a tailor in Bentworth, 4½ miles from the Herriard estate. A 'coat weskit and briches' – Blake's spelling is idiosyncratic – for servants James Sparrowhill and James Canons cost 12*s. 6d.* each in 1802, which did not include the cost of the fabric, buckram pockets and linings, 'rusha sheting [Russia sheeting] for the wasket sleaves', metal buttons and threads. Sleeved waistcoats and shorter jackets were prevalent among servants and workers, as were waist aprons (see figs 1.23, 2.23). Numerous entries, such as 'making a pare of nankin briches for Self, 3s.6d.', show that Blake made serviceable country clothing for George Purefoy Jervoise himself. Blake also made aprons with bindings round the edge, and mended breeches, greatcoats and 'frock waskits'.[34]

Fig. 4.9

James Ward, study for *The Deer Stealer*, 1820, pencil on paper. Ward's dynamic pencil lines convey the physicality of the poacher (who is lost in the final painting owing to its scale). His clothing – echoing that of the gamekeeper he aims to avoid – is rumpled with long wear, his stockings stout, and his pockets capacious enough to carry game. Yale Center for British Art, Paul Mellon Collection, New Haven, Conn.

Local tailors served a wide cross-section of tradesmen and those in service, who made country life run.

Joseph Vickery in the same village provided liveries to Herriard – that is, men's suits in the colours of a family or estate, which marked the wearer as being in its employ. In 1811 Vickery made for the Jervoise servants coat and waistcoat liveries for the coachman, huntsman, groom, helper, whipper-in and footmen, possibly for hunting, for a total of £5 15s. 4d.[35] The epithet 'knight of the rainbow' for footmen suggests 'the variety of colours in the liveries and trimming of gentlemen of that cloth'.[36] Livery announced the presence of a family employee in the commonest kind of civilian uniform, providing visual cohesion for disparately shaped bodies. The coat could have the family crest worked on it. Having servants in livery indicated living '"quite in style"', Austen tells us in *The Watsons*: '"The Edwards have a noble house . . . The door will be opened by a man in livery, with a powdered head"'.[37] Powdered hair was no longer in fashion by 1805, which highlights how livery was often of antique style. One reason why servant John Binns, of Austen's acquaintance, is supposed to have declined a new situation was that he refused to wear a livery that would have made him look the height of 1780s fashion.[38] Austen shows us livery as people encountered and understood it: Elizabeth Bennet recognises Lady Catherine de Bourgh's livery (*P&P*); Sir Walter Elliot's livery sports garish orange cuffs and capes (*Pers.*);[39] Sir Walter's cousin goes unrecognised at Lyme, as his groom wears mourning for Mr Elliot's wife instead of livery.[40] Both livery and mourning were an expense for the household purse, which helps to explain why even those further up the social scale worried about the cost of their employees' clothing. Dorothea Jordan relayed a message from her lover, the Duke of Clarence (1765–1837; later William IV), who wished his son 'to order Hale [the lad's manservant] a plain drab colour'd coat without any *facings*, as it is much more *fassionable* and lasts longer'. Two weeks later the duke was still interested in 'what sort of a coat' had been provided for Hale.[41] More modestly, Anna Larpent noticed economic changes through livery. A family 'rolling in prosperity' adds two rows of silver lace to the servants' livery; by contrast, impoverished by her father's death, her own servants had 'one row of worsted' taken off theirs.[42] 'Livery' appears in other contexts suggesting adherence to a patron through identical clothing, from followers of an aristocrat's style to female charity students whose benefactor replaced their old motley patched clothing with 'a livery of neat brown stuff gowns'.[43]

People throughout the countryside, no matter how remote, could buy clothing sundries from itinerant sellers such as pedlars, hawkers and packmen (selling textiles on credit for merchants and manufacturers). Pedlar dolls, popular from the early nineteenth century, show the range of small dress and textile items travellers might carry (fig. 4.10).[44] The sellers iterated their wares with distinctive cries: '"Do you want any pins, or needles, or threads, or tapes, bodkins or ironholders?" then in a much lower key "or staylaces, bootlaces, garters, or sus-pen-ders".[45] Some agricultural workers combined labouring with peddling. Ragmen collected old clothes and rags, and took away clothing deemed too decrepit to use. Dorothy Wordsworth described the old ragman she knew, sitting on his sack one spring

Fig. 4.10

Pedlar doll, 'Sarah Thrifty', 1820. An early example of a popular nineteenth-century genre, 'Sarah Thrifty', in her country cloak, print gown and common checked apron, carries a tray of useful items for dressing, listed on a printed bill. Platt Hall, Manchester.

afternoon, his coat of scarlet in a thousand patches and his breeches untied at the knees, with 'a round hat, pretty good, small crowned but large rimmed'.[46] She also portrays an itinerant Sheffield-ware seller, aged 83, in a 'rusty but untorn hat, an excellent blue coat, waistcoat, and breeches, and good mottled worsted stockings'. Because of his wanderings he has a fortnight's beard, unusual in an age of cleanshaven men.[47] Such solitary salespeople or 'travellers' would have been a familiar sight for Austen and her contemporaries (fig. 4.11). Jane bought 'six shifts and four pair of stockings' from the Overton 'Scotchman' (a generic term for all itinerant traders) in 1798.[48] In the next sentence she describes the Scotchman's 'Irish [linen], not so fine as I should like . . . It cost me 3s.6d. per yard. It is rather finer, however, than our last, and not so harsh a cloth', which shows that Austen bought not ready-made garments but a length of fabric to make shifts. The Woodforde household similarly bought linens at the door from one Mr Alldridge, who 'carries about Cottons, Linens, Muslins, Lace, Holland etc. in a cart and comes round regularly this way once in ten weeks'; or from 'a man who comes from Windham and carries about stuffs for Gowns etc.'[49] Alldridge was a trusted seller and source for garments. He sold the parson

> many divers things as under 3.10.11 [3 October 1811]. Viz. 8 Yards of Purple and white Cotton for a Morning Gown for myself at 2/3 [2s. 3d. per yard] 0.18.0 [18s.]. To 6 Yards & ¾ Callico Lining at 1/4 0.9.0. To 2 Coloured Handkerchiefs for my 2 Washerwomen 4.8. To 2 Waistcoat Pieces for my 2 Men, of Woolen but pretty Pattern, red, green and Brown in stripes about one Yard in length, each paid 0.14.0. To a Waistcoat Piece of my Boy, Robert Case also, about a Yard of Woolen 0.4.0 . . . . Paid also to Alldridge (omitted before) for 2 Cotton Gowns of my 2 Maids of Pink and White 17 Yards at 2/6 2.2.6.[50]

Fig. 4.11

David Wilkie, *The Pedlar*, 1814, oil on panel. Although this genre painting has a Scottish setting, rural customers across Britain would have experienced the pedlar's display of textile wares in their own homes. Yale Center for British Art, Paul Mellon Collection, New Haven, Conn.

The generous parson thought enough of Alldridge's wares to purchase for himself as well as his employees.

Settled country shopkeepers had increased enough in numbers by the 1780s to attempt to have the acts licensing hawkers repealed.[51] However, peddling grew again after 1800 with the development of the 'tally trade', which depended upon itinerant urban retailers paid on commission. Instead of goods for sale, they carried samples and took orders, supplied the items and accepted payment by weekly instalments. Before the smuggling trade declined after the wars (see chapter 7), pedlars often obtained and sold on their goods from the underground market.

Active Dress

Servants outdoors for hours at a time and pedlars tramping across miles of fields could attest how Britain's damp climate helped to determine dress. As Fanny Burney wrote, 'This *free-born weather* of our sea-girt isle of liberty is very incommodious to those who have neither carriages for wet feet, nor health for damp shoulders.'[52] Austen is brilliant in documenting how people's vulnerability to the weather shaped their lives in minute ways.[53] Men in more substantial clothes could scorn the weather, but it deeply affected women – in particular, their ability to take exercise outdoors. Everyone agreed that women *should* exercise. Men, who rode, walked and maintained a daily physicality outside the house, had less need to seek it. Although *The Mirror of the Graces* asserted '[Exercise] may be almost always obtained, either on horseback or on foot, in fine weather; and when that is denied, in a carriage', the reality was more difficult. The instruction manual outlines how few the 'proper hours' for beneficial exposure might be, if at midday it was too hot, and at evening too damp.[54]

Frail Fanny Price (*MP*) is buffeted by opposing views on exercise, so that she was either

> sitting at home the whole day with one aunt, or walk[ing] beyond her strength at the instigation of the other: Lady Bertram holding exercise to be as unnecessary for everybody as it was unpleasant to herself; and Mrs Norris, who was walking all day, thinking everybody ought to walk as much.[55]

Riding, even in a carriage, was an alternative form of activity. 'Carriage dress' was a common name for visiting dress but access to a carriage – expensive to set up and maintain – was a luxury; alternatively the traveller might depend on a carriage owned by others, but then had to wait on their itinerary and schedule, as so often happened to Austen when using her brothers' carriages.

England did have bright days, when sun protection from parasols and hats was essential to maintaining an untanned, pale skin, the epitome of beauty for centuries. Oil portraits show the effect of men's constant hat wearing on the complexion (see figs 3.6, 4.1): up to the temples their faces are ruddy; above the hatline their foreheads

Fig. 4.12

George Hunt and Henry Alken, *A Bath Coach*, 1820,
hand-coloured aquatint on paper. Hapless travellers
on the outside of the coach from London huddle
inside their caped greatcoats and use umbrellas to
ward off the Bath rain. Yale Center for British Art,
Paul Mellon Collection, New Haven, Conn.

are pale. Women sought to avoid this weathering. Not only did 'the ruddy peasant'
have the coarse brown skin that Miss Bingley (*P&P*) sees in Lizzy Bennet, there was a
feeling that 'only licentious women expose their skin', 'therefore all tanned women are
licentious'.[56] Although delicate white skin merging with delicate white fabric was the
aesthetic ideal, Lady Elizabeth Spencer-Stanhope (1795–1873) reflects the difficulty
of realising the ideal when describing a ball in 1807, where '*the pure white of the Calico*
[draping the ballroom] *made all the ladies look dirty*'.[57] Nor was it solely a feminine ideal:
Lord Byron's alabaster skin was a celebrated part of his looks and one he cherished.
Diana Sperling shows a man wearing a green 'half-bonnet' hanging from the rim of his
straw hat, suggesting an effort to cut the glare as well as protect his head.[58]

Parasols were a recent wardrobe addition, from the 1770s. These accessories had
wood, metal or bone sticks, with silk or linen covers and, like the rest of women's
dress, trimmings to taste, and changing length and proportion according to
fashion (see fig. 5.3). Generally small, they provided adjustable shade for the upper
body, while a bonnet or hat brim shielded the face.[59] Men preferred to carry an
umbrella, of dark-coloured taffeta or waxed silk. First introduced in 1750s London,

this was a novelty, and a sign that the owner could not afford to travel by chair or carriage. By the more energetic Regency period, its usefulness in deflecting rain from expensive clothing when walking was firmly established, and it was 'now made of such cheap materials that it is in the hands of every class', announced the *Universal Magazine* in 1810.[60] The multiple umbrellas kept for walking at Kellynch (*Pers.*) reflect its ubiquity. Captain Wentworth's umbrella in the same novel is a necessity in notoriously rainy Bath (fig. 4.12). Plainer than parasols, umbrellas had sticks of wood or metal, and were covered in silk or cheap cotton, usually of deep green but also found in brown, blue or red.[61]

At the other end of the body, keeping feet dry before the rubberisation of shoes in the 1840s was an issue for both sexes, though men had the advantage of tougher boots and shoes. Leather can be truly waterproofed only by repeated applications of oils, waxes and pitch, 'to prevent shoes from taking on water', as household receipt books have it;[62] but it cannot be fully treated on the soles as it interferes with grip. Thick-soled boots, and boiled leather or pitch-covered postillion's outer boots solved the problem for men in outdoor professions. William Wordsworth found a spontaneous solution when he stopped on his walk one rainy day to stuff straw into his shoes to protect his feet from icy melt.[63] External cork soles were another protective technique.

Middle-class women's footwear was flimsier. They did wear leather walking-shoes and short boots in plain leather, though few survive (fig. 4.13). Half-boots, at ankle height or just above, had a leather lower half (called a 'galosh') and a fabric upper to combine fashion and function. Lord Osborne (*Watsons*) recommends a 'half-boot; nankeen galoshed with black' (fig. 4.14); Emma Watson retorts that '"unless they are so stout as to injure their beauty, they are not fit for country walking"'.[64] Walking in Bath prompts an attack of gallantry in *Persuasion* centred on suitable footwear. Mrs Clay considers the rain a 'mere trifle'; 'she would hardly allow it even to drop at all, and her boots were so thick! much thicker than Miss Anne's', revealing a nice distinction between their incomes and class.[65] Mrs Clay's footgear perhaps resembles Maria Edgeworth's 'Sutton thick soaled boots'.[66] Mrs Topham bought ten pairs of walking-shoes (usually black) over fourteen years for between 7*s.* and 9*s.* 6*d.* a pair, suggesting that this elderly lady propelled herself around London as often on foot as in a carriage or sedan chair – those other preservatives against damp toes.[67]

Austen was a great walker. According to their nephew's recollection, she and Cassandra took long rambles in pattens as 'defence against wet and dirt' when the country roads surrounding Chawton were thick with mud.[68] Pattens (fig. 4.15) were wooden soles, resting on high iron rings, which fastened over the feet with straps. They raised the wearer out of street muck, though with only partial efficacy, according to diarist Agnes Porter (c.1752–1814), governess to the family of the 2nd Earl of Ilchester: 'You would smile to see me . . . who used to shrink from the least particle of humidity, now mounted upon high pattens which do not preserve me from the mud, wading half a mile through the dirtiest streets to pay an afternoon visit, and return home at night.'[69] Pattens were useful but not fashionable, associated

Fig. 4.13

Woman's shoes, 1806–11, leather. These shoes were probably made to be worn with walking-dress. By the beginning of the nineteenth century more practical footwear for both men and women was in demand, though fashion had to be taken into account as well. Fewer examples of walking-shoes survive than of evening slippers. Victoria and Albert Museum, London.

Fig. 4.14

Woman's half-boots, 1820–30, Scottish, fabric and leather. Half-boots reached above the ankle, and were made of fabric above, with the lower half or front 'galoshed' with leather. They were worn during the day and in winter. Collection of the Bata Shoe Museum, Toronto.

Fig. 4.15

Patten, early nineteenth century, wood and metal. Wooden-soled pattens were buckled over footwear with leather straps and raised the wearer above the ground on iron rings. This pair has a metal heel grip that would have helped to prevent the footing from slipping off the patten. Worshipful Company of Pattenmakers, London.

with working women, as were wooden-soled clogs. Devonshire clogs helped Maria Edgeworth and some friends to negotiate damp Welsh slate quarries; Eliza Jervoise bought a pair for 5s. in 1812; her husband's cost only 2s.[70] Diana Sperling recorded the awkward dignity of trying to walk in deeply rutted muddy autumn roads, and being carried over wet grass (fig. 4.16). She also depicted men and women wearing short white overboots, perhaps galoshes, for walking in snow.[71] Austen's attention to real details in fiction comes through in a letter advising her niece that a female character in the novel Anna was drafting 'ought not to be walking out so soon after Heavy rains, taking long walks in the dirt'.[72] Rural roads were unpaved dirt, muddy after England's frequent precipitation, and founts of dust in dry periods.

Countrymen's hobnails, hammered into shoe soles, provided traction for firm footing. In one gentry party's mountain excursion, those with unnailed shoes 'were obliged to descend by sliding' as 'the mountain heath and moss glaze the shoes in such a manner when without nails, it is impossible to stand, much less to walk with safety where the ground is not perfectly level'.[73] Although Grose records 'hobnail' as scornful slang for 'A country clodhopper: from the shoes of country farmers and ploughmen being commonly stuck full of hob-nails, and even often clouted, or tipped with iron', they must have been necessary for serious roaming outside.[74]

Austen's novels are full of shrubberies for flatter, genteel walking, sites for contained outdoor exercise, as replicated today at her old home, Chawton Cottage. Gravel walks, with good drainage, provided a safe path for strolling so gentle that even nervous Mr Woodhouse (Emma) will take a constitutional turn along them. The wrong clothing, like his daughter Isabella Knightley's thin shoes, and the wrong weather, 'the ground covered with snow, and the atmosphere in that unsettled state between frost and thaw, which is of all others the most unfriendly for exercise', could make even so healthy a woman as Emma Woodhouse 'for many days a most honourable prisoner' indoors.[75] Maria Edgeworth, underdressed during a sojourn in the country, encountered a 'desperately sharp wind – shawls blowing' when she is wearing a 'muslin gown – thin shoes', which brings on a violent headache and an attack of weakness close to fainting[76] – the kind of illness from exposure that Marianne Dashwood (S&S) experiences after spending two nights roaming a country estate at twilight. The 'imprudence of sitting in her wet shoes and stockings' gives her a violent cold, a possibly lethal malady at the time and one that Regency dressers strove hard to prevent.[77]

Men needed merely to add an extra outer layer in bad weather, as their clothing was loosely based on outdoor dress to begin with. Images of active Regency men show how far movement was absorbed into male clothing when compared with women's dress. Women amended, altered and covered up their normal clothing to go walking. Throwing a strong pelisse or any other kind of 'wrap' over day clothing was protection from the weather, even over stouter woollen walking-dress. Hooded cloaks made from red worsted or frieze were a feature of British country life for women ranging from the gentry to the poor (see figs 4.7, 4.16). Both Diana Sperling's gentry relations and John Dempsey's poor, working female subjects frequently wear a scarlet cloak in outdoor country situations – a garment

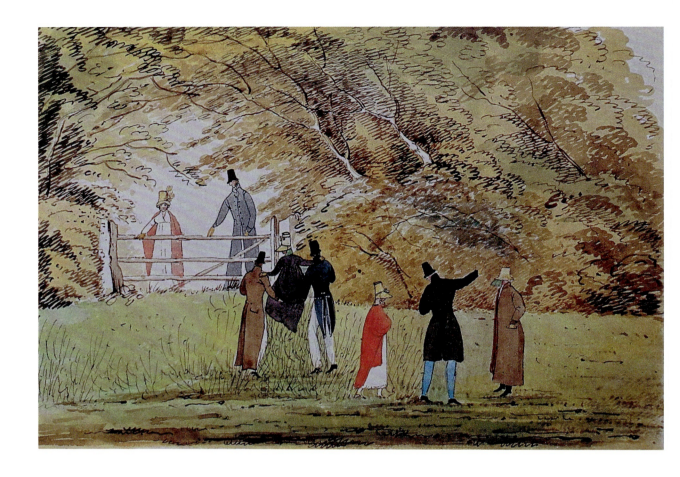

Fig. 4.16

Diana Sperling, *Charles Sperling's New Invented Method of Conveying Ladies Over Wet Grass*, c.1816, watercolour on paper. The Sperling girls wear the ubiquitous red cloaks seen throughout the English countryside. Charles's gallantry seems to negotiate some long, wet grass that would dampen the ladies' skirts and stockings. Private collection.

that nearly transcended class, and one foreigners thought peculiarly English. Less robust, more fashionable cloaks covered women in their daily lives, made from printed cotton, silks, muslins and purely decorative lace.

As horses, donkeys and their vehicles were valuable assets, required primarily for work or business, walking was popular for local errands, travel and sightseeing, providing pleasure in being out of the house, and social occupation to visit or spend time with acquaintances, reinforcing physical links with the immediate neighbourhood. Leisure walking for its own sake was of no small scale, either: 5 to 12 miles (8–19 km) was common. 'A walk of 11 miles – in deep mud – the pleasure of losing your way', as Diana Sperling described it.[78] Ellen Weeton ventured a full 20 miles (32 kilometres) in the Peak District.[79]

Sporting Clothing

A riding-dress or habit, in which masculine tailoring intersected with feminine fashions, was essential to gentry women's wardrobes (fig. 4.17). These heavy, durable woollen ensembles, comprising a habit jacket or bodice, skirt and optional waistcoat, required the same construction skill as men's coats. Tailors made habits and cloth pelisses because they had the existing skills to work wool, as instructions in early tailors' guides show (noting the delicacy required when fitting the bust).[80] The extra-long skirt of the habit hid the legs of a woman riding side-saddle. The jacket had long sleeves and a short peplum or basque skirt, with collar, cuffs and buttons, echoing men's fashions and their long-lasting materiality. Horsewomen wore this garment of 'usefulness, comfort, and familiarity' for riding or hunting, and travellers enjoyed its protection against the inconveniences of the road. Habits became informal daywear, 'for walking, visiting and at home as an alternative to . . . a nightgown, in which to spend the day until required to dress more formally'.[81] In 1801, for example, Dorothy Wordsworth found her friend Mary Hutchinson at home in her riding-habit, as all her other clothes were packed for travel.[82] The daughter of the Laird of Macdougall, 'a great bumping miss', paid Susan Ferrier (1782–1854) a morning visit in a blue riding habit.[83]

Habits even saw use as wedding outfits. Jane Austen's House Museum holds a scarlet wool jacket said to be made for Frank Austen from Mrs Austen's 'going away' habit after her wedding in 1764. In 1796 the future Lady Elizabeth Talbot was married in her parents' drawing-room 'dressed in a green riding habit, black hat and feather; a long white veil fell down over her face'.[84] Commentators long criticised the use of the riding-habit as fashionable rather than occupational wear, considering that to put it on 'when one pays a visit, or goes to church, is . . . a deviation from the original design' for riding.[85] The language of Classicism named women 'Amazons' or 'Dianas' in what was their most active and therefore masculinised dress. Habits were worn over a thin underdress, such as a plain silk or cotton 'body-lining' or slip, or a 'habit-shirt'.[86] 'Shirt' was a masculine term so adding 'habit' indicated a visible feminine, linen, upper-body garment. Diana Sperling illustrates this ensemble for riding a donkey, perhaps showing what the Austen sisters looked like riding or travelling in their little donkey cart.[87] Many of the Sperling girls' equine mishaps involve their falling off horses when dressed in riding-habits. 'Riding out for exercise on a dark, muddy, raining and windy day in November' caused Diana Sperling's bonnet to come off and her combs to fall out, loosening her side hair.[88] Riding was excellent exercise for Regency women who had 'the inclination, or the means', and it recurs in Austen's fiction.[89] Much of *Mansfield Park*'s action revolves around Fanny Price sharing her exercise pony with Mary Crawford.

Gentlewomen who followed a hunt wore habits in the hunt's colour, the ensemble tending to woollen cloth in shades of red, navy, green and the sombre colours prevalent in menswear. Preferences varied with fashion and season, lighter shades in lighter materials, such as nankeen, being worn during summer.[90] Maria Edgeworth's half-sister, in a new brown habit 'which fit to admiration', cantering in Hyde Park, was attractive enough a figure to catch the eye of the Persian ambassador.[91] Practically, horseriding required a hat with a veil to protect the complexion. The fabric could be suspended from a soft cap or high bonnet, seen in prints as a common riding-habit accessory. The new tall-crowned hats, which began to be worn around

1795, were another borrowing from men. However, the creep of jockey style into menswear during the Regency inspired a fashion for 'riding-hat shapes' for women (see fig. 4.4) with long low brims, as Austen greatly desired in 1811.[92]

Austen's lifetime encompassed growing interest in watery recreation through two kinds of bathing: in the sea and in natural springs at spa towns, among which Bath was prominent. Austen makes no reference to spa-bathing in the novels, and she seems never to have indulged in it.[93] Instead, when the Austen family lived at Sydney Place in Bath, they regularly spent long holidays in seaside towns such as Sidmouth, Dawlish, Lyme Regis and Worthing, though no letters survive from this period telling us about Austen's pastimes in those places.[94] Thomas Rowlandson's *Comforts of Bath* series (1798) shows men and women in spa-bathing dress: 'some are in fashionable hats and bonnets but some are still wearing linen caps'; the men have donned long-sleeved waistcoats with drawers of brownish linen, 'while the women are in high-waisted shifts with elbow-length sleeves'. Engravings of the baths between 1804 and 1806 portray people in 'long very loose-fitting garments of a bulky-looking fabric in a brownish colour, resembling . . . some kind of overalls'.[95]

The popularity of places such as Lyme, Scarborough and Brighton as seaside bathing retreats was heightened in the early nineteenth century by the wartime inaccessibility of the Continent for holidays, prompting Austen's creation of the seaside town of Sanditon. Spa-bathing clothes were a prototype for sea-bathing costumes, 'long, loose-fitting shifts, high to the neck with long sleeves', made of either linen or the stalwart flannel, for warmth and protection in chill water.[96] As the lively descriptions of a resort town in *Poetical Sketches of Scarborough* say, 'The ladies, dress'd in flannel-cases, show nothing but their handsome faces.'[97] If hypochondriac Mary Musgrove (*Pers.*) can bathe at Lyme in November, the flannel must indeed have kept the bather warm, though she may have been indoors in the public baths. Oil-silk caps gave long hair some water protection, and short hair relied on linen caps to filter out sand; according to the *Sketches*, some women bathed in their wigs. Ellen Weeton 'dipp[ed] three days' one May week, leaving her house already wearing her bathing-dress – perhaps the blue flannel she mentions later in 1810, of the kind illustrated at much more fashionable Brighton.[98] Diana Sperling illustrates similar loose, dark dress for private lake bathing. The presence of water affected even non-bathing visitors, who might don a relaxed holiday ensemble; Dorothy Wordsworth observed a man wearing 'blue jacket and trowsers' – sailor's or boatman's dress – when visiting Windermere.[99] The usefulness of the riding-habit apparently extended to sailing. Mr Campbell catches hold of Jane Fairfax's habit to prevent her being dashed into the sea at Weymouth, *Emma*'s coastal leitmotif.[100]

Overall, the Regency gentry were a vigorous lot, who adapted their clothing to many sporting pursuits. One of the joys of Diana Sperling's work is the range of situations her family is shown enjoying in her illustrations. A game of shuttlecock indoors sees Harry Sperling compete in trousers and a tail-coat, while the girls wear petticoats and habit-shirts. They play bowls and go fishing in normal day gowns.[101] To play cricket, the men change into white sporting clothing, probably of

Dress in the Age of Jane Austen

Fig. 4.17

George Chinnery, *Lady Louisa Duncombe on Horseback*, c.1824, graphite and ink on paper. Women's riding-habits changed style with fashion, retaining the key elements of dark colour, woollen cloth and tailored appearance. Yale Center for British Art, Paul Mellon Collection, New Haven, Conn.

linen and flannel. Many surviving coats and trousers in lighter, pale-coloured linen or nankeen may have been worn for activity, though the fabrics' weight also made them popular for summer dress (see fig. 5.6).

Other sources show varieties of Regency sporting attire. Parson Woodforde angled in a bespoke 'fishing Frock', and he had special shoes for his favourite sport: 'To one Garland, Shoemaker at Bruton, for a Pair of new Shoes for Fishing, lined with Flannell, paid him this Afternoon the exorbitant demand of 0.9.0. They were badly made besides.'[102] Henry Alken's *Sporting Sketches* (1817) shows the angling attire in action, among many sketches of hunting, and other scenes showing the range of active dress ensembles (see fig. 4.4). Ellen Weeton recounts a memorable foot race between four men after a regatta: 'Two of them ran without shirts; one had breeches on, the other only drawers, very thin calico, without gallaces [braces]. Expecting they would burst or come off, the ladies . . . turned away from the sight. And it was well they did, for . . . with the exertion of running, the drawers did actually burst,

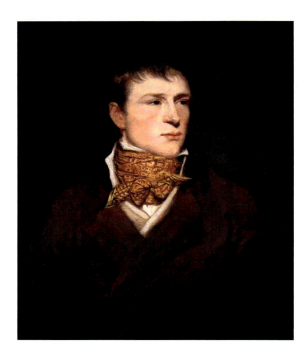

and the man cried out as he run – 'O Lord! O Lord! I cannot keep my tackle in, G–d d—n it! I cannot keep my tackle in.'[103] Similar undress was worn for other sports including leaping, wrestling and boxing. Lord Villiers, for example, wore a nightcap, and no neckcloth, waistcoat or coat to play tennis in 1803, apparently to comical effect.[104]

The popularity of boxing made a direct contribution to fashion in the form of the handkerchief named after Jem Belcher (1781–1811), boxing Champion of All England, 1800–05. A portrait of the pugilist shows him wearing his eponymous multi-coloured handkerchief around his neck (fig. 4.18), and belchers appear in images of working men into at least the 1830s.[105] Susan Sibbald encountered a boy she had known in childhood, all grown up and wearing 'a green Jockey or hunting coat, yellow buckskins and brown tops, buff waistcoat, a yellow and red silk handkerchief (then called "Belchers" . . .) and a broad frilled shirt'.[106] Her acquaintance is resplendent in the sporting-inspired dress that was the acme of youthful male fashion. If more letters between Austen and her brothers had survived, we might have better understood the men's sartorial engagements with the athletic age they lived in.

Fig. 4.18

Charles Allingham, *Jem Belcher*, c.1800, oil on canvas. The five times All England champion prizefighter wears the red and yellow handkerchief (to which he gave his name) as a prominent necktie under a broadcloth coat with velvet collar. National Portrait Gallery, London.

Travel Dress

The Regency period saw continuing improvements in the speed with which information and goods circulated around the country and the countryside, perhaps exacerbating people's anxiety about keeping up with fashion. An awareness of distance 'was an inevitable component of fashion culture's internal mechanism'.[107] Transport developments included better roads, and more and better post and private coach companies. An ever increasing number, frequency and quality of publications contributed to the movement of fashion and dissemination of ideas about clothes. As Edgeworth put it, 'Thanks to the printing press – the mail coach and the steam packet . . . we can all see and hear what each other are doing and do and read the same things nearly at the same time.'[108] Regency shopping habits and consumption choices, and long-distance gift exchange reveal how fashion became increasingly mobile during the era. Although efficient networks of acquaintances circulated clothing objects and information around Britain from at least the mid-eighteenth century,[109] what changes in the Regency is the increasing speed and lowering cost of transmission, and the quantity of movable goods available.

Improved transport networks inspired travellers to journey further in mail coaches and by post-chaise. Austen herself journeyed through fourteen English counties in her lifetime.[110] But travel was no easy matter: it involved piling oneself and one's luggage onto a conveyance with minimal suspension, at the mercy of unpaved roads, inns of uncertain quality, and tedious company if going by public coach (see fig. 4.12). Trunks and boxes containing new clothes, samples of textiles, or dirty laundry for home washing were stowed behind and above the passengers. The coaches also carried letters, some detailing new styles or answering shopping queries. As with any technology, mishaps and failures plagued the users of public transport, as Austen found when her 'writing and dressing boxes had been by accident put into a chaise which was just packing off as we came in, and were driven away towards Gravesend in their way to the West Indies.' After despatching a man and horse after the chaise 'they were got about two or three miles off'.[111] Many Regency letters concern the fate of boxes gone astray.

Clothing for travel needed to protect the wearer against the road's travails and be rugged enough to survive them (fig. 4.19). Much depended on whether the traveller was inside or outside the conveyance. For the drivers, coachmen, postillions and coach boy, a woollen greatcoat was an essential, the 'wrap of a traveller' as Austen calls it.[112] Also known as a 'box-', 'riding-' or 'driving-coat', the ankle-length greatcoat, with a large collar, emerged into middle-class fashion from the coachman's cloak, with its multiple capes over the shoulder to keep warmth in and wind and moisture out on long nights outside.[113] This coat enveloped the clothes worn underneath and could be very heavy, which was part of its effectiveness as a barrier. Museum examples can weigh upwards of 3 kilograms, probably explaining why Mr Allen (*NA*) 'had rather do anything in the world than walk out in a greatcoat', as it was a burden to wear.[114] The garment's heavy cloth served as a blanket if needed, as for General Tilney, in the same novel, whose greatcoat, 'instead of being brought for him to put on directly, was spread out in the curricle'. The greatcoat Mr Elliot (*Pers.*) drapes nonchalantly out of his coach is an essential part of his travelling equipment.[115]

'Ridingcoat' is glossed in an early nineteenth-century pronouncing dictionary as 'A coat made to keep out the weather'.[116] In this sense, it appears, outside of travelling, in the gentry wardrobe and on Austen's male characters. *Northanger Abbey*, begun in 1798–99, mentions greatcoats six times, a significant incidence for the clothes-reticent Austen, which tallies with the rise in its popularity from this time. The 'innumerable' shoulder-capes broadened the wearer's shoulders, increasing his active, masculine, physical presence and made him look 'becomingly important'.[117] The greatcoat was a male garment, though women could borrow its protection. Diana Sperling depicted herself wearing a pale grey caped coat as she leads a donkey carriage though mud.[118] Women's wardrobes encountered this heavy outer garment as a single- or double-breasted 'redingote', a genteel borrowing back of the French rendering of 'riding coat'. The pelisse's derivation from a fur-lined outer coat is found in the occasional reference to a 'pelisse-greatcoat', and in Nancy Woodforde's mention in November 1800 of friends 'very fashionably dressed' in 'brown Silk Pellices alias great-Coats'.[119]

Country

The concept of an extra cape layer around the neck and shoulders was popular in Regency dress (fig. 4.20). Cloaks for both sexes display the style, especially on men's 'hard' cloaks, made of tough worsted fabric. The ankle-length garments enveloped the wearer and usually featured a second, shorter cape over the top (fig. 4.21). They were lighter than coats and easy to put on and off without disturbing the clothing underneath or necessarily needing to put on one pair of sleeves over another. Women further covered their vulnerable necks and décolletage with tippets and pelerines, though the latter were made of light muslin as often as fur. Adding fleece to clothing was a sure way of keeping warm. Fitted kid gloves were no match for cold, so hiding the hands in a wool or fur muff provided cosy warmth, and offered the bonus of internal pockets for keeping letters, money and other useful items.[120] Muffs were vital winter and travelling accessories, as were fur-lined travelling boots worn over shoes. The wise traveller also brought their own slippers to avoid the worn-down, well-used communal indoor footwear offered to travellers at inns.

Keeping warm when travelling in bad weather was difficult, especially if sitting in an open carriage or on the outside of a coach (see fig. 4.12). A kind conveyance driver could forfeit his coat to an ill-prepared lady, as happened to a Scottish traveller who in '*dreadful*' cold, 'in spite of every covering I could contrive' and a large shawl bound around her head, found the carrier lending her 'his *great coat*'. Eventually, he could not endure without it and she returned it; 'this was a serious privation, for my "plaidy to the angry blast" was no defence'.[121] Unsurprisingly, she caught a cold. Mr Wise, a good-natured coachman, shared his greatcoat on either side with Austen's nephews Edward and George Knight, who wanted to travel on the outside of the coach; they were still 'much chilled when they arrived', though presumably they avoided trying to warm their feet up by pouring brandy into their

✸ ✸   Dress in the Age of Jane Austen

Fig. 4.21

Man's hard tartan cloak, c.1820, wool, worsted
and silk. 'Hard' tartan was woven from worsted,
the long-staple fibres from sheep's wool. Smoother
and tougher than short-staple wool, it repelled
water better, making the textile a practical choice
for outdoor clothing. Museum of London.

boots – so common a practice that a collection of household remedies warns people
against it![122] Frequent traveller Maria Edgeworth evocatively described what 'every
covering' might entail for an open carriage. When visiting a cloth manufactory
in northern England one chilly November, she was well 'wrapped up. 1st my grey
cloth gown – 2ly. furred pelisse – 3d. red shawl 4thly a large fur tippet . . . Besides
all these coverings . . . I had a great box coat over my knees. In short I was warm
as a dormouse.'[123] Thicker or woollen versions of normal garments proved stout
travelling companions even for the great. Harriet, Lady Frampton, was so eager
to meet Mrs Edgeworth that she came to greet her 'in worsted stockings just as
she alighted from her travelling carriage', without changing into her indoors silk
or cotton hosiery.[124] Apart from their temperature, open vehicles could damage
unprotected clothing. As Mrs Allen (*NA*), whose clothes are her first care in most
situations, observes, 'Open carriages are nasty things. A clean gown is not five
minutes' wear in them. You are splashed getting in and getting out; and the wind
takes your hair and your bonnet in every direction'.[125]

If not sheltering themselves from piercing cold, women used clothing to stave off
sun, winds and smaller chills when travelling. A lack of hat or bonnet prevented
Austen and her friend from travelling in a chaise in 1796.[126] 'Exposing themselves
unveiled, and . . . without bonnets', their heads and faces would have had 'no defence
against the attacks of the surrounding atmosphere', to the detriment of their
complexions.[127] Women used riding-hoods, calashes and 'uglies', a type of oversized,

boned, folding hood, large enough to cover a bonnet or hat underneath, during travel to bear off the rain. 'An excellent protection', 'these Calashes were made of black silk and cane, the shape of a calash over an open carriage. To prevent them blowing back there was a long loop of ribbon hanging from the front . . . held in [the] hands' reported Susan Sibbald.[128]

In general, women undertook journeys wearing a cloth pelisse or riding-habit (fig. 4.22). The report of the death of Mary Wollstonecraft's daughter Fanny Imlay (1794–1816) gives an unexpectedly detailed inventory of a woman's travel ensemble, as she journeyed from London via Bath and Bristol, before taking her own life in Swansea:

> She was dressed in a blue-striped skirt with a white body [bodice], and a brown pelisse, with a fur trimming of a lighter colour, lined with white silk, and a hat of the same. She had . . . a reticule containing a red silk pocket handkerchief, a brown berry necklace, and a small leather clasped purse.[129]

Agnes Porter conveys the wearying nature of long-distance travel on her 1805 expedition to her native Scotland from South Wales. After travelling all day, she 'arrived at York about ten at night. Out of forty hours I had been thirty-seven in motion – rejoiced to throw myself on the bed – quite a luxury to sleep with my cloaths off.'[130] Her preferred travelling dress was a pelisse.[131] These useful garments were made up in stuff such as the 'striped russette' advertised as 'a new article for travelling and for winter morning dress', and woven like satin to produce a glossy yet warm textile.[132] Dress could help ease travel's rigours by accommodating necessities in reticules and pockets. Lady Frampton of the worsted stockings travelled with 'sandwiches in one pocket and letters and gloves stuffing out the other'.[133]

Transport affected people's relationship with clothing in other ways. The disposition of trunks was crucial for Regency travellers, determining where and in what state one's clothes arrived at the other end of a journey. Trunks were often sent separately on a public carriage, while the traveller went in the smaller vehicle of a friend or relative. Before returning from London in 1813, Austen pondered these logistics: 'I have not quite determined how I shall manage about my Cloathes; perhaps there may be only my Trunk to send by the Coach, or there may be a Bandbox with it.'[134] Relying on clothing for a stay to turn up at its destination independently could be chancy. When Austen's trunk did not arrive with her in London in March 1814, she was put to the trouble of 'borrow[ing] Stockings & buy[ing] Shoes & Gloves for my visit. I was foolish not to provide better against such a possibility.'[135]

Packing for travel required conscientious thinking about the clothing required for a visit, stored in a way that reduced wrinkling, concealed valuables and conserved space. Further consideration provided for one's needs immediately upon arrival: Catherine Morland (who travels in a habit) carries with her a 'linen package, which the chaise-seat had conveyed for her immediate accommodation' before servants unpack her trunk at Northanger Abbey.[136] People exercised greater care for things that were more expensive and troublesome to replace if damaged. Merely to iron a gown crumpled

Dress in the Age of Jane Austen

by packing required the availability of a flat iron, a fire and a skilled laundress, and the time to heat the iron on the fire. Gowns were laid lengthwise and folded in the trunk (except for velvet which was rolled), and there was an art to doing it well. Men's harder clothing fared better in the folding. Lady Catherine de Bourgh (*P&P*) gives her parson's guests 'directions as to the best method of packing, and was so urgent on the necessity of placing gowns in the only right way' that Maria Lucas thinks herself obliged 'to undo all the work of the morning, and pack her trunk afresh'.[137] Maria Edgeworth was kinder in complimenting her niece, 'dear packer and gauger', 'for all the care you took in putting up my clothes so nicely', grateful when 'dressing in a desperate hurry' for the sensible organisation of her travelling trunks, although, on the same trip, Edgeworth lost her dressing-box containing 'every trinket and keepsake'.[138]

A delightful poem printed in one of Fanny Knight's pocket-books tells readers 'How to Pack a Gentleman's Portmanteau'.

> Coat, Waistcoat, and Breeches, shirts, stockings and shoes,
> With Handkerchiefs, Nightcap and gown,
> A Comb and two Razors, and Tooth-brush compleat,
> All you want, when you travel to Town.

Women are next instructed:

> With linen and stockings, and shoes first begin,
> Then your Night-cloaths and Petticoats neatly put in.

Next your Dresses compleat, for each part of the day,
With your Handkerchiefs, Caps, all in Gala array,
Then your Ribbands, Fans, Flowers and Gloves long and short,
With your Coombs, and your brushes of every sort,
And snug in your corner your Trinket-box place,
No Cosmeticks you want with that beautiful face,
Some Needles, and Thread, with your Thimble combine,
For one stitch timely set in the end may save nine,
A spare pair of Garters and Lace add to these,
For the rest I will leave you to do as you please.[139]

The lists incidentally reveal the greater number of essential items required for Regency women to dress. How and when to get one's clothes washed could be a matter of some difficulty when travelling, and Austen mentions this problem in her letters. Local washerwomen's skills were trusted, but those of another locality were an unknown quantity. Men moving between properties or on business might send their washing back home to be cleaned and returned to them. Austen sent dirty laundry home for washing, perhaps because it was cheaper than the services of London washerwomen. Eliza Jervoise's accounts, as she travelled between her homes in Hampshire and Wiltshire, show how women – with more frequent washing needs and more garments to wash – hired the services of laundresses in towns they passed through.[140]

Shopping at a Distance

One of the by-products of business or pleasure travel was to aid the widespread, established practice of proxy or 'agency' shopping, where people bought on behalf of others. All the extended Austen family and circle of acquaintance (servants included) participated in proxy shopping, mostly when people visiting metropolitan areas obtained articles of dress for their friends and relations country-wide. A letter to Cassandra shows the level of detail involved:

> I shall want two new coloured gowns for the summer . . . I shall not trouble you, however, to get more than one of them, and that is to be a plain brown cambric muslin, for morning wear; the other, which is to be a very pretty yellow and white cloud, I mean to buy in Bath. Buy two brown ones, if you please, and both of a length, but one longer than the other – it is for a tall woman. Seven yards for my mother, seven yards and a half for me; a dark brown, but the kind of brown is left to your own choice, and I had rather they were different, as it will be always something to say, to dispute about which is the prettiest. They must be cambric muslin.[141]

Miles Lambert has looked at the distribution of clothing in northern England. He explains how

Fig. 4.23

Muslin gown, c.1812 (detail of the bodice). The fabric, white muslin with red crewel spots, illustrates the material that Austen bought for herself and her sister in 1811: 'In texture it is just what we prefer, but its' [sic] resemblance to green cruels [crewel two-ply embroidery wool] I must own is not great, for the pattern is a small red spot' (Letter 70, 18–20 April 1811). Museum of London.

regional consumers, particularly women, might occasionally visit London or a major city, but fashionable consumption required more continual contact, and in the absence of a close contact they could solicit the assistance of business colleagues or even mere acquaintances . . . Through a connection with fashionable goods, regional consumers could acquire social cachet and appear as arbiters of taste in the localities.[142]

Acquiring goods relied on networks of individuals, making shopping a collaborative act that depended on shared knowledge. The practice could involve a number of people. In 1813 Austen wrote to Cassandra that her friend Harriot, in a letter to their niece Fanny, was inquiring 'whether they sell Cloths for Pelisses at Bedford House', and wanting Cassandra to get the drapers 'to send her down Patterns [samples of textiles], with the Width & Prices', but only if the house dealt in credit, not ready money.[143] The first responsibility of the proxy shopper was that of disposing of the commissioner's money on appropriate goods according to their fiscal situation. As Austen told Cassandra from London, after making some speculative purchases: 'I am sorry to tell you that I am getting very extravagant, and spending all my Money, and, what is worse for you, I have been spending yours too', on the kind of red crewel-spotted muslin seen in figure 4.23. Proxies

were economic agents, but their equally important role was as aesthetic agents, a responsibility requiring trust equal to the monetary one, but of more nebulous character. It was an anxious task to find a 'pretty' cambric or a 'quality' muslin for another, requiring an understanding of what the commissioner meant by these definitions. Family members therefore made good proxy shoppers because of their shared aesthetic understanding.

Proxy shopping was an arrangement not only between women. Men bought for their social and familial networks, including male acquaintances, exercising their personal experience of material culture, engaging 'in both the pleasurable and the skilled aspects of shopping. They do not seem to have been any less efficient at shopping or less interested in it than women, and they spent as much time comparing and contrasting and shopping around' (fig. 4.24).[144] *Northanger Abbey* provides a famous example of male proxy shopping. The marvel of Henry Tilney's understanding of muslin is not just his interest, but his informed tactile knowledge of muslin's qualities and his ability to determine its place in the hierarchy of consumer worth; his sister often trusted him in the choice of a gown (length of fabric), and on one triumphant occasion he made such a purchase on her behalf, giving 'but five shillings a yard [for it].'[145] Regency people were accustomed to touching as much as seeing the components of dress, and proxies provided substitute bodies for those at home. Sometimes the body of the shopper could literally stand in for the commissioner. Austen sent Cassandra a pair of emergency mourning shoes and hoped they would fit, as both Jane and their friend Martha had tried them on, comparing their knowledge of the similarities between their own feet and Cassandra's to judge the size. Other communications from agency shoppers might include up-to-the-minute fashion information. These networks connected 'the local to the national, the rural to the urban, and the consumer to the market'.[146]

Proxy shopping could be a courtesy from those with mobility to those without. Witness Mr Knightley (*Emma*) offering to undertake tasks in Kingston for Miss Bates. When she deflects his offer to Mrs Cole, Knightley reminds her that the latter has servants to send – another common way to obtain goods at a distance, though one tempered by a less personal knowledge.[147] 'Many commissions were interwoven within business correspondence', notes Lambert, 'requesting the duty of agency work as a corollary to continued patronage.'[148] The commissions undertaken by agents, bankers, servants or tradesmen were 'correspondence shopping', carrying less sentiment and more duty, but still reinforcing valuable networks across the country.[149] In one of countless instances, Agnes Porter sent her travel schedule to a friend to aid her shopping planning, asking her to 'let me know whether you have any commissions for London. In my way to Norfolk I only pass through it, but towards the end of July I shall be there for a week.'[150]

The third, and least certain method of acquisition at a distance was dealing with retailers and manufacturers directly by correspondence. Old clothes, or the patterns taken from them, could be sent to a trader as a model for new items. The process was 'prone to confusion and delay', and worked better when there was an

Dress in the Age of Jane Austen

existing relationship with the supplier.[151] The sending out of 'patterns' or samples of fabrics (see fig. 6.5) allowed a consumer to feel the textile's qualities before buying, and the tradesman to market goods and services to the customer at the same time – an opportunity that was lost when shopping was done by proxy.

Letters were a prime means of spreading information about clothing across the country. Many of Austen's letters discuss new clothing ideas with Cassandra, imparting knowledge of novelties, agreeing on alterations or assessing the state of their wardrobes. Writers highlighted those elements of dress relevant to sender and receiver, giving an individual perspective on the morass of available taste. Maria Edgeworth's correspondence can be a rich fund of dress detail:

Fig. 4.24

A leaf from Barbara Johnson's album, 1746 –1823, showing a piece of the silk sarsenet bought by her brother in February 1803. Her brother frequently bought her fabric for gowns, either as a present or perhaps on commission. The accompanying images are all from pocket-books, not fashion periodicals. Victoria and Albert Museum, London.

Fanny wore her green silk and it looked beautiful. All the fashionable trimmings are of that rolled sort of flounces. Lady E. Whitbread has one a Spanish flounce she says – so pretty and so easily made that I will send the pattern in my next. The hems tell Millward are run with packthread which [Lady W.] says is used because stiffer and sits better than bobbin. I wore one day Emma's turban and another day brown and white net. Both days I looked lovely I am confident. We called on Miss Brooke. The bonnets were very pretty and elegant but far too large both in crown and leaf. She was very civil and will make them exactly to our tastes.

Mrs Roberts too was very civil. Sitting with her I found an elegant lady with nice bonnet and long shawl held prettily *over the opposite arm* . . . She was so exquisitely accoutred.[152]

From these paragraphs we glean that flounces were in, her correspondent's servant Millward does dressmaking, how materials affect a gown's finish, that Edgeworth borrows accessories to extend her wardrobe and has bespoke bonnets from a milliner, and how the arrangement of a shawl could distinguish a well-dressed woman. How much more its recipient would have understood. Other of Edgeworth's letters are staccato in their transmission: 'Steel buckles and ornaments in silk and velvet bonnets very fashionable – No long ends to sashes at your peril – Steel buckles to belts in the morning gold in the evening preferred to sashes'; five ladies out of eight wore ruby gowns at dinner one night; three-quarters of the stylish women in Hyde Park wore 'black bonnets silk or leghorn or velvet' and the rest 'drab or dove' beaver bonnet-hats.[153] Edgeworth's clothing descriptions throughout her correspondence illuminate the scantiness of Austen's by comparison, and how concerned with her personal wardrobe she was instead of the wider fashion scene.

The Austen sisters more often recorded the logistics of moving clothing around the country. They used Collier's (or Collyer's) Southampton Coach to transport items to and from London, as when Jane asked Cassandra to 'send up my Silk Pelisse by Collier on Saturday', while staying with their brother Henry. She adds 'and be so good as to put up a clean Dressing gown which will come from the wash on Friday'.[154] It is clear that, even when she is away, Austen knows the disposition of her clothes relative to the laundry schedule. Some of the exasperation attending on leaving what one needed elsewhere is conveyed in a letter of 1813 from Godmersham. 'It is hoped', wrote Austen, 'that the portfolio may be in Cant[erbur]y. this morning. Sackree's sister found it at Croydon and took it to town with her, but unluckily did not send it down till she had directions . . . there are parts of workbags in the parcel, very important in their way.'[155] How irritating to have vital parts of sewing projects or ensembles dancing about the countryside at the speed of other people's goodwill.

Parts and parcels of dress appear in innumerable examples of the use of postal services to transmit clothing. Agnes Porter sent 'some *patterns*' to a friend, themselves 'just received' from her acquaintance at Sarum, with a letter stating that they were to be returned through Agnes.[156] Nancy Woodforde showed off her new 'Pick-Nick' bonnet,

Dress in the Age of Jane Austen

which she had had sent from London, to Mrs Custance, whose opinion was that 'it was very handsome and [she] had seen nothing like it at Norwich yet'.[157] Ellen Weeton wrote home to get some clothing sent to her:

> a black Chambray gown, A silk petticoat, A cambric muslin petticoat and a blue flannel bathing-dress; in the middle drawer is some black lace net, wrapped in a piece of black mode, and a black silk workbag with some crape and the blue duffil coat, which will be very useful when sailing.[158]

Textile care whizzed between women at home and their men away from it, as the Longsdon family demonstrate. William Longsdon asked his mother to send him and his brother their nankeen summer clothes, with some nightshirts for John, as she had sent him only one in the box, and 'cloth to mend his own light coloured pantaloons'.[159] A month later brother John wrote thanking her for the clothes, telling her he needed more shirts, and passing on the news that William had received a pair of shoes from an acquaintance that fitted well.[160] John Longsdon thanked his sister for the four shirt ruffles she made, which came safely in 1811.[161]

Coaches trundling though the country full of these packets, along with letters, trunks and people, were the physical links that bound gentry communities together. Productive agriculture from the estates populating Austen's life and works underlay the increase of prosperity and material consumption in the new century, along with the speed and coverage of Regency horse-drawn mobility. Throughout the countryside people moved about in clothing, and clothing moved about with people. The state of the roads and the weather were not just topics for polite small talk: they were vital qualities of the landscape that influenced what people wore day to day, how they got it, and how they told others about it. Much of gentry dress responded to place, to the environment of a damp island combined with a national love of outdoor activities, especially those of the English gentleman, riding out from his country house, with his horse and hound, sporting his country-style attire. To be rural was not necessarily to be isolated. Dress could travel across the country and encompass hundreds of miles through acquaintance networks, along whose routes travellers gamely bounced, with fashion an extra passenger on each journey.

Chapter 5

City

Here I am once more in this scene of dissipation and vice, and I begin already to find my morals corrupted.[1]

Lydia Wickham stayed with her sisters when her pleasure-loving husband was gone to London or Bath – *the* places to enjoy oneself. Jane Austen also spent time in the great metropolises of her day, hubs of consumption and sources of novelties, vulgarities and necessities for dress. London, especially, was the heart of *ton*, the centre of fashion, finance and court, touching people's lives and experiences of clothing across the country as its urban sophistications radiated outwards.

Visiting London was a brilliant variation from the rhythm of daily lives, a place to partake of social ease and elegance and saturate oneself in culture, especially during the 'season' – April to August – though it is notable that Austen's heroines often arrive there heartsick rather than brimming with anticipation. Bath's pleasures were comparative:

> 'those who go to London may think nothing of Bath. But I, who live in
> a small retired village in the country, can never find greater sameness
> in such a place as this than in my own home; for here are a variety of
> amusements, a variety of things to be seen and done all day long, which
> I can know nothing of there.'[2]

The urban experience of clothing is this chapter's subject, which delves into the fraught delights of shops and shopping and the visual pleasures that accompanied moving in society. The business of commissioning new clothes from professionals was best undertaken in a city, as was the equally important business of wearing them to go out. The lucky provincial visitor might glimpse members of the beau monde, the forge of fashionable invention: their pursuit of style created tastes for the respectable gentry sort to aspire to, shun or dismiss – yet secretly desire.

❀ ❀

Fashionable Cities

In 1801 about 30 per cent of Britain's 11 million people lived in urban areas.[3] Cities such as Bristol, Manchester, Cardiff and Edinburgh were exchange centres for information, trading hubs for regional areas, and the source of changing customer needs that caused dress and textile producers to develop innovations in response.[4] The heady pell-mell, Pall Mall jumble of high and low life that was Regency London has attracted much scholarly attention, but the London

> which occupies Sir William Lucas's fantasies, Mrs Bennet's shopping dreams, and the Bingley sisters' social aspirations, is complemented in Jane Austen's novels by the London of commerce and business. Austen anticipates a time of bourgeois advancement, tying status to money rather than family and estate, but many of her characters have not yet reached that insight.[5]

Although Bath's star was waning by the early nineteenth century, it retained some of its heyday twinkle and still attracted good society, eager to mingle, socialise and take the waters. Austen knowledgeably advises us that 'Bath, compared with London, has little variety, and so everybody finds out every year'; a six-week visit was pleasant enough, but the town soon palled, to become 'the most tiresome place in the world'.[6]

London had 1.4 million people by 1815.[7] It was expanding rapidly and absorbing outlying villages and their country ways into the urban mode. Conversely, the city adaptation of country dress, and the creation of new parks during the Regency brought rural influences into urbanity. Country folk longed for the city and vice versa, in a controlled naturalism that contained burgeoning Romanticism. Places like Brunswick Square, where the Knightleys have a house (*Emma*), featured elegant accommodations in a compact space, surrounding what was still essentially a village green. In Austen's fiction, 'the map of London functions as a textual substitute for first-hand experience. The addresses of the various families in London are presented as designations in the social topography of the city.'[8] The spaces of London were 'a historical construction, the expression of specific social and cultural circumstances' that affected how people dressed for moving about its streets.[9] The physical structure of a town or city and the state of its streets had a major influence on how footwear was constructed.[10] 'Nice pavements', of the kind Austen attributes to Bath, created modern, designated pedestrian spaces alongside the streets, yet their hard surfaces wore down leather soles more quickly.[11] The output of thousands of chimneys deposited soot smuts on pale clothes, and created black snow in winter, calling for the protection of a carriage, the wearing of walking-dress, or easily cleanable gowns and waistcoats – a need met by the increase in washable cotton fabrics. The maelstrom of horse-drawn traffic splashed unsavoury liquids onto passers-by all year round.

Austen introduced London (about which she was ambivalent) into her work 'as a background presence, a constant threat to country life'.[12] *Sense and Sensibility* best exploits Austen's knowledge of the city, gained through regular visits to her brother

Henry, a banker.[13] She writes about real shops and places her readers recognised as the most elegant emporia and residential addresses. Austen's relationship with Bath was similarly ambiguous. She lived with her family in the city she is believed to have disliked between 1801 and 1806, and many authors have explored her Bath connections in detail.[14] *Persuasion* and *Northanger Abbey* are set extensively there. Bath's position as a place of health and social pleasures differentiates it from London's trade and mercantile centres. Fashions and fripperies, shopping and shows, gained more importance in the smaller cosmopolitan hub.

The mirror of crowded city environs magnified village clothing concerns and the sharp inspection of others' dress and public image. For every local shop in the country there were ten or twenty specialist retailers in town. For every voyeuristic visit to church or walk down the high street there were passages thronged with people, ripe for observation. *The Microcosm of London* (1808–10), published by Rudolph Ackermann, shows, throughout, the spectacle of massed dressed bodies (fig. 5.1). Drapers and milkmaids crossed paths with duchesses and bankers. Full public display meant that one's appearance was consumable by any viewer's gaze. The 'public or semi-public

Fig. 5.2

Unknown artist, 'Promenade in Kensington
Gardens', *Fashions of London and Paris*, July 1804,
hand-coloured stipple engraving on paper.
A realistic fashion plate, combining male and
female figures displaying their London walking-
dress. The long trains of the women's gowns were
to disappear from stylish day apparel in the next
few years. Victoria and Albert Museum, London.

events – assemblies, balls, supper parties, country-house gatherings' – 'the crucial
events of an Austen plot [which] take place indoors or in the confining presence of
a number of people', were just part of the urban array of theatres, shops, pleasure
gardens, entertainments, exhibitions and more. The Regency person, especially if
female, was rarely alone, and this 'sense of being watched, hedged in and discussed
by a whole community informs all Austen's novels'.[15] Someone was always there
to observe one's appearance. The main difference in the urban environment was
that strangers were the observers, instead of (or in addition to) an acquaintance
network. Suddenly, the attractions of long private walks become clearer.

Dramatic, urgent change throughout the eighteenth century had transformed
London's built landscape, redefining its space to 'embody new notions of politeness
by providing "synthetic" replicas of the countryside and garden environments . . .
In town, [walking's] only purpose was to see and be seen' (fig. 5.2).[16] Both London
and Bath had their fashionable outdoor spaces, accessible to all. Londoners took
to Hyde Park; the denizens of Bath promenaded in crowds along the Crescent.
New buildings, new squares and open carriages, such as landaus and barouches,
allowed maximum visibility for and of the fashionable populace. As Austen wrote
with customary amusement, 'The driving about, the carriage being open, was very
pleasant. I liked my solitary elegance very much, and was ready to laugh all the
time at my being where I was. I could not but feel that I had naturally small right
to be parading about London in a barouche.'[17] Carriage dress was essential London
wear for the hackney cabs, sedan chairs, shorter journeys by stage coach and trips
by other wheeled transport for shopping and sightseeing.

Visitors could watch the royal family at home, or spot them in the street. One morning
in 1795 Mrs Caroline Lybbe Powys (1756–1808) of Hardwick House, Oxfordshire,
went to Mrs Dawson's, the famous milliner in Pall Mall, to see the new Princess of

Dress in the Age of Jane Austen

Wales go for the first time to the official Drawing-Room in her
new state coach, and afterwards recorded that Her Highness wore
a pink petticoat under a clear muslin gown, a purple sash and
hat, and a black lace cloak.[18] Austen saw the ladies go into court
on 4 June 1808, though Sackree, the Godmersham nurse, had the
advantage over her of being in St James's Palace to watch.[19] Even if
one did not catch a glimpse of the famous (and infamous) directly,
the numerous print-shop windows were the Georgian equivalent
of television.[20] The satirical and caricatured figures stuck up in
comic engravings emphasised the beau monde types seen around
the metropolis, reinforcing their notoriety even as they mocked.
Northanger Abbey's characters may be related to notables and
types seen in comic prints.[21]

On a smaller scale, fashion was Bath's glory. Provincial ladies
observed the ensembles of the great, good and notorious attending
the spa town, then amended their own dress and reported its
novelties to their friends. *Northanger Abbey* arguably reveals its
youthful composition by being the chattiest about clothes of
all Austen's novels; no other is so direct about what people are
wearing, or includes characters who relate their visions of dress.
'"There goes a strange–looking woman! What an odd gown she has
got on! How old–fashioned it is! Look at the back."'[22] The focus
on the back detail suggests that the oddity lies in the remains of
earlier 1790s fashion, remade or altered to meet early 1800s trends, as may be seen in
many historical objects.

Visitors to London, Bath, Brighton and other places of fashionable density savoured
what they saw to relate later. On occasion, Austen could detail noticeable changes:
'the coloured petticoats with braces over the white Spencers and enormous Bonnets
upon the full stretch, are quite entertaining . . . The broad-straps belonging to the
Gown or Boddice, which cross the front of the Waist, over white, have a very pretty
effect, I think' (fig. 5.3).[23] Austen was a lively observer of people and their dress,
once spending time in London watching for '*Veils* as we drove through the Streets, &
had the pleasure of seeing several upon vulgar heads'.[24] The latest London fashions
rippled into Hampshire at the speed of post.

Shops and Shopping

Shopping was essential to viewing and interpreting fashion through the latest
consumer goods. When Mrs Allen and Catherine Morland (*NA*) arrive in Bath,

> our heroine's entree into life could not take place till after three or four
> days had been spent in learning what was mostly worn, and her chaperone

City

was provided with a dress of the newest fashion. Catherine too made some purchases herself, and when all these matters were arranged, the important evening came which was to usher her into the Upper Rooms.[25]

Wiltshire style would not do in Bath. Here the older woman shares, through co-shopping, her own hard-won expertise in constructing the right social body through dress, and imparts the complicated business of understanding hierarchies of taste and quality among Bath shops – new geographic and social spheres for the country girl unused to the demands of town clothing. Age conferred some authority: Isabella Thorpe, only four years older than Catherine, could compare Bath's fashions 'with the fashions of London; could rectify the opinions of her new friend in many articles of tasteful attire'.[26] The experiential knowledge of friends and relations could disseminate fashion by demonstrating where to obtain and how to apply it to one's dress. They show the newcomer how to 'see' then consume the right fashion.

Many scholars have identified the 'consumer revolution' of the long eighteenth century that flowered in the age of Austen.[27] Shopping as a pastime (and verb) developed in the eighteenth century, with clothing identified as the single most important category of material culture in expanding consumption.[28] Scholars have also looked at *how* people consumed clothing and developed material literacy. Close understanding of the textiles, workmanship, quality and suitability of the goods they purchased was central to shopping practice.[29] Proxy shopping could take a long time in the capital, as Austen found when she spent 'From half-past 11 till 4 in the streets, working almost entirely for other people, driving from place to place after a parcel for Sandling, which we could never find, and encountering the miseries of [drapery warehouse] Grafton House to get a purple frock for Eleanor Bridges.'[30]

The sheer number, in London, of 'so many shops to dispose of one's money in articles one is apt to think cannot be got in the country' could dazzle the casual visitor and absorb endless time. Mrs Lybbe Powys 'traversed the streets from eleven to three, and again in the evening', noting that 'even in Bond Street [there was] hardly a coach to be seen'.[31] Bond Street was a masculine domain in the early nineteenth century, home to hatters, tailors, hairdressers and perfumers, jewellers and other tradesmen catering for fashionable gentlemen. It was considered indiscreet for a lady to be in Bond Street in the afternoon. The Prince Regent instigated Regent Street in 1813, which swept from his residence at Carlton House to the new Regent's Park. Its 'palace like shops' and 'broad shewy windows' epitomised London's role as pinnacle of British wealth and fashion.[32]

One German tourist was overwhelmed by the 'richness and elegance . . . the splendour of the shops and larger stores . . . the beautiful draperies the merchants show to the public behind large plate glass windows' in the 1790s.[33] Using windows to display goods was a recent innovation. Drapers' shops in particular enticed customers with elaborate displays of fabric falls, imitating their finished effect. Once inside, customers asked for the articles they wanted – a bolt of fabric, a reel of ribbon, a card of lace. The shop attendant extracted the articles from shelves, or under the counter, for the

Fig. 5.4

Unknown artist, 'Messrs. Harding Howell &
Co.' Repository of Arts, March 1809, coloured
engraving on paper. The arrangement of drapery
stores gave sellers the power of choice over what
the customer saw, as most of the stock was
behind or under the counter. The ladies on the
right in this London draper's shop wear cloaks
matching their hats.

customer's approval (fig. 5.4). Austen once waited half an hour at drapery warehouse
Grafton House for the free attendant she depended upon to buy anything.[34]

The City proposed and the West End disposed of textiles. Many wholesalers and
importers were based in and around Cheapside and St Paul's. According to an 1803
guidebook, two sets of roughly parallel streets, forming an almost continuous line
of shops, stretched 3 miles from Mile End through Cheapside and the Strand to
Charing Cross; and 4 miles from Shoreditch through Holborn to the end of Oxford
Street.[35] Gracechurch Street, where Mrs Bennet's brother plies his unnamed trade
(P&P), was noted as one of the finest secondary trading streets. By living above his
premises, Mr Gardiner is typical of clothing and textile traders at the time.

Customers selected the components of dress and accessories from an enormous range
of establishments. Linen drapers, drapers, haberdashers, milliners, mercers, furriers,
hosiers, wholesale and retail, warehouses and small shops all clamoured for business.
Specialist makers often retailed finished goods, which enlarged the potential
shopping arena to shirtmakers, tailors, mourning outfitters, glovers, hatters and
their ilk. Such a plethora of options could befuddle the unwary. Mrs Bennet panics
at the thought of Lydia left to buy wedding clothes in London because she does not
know the best warehouses of the thousands available, and her mother is unavailable
to guide her through the maze of quality. Mrs Bennet starts to dictate her orders
by letter, doing her best to share her knowledge textually through the proxy of her
sister-in-law, Mrs Gardiner. Since Mr Bennet does not like London, his wife must
have spent time there without him in order to feel so certain of her chosen suppliers.

A significant difference between town and country shopping was the specialist shops dealing in particular kinds of clothing components. A 'manufactory' sold goods made on the premises. A 'warehouse' was any large retail or wholesale establishment, selling commodities – not necessarily made on the premises – cheaply and in quantity; it might sometimes be a distributor for a number of suppliers, more like a store than a shop.[36] In economic and social terms, warehouses occupied the middle ground, so Austen's connecting them to Mrs Bennet signifies attempts at economy.

Bath fulfilled a similar role as a centre for goods unobtainable locally. The city was second only to London in the variety and fashionability of the available merchandise, a retail offering skewed by the wealthy visitors and holiday spirit of the place.[37] 'Half of the inhabitants do nothing, the other half supplies them with nothings', as one traveller saw it, through 'a multitude of splendid shops, full of all that wealth and luxury can desire, arranged with all the arts of seduction.'[38] Bath had traditional and more exclusive shops, and 'highly reputed services in bespoke tailoring, dressmaking, staymaking, quality shoemaking, jewellery, hairdressing', alongside large warehouses, and many small milliners' shops, 'where the personal touch and the subtleties of the mode were all-important'.[39]

Putting together a Regency ensemble took time and thought. Each piece required selection and separate purchasing, and then it might need making up or alteration. A *Commercial Guide* of 1817, listing the following retailers of women's dress on Oxford Street alone, gives some idea of why dress shopping could be arduous.

33 Linen drapers
2 Silk and satin dressers and dyers
10 Straw bonnet manufactories
2 Drapers and tailors [excluding those tailors
    who sold textiles but did not term themselves drapers]
6 bonnet warehouses
1 India muslin warehouse
6 Lace warehouses
3 Fancy trimmings and fringes manufactories
5 Woollen drapers
1 Button manufactory
3 Plumassiers [feather merchants]
2 Calender [linen smoothers] and dyers
24 Boot and shoe makers
5 Perfumers
17 Hosiers and glovers
1 Patent manufactory
4 Silk mercers
1 Tailor
1 Silk weaver
3 Stay and corset warehouses
4 Furriers

1 Stocking warehouse
12 Haberdashers and hosiers
1 Ready made linen warehouse
1 Ribbon warehouse
4 Umbrella manufactories
1 Muslin and shawl warehouse[40]

Men's clothing suppliers were slightly less numerous than women's but equally diverse. Any cursory glance at other sources covering the City and the West End reveals the list's partial reporting. Advertisements, accounts, invoices, trade-cards and insurance records map London's dense consumer environment for bespoke and ready-made clothing.[41] Smaller accessories, rather than body garments, had also long been available to purchase ready-made, and helped to provide the delights of browsing and window-shopping. Such were the 'many pretty Caps in the Windows of Cranbourn Alley!'; Austen hoped that when her sister came to London they should 'both be tempted'.[42] A finished cap is easier to desire than one made from muslin and ribbons in the imagination.

By contrast with drip-feed purchases of small haberdashery, utilitarian fabrics such as flannel and Irish linen were bought in large quantities, in 'pieces' of 9 to 25 yards. Needlework guides stress the advantage of piece-buying, as the length usually varied somewhat, offering better value for money than buying 'by measure'. Warehouses provided these textile staples as well as fashion fabrics. The warehouses Austen is known to have frequented were Layton & Shears in Bedford House, Grafton House, Newton's in Leicester Square and Christian's. Numerous letters discuss buying dress fabrics because Austen was sending information back to Cassandra in Kent or Hampshire, or vice versa. Shops either took credit, requiring the buyer to be known to the seller or to come with references, or took ready money.

Another source for finished clothing was the extensive network of second-hand sellers, though there is no mention of Austen or any of her characters dealing with them. For a large percentage of the Regency population, however, the used-clothing trade helped them to realise cash from old clothes, or offered clothing at bargain rates, 'as long as the cost of new materials kept those items out of their reach'.[43] Old-clothes sellers, often Jewish, walked London – the trade's hub – buying at doors, then selling to individuals, or to merchants who repaired the clothes and then sold them on. Clothes brokers and salesmen carried out their trade from fixed premises, and used tailoring skills to improve their stock. Theirs was considered a respectable trade, unlike that of the pawnbrokers, whose pledges ranged from the owner's second shirt, to noble court robes.[44] Second-hand clothes – the capital's cast-off consumption – trickled through a series of middlemen to rural communities, who preferred 'clothes a year or two old' to the latest fashions. 'Thus clothes outmoded by the calculations of one group would be in demand by another', exploiting the value and utility inherent in clothes.[45] The second-hand clothes market benefited those who used it to create the essential respectable appearance that could be a leg-up to a better income. At the end of the chain, gentry women gave their old clothing to their parish poor, but disposed of rags worn beyond usefulness to collectors, who sold them on to the paper-makers. Jane Austen's novels were written and printed on the final vestiges of Regency clothing.

Making Style

Menswear achieved modernity in the Regency, when the popularity of dull, dark wool for outerwear merged with the idea that a coat should display its quality through excellent fit, improving the figure. London had the best tailors. Some firms that existed during the Regency still survive in London's Savile Row and its environs, and the principles that informed early nineteenth-century tailoring have never left dress.[46] Anne Hollander identified the greatest neo-classical contribution to dress history not as the white columnar woman, but as the English tailored male.[47]

Another change emerged in the idea that 'it is no longer sufficient to wear well-made clothes, but they have to be from a certain maker'.[48] The discerning customer patronised one tailor for his coat, another for his trousers, and a third for his waistcoat, depending on their specialist expertise. He also shopped for the suit cloth himself instead of leaving it to the tailor, who might use cheaper, marked up, or sun-faded cloth, furnished by 'mercenary and unprincipled tradesmen'.[49] Those

Fig. 5.5

Bill to George Purefoy Jervoise from William Coward, tailor, 1811. Purefoy Jervoise received detailed yearly bills from the tailor he patronised faithfully for his coats, waistcoats and breeches. Garment for garment, his clothing is more expensive than his wife's (fig. 5.11) though he bought less. Hampshire Record Office, Jervoise of Herriard Collection, Family and Estate Papers.

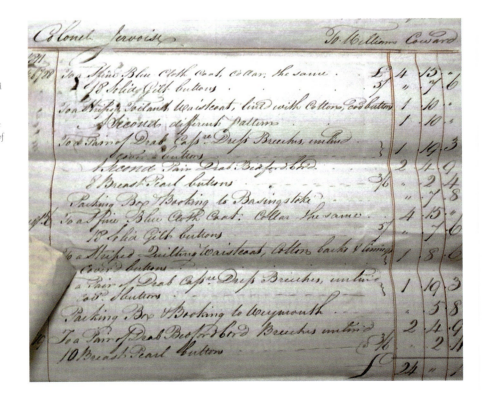

who were 'no judge of cloth' soon learned to be if they aspired to taste. Hampshire MP George Purefoy Jervoise bought his good clothes from his tailor, William Coward at 2 Hanover Street, whose yearly bills detail his spending (fig. 5.5). They also reveal that each element of Regency men's dress cost roughly double its female equivalent. Men shopped less often, but spent more when they did – a fact that is not brought out in contemporary critiques of fashionability.

Austen is understandably reticent about tailors and men's dress, as it was a masculine world, into which men inducted men, fathers taking their sons to be measured. Purefoy Jervoise's bills throw light on Colonel Brandon (*S&S*), 'a respectable man . . . with more money than he can spend', having 'two new coats a year'.[50] Purefoy Jervoise averaged four a year, demonstrating Brandon's restraint in spending. Bingley and Wickham (*P&P*) both wearing blue coats and Willoughby (*S&S*) a shooting-jacket in the country represent the total of the fictional references to coats in Austen's writings. Austen's brother Edward was mentioned wearing a shooting-jacket in 1796 and the congruence with Willoughby may be an in-joke.[51] The *Pride and Prejudice* coats, surviving from Austen's original draft of the novel as *First Impressions* in the 1790s, may be a sly nod to the fashion for blue coats established by Goethe's phenomenally popular *Sorrows of Young Werther* (1774), or an oblique reference to the Whig uniform of blue coat and buff breeches.[52] Closer to home, Austen made fun of her speculative love Tom Lefroy (1776–1869) for finding fashion inspiration in a picaresque novel. His '<u>one</u> fault' was that 'his morning coat is a great deal too light. He is a very great admirer of Tom Jones, and therefore wears the same coloured clothes [a white coat], I imagine, which [Jones] did when he was wounded.'[53] Lightweight coats made of linen or paler browns were advised for summer, as the colour disguised accumulating dust (fig. 5.6). Otherwise, a coat's 'chief beauties' resided in colour, surface texture and make. The colour was usually dark – black, blue, dark brown or green; gilt buttons were preferred for evening coats, self-covered or silk thread buttons for garments to be worn at other times (fig. 5.7). The fabric should never be 'too satiny', as the best cloths were dull. The cut of day-coats sat close, but easy to the shoulders instead of tight, the skirts hanging smoothly.[54] Richard Dighton began his decade-long series of engravings of men in the City and the West End in 1817 (fig. 5.8). Over a hundred portraits taken from life show, cumulatively, the possible combinations of coat, waistcoat, legwear and hat – remarkably varied even with the comparatively restrained Regency colour palette.[55] Professional men such as doctors, lawyers and bankers stand out in their wholly black suits, of the kind in Thomas Coutts's wardrobe.

The tailor's art was in manipulating cloth (fig. 5.9). Wool stretches, shrinks and accommodates shaping like no other fibre. Adding careful interior padding and tactical darts created coats that, at their best, enhanced the male form into a better version of its natural self, one of the Regency's constructed naturalisms. Charles Bazalgette has amassed a wealth of information on Regency tailors while researching his ancestor, who ran a successful London firm with royal patronage, providing a rare insight into the art's practicalities.[56] On a quotidian level, tailors differed widely in skill and quality. The authors of *The Taylor's Complete Guide* make

City

clear why attention to tailoring was such a revolution. They recall tailors, fixed in their habits for twenty years or more, who cut and roughly fitted garments with no attention to the niceties of smoothness, ease and elegance.[57] New Regency fashion ideas influenced tailors to focus on fit and the particulars of cut, which distinguished an elegant coat from a bad one. The coat that fitted the wearer like a second skin should have been unnoticeable when compared to an ill-fitting one. Tailors started to publish patterns during the Regency in an attempt to pass on knowledge gained from years of experience (fig. 5.10). The publications emphasise the gap between the work of male tailors, who created hard silhouettes with curved cutting, and engineered and moulded woollen fabrics to fit the figure, and the skills of female seamstresses and dressmakers, who draped soft garments in linen, cotton and silks, often using straight lines for the cut.

Jane Austen wrote in 1799 that she had 'got over the dreadful epoch of Mantua-making much better than I expected'.[58] A mantua-maker, named after the mantua gown established in fashion from the 1690s, made women's outer clothes. These professionals ranged from women with formal training through apprenticeship to an experienced maker, to those earning a living from their sewing abilities in a

Fig. 5.6

Summer coat, 1815–20, linen and flannel. A gentleman's light country coat, buttoning from neck to waist, with turned-back collar, narrow sleeves, deep pockets inserted at the waistline, two further deep pockets inserted into the rear skirt, and the upper half of the coat lined in soft flannel; it is possibly a sporting coat. Private collection.

✳ ✳   Dress in the Age of Jane Austen

Fig. 5.7

Coat, 1803, wool, silk and metal. This slim- fitting, double-breasted outer coat, of high-quality British wool facecloth, with a silk velvet collar, was made by John Weston, tailor and draper to the Prince Regent, later George IV. The prince was passionately interested in clothes and patronised London's most skilful craftsmen. Museum of London.

reasonably respectable trade.[59] They occupied the middle ground between seamstress and tailor, and could be found everywhere in London. The term 'dressmaker' came in with the nineteenth century; it was in use by 1799 and established by the early 1820s. Edgeworth addressed the new phrase with a certain asperity in 1813: 'I have half an hour before the cursed mantuamaker, I beg her pardon dressmakers appointment.'[60] Professional dressmaking appears only in *Northanger Abbey* and *Persuasion*, the latter in discarded draft chapters.

The longest passage on clothing from Austen's pen describes a gown the mantua-maker Mrs Mussell is making for her:

> It is to be a round Gown, with a Jacket, & a Frock front, like Cath: Bigg's, to open at the side. – The Jacket is all in one with the body, & comes as far as the pocketholes; – about half a quarter of a yard deep I suppose, all the way round, cut off straight at the Corners with a broad hem. No fullness appears either in the Body or the flap; – the back is quite plain in this form; ⛛ – and the sides equally so. – The front is sloped round to the bosom & drawn in – & there is to be a frill of the same to put on occasionally when all one's handkerchiefs are dirty – which frill must fall back. – She is to put two breadths & a half in the tail, & no Gores; – Gores not being so much worn as they were; – there is nothing new in the sleeves, – they are to be plain, with a fullness of the same falling down & gathered up underneath, just like some of Marthas – or perhaps a little longer. – Low in the back behind, & a belt of the same.[61]

Fig. 5.9

Unknown artist, a tailor at work, from John Souter, *The Book of Trades* (1809), hand-coloured engraving on paper. The tailor's tools include shears, patterns, pressing irons and individual measuring strips (shown here hanging on the back wall). Rijksmuseum, Amsterdam.

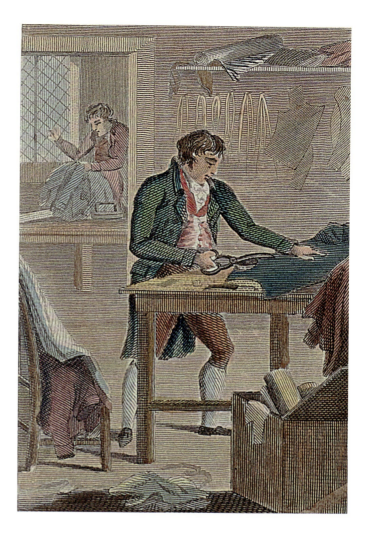

Style and construction were synonymous for the materially minded Regency woman. The letters' irregular survival precludes tracing the Austen women's preferred mantua-makers. Austen mentions Miss Small, Miss Summers, Mrs Mussell, the Misses Bakers (who also did millinery), Miss Burton and Miss Hare – a line-up of employed, mostly unmarried women rare for the day.[62] Mrs Mussell had 'made my dark gown very well & may therefore be trusted I hope with Yours', but Austen noted 'she does not always succeed with lighter Colours. – My white one I was obliged to alter a great deal.'[63] Although she is in the fashion hotspot of Bath, Mrs Mussell's skills do not produce a predictable product, and Austen needed her own nimble fingers to amend the gown into suitability. The impression overall is of Austen using local, affordable makers, not fashionable establishments, like one Maria Edgeworth patronised – a Mrs Ducks in London, possessing the 'elegant luxury' of a room with an excellent fire.[64] Warmth was important for women in their underwear for fittings.

We lack a detailed understanding of how these clothing clients and makers decided on the final style, the actual 'fashioning'. The 'production of commissioned garments

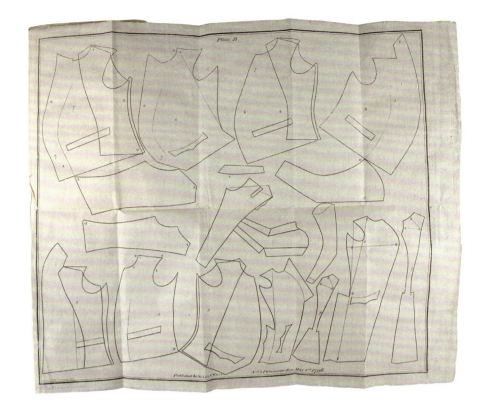

was intensely confidential and intimate, at both a bodily and, potentially, a personal level . . . The producer would be privy to knowledge of any physical deformity or flaw which, by contemporary standards of beauty, the consumer might desire to be hidden',[65] just as, according to Francis Place, tailors were party to the secrets and indiscretions of their male clients.[66] Austen is also silent about how her own preferences shaped the new garment. The final result seems to have been a balance between 'my own thought', as Isabella Thorpe (*NA*) proclaims of her new sleeves,[67] and the dressmaker's professional experience of new styles and current taste, filtered through tact and flattery to suit the customer's figure and budget. If they had space, dressmakers displayed samples or finished work for other customers in their rooms, inspiring new orders and allowing a client to pry deliciously into other women's new clothes. Mrs Palmer (*S&S*) hunts out the London warehouse where Miss Grey's clothes are on view before her wedding to Willoughby; perhaps the bride ordered on the scale of a Miss Brownlow's sixty-two dresses, 'a new morning and evening gown for every day of her honeymoon'.[68] Dressmakers promised good customers not to exhibit their gowns in progress, so as to retain their freshness and novelty when worn.

Eliza Jervoise's accounts detail one gentry woman's continuing relationship with her London dressmakers and the full costs involved. She first consistently employed Esther Crowther of Marylebone, letters from whom show the scope of the dressmaker's business with her client beyond mere construction, including buying pre-made gowns at a discount. By 1806 Mrs Jervoise had moved to a Mrs

Dress in the Age of Jane Austen

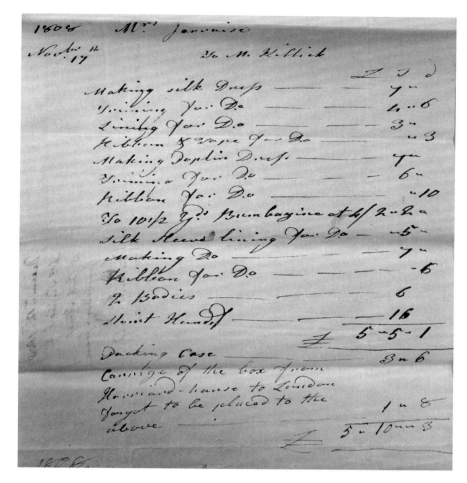

Killick and her daughter, also in London.[69] Professional tailors' and dressmakers' bills frequently include the work of refreshing and remaking existing clothing. Mrs Killick's 1808 bill shows how those costs broke down, and how small a part labour was of the final sum (fig. 5.11). The material components contributed most to the price, including a handkerchief worth nearly twice the gown-making cost. Note that the '2 bodies' are itemised separately, perhaps owing to the different fabrics or separate fitting requirements. When Cassandra came into 5 guineas and contemplated buying a gown, Austen offered to give her the price of the body lining because it was a separate cost.[70]

Austen mentions a making price only once, when during a stay in London she and Cassandra had pelisses sewn by a 'young woman in the neighbourhood'.[71] The maker charged 'only' 8s., which Austen considered reasonable. In fact, 7s.–8s. is the remarkably consistent cost for making female dress between about 1800 and 1815 across southern England. In 1801 Miss Crowther charged 7s. for making a 'Cambrick Muslin Robe', and a 'Round Gown', as did Mrs Killick in 1806 for a 'Bombazine dress', while making a 'pelice' was 10s. 6d. – still less expensive than making a crape handkerchief at 12s. By 1819 Mrs Killick charged 10s. 6d. for 'Making Black Satin

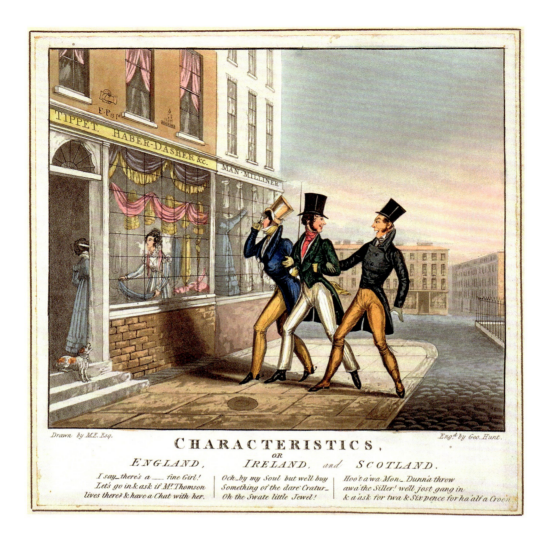

Drawn by M.E. Esq.   Eng.d by Geo. Hunt.

CHARACTERISTICS,
OR
ENGLAND,   *IRELAND, and*   *SCOTLAND.*

I say_there's a ___ fine Girl!	*Och_by my Soul but we'll buy*	*Hoo't a'wa Mon_ Dunnä throw*
Let's go in & ask if M.r Thomson	*Something of the dare Cratur_*	*awa' the Siller! we'll jost_gang in*
lives there? & have a Chat with her.	*Oh the Swate little Jewel!*	*& a'ask for twa & Six pence for ha'alf a Croon*

Fig. 5.12

M. Egerton, *Characteristics*, 1825, coloured lithograph on paper. The three gentlemen representing countries of the United Kingdom are outside a millinery and haberdashery shop, ogling the female haberdasher on display in the window with her textile stock. The next-door window shows a rare view of how gowns for sale were displayed.

dress', an increase of 50 per cent over the usual price, perhaps because of the extra amount of fabric in gown skirts by that date. But 'Making a pelisse' and a muslin dress cost the same. Occasionally Mrs Jervoise used a Miss Small of Basingstoke, who charged only 5s. for making up a dress.[72] She may be the same Miss Small who took on apprentice Lizzie Bond in 1798, according to Austen.[73]

The total price for garments for gentry and middling sorts of women – that is, for materials and making together – was from around £1 to as much as £8. How long did it take to make these garments? While the dressmaking *business* could be profitable, 'the mere work-women do not get any thing at all adequate to their labour . . . the recompense for extra work is, in general, poor remuneration for the time spent'.[74] Did dressmakers compensate for shortfall through judicious mark-up on the extras? Selling 'fancy' haberdashery generally had an 'exorbitant profit' attached to it, according to one Bath warehouseman.[75] In this way, the work of milliners and dressmakers was often combined, and perhaps clients who bought their own trimmings did so for economy (fig. 5.12).

Full Dress

The biggest distinction in Regency sartorial convention was between 'undress' day clothing, and evening and 'full' dress, often just called 'dress' (fig. 5.13). The *Lady's Magazine* outlined the regulations of custom according to the time of day. 'In the morning, the arms and bosom must be completely covered to the throat and wrists', while in the evening arms could be bare above the elbow, and neck and shoulders unveiled, creating an enduring template for female evening dress.[76]

At minimum, one 'dressed' for dinner, even with family or friends, as Austen's heroines frequently do. The Bingley sisters (*P&P*) retire to dress at five o'clock 'and at half-past six Elizabeth was summoned to dinner', giving a full hour and a half for dressing.[77] Austen's view of the effort involved is palpable in a letter: '*I was very glad to be spared the trouble of dressing & going & being weary before it was half over, so my gown & my cap are still unworn.*'[78] The evening change of clothes must have been a rare chance for solitude, as when Lizzy hurries away to dress, 'eager to be alone'.[79] General Tilney (*NA*) allows Catherine only half an hour to dress with '"No theatre, no rooms to prepare for."'[80] Miss Tilney entreats her to 'make as little alteration as possible in her dress' in order not to be late, though Catherine does change her gown.[81] The change of clothes is explicit in an episode in *The Watsons*, where characters are 'accosted by a young man in a morning-dress and boots', who tells them '"I am this moment going to dress . . . I am waiting for my stupid fellow,"' meaning his valet, who will help him dress.[82] Good help was essential to both sexes for creating an evening look elegant in all details. Betsey (Wynne) Fremantle described a general, dressed for dinner, who looked 'as if he had come out of a band-box; so excessively neat; white kerseymere waistcoat and small clothes, dark blue coat, white silk stockings, with very glittering shoe and knee buckles, frilled shirt, and white plaited stock, buckled behind'.[83]

Mis-dressing could create awkward moments. An acquaintance of Susan Ferrier's went to what she thought was a family dinner at General Maxwell's, and found herself in 'rusty fusty worsted robes' amid a society assemblage full of 'belles' and 'beaux'.[84] Austen's evening gown, brought to Godmersham for special occasions, was insurance against any faux pas as to levels of 'dress', and would have been low necked. Commentators despaired of the quantity of female flesh on display in full dress, and played on the tensions between 'dress' and 'undress'. Moral concern centred on how to be appropriately dressed yet covered, as the father of a '*fashionable nude*' wrote in a published letter:

> I would be glad if you would send for your dress maker, and with all your ingenuity invent a dress which should be thoroughly beaming, and perfectly decent at the same time. I have been asked, how I could suffer my daughter to dress so improperly; what could I answer but that fashion bears down every thing before it?[85]

Austen found the style amusing: 'Miss Langley is like any other short girl, with a broad nose and wide mouth, fashionable dress and exposed bosom.'[86] However,

by 1814 she too had altered her evening dress by lowering the bosom of her gauze gown; on the night she wore the altered gown she also experimented with the new long sleeves to see if they were 'allowable', though Mrs Tilson also wore them and 'assured her they are worn in the evening by many'.[87] Sleeves could be made separately to match a dress (Eliza Jervoise had a pair, costing 7s.). The long sleeves Mrs Bennet is 'very glad to hear of' in *Pride and Prejudice* (set in 1812) may be the result of this same change.[88] At the other extreme, in 1803 'Lady Meredith was . . . turned out of the Rooms at Bath by the Master of the Ceremonies for having *no* sleeves to her cloaths – the naked elbow appears every where with impunity, but the arm above it is not tolerated as yet.'[89] The health aspects concerned Regency people in the cumulative effect of 'naked arms and bosoms, thin shoes, short

Dress in the Age of Jane Austen

Fig. 5.14

Evening gown, c.1820, muslin. Muslin gowns embroidered with gilt or silver thread are common in collections, but untarnished examples are relatively rare. This gown retains the original sparkle of the embroidery, highlighted by the soft, dull cotton ground. The waistline has descended nearly to the natural position by 1820, and sleeve size is increasing. Los Angeles County Museum of Art.

drapery, and sudden changes of climate' in causing influenza, consumption and other respiratory ailments.[90] Fanny Burney declined an invitation to a party after illness, because 'I cannot yet risk an evening, and a dressed one too.'[91]

Anxieties about male evening dress involved tightness. While *The Whole Art of Dress!* advised that a dress-coat, distinguished by its cut, 'should never be made to button [but] should, if any thing, be even too small to meet across the waist and chest, so that it may sit open and display the waistcoat, shirt, and cravat to the utmost advantage', others perceived this as a man's coat fitting so closely that he could scarcely draw breath, 'laced within an inch of his life'. In colour, 'Black and blue are the only full-dress colours: night will not allow a dark green to be discriminated from them.'[92] The rise of black in menswear dates from the Regency, seen in every image of male evening dress. Scholars and contemporary commentators stressed black's sombreness; but the colour is attractive, John Harvey argues, making the person look thinner, setting off the face, perhaps suggesting intensity with a 'glamorous and dashing smartness' evident in the 'elongated and elegant languor' of some and the 'charged uprightness' of others.[93] His phrase recalls Emma finally noticing Mr Knightley's 'tall, firm, upright figure' and 'natural grace' when dressed for a ball.[94]

Fig. 5.15

Rolinda Sharples, *The Cloak-Room, Clifton Assembly Rooms*, 1818, oil on canvas. Sharples's accomplished and detailed painting provides myriad details of Regency ball dress, from the satin slips of women worn under gauzy outer gowns, cut with the very small bodice of the late 1810s, to the dress uniforms, evening coats and fine legs of the gentlemen. Bristol Museum and Art Gallery.

For women, textiles for 'dress' either absorbed or reflected light. Lamps and candles lit evening gatherings, leading to a preference for bluer tones to neutralise the yellow light.[95] Fashion writers noted that a 'pale yellow colour, which is extremely elegant in the day . . . appears soiled in the evening', and diminished the 'brilliancy of the complexion'.[96] Metallic ornaments and embroideries glinted in the flickering candlelight, coming to life in a way electric light eclipses. White muslin provided a foil to the glitter of gilt-thread embroidery (fig. 5.14). Silks continued popular, forming 'a crowd of sattins and laces' in the evening.[97] There are significantly more silk evening gowns in museum collections than those made of other textiles. Fashion magazines contain many resplendent descriptions of full dress, but white silk dresses prevail among records of actual wear (see fig. 5.13). In 1813 Fanny Knight wore white sarsenet with silver in her hair to the Canterbury ball.[98] Other documented examples include white merino trimmed with satin for dinner, and a twelve-year-old white satin dress, now unfashionable, which had been worn at the lady's wedding.[99] As translucent fabrics became popular for full dress, women adopted a white (fig. 5.15) or coloured silk slip or petticoat worn under gauzes, nets and muslins, which changed the hue of the gown; Susan Ferrier remarked on the 'great beauty' of crimson gauze over sky-blue satin observed at a ball.[100] Evening slippers of pale satins and silks, sometimes finished with ribbons crossed up the legs, matched or contrasted with the gown (fig 5.16). Men wore pumps of black or patent leather, which appeared to lengthen their legs, especially when combined with the cream breeches and stockings usual in the evening (though both in black were acceptable). Incredibly slim to modern eyes, shoes fitted tightly as part of fashionable style, offering ample fodder to satirists to ridicule the forcing of reality into the narrow ideal foot. Shoes were Regency consumables, constantly entering and departing the wardrobe, their lives eked out by frequent cobbling and repairs. Ladies' delicate fabric dancing slippers could disintegrate in an evening – a pair of Harriet Wynne's split at a ball.[101] Leather soles wore out fast, no matter how well made, and required frequent replacement.

Dress in the Age of Jane Austen

Fig. 5.17

Austen highlights the importance of headwear in creating the right evening look. At a concert in Bath in 1805, she wore a gown with crape sleeves 'put in on the occasion; on my head I wore my crape & flowers but I do not think it looked particularly well'.[102] Evening caps were, again, a way of refreshing ensembles, and the Austen women used London trips to acquire new ones. In 1813 a Miss Hare had some pretty ready-made caps in her shop, and Austen bespoke 'one like one of them, only white satin instead of blue. It will be white satin and lace, and a little white flower perking out of the left ear, like Harriot Byron's feather. I have allowed her to go as far as [£]1.16s.'[103] This is clearly an evening or visiting cap, by the quality of the materials and the price – more than the guinea that a first edition of *Emma* would later cost. The Austen sisters often had dresses made in the same fabric, for evening as well as daywear; the two gowns supposed to have been worn at the Duchess of Richmond's famous Waterloo ball by a pair of sisters (fig. 5.17) provide a wonderful comparative example of this practice.[104]

The Regency evening social activity *par excellence* was dancing, covered in many books about Austen's life and times.[105] In the country, dances could draw together people from up to 20 miles' radius (more than 30 km) – a travelling distance of around four hours.[106] Private balls, of the type Austen fictionalises most memorably at Netherfield Park, were an opportunity for sociability, entertainment and exercise. These were attended by invitation, but ticket purchase allowed anyone with the money (and the right appearance) access to public balls held in assembly rooms from the local, as in fictional Meryton, to the splendid, as in real-world Bath.

Dancing was a near universal skill for the middling sorts – '"Every savage can dance,"' as Mr Darcy snarls.[107] Beside the pleasure of different company, the dance floor was, in Austen's time, 'the best opportunity for identifying romantic partners and for advancing a courtship, for testing relations between the sexes.'[108] Dressing for a ball, no matter where, was a careful business, as both single and married attendees were presenting their best personal display. But dancing took its toll on delicate evening attire, as Susan Sibbald found when she danced so much one night that she wore a hole in the sole of her shoe that made her foot bleed.[109] How to balance comfort and elegance, and secure coiffures and their decorations in place to survive long, active hours occupied women's thoughts for many days beforehand. Both sexes carried dancing shoes in bags and changed their footwear once indoors, as depicted in fig. 5.15.[110]

In the sense of the amount of exertion required of them, ballgowns may be considered a kind of decorative

THE FIVE POSITIONS OF DANCING.

1   2   3
4   5

The Figures shew the positions of the Learner, and the Feet that of a finish'd Dancer.

sporting dress. Illustrations of ballgowns in fashion plates show shortened hems to allow freer movement of the feet (fig. 5.18) (in dress collections, when such a gown is presented on a mannequin as though full length, it distorts the perception of women's height in the period.)[111] Dance dresses often feature a slimmer, almost tubular skirt that would be lighter to wear. Maria Edgeworth's sisters wore white Paris gauze gowns at an annual ball in Dorking – 'very genteel'. Fanny had her hair done in 'perfect taste – a tress added to her own and plaited with puffs of her own hair in its centre and pomegranates and white flowers happily mixed [with] her gold and pearl comb in front of the tress'; she ended up being considered the second best-dressed woman in the room, after the hostess.[112] Fanny Knight went to a ball in 1811, probably with her sisters, wearing sprigged muslin trimmed with Honiton(?) lace (her writing is often illegible) 'over satin slips & ornaments, & flowers in our heads'.[113] The ballroom was one place where women's lighter clothing was an advantage. Combining a crush of energetic bodies in a room lit by hot candles meant that ballrooms were stifling, even in the middle of winter, and fans were essential for cooling the face (see fig. 5.18). No wonder the dancers at the Crown Inn in Highbury (*Emma*) want to throw open the windows, to Mr Woodhouse's horror.

Light fabrics and revealingly cut gowns allowed women to 'glow' off their exertion, while their companions perspired manfully into the layers of linen and wool encasing their bodies, neck to wrist and knee, though breeches and pantaloons made from stretch material like black silk jersey could make moving a little easier. One of the advantages of breeches as evening wear was a full bend at the knee; the tightness of non-knitted pantaloons somewhat curtailed nimbleness. Rules for the Bath assembly rooms decreed no boots or half-boots were to be worn in the ballroom (though after 1800 officers on duty were exempt), and ladies who wished to dance minuets were required to wear court dress (see below).[114] The lady patronesses at Almack's, London's most exclusive establishment for balls and suppers (Eliza de Feuillide was a visitor), were rigorous and inflexible in their rules for dress. Famously, Arthur Wellesley, Duke of Wellington (1769–1814) was once turned away for wearing trousers instead of breeches.

Maria Edgeworth tells a story illustrating the fluid consumption practices and the importance of alterations in obtaining appropriate dress. She and her half-sisters went to Almack's in 1822:

> A long story about a wedding dress that cost 20 pounds and that I got for three guineas . . . Suffice it that said dress was made in Paris of silk *pattinet* gauze or something like it[,] was trimmed at bottom with two flounces and two rows of vine leaves and bunches worked in white chenille and glass

beads . . . The body with 3 festoons of ditto in front – sleeves beautifully worked to match – and steel bugle belt. I [cut out] one stripe of the trimming and one flounce to trim a fellow dress for Harriet. The gap was filled up with plain pattinet gauze and two folds of white satin over the joinings and this bobbery of Fannys gown made a complete trimming of a ditto dress for Harriet. Body and sleeves were made *nearly* to match and bugle belt. The whole was performed by our incomparable maid who . . . executed it with wonderful celerity. The two dresses cost F and H only £2–17 apiece.[115]

The same dresses served them on one evening for dinner at Lady Swinburne's, a concert at Mrs Haldimand's and a grand party at Lady Londonderry's.[116] Their only regret was that the beautiful hem trimmings were displayed only upon entering, when each person was 'completely seen and passed in review by all the nice judging many'.

Elites and Excess

The wild, eccentric lives of the Regency beau monde and *haut ton* have drawn many authors to their flame. It was an age of expensive *joie de vivre*, the figures of Lord Byron, the Prince Regent and his numerous mistresses, idiosyncratic Lady Caroline Lamb and the socialist Shelley–Godwin–Wollstonecraft enclave epitomising the éclat of Regency London's high society to following generations. Walter Scott summarised the set as the 'heroine from Grosvenor Square, and a hero from the Barouche Club or the Four-in-hand, with a set of subordinate characters from the elegantes of Queen Anne Street East, or the dashing heroes of the Bow Street Office'.[117] Romping historical fiction, such as Georgette Heyer's, celebrates these bucks and Corinthians, ultras and exquisites.

However, this elite was a very small set. The titled nobility numbered around 1,000 men and their families, but 'fashionable society was not commensurate with the peerage in its totality or simply the nobility in a new guise'. Only a proportion of the aristocracy embraced the life of the beau monde, 'the cohort of privileged individuals who enjoyed public prominence within the framework of the London season'.[118] Austen's writings about the upper gentry edge into its higher echelons, reflecting her experience. After her youthful creation of the amoral and libertine Lady Susan, the flash coves and fast women of the beau monde appear only peripherally in Austen's mature works, in the persons of gambler and pleasure-ruined Mr. Willoughby, Colonel Brandon's first love (both *S&S*), Mr. Wickham (*P&P*), and Mrs Smith's husband (*Pers.*).

At the head of all trendsetting was George 'Beau' Brummell (1778–1840; fig. 5.19). Three years younger than Austen, he helped to transform Regency men's dress to its modern form, much as Austen transformed the novel. He did not single-handedly invent the new regime of masculine dress, but he best distilled it, fusing the wearer and the dress in his person. Around him it spread in society so successfully that 'its aesthetic protocols have lasted until the present time'.[119] No single person affected early nineteenth-century clothing more than Brummell. The revolutions

of fit, sobriety and perfection that this non-aristocratic wit achieved marked the rise of the gentry class as tastemakers, a new beau monde, whose influence Austen was already recording in *Sanditon*. His force of personality and capacity for style setting allowed him to dictate to the Prince Regent himself. Brummell epitomised a new standard of elegance and ideal of perfection in male dress without being a flamboyant dresser.[120] He helped to strengthen the reputation of the English as standard setters for fashionable male dress by introducing 'a perfection of restrained taste', and 'a nice blend of careless ease and absolute control', the studied epitome of the unstudied riding-dress style seen as English taste.[121]

Brummell's sartorial sobriety comprised eschewing

all ornamentation apart from brass buttons on his plain cloth coat, and a heavy gold watch and chain. He shunned patterns and bright colours, limiting himself to plain coats of blue, or perhaps green, with contrasting waistcoat and buff breeches or pantaloons. Evening wear comprised a blue or black coat, white waistcoat, black pantaloons, and pumps. Apart from plain dress with immaculate cut and fit . . . his linen was always whiter than white; his neckcloths starched and uncreased.[122]

Surveying images of Regency men shows how deeply his style maxims reflected correct dress. Brummell is the first to be credited with starching his neckcloths – in his case, to the stiffness of fine writing-paper; but imitators, satirised in endless plates, wearing excessively high collars and a vast yardage of neckcloths, missed the crisp, clean point of Brummell's perfection. Lord Byron actually followed Brummell's upright stiffness. Earlier portraits of the poet afterwards had his neck-containing collars painted out and replaced with an open-necked, poetic style that he appears not to have adopted in everyday wear.[123] Starching was a cost in materials and time, making it a luxurious affectation ripe for targeting by critics of dandyism. Other innovations attributed to Brummell include straps passing under the foot to hold the trousers taut.

Some argue that Brummell was the ultimate dandy; others that he was the opposite of the dressed ostentation characterising later nineteenth-century dandies. The word was applied to Brummell only after his apex of influence. Ian Kelly, in a biography grounded in an understanding of the material qualities of Brummell's clothes, pinpoints the Beau's candidature for both camps through his 'theatricality of understated chic'.[124] Dandies were self-created to construct an elegant surface transcending social background. Francis Grose's *Classical Dictionary of the Vulgar Tongue* defines dandy as 'the ton, the clever thing', implying a smartness of person and attitude, 'united in a stance of combined disdain, provocation, and indifference towards the world' (fig. 5.20).[125] 'Dandy' was also a label for a man greatly concerned with his appearance, or displaying vanity in dress, like Sir Walter Elliot (*Pers.*). Austen's broad satire of an ageing dandy had similarities with representations of the Prince Regent.[126]

Grose relishes other slang words for men's appearance. He defines, and Austen uses, 'quiz' and 'coxcomb', which she deploys pointedly. Isabella Thorpe (*NA*) dismisses the man she actually has her eye on as '"the greatest coxcomb I ever saw"'.[127] Unintentionally, Lucy Steele does the same thing with her future husband Robert Ferrars (*S&S*), calling him '"silly and a great coxcomb"'.[128] Ferrars is introduced fussing over ordering a silver toothpick in fashionable Bond Street, and his character fulfils Grose's definition of 'a fop, or vain self-conceited fellow'.[129] Ferrars's easy civility, and the quality of his bow assure Elinor Dashwood 'as plainly as words could have done, that he was exactly the coxcomb she had heard him described to be'.[130] Frank Churchill (*Emma*) merely affects the '"ostentation of a coxcomb"', as his father chaffs him, concealing the real purpose of his trip to London – to buy a gift for his beloved – behind the foppish excuse of getting a haircut.[131]

Northanger Abbey uses 'quiz' – 'a strange-looking fellow, an odd dog' – in both senses of the object and its appearance.[132] Isabella Thorpe could 'point out a quiz through the thickness of a crowd', she and her sisters being the greatest quizzers in the Bath assembly rooms.[133] Her brother John is impolite enough to critique his mother's 'quiz of a hat' to her face, bringing out the sense of an eccentric, peculiar or ridiculous appearance.[134] Specialist quizzing glasses 'made a fashionable virtue out of staring', turning polite sociability on its head.[135] 'Quiz' was Oxbridge cant, so Austen may have heard the phrase from her brother Henry, who attended Oxford between 1788 and 1793, just before the novel was drafted, and where, in the story, James Morland is studying.

Churchill's lack of 'conceit or puppyism' highlights another (canine) word for the overdressed man.[136] Maria Edgeworth's friend Lady Elizabeth Whitbread (1765–1846) declared she could not bear 'those fine puppy-men', after seeing one 'strutting before me with his great coat gathered behind *nicely* . . . like a woman's between button and button and I am sure he thought as much of his dress as the prettiest girl of 16 in London'. A neat waist and full skirts were feminine details. Other critics of fashionable men find an echo in the core of Lady Elizabeth's complaint: '"Are you not ashamed of yourself? You a man! And an Englishman!"'[137] Suspicions against men concerned with dress centred around their masculinity: 'Ye epicene non-naturals who trench upon the petticoat, to furnish you with trousers, and on the fair ones' stays, boddices or corsets.'[138] Dress attention was womanly, unbecoming to an Englishman and smacking of the Continental foreign. Effeminate behaviour was criticised in the same breath: 'you boot-brushing, tooth picking, drawling, dancing, riding, driving, simpering, sauntering, ogling, staring, d—ing, swearing and troublesome animals' (the 'tooth picking' reference reinforces the portrayal of Robert Ferrars as dandiacal).[139] Scorn for dandies extended to shopmen essaying fashionable appearance: 'There is not a more obtrusive, impertinent, more improperly dressed being in town than our linen-drapers, haberdashers, and their men', and, even worse, the man-milliner (fig. 5.21),[140] whose preoccupation with dress, conceit, affectation and presumption and their association with feminine materiality compromised their social masculinity.

Tom Bertram and Henry Crawford (*MP*) can be seen to embody, respectively, the two types of fashionable men, the sportsman and the dandy.[141] Crawford displays a 'nonchalant minimalism' in his speech and gesture, though we are never told of his clothes. His ability to seem attractive through careful cultivation of manner and attitude also bespeaks the dandy's 'entirely personal excellence', which captivates through insolent charm.[142] One could not be a dandy without an audience: *ton* was a performative art. Whereas dictums on genteel fashion emphasised appropriate modesty, respectability and inconspicuousness, dandies gloried in visibility. '"My natural taste is all for simplicity; a simple style of dress is so infinitely preferable to finery,"' declares Mrs Elton (*Emma*). '"But I am quite in the minority, I believe; few people seem to value simplicity of dress, – shew and finery are every thing,"' which draws attention to her own simplicity while undermining its supposed effect, and making her a female dandy.[143] Throughout *Emma*, Mrs Elton's clothes substitute for character, a complaint also repeatedly levelled at men: 'In dress consists his fortune, wisdom, wit; / His fame's in dress' proclaims a satirical poem.[144] Dandies had the appearance but not the benefits of true aristocracy, as does Mrs Elton, further qualifying her for the label of 'dandy'. Daughter of a Bristol merchant, she flaunts her provincial town fashions among Highbury inhabitants with a supposedly London air.

Austen is mistress of economy; when she describes dress, it is laden with significance. 'Mrs E.' attracts more dress adjectives than any other Austen character, and they are all relevant. Her fame is in dress, to which she constantly draws attention; its trimmings, too rich for local fashionability, stand in for the wisdom and wit she does not possess. The accessories vulgarise Mrs Elton's appearance beyond what is respectable or suitable. 'All her apparatus of happiness, her large bonnet and her basket', are things put on, an externalised happiness because she has no inner character.[145] Something as small as a handbag speaks volumes under Austen's

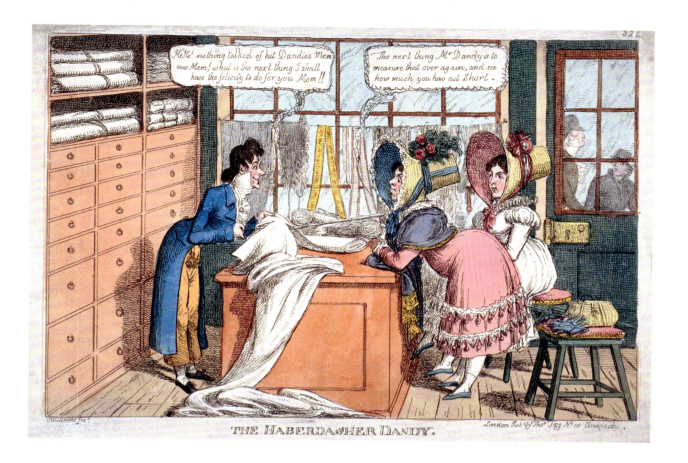

THE HABERDASHER DANDY.

Fig. 5.21

Charles Williams, *The Haberdasher Dandy*, 1818, hand-coloured etching on paper. Men working in the highly female trades of haberdashery and millinery attracted their own brand of scorn. The haberdasher dandy is here accused of using flattery and charm to distract customers from noticing that he has given them short measure. Lewis Walpole Library, Farmington, Conn.

pen. A 'purple and gold ridicule', though fashionable, is also gaudy, vulgar and too loud, summarising Augusta Elton's personality perfectly. Austen never has a positive word to say about purple in fiction or letters – she poked fun at a purple mantle, gown and pelisse in 1814–15, during *Emma*'s composition period. And her spelling is deliberate: 'reticule' was the alternative, but Austen plays on the 'ridicule' of its owner implicit in the object. Mrs Elton is, after all, only 'as elegant as lace and pearls can make her', having no natural refinement – unlike Emma or Jane Fairfax. Emma's politeness allows her to get away with describing the 'vain woman, extremely well satisfied with herself, and thinking much of her own importance' with the 'nothing-meaning terms' '"elegantly dressed, and very pleasing"'.[146]

Aristocrats and Royalty

Aristocratic and highly fashionable dress was fair game for critical skewering, and nobody resisted. Like Lady Catherine de Bourgh (*P&P*), aristocrats were felt to have a duty to preserve the dignity of rank in their person. When people met 'a royal Duke and his groom so habited alike, all pepper and salt', the similarity was offensive. Instead, 'without putting himself much out of his way, without being over-

Fig. 5.22

After George Dawe, portrait of Princess Charlotte of Wales in Russian dress, 1815, oil on canvas. This is the second of three versions of this portrait, which show Charlotte in increasingly elaborate shirts, culminating in sleeves made entirely of lace. The bodice sleeves of her plain petticoat are visible under the filmy material. Her gown is made of blue silk, with gold 'lace' (braid) trimmings. The Royal Collection.

dressed in a morning, or under dressed in an evening, a nobleman of taste and of discernment might continue to dress like what he is'.[147] Even Emperor Alexander I of Russia (1777–1825) wore a plain blue coat when visiting London and looked 'like a gentleman – but a country gentleman, not an Emperor', Edward Stanley opined. So much relied on a nicety of detail, of cut, fabric and quality. His sister the Grand Duchess of Oldenburg (1788–1819) on the same visit wore an 'extreme simplicity' of dress – 'she had nothing but a plain white gown and plain straw hat, with no ornament of any sort . . . [which] made me doubt whether it was really the Duchess; but it was'.[148]

The paradox was that 'whatever you unnecessarily expend on yourself, you take from the needy and distressed', yet 'the rich must spend to encourage trade'.[149] The making and circulation of fashion by the wealthy was considered an economic benefit. As a didactic text explains, 'Even some things that are merely ornamental, furnish employment to thousands of industrious families and, for those who can really afford it, to encourage them is a far more effectual method of supporting the poor than indiscriminate alms-giving.'[150] Similarly, Queen Charlotte (1744–1818) complained she 'had to order more clothes than she could wear, with more lace than was necessary, as they were perquisites for her servants' (which included Fanny Burney for a while).[151] Used royal clothes were passed on to, or inherited by, court officials or servants, just as the clothes of the gentry were given to servants in private houses. The recipients could wear the garments, or realise ready cash by selling them on. Though unconnected with the royal family, anyone could view and purchase clothing at a public auction of their clothes after death. Queen Caroline's clothing was sold in this way in 1821. It was 'a melancholy sight – All the Queens dress – even her stays laid out – and tarnished finery to be purchased by the lowest of the low.'[152] After his death in December 1830, George IV's clothes and accessories were sold at knock-down prices, the proceeds going to his household. Some of the dispersed items survive in museum collections.

The Prince of Wales's appointment as Regent on 5 February 1811 had a striking effect on fashionable nomenclature. As Dorothea Jordan wrote from Coventry only twenty-two days after the event, 'That not only the Regent but *Regency* is gaining popularity every day is very evident. All the milliners here have got Regency caps and gowns, and even the ribband weavers are beginning to produce Regency *devices*.'[153] A chapeau-bras could have a 'Regent fold' and a 'Regency hat' for women was fur, with the rim turned up, and a broad gold band.[154]

In his person, George, Prince of Wales, combined the fashionable appearance of wastrel wealthy aristocrat, dress-obsessed dandy and the acme of British rank. Austen was not a fan. The clothes-mad Prinny used a French tailor almost exclusively until about 1795, after which he patronised English makers such as John Weston and Schweitzer & Davidson, under Brummell's influence, and because his tailor was his largest creditor.[155] He racked up extraordinary debts on clothes, but by his middle age the once dashing prince had become a figure of ridicule, which increased at the same rate as his waistline. To Thackeray, George IV was best remembered as an empty heap of clothes; to his estranged wife, Queen Caroline, the monarch 'would make an excellent tailor, or shoemaker, or hairdresser, but nothing else'.[156]

While the royal princesses were not notably fashionable, the Regent's only child, Princess Charlotte, was genuinely celebrated for her youth, beauty, manners and spirit (she fancied herself like Marianne Dashwood in temperament). Many items of her clothing survive, including the Russian-style dress she wears in a portrait of 1815 (fig. 5.22).[157] Her clothing includes shirts of some of the finest-quality surviving Regency muslin – and gowns with some of the worst-quality stitching: hurrying to

Fig. 5.23

George Dawe, portrait of Victoria, Duchess of Kent, mother of Queen Victoria, 1818, oil on canvas. Her black velvet mourning evening gown, with delicate lace decoration and modishly small bodice, could have been worn for Queen Charlotte (d. 17 November 1818). Two years later, she would be mourning the death of her husband, the Duke of Kent. The Royal Collection.

finish a garment affected even the royal family. The princess had £800 yearly from her negligent father to dress herself, which barely covered the clothes required in her position. Skilled staff contrived, by altering Her Royal Highness's wardrobe, to give 'the appearance of novelty at a very trifling expense', the same tactical amendments that the Austen sisters employed further down the social scale.[158]

After a love marriage, Princess Charlotte died in 1817 in appallingly mismanaged childbirth. The death of a member of the royal family threw the whole nation into mourning (fig. 5.23). A run of deaths in the 1810s turned fashion plates in magazines black, and singed the edges of everyday dress, including Austen's. She wrote to Cassandra in 1805: 'I suppose everybody will be black for the D. of G. [Duke of Gloucester, a brother of George III]. Must we buy lace, or will ribbon do?'[159] Queen Charlotte died in 1818, the Duke of Kent (Queen Victoria's father) on 23 January 1820, promptly followed on the 29th by George III.[160] The king's death had been long anticipated; its imminence sparked the Regency, and was believed certain enough to make Anna Austen and her friend Harriot walk to Alton one June day in 1811 'to provide mourning against the King's death', collecting Aunt Jane on the way. They also bought 'a Bombasin' for Mrs Austen, who thought she 'should get it cheaper than when the poor King was actually dead'.[161] She cheerfully continued 'If I outlive him it will answer my purpose, if I do not, somebody may mourn for me in it – it will be wanted for one or the other . . . before the moths have eaten it up.' After George III's health scare in 1812, Elizabeth Grant's mother also feared black fabric prices would rise and bought a quantity of material on sale. When he survived, the family 'just had to wear it' anyway, 'and plentifully trimmed with crimson it did very well'.[162]

Retailers further profited from mourning consumption after the monarch finally departed. Mrs Topham bought a whole new mourning outfit for the king early in February 1820. Her gown comprised 10 yards of bombazine (£2 10s.) embellished with 3½ yards of trimming at 5d. per yard, 1½ yards each of ribbon and lace, another 1¼ yards of black lace, and the making cost of 8s., plus trimming and body lining at 10s. The widow also bought a remnant of crape (spending 8d. for washing it), another yard of black crape (7s.), a pair of slippers, ½ ounce of black silk, two skeins of floss, black cotton, needles, a muslin frill and cap, a crape cap and a pair of gloves. Her total personal expenditure was £6 1s. 11½d., and she would also have provided mourning for her household servants.[163] Eliza Jervoise bought her royal mourning 'Black Gros de Naples bonnet trimmed with a flower' for a considerable £2 5s., not sacrificing style to sadness.[164] After the funeral came the coronation and a fresh rush of spending. The pretty evening gowns surviving today match the 'fine glittering gauze, spangled and pedigreed with lace and gum-flowers' on display at a London mantua-maker's as examples of coronation fashions.[165]

Austen's letters emphasise how headwear responded to noble fashions and passing cultural events for less expense than a gown. Nearly all her references to aristocracy and clothing concern a hat or cap connected with a lady, or comment on their appearance. In 1798 she changed the trimmings of a cap on Cassandra's advice, so

Fig. 5.24

that 'it makes me look more like Lady Conyngham now than it did before, which is all that one lives for now'.[166] The tongue-in-cheek reference was to Elizabeth Conyngham, future mistress of the Prince of Wales. Writing from Bath, Austen reported that 'Bonnets of cambric muslin on the plan of Lady Bridges' are a good deal worn, and some of them are very pretty'.[167] Another style, the Oldenburg bonnet, made after the duchess's 'curious' design, with a tall crown and hiding the face, swept through England and France in 1814 and stayed in vogue for some years.

Court dress was the highest Regency clothing etiquette, and was subject to strict convention:

> The court dress for ladies is now distinguished only by the hoop, lappets, and full ruffles; for the mantua is now made exactly like any other open gown, and differently in shape before, according to the fashion of the year: the petticoat also is plain or trimmed, according to the fancy of the wearer.[168]

Trimmings and embroidery were gold or silver, and though feathers were not necessary, 'young ladies very seldom go without them', as may be seen in myriad fashion plates of court dress.[169] Periodicals regaled readers with lists of ladies attending court events and summaries of their dress. Lady This and the Duchess of That sparkle with golden tissue, expensive lace and silks of every hue and weave.

As women's waistlines rose, so did the waists of court gowns. Unfortunately, traditional Queen Charlotte insisted on retaining the eighteenth-century hoop petticoats as an obligatory part of court dress. Until 1820 the hips of women attending court started at their ribcage (fig. 5.24). Eliza de Feuillide could have told Austen first-hand about court fashion after her visits, and complained of standing at court for two hours 'loaded with a great hoop of no inconsiderable weight'.[170] They caused difficulties fitting into carriages and sedan chairs. Happily, the new George IV dispensed with hoops immediately.

Men's court clothing was the last bastion of eighteenth-century styles. Sir William Lucas (*P&P*), visiting his beloved St James's Palace, would have donned the appurtenances of court elegance such as gleaming white stockings, buckled shoes and embellished coat and waistcoat. *A Book Explaining the Ranks and Dignities of British Society* explains gentlemen's dazzling appearance: 'The court dress . . . is what is commonly called a full dressed coat, without collar or lappels, made of silk, velvet, or cloth, and often richly embroidered in gold, silver, or coloured silks. Any naval or military uniform is reckoned a full dress.'[171] The combined effect was the most vivid, brilliant gathering of clothes possible in the early nineteenth century (fig. 5.25).

Fig. 5.25

Thomas Rowlandson, Augustus Charles Pugin and Joseph Constantine Stadler, 'Drawing Room St James's', W. H. Pyne and William Combe, *The Microcosm of London* (1809), pl. 76, hand-coloured etching and aquatint. In official gatherings at St James's Palace, the last vestiges of eighteenth-century ostentation in dress – pale grey wigs, embellished silk suits for men and heavily decorated gowns with hoops for women – were paraded in formal splendour. Metropolitan Museum of Art, New York.

Such brilliance epitomised the city glamour people sought to add to their fashioned selves. Urban environments were a sphere that most people stepped into for a while, borrowing some of their dazzle on returning to village and country life, especially at more elevated social activities such as balls and dinners. Those who lived in towns often made a living selling the makings of metropolitan style. If the countryside was an extended web for the wide dissemination of Regency fashion, cities concentrated fashion's essence, offering a heady brew from which the gentry tried to sip moderately, preserving a distance between court and beau monde 'gaudy attire' and 'the becoming garb of a gentleman'.[172] Jane Austen expressed her era in her love of neat, appropriate dress, but with a penchant for prettiness. London and Bath were the main places where people tried to combine both, buying dress from myriad shops and warehouses in intensive bursts of shopping, and modelling their ensembles on the vivid, vulgar and varied creatures surrounding them in the crowded city streets.

❊ ❊

Chapter 6

Nation

A Most Glorious Wad of News! Buonaparte vanquished & dethroned & the Bourbons reestablished! Vive le Roi! Et Dieu soit beni!![1]

Looking out of the window of Chawton Cottage one June day in 1814, Jane Austen could have witnessed the august Alexander I, Tsar of All the Russias, rolling along the main road from Alton to Winchester. The allied sovereign's British visit celebrated the (apparently) final victory over Napoleon. Locals rumoured that the imperial carriage would pass through; the mail route from London to Portsmouth suggests against it. Watching for the tsar was briefly London's favourite pastime, and Austen cautioned Cassandra: 'Take care of yourself, and do not be trampled to death in running after the Emperor.'[2] Thus, ordinary Britons might see for themselves the directors of the great theatres of war that so shaped the Regency.

These two final chapters of the book step further from Austen's direct experience into the wider arenas of her age, and her family connections, which encompassed a significant amount of the world. Brothers Frank and Charles sailed in the Royal Navy, saw direct action in the Napoleonic Wars and traversed the half the globe. Henry Austen became a militia captain. All of them served and defended Britain. One sister-in-law was born and raised in Bermuda; another, Eliza de Feuillide, was born in India and married a French aristocrat as her first husband. Three brothers – James, Henry and Edward – travelled through France and the Continent. Constant foreign correspondence, and information shared when the travellers came home were a source for Austen's fiction.

✳ ✳

In this chapter British identity and cultural position through clothing are first considered, and then the influence of the Napoleonic Wars on fashion and the trade in dress goods. The burgeoning empire that would define the nineteenth century appears in the textile manufacture that spread within the country and outwards from it to encircle the globe. The longer-lasting style wars between Britain and France emerged from the interrelationships between nations and nationalisms in the ways their citizens clothed themselves. And how Britons wore the world is furthered explored in chapter 7, through dress connections made by sea and in the British colonies.

Britain

The Act for the Union of Great Britain and Ireland, passed in 1800, created the United Kingdom. Of the 10.9 million Britons recorded in 1800, 76 per cent (8.3 million) were English. Although Austen never uses the words 'Britain' or 'British', her novels, especially *Mansfield Park*, ring with a sense of the whole nation. Like other authors, she writes of 'England' and considers Englishness. I interchange the two, to reflect the fluctuating national identities at play, following Napoleon, who banned 'All commerce and all correspondence with the British Isles' and – in the Berlin Decree of November 1806, the first of a series of reciprocal trade embargoes, causing many of the major conflicts – ordered that 'Consequently letters or packages directed to England or to an Englishman or written in the English language shall not pass through the mails and shall be seized'.[3]

The long belligerent period from 1794 to 1815 was an excellent forge to shape the new nation's ideas of itself (fig. 6.1). Indeed, Linda Colley argues that British identity emerged in these years from the nation's need to defend itself against the non-British.[4] The material culture of middling English homes was the outcome of a successful, stable economy, manifesting itself through increasing amounts and qualities of clothing across all classes. The meanings associated with clothing morphed according to new cultural situations and changing social practices. Hence *Sanditon*'s 'Blue shoes, and nankin boots!', visible in the Norwich shoe shop (see fig. 3.10), indicate the increased novelty, quality and distribution of fashionable consumer goods that Austen was already noticing in the two years after the peace and before her death.[5] England, hence Britain, developed from a marginal economy to a major European power, and France's only real competitor. 'Ideas of democracy . . . were often expressed through consumption', 'a uniquely British maxim, the secret of the nation's success', as intellectuals and politicians at home and abroad repeatedly asserted.[6] There was more to buy, more to wear, and both actions reinforced Britain.

Scotland and Wales comprised 14.6 per cent and 5 per cent respectively of the new unified population. In 1811 Glasgow and Edinburgh were the largest cities in Britain after London, with populations of c.100,000 each, followed by Manchester and

Fig. 6.1

George Livesay, Grand Review at Hatfield House
before George III in 1800, *1803, oil on canvas.
A large-scale painting conveys the splendour of
massed British troops, a spectacle for the local
Hertfordshire inhabitants. The old gentleman
in the long coat was 102, so had lived in three
centuries at the time of painting. The artist and
his family are the group on the left. Hatfield
House, Hertfordshire.*

Liverpool. Dublin was the sixth most populous city in Europe, and Ireland held 9.4
per cent of the Union's population, though it was not part of Great Britain. The
older and wealthier a town was – notably Edinburgh – the more similar its dress
production and consumption patterns were to London's, though imported London
fashions trumped the prestige of local wares in all British metropolises. Elizabeth
Sanderson's work, for example, shows Edinburgh milliners travelling south to buy
fashionable goods from metropolitan wholesalers.[7]

Other research demonstrates fairly uniform clothing acquisition and making
strategies among the non-English urban gentry, as the men in figure 5.12 show.
The class-based systems of acquaintance and respectable society spread across the
country. British regional connections could cover large geographical areas. The
collective social networks of the county town of Chester 'encompassed London,
Dublin, Cork, Edinburgh, Nottingham and Oxford, plus seventy-eight other
towns. Even small towns in Lancashire and Cheshire showed surprisingly common
connection with London.'[8] *Where* genteel consumers were in Britain had less impact
upon their dress than *who* they were and *whom* they knew. Alexander Carse's
painting *The Arrival of the Country Relations* shows modish Edinburgh dress that
would have been suitable among the British gentry anywhere (see fig. 4.7), as does a
portrait of three stylish Welsh girls (fig. 6.2). The diaries of Agnes Porter, governess
at Penrice Castle in south Wales between 1799 and 1806, also show middling and

Fig. 6.2

Unknown artist, *Three Hughes Sisters*, 1815–19,
oil on canvas. Nothing about the sisters' dress
suggests their provincial origins, which is
intimated only by the less sophisticated painting
style. Their gowns are lovely examples of stylish
evening dress for the late 1810s, with fashionable
frills, diagonal buttons on the bodice and
roundly puffed sleeves. National Museum
of Wales, Cardiff.

elite Welsh people practising normative Regency dress habits. Irish writer Maria
Edgeworth's letters home transmitted London's social whirl to her relatives. Henry
Austen spent time in Ireland but the only Irish references in Austen's fiction relate
to Jane Fairfax's invitation there in *Emma*.

Austen's social peers towards the edges of Britain were inclined to think of their
taste and dress as the benchmark, determining clusters of respectable, provincial
urbanity among picturesque rural and regional clothing on a par with curious
foreign attire. By 1822 Edgeworth had to double-check how, by 'dress and person',
artist David Wilkie could mark someone out as Irish.[9] English (or Anglicised)
perceptions of regional dress combined curiosity about native customs with an
inherent superiority of status and aesthetic sense, yet reveal how traditional
clothing modified general Regency dress forms. Elizabeth Grant's family moved to
Scotland from England and her memoirs record the differences that were striking

to her. She wrote of Scottish people in church 'all in the tartan', but remarked that it was used idiosyncratically: by men 'as a wrap, the plaid as drapery, the kilt to match on some, blue trews on others, blue jackets on all', 'the women were plaided too', looking '*picturesquely* matronly in their high white caps' (emphasis added).

> The girls who could afford it had a Sabbath's day gown of [linsey-woolsey] and very bright colour . . . some had to be content with the best blue flannel petticoat and clean white jacket, their ordinary and most becoming dress; a few of these had neither shoes nor stockings, but they all wore the plaid, and they folded it round them very gracefully.[10]

Novelist Catherine Hutton, encountering a wedding near Llanberis in 1796, saw all the women wearing wool, and men the tall-crowned beaver hat that became an emblem of traditional Welsh dress.[11] At a Caernavon wedding, the town women wore such hats, with the same 'printed cotton gowns, white petticoats, and white stockings' the gentry favoured.[12] Wool-producing regions tended to wear woollen cloth – the same textiles that contributed so much to Britain's prosperity – and its prevalence, especially unshaped and draped, struck travellers as a manifestation of the landscape on bodies, but also as bodies being part of the landscape's visual attractions (fig. 6.3).

Tartan's distinctiveness best combined British regional identity, manufacturing prowess and Regency aesthetic nostalgia. Scotland's dual identities were organised around Lowland and Highland areas. The post-Culloden proscription of Highland dress was repealed in 1783, and thereafter tartan and its associations were promoted as a constructed picturesque symbol. Where Elizabeth Grant's family had worn pelisses and beaver bonnets as their outer wraps in England, their Scottish replacements were

Fig. 6.3

James Ward, *Scottish Peasant Women*, early nineteenth century, watercolour on paper. Ward's sketches of women working outside emphasises the woollen plaid of their dress, as well as the unfashionable lower waistlines. The regional use of unshaped lengths of cloth, shown here forming an apron and child carrier, registered as quaint, picturesque costume to gentry eyes. Yale Center for British Art, Paul Mellon Collection, New Haven, Conn.

'cloaks with hoods, made of tartan spun and dyed by Jenny Dairy, the red dress tartan of our clan, the sett originally belonging to the Grants'.[13] The idea of clans having particular tartans was part of yet another romanticisation and has no historical basis.[14] In 1795 only military regiments had fixed tartans, and throughout the Regency all tartan was of Lowland or English manufacture, wholly led by commercial demands. Emotive myths of ancient traditions were 'inevitably more appealing than the pattern books of a Lowland retailer or the fleshy thighs of a German king' – a reference to George IV's disastrous 1822 visit to Edinburgh, where he wore a kilt.[15] But by then, tartan blended Lowlands and Highlands into a perception of a single 'Scottish' national dress, while simultaneously spreading across British fashion (see fig. 4.21).

Sir John Sinclair, head of the Highland Society, designed tartans and promoted the new Scottish identity through dress. The multi-coloured and mixed tartans then in existence excited the disfavour of antiquarian John Pinkerton who believed that 'nothing can reconcile the tasteless regularity and vulgar glow of tartan to the eye of fashion'. He insisted Sinclair wear 'a single . . . and restrained tartan', 'of a colour proverbially mild, and without glare'.[16] Like Orientalism, the exotic cloth had to be filtered through modern English 'correct' taste to render it acceptable. Sinclair influenced later ensembles that display only single tartans, which are seen whenever tartan appears in women's fashion (fig. 6.4). Others emphasised men in tartan as part of the picturesque tradition, an appropriated antiquarianism comparable to classically inspired dress.[17] Authors like William Gilpin compared Highland dress with Roman fashions, pursuing the strong, martial masculinity line that Highland elites sought to establish through their regimental uniforms.[18] Tartans and plaids in Regency fashion helped to promote the imagery of a militarised Highlands, based on a local pastoralism, and to forge a connection between Scottish and British values by demonstrating 'an unerringly "British"' social hierarchy.[19]

British Textiles

Regency textiles were made of only four fibres: wool, silk, linen or hemp, and cotton; Britain produced cloth from them all, along with leather and fur manufacturing. The growing quality of textiles and their increasing market share were key markers of the industrial revolution that transformed Britain and the nation's dress, especially across the Midlands and northern areas. In Ireland, a large part of Dublin's industry was devoted to silk-ribbon manufacture. The country produced silk and union cloths for dress, exported around the world.[20] Irish linen, consumed across Britain, was so ubiquitous that it was simply called 'Irish'. Austen's purchase of Irish in England from the Overton Scotchman was an accidental minor act of union.[21]

Fig. 6.5

Wool was the greatest British fibre, traditional heart of its national textile identity, and backbone of its internationally acclaimed menswear. The nuances of various superfine, broadcloth and kerseymere cloths bespoke the quality of men's coats to observers, and wool was the foundation of English tailoring as much as of everyday Regency undergarments. Wool was Britain's glory (fig. 6.5), no matter how the Spanish merino industry tried to compete for the high-end market. It is a daunting task to summarise the breadth and variety of British wool fabrics. The woollen goods manufactured in every county of the nation, consisted, as the *General Dictionary of Commerce* informs us, of 'cloths of every description in regard to quality, size and colour; serges, kerseys, baizes, perpetuanas, fri[e]zes, swansdowns, flannels, blankets, stockings, &c. &c.'. Even Austen's nearest small town, Alton, manufactured 'druggets and serges, white yarn and a variety of worsted articles dyed in the wool of peculiar quality'.[22] Every area of the nation has its own equally specific specialities listed. Wool hides behind other textile words. 'Cloth', as in the 'Cloths for Pelisses' that the Austen family sought from Bedford House in London, always meant a woollen textile, as did 'stuff', any light woollen textile, often made of worsted, in which the Austen sisters had morning gowns.[23] The fibre's qualities suited all climates, so British wool was traded across the globe.

Cotton and linen manufactories were increasing their incursions into the Regency wool-producing landscape. In a Staffordshire tape manufactory in 1800, Mrs Lybbe Powys witnessed these flourishing technological changes in a noise of machinery 'hardly to be borne' and the transformation of 'tumbled' and 'dirty' tape coming off the machines into 'perfectly smooth and glossy' rolls. as bought at the haberdasher's.[24] Imported cotton had long been a desirable luxury, affecting general Western fashion from at least the 1770s, and Britain soon started competing for export markets with foreign products. By the 1810s cheaper English cotton fabrics started to achieve Indian quality and imitated their decorative weaving techniques of motifs and patterned borders (see chapter 7).

The new British cottons – muslins, cambrics and other weaves – were external fabrics, visible to others when worn. Looking at the material record reveals the specific effects on garments during the Regency of changes in textile manufacturing; and incidentals like humble tape can point to bigger changes. Non-decorative, functional use of cotton appears from the 1790s, when cotton shifts, corsets, cravats and nightwear began to slip into cupboards across the nation. Linings for breeches and pockets from the late 1790s onwards are often made of coarse cotton, as is the countryman's beloved fustian, or 'Bedford cord[uroy]'.[25] The drawstrings around the neck or waist of women's gowns, essential to many Regency styles, were cord, or the flat tape that Mrs Lybbe Powys saw. After the mid-1810s, these tiny functional elements of dress began to be made of cotton instead of linen, increasingly so in the gowns of the 1820s. Cotton's presence in the cheapest parts of clothing shows British manufacturers moving to cotton as the basic vegetable fibre. The growing amount of decorative cording – fine cord covered with fabric, now called 'piping' – at the edges of clothing from about 1815 is another sign of cotton products transforming fashion. It must have been affordable to be used so copiously (fig. 6.6).

The year 1815 recurs in the history of British dress. Many clothing trends changed around this time, and a demarcation between retail and wholesale selling began.[26] The material and the ideal in dress coalesced differently after the wars, especially in that there began to be more emphasis on decoration and trimmings. In 1800 a gown's appeal and value centred on the fabric. The primary labour value of ornamentation created by printing or embroidery was embedded into the textiles during manufacture, or was added after purchase through needlework. The use of applied haberdashery ornamentation soared after 1815. The main emphasis of hand labour thus generally moved towards manipulating a gown's fabric into fashionable shapes and trimmings, and adding a range of embellishments to finished gowns. The raw and finished textile goods available from Europe after the wars affected prices, and expanded quantity and choice in these dress components. Lowered production costs of items like silk ribbons made them newly affordable and promoted their abundant use. Comparing examples of gowns remade from older ones in 1800 and 1820 shows that, to be stylish, the later garment required more prolific additions, like contrasting satin and covered cording (figs 6.7, 6.8). Haberdashery spread across gowns in the form of bobbin and blonde laces; ribbons were wrought into geometries and rosettes; 'gum flowers' and leaves decorated hems stiffened with French wadding; cheaper, coarser satins were rolled into bias-cut 'rouleaux' tubes applied in patterns; and little belts were added. Gowns were sprinkled liberally with cartisanes – card shapes wrapped in silk floss (fig. 6.9). The cost of trimmings in extra spending, and fiddly sewing, obvious to contemporary observers, has been eclipsed to the modern eye by its aesthetic effects.

Nets were a triumph of Regency technical ingenuity. Muslins and gauzes had accustomed wearers to transparency in clothing since the 1780s. Then John Heathcoat's invention (1808) of a net-making machine that exactly reproduced the twist-net (diamond-shaped) ground of bobbin lace, in cotton or silk, was perfected in 1809. Others followed, with variations of net- and lace-making machines. Britain sought to retain its domination of the international market by restricting the export of new machinery and the loss by labour movement of its skilled operators.[27] After manufacture, the nets were further hand-spotted, embroidered and tamboured by thousands of women and children working around English towns, and in Ireland and the colonies. When Austen observed a Miss Debary 'netting herself a gown in worsteds' (coloured wools) in 1798, the lady reproduced in her handwork a nation-wide Regency passion for netted clothing (fig. 6.10), which sprang from industrial innovations particularly of the late 1790s.[28] Airy silk gauzes, tulles, bobbinet(te)s and other cheaper patent nets, of the kind Fanny Knight bought from Grafton House in 1813, appear frequently in the material record in the 1810s. By about 1818 it was possible to confect a gown of nearly nothing topped with a profusion of trimmings.

Fig. 6.6

Spencer, c.1815–20, silk satin. The ivory-coloured
cropped jacket, fastened at the centre front, is
adorned with tabs that echo uniform styles,
piping at the edges of the collar, cuffs and applied
decoration, and domed silver purl-wire baubles.
Private collection.

Fig. 6.7 Above Left

Evening gown, c.1820, remade from older blue silk brocaded in white (detail of the bodice). The extra trimmings, added to finish the gown, include cording along the seams, silk binding around the neck, and decorative strips of folded fabric up the sleeves and around the cuffs. Victoria and Albert Museum, London.

Fig. 6.8 Above Right

Evening gown, 1800–05, silk (detail of the bodice). The fall-front gown is made from late eighteenth-century silk, and may be an alteration of an existing gown. The bodice, which is lined with linen, has been trimmed with looped braid at the neckline and sleeves. Victoria and Albert Museum, London.

Fashion became modular, a diaphanous outer garment worn with a lining gown or 'slip' petticoats, meant to be seen, as two separate yet connected pieces. Clever rotation could change the appearance of an overdress (see figs 5.15, 6.11), and muslin lined with coloured silk appears more often in garments dated after c.1815.

Lace-lovers benefited from mechanised netting. Handmade lace was a phenomenally expensive status symbol (see fig. 5.13), but machine-made lace was very accessible. Eugenia Wynne described her wedding dress as 'patent-net', while her sister Betsey called it 'lace', showing consumers' perception of the equivalence between the fabrics.[29] After the invention in 1778 of a 'point net machine' producing hexagonal mesh lace, prices decreased rapidly. From around 1795, open-work fabrics and goods, including knitted lace stockings, were produced on adapted machines. Demand for lace spanned virtually the full spectrum of society, and could absorb the huge assortment of qualities and prices available. As early as 1789, caps for the poor contained cheap 'Hanover' lace.[30] Austen's letters reflect the prevalence of lace throughout Regency dress in her acquisition of lace veils (costing 16s. in black, apparently a good price), a cloak made of, or trimmed with, lace, and lace on caps for evening and morning carriage wear.[31] 'Blonde' – a particular sartorial favourite – was made of undyed creamy silk, similar to the 'very cheap' and 'very nice plaiting lace' used for edgings that Austen bought for 3s. 4d.[32] In Sanditon's consumer-minded terrain, 'straw hats and pendant lace' in deserted shops evoke the cheaper fashion goods available in the late 1810s.

In fiction, Austen uses a focus on lace – a textile defined by its empty spaces – to symbolise triviality. Mrs Allen (*NA*) discovers 'that the lace on Mrs Thorpe's pelisse was not half so handsome' as hers; Mrs Wallis in *Persuasion* is '"a mere pretty, silly, expensive, fashionable woman [with] nothing to report but of lace and finery"'.[33] Mrs Elton's dismissal of Emma's wedding ensemble as containing very little lace is attached to its status value.[34] A set of rose-point lace given by Edward Austen's adoptive mother, Mrs Catherine Knight (1752–1812), to his aunt Mrs Jane Leigh Perrot in October 1812 still survives in the family.[35] Machine lace emulated the classic styles of the handmade lace industry, centred in Buckinghamshire and Honiton in England, so after mechanisation makers changed their techniques slightly to alert the connoisseur to the real thing. Exquisite French and Low Countries lace was always highly prized too.

'Estimating her Lace' and deciding if it was 'real' or not must have been a pleasant (private) pastime for more women than Jane Austen.[36] After meeting the Bingley sisters, Mrs Bennet thinks she '"never in my life saw any thing more elegant than

Fig. 6.9

Evening gown, 1820, machine-made bobbin net (detail of the skirt). The gown is decorated with silk satin flowers, embroidered with chenille, and trimmed at the hem with silk satin binding. Small silk-wrapped cartisane crescent shapes are applied all over the skirt fabric. Victoria and Albert Museum, London.

Fig. 6.10

Open robe, 1797–98, cotton filet mesh. The cross-over bodice has inner panels, and the sleeves and skirt with a generous train are edged in yellow silk ribbon. The robe embodies the Regency passion for net clothing and accessories. Private collection.

their dresses"', but stops her sentence, '"I dare say the lace upon Mrs. Hurst's gown—"' before she vulgarly blurts out her valuation aloud.[37] The price of handmade lace could be staggering. Mrs Topham dropped £8 on a 'drap'd white Lace handkerchief' in 1814. It cost as much as an entire silk pelisse she bought later, and the expense continued in the 5s. 6d. she paid to have it washed.[38] Eliza de Feuillide reported that the actress Miss Farren ordered 'thirty muslin dresses each more beautiful than each other', for her marriage to the Earl of Derby, 'all trimmed with the most expensive Laces, Her Wedding Night Cap is the same as the Princess Royal's and costs Eighty Guineas'.[39] Lady Grenville marked out her wealth and position one morning when her 'Valenciennes lace – ruffs and scarf and cap' – cannot, by Maria Edgeworth's estimation, have cost 'less than 200 guineas.'[40] If this was her morning dress, what splendour must her evening attire have attained?

At the other end of the fashion spectrum, hat-making was a more solid and mundane mainstay of British industry. Even the poorest people wore headgear, to keep weather out and warmth in, adhering to an etiquette so deep it was never questioned. A man taking off his hat was a mark of respect to a lady or a superior, and signalled hierarchies of class and status. The Dashwoods' servant Robert displays the convention by removing his to speak to Lucy Steele in her carriage after her elopement (S&S).[41]

Thomas Mortimer summarised the breadth of hat manufacturing for his dictionary:

> The hats made from the fur of animals, consists [sic] of castors or beaver hats, the bodies whereof are composed of a mixture of hair, coney [rabbit] wool, hares' wool, and finally beaver intermixed with a small portion of floss silk: plated hats which are only thinly covered with beaver; cordies, a sort of coarse hats chiefly used by farmers and the middling classes;
> . . . prevailing [colours] are black, and drab, or drab with green undersides; women's and children's beaver and woollen hats or bonnets are of all colours, but principally of black, drab, white, green, purple, blue, brown . . . and fawn colour. There are many other kinds of hats . . . such as silken hats of every description and colour . . . these hats are water-proof, and for a time appear very beautiful, but a shower of rain spoils them, and being lined with a sort of cane, and consequently stiff and heavy, are decidedly inferior . . . to beaver hats.[42]

Historically, the best hats were made wholly of beaver fur imported from North America.[43] Declining beaver populations, import costs, and war with America and French-controlled Canada contributed to the rise in woollen imitations. Thus when Austen hoped Mrs Chamberlayne might sell her black beaver bonnet, the headwear's 'ugly' form condenses hundreds of years of British foreign trading.[44] Hats' durability made them a valuable second-hand commodity, as Austen intimates.

Lock's the hatter still occupies its original premises in St James's Street, off Piccadilly. Regency luminaries, such as the Duke of Wellington and Lord Nelson, ordered headwear there. Hats were as important to men as bonnets were to women as sites for fashionable expression – and more expensive. A highly fashionable chapeau-bras or opera hat with silk and gold tassels cost £3 8s.[45] These foldable articles were designed to be carried under the arm, an affectation equal to any feminine novelty (see fig. 5.18, top right).

Hats had a particular influence over 'the countenance and figure in regard to shape and method of wear', affecting 'both the appearances of age and stature, sobriety and rakishness in the individual'.[46] One of Emma Woodhouse's many misreadings is to interpret Mr Elton's air, and 'the very sitting' of his hat, as proof of his supposed love for Harriet Smith.[47] Many Regency observers thought the character of a hat could convey some of its wearer's character, just as gait leaves its imprint on shoes. Richard Dighton's series of prints 'City Figures' bears out such observations. Each man's hat and manner of wear is particular to him and evokes his identity as strongly as does his stance or figure (see fig. 5.8), allowing the modern viewer to experience something of the Regency manner of close dress observation. Hatter Robert Lloyd played on the congruencies between identity, individuals and national concerns in

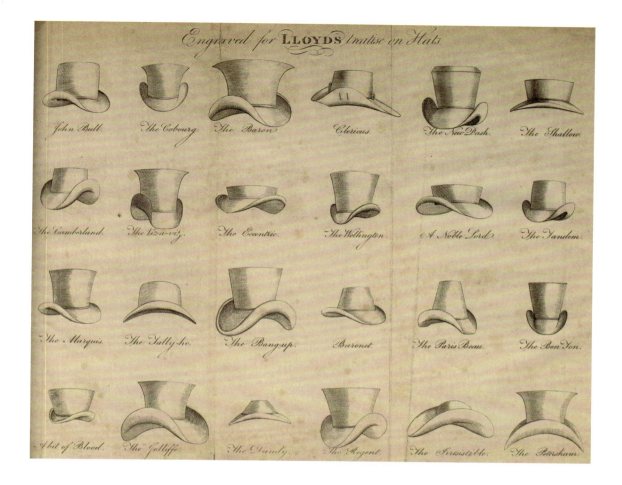

Engraved for **LLOYDS** treatise on Hats.

John Bull.   The Cobourg.   The Baron.   Clericus.   The New Dash.   The Shallow.

The Cumberland.   The Viz-a-viz.   The Eccentric.   The Wellington.   A Noble Lord.   The Tandem.

The Marquis.   The Tally-ho.   The Bang-up.   Baronet.   The Paris Beau.   The Bon Ton.

A bit of Blood.   The Jolliffe.   The Dandy.   The Regent.   The Irrisistible.   The Petersham.

Fig. 6.12

Unknown artist, twenty-four named designs for men's hats, from Robert Lloyd, *Lloyd's Treatise on Hats* (1819), engraving on paper. After the top hat emerged in the 1790s, high-crowned hats became established in menswear and remained current through the nineteenth century.

his *Treatise on Hats* (1819), where each hat's description matches the qualities of its name (fig. 6.12). The 'John Bull', like the British everyman character, is independent, has gravity and a bold but manly dignity, a 'combination of rare qualities not often met with'.[48] The 'Regent' is 'decidedly elegant' and on a large scale; the 'Cumberland' (that is, the Prince Regent's brother) 'will always have a number of admirers' but is 'much *shallower*' than the 'Regent'.[49] Since all the hats were Lloyd's invention, and his business success is documented, we can assume either that his customers enjoyed the joke, or that the pamphlet was a gimmick, intended more to raise awareness of his business than to advertise specific items of stock for sale.

Jane Austen's nation provided amply for the fabrication of the bonnets so closely associated with her in the popular imagination.[50] Straw hats and component parts for 'Village hats of straw or chip', and Grecian, round and poke bonnets were made in the south Midlands, centring on Luton, and north Essex. In 1800 Austen and her mother ordered new bonnets in Bath, both of 'white chip trimmed with white ribbon'; chip, made from fine lengths of wood shavings plaited together was, with straw, the commonest bonnet material. Austen described the final articles as 'very much like other peoples, & quite as smart', in the same comparative noticing she applied in 1807 to an acquaintance who wore 'one of the prettiest Straw Bonnets'

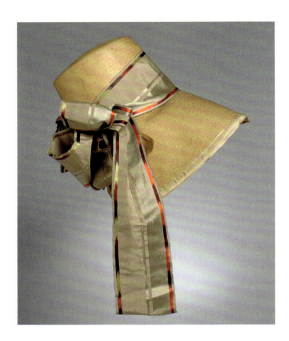

in Southampton.[51] Such headwear and Austen's 'pretty style of hat' of a year later, 'something like Eliza [de Feuillide]'s, only, instead of being all straw, half of it is narrow purple ribbon', probably had Midlands origins.[52] In 1811 a young lady in London made Austen a straw hat for a guinea, which she considered a reasonable price.[53] English woods offered willow or cane frameworks for bonnets. 'Willow sheets' or 'willow squares' were pieces of plaited willow sold ready prepared for hat making, for one of which Austen paid a shilling in 1814 in London.[54]

Desirable 'Leghorn' articles came from Livorno in Italy and were made of a finer plait than English straw sources could provide (fig. 6.13). Mrs Elton's style is conjured up by articles such as a 'Hat of Leghorn straw, in the Gypsey fashion, and tied under the chin with an India silk handkerchief'.[55] The fashion magazine's description dates from the turn of the century. During the subsequent conflicts, imports of genuine Leghorn dropped off, stimulating the industry undertaken by wives and children of agricultural labourers around Bedfordshire, Buckinghamshire and Hertfordshire (the Bennets live in the prime bonnet territory of the latter county).[56] Despite many attempts to find a grass to match Leghorn's pliable delicacy, the Italian product regained its market share after trade resumed in the 1810s.

The Military

Apart from the brief Peace of Amiens (March 1802 – May 1803), Britain was at war with France from 1793 to 1814, followed by Napoleon's Hundred Days, and then the final victory over him at Waterloo on 18 June 1815 – nearly half Austen's lifetime. Military clothing (which has been studied in greater detail than any other area of Regency dress) was one of the strongest influences on civilian style.[57] Fashion absorbed the insignia of war, and martial male bodies dotted the British sartorial panorama. Britain's military and its commercial and fighting sea presence – the army, merchant seamen and the navy – equalled the Welsh population (540,000). A continual presence of militias and regiments in local towns, backed up by prints delineating the particularities of their uniform, made Regency consumers very aware of military style.[58] The creation of the British 'redcoat' soldier was something of a branding exercise, 'a way of uniting the ideals of patriotism with the monarch', especially George III, himself often painted in a red military coat.[59] The red coat became 'a potent symbol of the British army and hence by implication Britain itself'.[60] Handsome Henry Austen joined the Oxfordshire militia in 1793, newly embodied to fight in the French Revolutionary wars, though it never saw action. He became captain, and served until the militia was disbanded in 1800. His service coincides with the period during which Austen drafted *First Impressions* (c.1796–7), which became *Pride and Prejudice*, and her favourite brother's martial experience fed into her depictions of militia life and characters.

The Regency world was full of soldiers. The visual impact of 'lobsters' (Thomas Lobster was the counterpart of nautical Jack Tar) among the ranks of pale muslin-draped ladies and sombre gentlemen packed a punch (fig. 6.14).[61] Austen peppers her novels with red coats. Clothes could maketh the man, as Mrs Bennet (*P&P*) sighs: '"I remember the time when I liked a red coat myself very well – and, indeed, so I do still at my heart; . . . I thought Colonel Forster looked very becoming the other night at Sir William's in his regimentals."'[62] Lydia, the daughter who is most like her, indulges in reveries of Brighton's delights, 'the glories of the camp', 'the young and the gay, and dazzling with scarlet', a scene in which Lydia sees herself attracting tens and scores of uniformed men.[63] Wags called this bewitchment 'scarlet fever'.[64]

Looking at soldiers is a rare example of Regency women frankly appraising the physique of the opposite sex. The younger Bennet girls watch the militiamen in the street; we find the same glamorised bodies of healthy young men in *The Watsons*, stationed in provincial towns and waiting for action but with not much to do, surrounding local girls at balls. Their clothing became a substitute for the man himself, conveying the 'heroism, danger, bustle, fashion' of soldiers.[65] The 'glamour' (a word popularised by Sir Walter Scott) covered styles such as the regulation regimental pigtails that soldiers wore long after they had fallen out of fashion.[66] Betsey Wynne's dinner with a general who wore 'his hair powdered with a queue' in 1801 suggests that General Tilney (*NA*) would wear such a style, though perhaps his son Captain Frederick Tilney is more modern.[67]

Henry Austen bought his commission, as Mr Darcy buys Wickham's (*P&P*). Officers were then expected to provide their own uniforms, produced by their tailor to regulation style.[68] Travellers exploring the Waterloo battlefield in 1816 found 'an English officer's cocked hat, much injured apparently by a cannon shot, with its oilskin rotting away, and showing by its texture, shape, and quality that it had been manufactured by a fashionable hatter, and most probably graced the wearer's head in Bond Street and St. James's'.[69] Even within uniformed ranks, individual taste and income were immediately apparent. 'The regimentals of an ensign' displayed a man's financial attractions along with his physical charms.[70]

George Purefoy Jervoise became a captain in the North Hampshire militia in 1794, and was promoted to lieutenant-colonel in 1798 and colonel in 1800, serving until 1811. His uniform bill for 1805 reveals the full cost of outfitting a commission. A pair of leather breeches: £3 13*s.* 6*d.* A 'Superfine Scarlet Cloth Regt'l Coat . . . Lin'd with White Sattinett Black Genoa Velvet Cuffs and Collar', £5 5*s.*, the velvet an extra £1 4*s.* The forty-two '2 Breast Sollid Gilt' buttons added 19*s.* 9*d.* – the cost of one of his servant's livery ensembles – to the price of one coat, for which he paid £7 8*s.* 9*d.* in total. Next comes 'A pair Very Rich gild Reg'l Epauletts' for £7, skirt ornaments for 6*s.* 6*d.*, and a 'Rich Army Sword Knot', 14*s.* The ensemble was topped off by a cocked hat and cockade (9*s.* 6*d.*). If we add £2 2*s.* for London-made boots, Purefoy

Jervoise paid £19 14s. 5d. for the uniform (over one and half times a housemaid's yearly wage), before adding £3 5s. 8d. for 8¾ yards of saddle-cloth lace.[71] As the *London Magazine* asked:

> What would the pomp, pride, circumstance of glorious war, nay, the very army itself be, but for the tailor. It is not the man, but his coat, that fights; the courage lies in the uniform; it is the courage of the 42d suits of clothes; and hence also the burning valour of the 10th dragoons, the valour of its sabretashes and gilded boots . . . Strip the army, and what is an army ? – Nothing. It is the tailor who makes armies and conquers victory.[72]

Army uniform was a permissible place for men to express interest in clothes and their appearance without having their masculinity questioned. Even so, dandy officers attracted satire, as could the trappings of display. The Royal Lancers were roasted for their 'manly limbs concealed beneath a bale of crimson cloth and a web of gold lace [braid]. The body compressed in stays, reminds you of a funnel, and its covering of a mad-house strait jacket bedaubed with embroidery and filigree fancies.'[73] When Edward Ferrars (*S&S*) dismisses the army as 'a great deal too smart' for him, the reference is to his potential brother officers, drawn from the non-inheriting sons of the gentry or merchants with money, who often merged society and soldiery to be '"dashing and expensive"', as Ferrars puts it.[74] It was the prospect of constant, good society (read: 'drinking', 'gambling' and 'womanising') that first tempted Wickham (*P&P*) to join the militia. Henry Crawford (*MP*), playing a young soldier in *Lovers' Vows*, would have been wearing regimental costume, thus increasing the desirability of his person, and contrasting his play-acting for pleasure with the men labouring in real theatres of war simultaneously. He merely 'seems', like a dandy; others truly acted.[75]

Besides its decorative effects, army uniform was a tool of war, leading to tensions between ceremonial convention and effective functionality. On one hand, military uniforms 'were used as totemic objects, inculcating pride, courage, self-esteem and subordination. As a leading writer on the organization of infantry units, wrote, "once a soldier can be brought to take a delight in his dress, it will be easy to mould him to whatever else may be desired".[76] On the other, doctors criticised the physical constraint of regimentals, expressing concern for their sex regarding the affectation 'of what is called military smartness', which 'seems to have converted their whole apparel into a system of bandages'.[77] Advice for soldiers themselves also warned about uniformed constriction:

> The stiff bandage that surrounds the neck, and the tight ligatures that constrain the articulations of the loins and of the knees, should if possible be avoided. Freedom of respiration is no doubt also impeded by the pressure of the belts crossing upon the chest; and in hot weather the soldier's flesh is often excoriated by them.[78]

The operational suitability of military uniforms was of less concern to domestic watchers than to men on campaign, whose clothing could enhance or impede their

fighting function.[79] 'Woollen clothing will be found the best defence against the cold, . . . or the bad consequences of encamping in damp situations,' Dr Blair advised, recommending 'Flannel drawers and under waistcoats'.[80] Fighting veterans agreed; even Napoleon wore flannel underwear. The Duke of Clarence told his newly martial son that in the event of a sudden mobilisation, 'leave all finery: boots and flannel are the best and most useful things'.[81] Colonel Brandon's flannel waistcoat represents a practical military man fighting in adverse conditions and his loyal service to the crown, not the decrepitude that Marianne Dashwood carelessly infers (*S&S*).[82]

Military Fashion

The erotic appeal of uniforms was not lost on civilian men. 'During the war we had military Exquisites ad infinitum. Some of our young Ladies bestowed so decided a preference on these merveilleux that they would not dance with a man without mustachios, nor walk with one unless he had fixed spurs', which destroyed fragile gown fabrics. The appeal that military dress lent a man caused linen drapers and 'other counterfeits of the gentleman' to sport 'cossacks and brass spurs in war-time with impunity'.[83] However, men's general fashion absorbed permanent soldierly

Fig. 6.15

James Ward, *Cossack Gregory Yelloserf*, July 1814, graphite and watercolour on paper. Ward drew the Russian soldier from life at King Street Barracks, clearly depicting the gathered trousers that inspired the 'Cossack' style that swept through men's fashion after the troops visited London. Yale Center for British Art, Paul Mellon Collection, New Haven, Conn.

details. The military armoured gorget protecting the throat is thought to be the origin of the stock that aided men's quest for collar height. Unlike soft cravats, stocks could be a neckpiece stiffened with buckram or whalebone, covered in a fine fabric, often black or white satin, and buckled at the back. George IV particularly popularised stocks after 1822, as they held in his abundant neck.

After a genuine Cossack troop visited London with the Russian emperor in 1814, their legwear inspired 'Cossacks' (fig. 6.15), a style of wide, loose trouser, of 'rude shapelessness', as a tailor complained, pleated into a waistband at the top and drawn round the bottom with a 'ribband'.[84] Body-hugging pantaloons, ankle to three-quarter length, came from military into common use, ornamented with symmetrical gold braiding around the frontfall. They were made of cotton or wool and extended 2 or 3 inches (c.5–8 cm) up under the waistcoat. George Purefoy Jervoise had a 'pair of Drab Colour Worsted Stocking [knitted fabric] Pantaloons with covered buttons' in 1802.[85] Cream and pale colours echoed classical statuary most effectively (fig. 6.16), though by the 1810s black pantaloons in kerseymere or silk jersey were acceptable full dress. The skin-tight garments showed off muscled soldierly legs, and left no doubts as to the wearer's masculinity.

Close pantaloons slipped easily into boots, the new fashion footwear of the late eighteenth century (see chapter 4), and the two formed a harmonious combination, another factor in the widespread adoption of both. The English esquire became an officer during wartime, and his riding-boots accompanied him, acquiring martial allure.

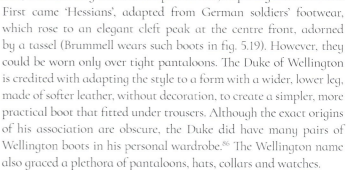

First came 'Hessians', adapted from German soldiers' footwear, which rose to an elegant cleft peak at the centre front, adorned by a tassel (Brummell wears such boots in fig. 5.19). However, they could be worn only over tight pantaloons. The Duke of Wellington is credited with adapting the style to a form with a wider, lower leg, made of softer leather, without decoration, to create a simpler, more practical boot that fitted under trousers. Although the exact origins of his association are obscure, the Duke did have many pairs of Wellington boots in his personal wardrobe.[86] The Wellington name also graced a plethora of pantaloons, hats, collars and watches.

If military dress effected deep change in Regency men's clothing, Hussar this, Janissary that, and Wellington the other flickered through women's dress for twenty-five years (fig. 6.17). Military styles, including Highland tartans, came to be reflected in women's fashion from the 1790s, as upper-class ladies embraced the social associations of uniforms, emulating husbands, supporting relatives and whipping up novelties out of patriotic fervour. Women connected with a regiment might attend formal events in clothing that alluded to regimental colours and mascots. Soon after Eliza de Feuillide married her cousin Henry Austen in 1797 she joked that she would 'bespeak [her] Regimentals without delay'.[87]

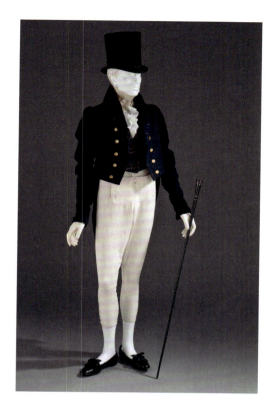

Fig. 6.16

Man's pantaloons, 1820s, silk crepe, made in Scotland. The slightly stretchy crepe ('crape') weave allowed these three-quarter-length pantaloons to cling tightly to the wearer's legs, outlining their form. Los Angeles County Museum of Art.

Foreign, topical names helped to sell the latest fashions. Braid, cords, tassels and frogging mimicked uniform decorations on spencers, pelisses, hats, redingotes and anything else that could be decorated. The pelisse itself had a military origin. British light dragoon regiments had started adopting hussar elements in the 1790s. Four converted fully by 1807 and their spectacular attire, from the cavalry's Hungarian beginnings, exploded into everyday dress. Theirs was the original pelisse – a fur-lined jacket worn over one shoulder like a cape, fastened with a cord, and festooned with gilt braids and buttons. Furred shakos sat atop heads, and luxurious moustaches adorned faces above necks that emerged from braided dolmans (tunics) (fig. 6.18). How could women resist? Elizabeth Grant maintained that she set an Edinburgh fashion after walking out in 1815 'like a hussar', wearing 'a pelisse trimmed with fur and braided like the coat of a staff-officer, boots to match, and a fur cap set on one side, and kept on the head by means of a cord with long tassels'.[88] The silk cord on Austen's pelisse is a sedate nod to the trend, and the piping popular from the 1810s appeared first on uniforms.

Grant's comments on post-peace fashions are revealing. Of 1816, she wrote:

We were inundated this whole winter with a deluge of an ugly colour called Waterloo blue, copied from the dye used in Flanders for the calico of which the peasantry made their smock-frocks or blouses. Everything new was 'Waterloo', not unreasonably as it had been such . . . a victory after so many years of exhausting suffering; and as a surname for hats, coats, trousers, instruments, furniture, it was very well – a fair way of trying to perpetuate tranquility; but to deluge us with that vile indigo, so unbecoming . . . ! It was really a punishment; none of us were sufficiently patriotic to deform ourselves by wearing it.[89]

The long conflicts further influenced clothing by causing shortages in leather, used by large-scale boot production, and wool and linen required to outfit military and naval bodies.[90]

British clothing adopted many notions of foreign garments through war reportage.[91] 'By this period, expressing visual fantasy *in dress* was an entirely female privilege', argues Anne Hollander, referring to how women revamped and incorporated a diversity of outside influences into fashionable confections.[92] I contend that military conventions in male dress were equally expressive of romantic fantasies. The ideas were merely subtler in expression. The campaigning world infiltrated dress in adjectives preceding every kind of novel component of fashion, from cap to shoe ribbon: 'Spanish', 'Flemish', 'Vittoria', 'Pyrenean', 'Tyrolese', 'Polish', 'Hungarian', 'Russian', 'Janissary', 'Algerian'. A quick scan of fashionable Regency textile colours

reveal similar influences: the classical world tinted shades called Apollo (1823), Trocadero (1824), and Pomona (1811), Roman goddess of flowers. Fascination with royalty and prominent aristocrats generated hues named Clarence (1811), Princess Elizabeth, Esterhazy (1822) and Marie Louise (1812). Military campaigns introduced fads for Egyptian Brown (1809) and Russian Flame (1811); wistful history for Dust of Ruins (1822) and Terre d'Egypte (1824); and the wider world for Mexican Blue (1817) and Naccarat (1800).[93] War, tourism, exploration and colonisation were entangled in ostentatiously exotic dress influences. Campaigns in Prussia, Poland and Russia saw an influx of fur into women's dress.

The Egyptian engagements (1798–1801) helped fuel Regency women's passion for turbans, from cap size to imposing widths (fig. 6.19). The style certainly appealed to older women, such as Mrs Topham, who, during her sixties, when her head was being shaved regularly, bought at least six turbans, in gauze, white satin and silk, and one with a tassel. Perhaps the ease of covering less than youthful locks increased their popularity, when wigs alone could shift easily out of place. Elizabeth Grant recalled her great-aunts wearing 'dress turbans' in 1808, made of rolls of muslin folded round a catgut headpiece and 'festooned with large loops of large beads ending in bead tassels after the most approved prints of Tippoo Sahib', a directly East Indian inspiration.[94] Her mother had brought the 'extremely beautiful as well as fashionable' headgear from London. Younger women adopted turbans freely: appearance-obsessed Isabella Thorpe writes to Catherine Morland (*NA*) about a rival, who 'had tried to put on a turban like mine, as I wore it the week before at the concert'.[95] The style suited the draped, windswept fashions of the late 1790s and continued to evolve through the Regency.

Of course, some commentators lamented the drawing of fashions from every popular occurrence: '[The T]reaty [of the Dardanelles] with the Sublime Porte [the government of the Ottoman Empire] will doubtless introduce amongst our spring fashions a profusion of Turkish turbans, Janizary jackets, mosque slippers and a thousand similar whimsicalities; all of which . . . must speedily give way to Russian

cloaks, hussar caps, Cossack mantles, Danish robes, &c.'[96] At Brighton in October
1810 could be seen the 'Arabian coat, Arcadian mantle, Persian spencer, and Grecian
scarf, with French cloaks and tippets'. Hidden in these names is Britain's complicated
relationship with Europe, and with itself as a nation, mobilising outwards through
war to create new inward visions of itself, all expressed through dress.

The Continent

Fashion histories have sometimes stressed a cessation of the trade in fashionable
styles and information on dress during the belligerent period between Britain and the
Continent. But this idea needs reconsideration. Leisure travel and official trade were
prohibited during the Napoleonic Wars, and letters from civilians, such as Fanny
Burney, caught in France by sudden decrees, show their desperation at being marooned
on the 'wrong' side of the Channel. Nevertheless, throughout the martial era, fashion
goods and information passed regularly to Britain via thriving black markets (see
chapter 7) and trade routes through whichever countries were currently allies, despite

an escalating series of reciprocal embargoes and blockades. Napoleon's economic Continental System attempted to block British textile imports to Europe and vice versa, while Britain similarly strove to undermine French commerce. Some trades actually profited by filling the gap for European products in British and foreign markets. For example, the lack of continental ribbons caused a boom in Coventry in 1812–15, when manufacturers responded to the fashion for novelty ribbons like the 'black sattin ribbon with a proper perl [purl] edge' that Austen tried to make a 'kind of Rose' with.[97]

An alternative view to isolated Britain is that the mobilisation of thousands of men around the Continent created new opportunities for travel, and increased British women's access to desirable fashion goods. Sweethearts and husbands, brothers and sons, on leave and at a loose end in foreign cities, became martial tourists and shopped for their womenfolk at home. They could take these collateral spoils home as presents or send them back, in a different mode of fashion dissemination. Charles St George, for example, sent his mother, Irish writer and poet Melesina Trench (1768–1827) 'The most beautiful, and the most superb Brussels veil – the prettiest, the best chosen, the newest – in short, a present in the most excellent taste'; it was sent direct and was therefore cheaper than any official import.[98] Their letters discuss the comparative cheapness of continental goods and set up lively negotiations for proxy shopping while Charles was on official business. Historians have started considering the experience of martial young men abroad and how their tours of duty echoed the Grand Tours that were previously the privilege of the wealthy.[99]

William Price (*MP*) is, similarly, a source of international fashion dissemination. He notices Fanny's 'head' – either hairstyle or ornament – and says:

> 'Do you know, I begin to like that queer fashion already, though when I first heard of such things being done in England, I could not believe it; and when Mrs. Brown, and the other women at the Commissioner's at Gibraltar, appeared in the same trim, I thought they were mad; but Fanny can reconcile me to anything.'[100]

The young midshipman, who had been active in the Mediterranean Station twice over the previous seven years (the novel's chronological setting is debated) and often on shore, had *heard* of fashions from England, perhaps from Fanny, and *observed* how women in the British outpost were keeping up with their domestic compatriots. As *Mansfield Park* was finished before the 1814 peace, the incident shows one of the ways in which fashion information travelled between people during the conflicts, through seeing and writing – a pattern that is perhaps based on Austen's own fraternal correspondence. Colonel Brandon's sister at Avignon can send for him, before 1811, knowing his military position will allow him to get to France (*S&S*).[101]

As part of the general increase in Regency printed media, and alongside books on figures and costumes, the continental travel memoir became a popular genre.

Together with material gifts, print culture transmitted information about the manners, customs and costumes of continental nations to the reading British. The flood of costume books with elucidating titles such as *Sketches of the Country, Character, and Costume, in Portugal and Spain, Made during the Campaign, and on the Route of the British Army, in 1808 and 1809* provided armchair experiences for domestic readers, and inspiration to fashion makers.[102] Instead of isolating those left at home, war sparked new interest in clothing cultures outside the isles. British eyes absorbed details of the dress of peoples very different from themselves, with a new attention

to accuracy, though always tempered with a picturesque air (fig. 6.20). Britain's expanding spaces for conflict, trade and colonisation allowed the country to nourish a national self-image with fresh vision, against new revelations of the foreign and exotic, creating styles from this jumble of sources that other countries nonetheless identified as 'English'.[103]

The French

The battle between London and Paris over fashion lasted much longer than the Napoleonic conflicts. Paris was the bastion of elegance, yet Anglomania across the Continent had influenced male dress for many decades. Many authors have covered French style, and the two nations' long, ambivalent engagements in the fashion arena before the Regency, so this section focuses on how the British perceived, consumed, competed with and desired French fashions.[104] The French view of the English, in turn, helps to characterise national taste. In the popular imagination, the English adopted simplicity and modesty (Plain! Dull! said the French); the French ostentation and indecency (Non! This is true style, they riposted). Aileen Ribeiro characterises the conflicting influences as 'uniformity' and 'individualism', arising from England's greater social mobility and less court-centred society.[105] The schism between the countries' Anglican and Catholic faiths further reinforced their style contrasts.

Austen's first cousin Eliza had extensive French elite connections from her first marriage to the Comte Jean-François Capot de Feuillide (1750–1794), who was guillotined in 1794 for monarchist loyalty, leaving Eliza widowed in London with first-hand knowledge of the Revolution's Terror. James Austen had visited the Comte de Feuillide before the Revolution, and Edward Knight travelled the Continent on the Grand Tour (1786–90). The English flocked to France during the Peace of Amiens (1802–3), during which Eliza returned with her second husband, Henry Austen. While Henry left in good time, family tradition says that Eliza narrowly escaped the sudden detainment of English citizens after hostilities broke out again only thanks to her perfect French. Napoleon's first defeat reopened Paris between April 1814 and March 1815, and normal traffic resumed in July 1815 after his final vanquishing at Waterloo in mid-June. The Austens' neighbour Christopher-Edward Lefroy toured France in August 1816, and after he visited the family on his way back, Austen wrote that she was pleased to find him 'thinking of the French as one could wish – disappointed in everything'.[106] Tempting as it is to imagine that he distributed Parisian fashion trifles, no continental consumption appears in Austen's letters.

Despite the official embargoes, details of the Parisian fashion scene appeared in English publications some months or a year after their debut in popular magazines such as *Le Journal des Dames et des Modes* (published every five days, 1797–1803) and its successor *Costume Parisien*.[107] London engravers copied and adapted Parisian fashion plates for local distribution, and anonymous correspondents provided textual reportage every month throughout the wars. Despite the flow of visual and written information, it was not until people went, saw for themselves, and returned wearing or carrying styles that British fashion changed significantly, a sequence that reinforces the importance of first-hand fashion viewing. After Napoleon's abdication in 1814, gowns showed 'a more marked *change* than one has lately seen', as Austen noticed. The 'enormous bonnets', long sleeves, 'Waists short, and as far as I have been able to judge, the Bosom covered', as well as the appearance of flounces 'at Mrs Latouche's, where dress is a good deal attended to', match the elements of French style that artists, travellers and correspondents remarked upon.[108]

Proxy shopping helped the acquisition of bespoke French goods for those who could not be fitted *in situ*. Maria Edgeworth sent a parcel to her stepmother in Ireland containing a black velvet gown and spencer 'made by the very best dressmaker in Paris by a pattern body' taken from an existing garment the previous summer. The novelist had a matching gown. She assures her relation that 'the connoisseurs . . . pronounce them to be the handsomest gowns . . . brought from France. Madame Gautier said she was determined to send me the best specimen of Parisian manufacture and Parisian taste.'[109]

Each nation had definite opinions about the other's dress. For the English, French fashion was daring, immodest, revealing and overly decorated. The typical 'Frenchwoman' was dark-haired and -skinned, petite and vivacious, affecting gold earrings. Her male counterpart was tall, also dark, and was presented as simpering, insincere, deceptively charming, and overdressed. Social anxiety about Frenchmen maps closely onto dandies – too concerned with clothes to enact a trustworthy masculinity. Scholars have studied the correspondence between Frank Churchill in *Emma* and French deceptiveness, contrasting this with Mr Knightley's explicitly English stability. The Crawford siblings (*MP*) are similarly fascinating and disruptive foreign characters. The character of Henry Crawford was inspired by the short, dark, fiery Irish actor Edmund Kean.[110] A number of scholars have discussed Mary's possible origins in Austen's extremely pretty, pleasure-loving and flirtatious cousin Eliza.[111] I add that Austen's presentation of Mary Crawford's appearance aligns closely with satirical and popular depictions of Frenchwomen, having a 'lively dark eye, clear brown complexion, and general prettiness' – petite, coquettish and brilliant, in contrast to the quintessentially English, less dynamic 'tall, full formed, and fair' Bertram sisters.[112] Olive skin often features as 'French' against the pink-and-white complexioned English.

Mary Crawford contends that '"If you can persuade Henry to marry, you must have the address of a Frenchwoman. All that English abilities can do has been tried already,"' a belief in the French superiority of seeming that Fanny Price again undermines by genuinely attracting Mary's dandiacal brother with her quiet, steady character.[113] The situation again sounds much like that of cousin Eliza, an Englishwoman with the address of a Frenchwoman, who married another Henry, Austen's brother. 'Address' is hard to quantify – a stylish French *je ne sais quoi*;

Fig. 6.21 Above Left

Horace Vernet and Georges Gatine, 'Merveilleuse no. 8', from *Incroyables et merveilleuses* (1814). A set of thirty-three coloured engravings depicting the height of French fashion. The high bonnet crown contrasts with English fashion at the same time, and French hems were a little shorter than the English, revealing the ankle. Victoria and Albert Museum, London.

Fig. 6.22 Above Right

Horace Vernet and Georges Gatine, 'Merveilleuse no. 21. Chapeau à l'Anglaise. Spencer à l'Anglaise', from *Incroyables et merveilleuses* (1814). The 'Anglaise' style is softer and more countrified than the French, expressed through a poke bonnet, a lower-waisted gown and half-boots. Victoria and Albert Museum, London.

'"a certain something in her air and manner of walking, the tone of her voice, her address and expressions"', which Caroline Bingley feels to be so essential to elegance (*P&P*).[114]

The stance and manner of fashion-plate figures may have been part of the attitude Frenchwomen tried to convey, along with dress details. 'French style' was evident to Regency audiences, but is harder to reconstruct for the modern eye. Small details created the bigger picture: an embroidered shirt, the shape of a shoe front, the height of a bonnet. The engravings in figures 6.21 and 6.22 show, respectively, French high fashion, and the French take on English fashion. To the alert Regency viewer, the difference was clear. Frenchwomen wore bonnets with higher brims and their waist started directly under the bust (which may account for the fluctuating position of the waistline in British dress from c.1812 to 1819, when it started to drop again towards the natural). French hems started broadening earlier than English ones, and were a little shorter, revealing the ankles.

Fanny's gaining Edmund's affections is echoed in declarations, along similar lines, that 'The spirit of British fashion has triumphed over the French, and has produced this advantageous change, that neatness and cleanliness in dress are now preferred to dirty pomp, and the quality and fineness of stuffs to tawdry edging, lace, and decorations.'[115] *Mansfield Park* establishes the triumph of Fanny's neat, clean morals over Mary's tawdry, suspiciously foreign ones, in a congruence of soul and body so often thought to be linked in Regency dress. As Edward Stanley observed of Paris, 'The people are like the Town, and the Town is like a Frenchman's Chemise, a magnificent frill with fine lace and Embroidery, but the rest ragged.'[116] British dress and British bodies were considered plain but dependable stuff.

French and English Taste

Fashion searched for novelty and fresh change, yet contained ambivalence – between desire and disapprobation – over the consumption of Parisian style. Women returning from France flaunted their style *à la Française* from head to toe. Edward Knight took his daughter Fanny on her first trip to Paris in May 1817, and she surely must have enriched her wardrobe with a French article or two. As English male style was considered superior to continental, men would only sparingly add foreign items to set off the Bond Street ensemble. How to acquire taste but retain principles seems to have been at the heart of the problem. Paris exaggerated, and exaggeration was vulgarity. The implication is that French quality goods tempered by English restraint would create the best outcome. Thomas and Co. in London, for example, advertised 'the most extensive, elegant and novel stock' of summer fashions to magazine readers, combining 'in a peculiar degree of style, the English with the French taste'.[117]

By the 1810s, the English tended to think Frenchwomen overdressed and over-rouged – they daubed the colour on 'from the bottom of the side of the face up to the very eye . . . all over the temples'.[118] The excessiveness of their dress in the matter of proportion, volume and quantity of trimming attracted comment, but was still ripe for emulation. The Miss Smiths, who had 'all lately been at Paris' and had 'fine remains of their Parisian toilettes' contrasted, to Maria Edgeworth's fond eye, with her half-sisters, who 'looked as well dressed as they did . . . the materials and make better and no flowers or frippery'.[119] The Miss Smiths' attire was perhaps like that of an English girl dressed out by her French governess (satirised in fig. 6.23). However, the author acknowledged the successful translation of French style in the case of Lady (Louisa) Georgiana Bathurst, who

> has been in Paris – speaks French well and *enough* French air and French flowers – not too much. The simplicity of [her] dress indeed struck us particularly after all the turmoil the Bath ladies and Bath Dress-makers make in vain about this business – plain French white silk frocks with a plain short sleeve like Fannys and plaited blond round the neck and a blond flounce and thats all.[120]

English taste sought moderation in all things. The British could demonstrate superior aesthetic judgement by their discriminating application – not slavish adoption – of foreign taste according to British lights.

Fig. 6.23

George Cruikshank, *Le Retour de Paris or, the Neice presented to her Relatives by her French Governess*, 1819, etching on paper. Cruikshank's rendition of French fashion lampoons the extravagant bonnets, raised hemlines, numerous flounces, decorative collars and abundant floral embellishment that Englishwomen regarded as excessive. Wellcome Collection, London.

The French were repeatedly accused of ditching their stays and petticoats, especially by visitors in 1802–3, when classical simplicity was at a height more enthusiastically adopted in France than in England. Caricaturists and satirists had a field day showing Englishwomen similarly dishabille; but the new nudity was 'limited to the more raffish members of the demi-monde', as Fanny Burney found.[121] The contrast of semi-transparent muslins with older opaque silks fuelled the cries of nakedness.[122] It is important to note that French adopters of naked style often 'found themselves so rudely treated whenever they appeared, by the sovereign multitude' that they changed their dress, or wore it in private – which hardly suggests a universal fashion.[123] Traveller Edward Stanley riffed on the naked French theme when he wrote to his family: 'As I cannot find my Cloaths am sitting in a Dress à la Mode d'une Dame Française', meaning his shirt or nightshirt.[124] Perhaps male and female observers perceived 'nudity' in French dress differently.

There is a wealth of 'French' style information in Maria Edgeworth's description of her sister Harriet's costume for a family masquerade. Although the intention was to dress her as 'a pert travelled young lady just returned from Paris at the height of the fashion', her 'ease of motion unencumbered by her finery' meant that instead of 'looking like a vulgar fine lady . . . she looked like a real fine lady overdressed by some mistake' – another perceived triumph of British natural grace. Frenchness was expressed in a figure 'crowned with feathers of all colors to an amazing height with a gold diadem and profusion of artificial flowers – a nosegay of vast size – rose colored gauze dress with a border of roses – scarlet sash and a waist of peaked length – And ringlets of dark hair and dark eyebrows.'[125] The size of Frenchwomen's hats astonished English visitors. Although the tall-crowned Oldenburg bonnet was popular across England (fig. 6.23), in Paris at the same time it was 'broader and more loaded with flowers, bunches, bows, plumes than any we saw in London, and would you believe it I am already not merely getting reconciled but absolutely an admirer of them', wrote Edward Stanley, incidentally showing how exposure to new

Dress in the Age of Jane Austen

fashions helped to establish their novelty as normal.[126] Four days later, however, he sounds less convinced: 'how you would stare [at] persons almost extinguished in their enormous casques of straw and flowers. I have seen several bearing, in addition to other ornaments, a bunch of 5 or 6 lilies as large as life.'[127]

Real flowers were 'nature's ornament', conjuring up fashionable Arcadian pastoral simplicity. Artificial flora and fruit recur as features of French dress, again expressing conceptual anxieties around natural versus imitation. After the Stanleys' visit to France in 1816, Mrs Stanley was 'dressing herself à la Française' thanks to the purchase of 'a large box of flowers'.[128] To wear fake flowers tastefully again required a sense of harmony achieved through English moderation. As *The Duties of a Lady's Maid* expressed it in 1825, imitations 'will always be more or less fashionable as ornaments of dress; though nothing can be in worse taste than a profusion of them, particularly when glaring and high coloured',[129] a view of French dress endorsed by commentators in the *Lady's Monthly Museum* and other fashion journalists. Other nature-inspired decorations embellished fashion. Austen wrote home fifteen years earlier of the 'Flowers . . . very much worn' in Bath, but how 'fruit is still more the thing. Elizabeth has a bunch of strawberries, and I have seen grapes, cherries, plums, and apricots.'[130] She declined to buy an Orleans plum at the 'cheap Shop' as it cost the same as 'four or five very pretty sprigs' of flowers. 'Besides', she concluded in pure Austen style, 'I cannot help thinking that it is more natural to have flowers grow out of the head than fruit.'[131] Fashion observers recorded grasses, wheat, acorns and other natural products decorating hats, and declared Englishwomen particularly fond of feathers.

The French had their own views. French corsets were shorter in the body than the English long stays – perhaps one reason why visitors assumed that Frenchwomen wore none. Engravings in *Le Bon Genre* ridicule Englishwomen's straight waists under long stays, contrasting the effect with sprightly high French busts (fig. 6.24). The series also burlesques the sartorial historicism beloved on the other side of the Channel, though the French were equally enamoured of the medievalesque *le style troubadour*.[132] The eccentric 'gothic Anglaise' style of dress that Fanny Burney accused herself of wearing merely took a different form in France.[133] Surprisingly, Napoleon and his empress Joséphine de Beaharnais (1763–1814) were Scotophiles. They adored Scott's epics and Joséphine incorporated romanticised tartan elements into her wardrobe well before picturesque Highland troops helped to occupy Paris in 1814. Fashion plates from Britain and France are scattered with Scotch bonnets and scarves, shawls and tunics in plaid, responding to the new interest in Scotland (fig. 6.4).

French visitors admired Englishwomen's deportment, which they attributed to a love of riding and exercise.[134] Riding-habits were Britain's most successful female dress export. The understated elegance of English wools and masculine tailoring found their counterpart in the habits that epitomised *le style anglais*. Horseback was where to be said to 'look English' was a compliment. Otherwise, mourned a fashion writer in the *Repository of Arts*, 'Foreigners observe that there are no ladies in the world more beautiful, or more ill dressed, than those of England', a generalisation to be taken with a pinch of salt.[135]

Fig. 6.24

Unknown artist, 'Costumes Anglais', *Le Bon Genre*, October 1814, pl. 72, hand-coloured engraving on paper. The French retaliated for English censure by mocking English historicism, low waists, and longer less bell-shaped skirts. Victoria and Albert Museum, London.

English beauties were not without local Gallic assistance. Revolutionary upheaval in 1793 had landed French fashion on British shores in the form of émigré embroiderers, dressmakers and other skilled workers of the materials of fashion, including Rose Bertin, the famous *marchande des modes*, who styled Marie-Antoinette so successfully.[136] Some did not return until 1814. The style and élan of refugee aristocrats selling millinery, and making, instead of wearing, the latest fashions stimulated London women to greater heights of dress.[137] Eliza de Feuillide employed her London lady's maid and housekeeper from among the refugees, giving Austen regular contact with the dispossessed French at her brother's Manchester Street house, in the district of the exiled noble community. Austen also socialised with the Comte d'Antraigues – 'quiet manners, good enough for an Englishman' – in Eliza's circle of London friends.[138]

Back and forth went the snipes. Frenchwomen wore no stays; Englishwomen's bosoms were half covered. Frenchmen were unwashed and affected; Englishmen had no grace. After pointedly throwing in French phrases for 'false taste' and 'false manners', the author of *Dress and Address* sums up the French problem: 'all falsities and borrowed materials, are unnatural, unsafe, and do not pass current with an experienced eye'.[139] Dubious yet seductive Frenchness undermined Britishness. The French were always a little too much.

Despite internal competition, between them, France and Britain dictated style for the rest of the Continent. 'London and Paris', writes Riello, 'performed a unique international role in the clothing sector through the co-ordination of distribution channels, the circulation of ideas, innovations and techniques, and the creation of perpetual fashion changes'.[140] The two cities determined the tale of fashion across Europe. In London, for example, Countess Ludolf, 'a grecian lady' from Corfu, was observed to 'look more like a little Frenchwoman – with pretty artificial flowers in her cap'.[141] Elsewhere in Europe, German fashionable society considered London and Paris equal as sites of fashion production. Idealised figures of fashion were agents for a new look: either the 'slim, darkly dressed English Lord', representing 'fashion articles that are more tasteful, elegant, solid and graceful', as the Berlin *Mode Journal* described British goods; or a young Parisian coquette, 'more delicate, dainty and frivolous', as well as 'more stiff and overly ornamental'.[142] Betsey Wynne noted this in practice. In Hamburg, 'the Ladies dress very elegantly, the men ape the English fashion'.[143] Part of the success of the English male clothing regime was that its 'comfort and simple elegance' created style permanence, meaning that someone 'dressed in an English suit, in whatever country he may travel, will not fall out of fashion. He dresses like an Englishman! they will say by way of praise, not mockery.' Although this observation is from a German magazine of 1786, it holds true throughout the Regency. Englishmen's dress was paradoxically in fashion, while standing aloof from fashion, and acceptable anywhere. The German editor believed that the appeal of English goods was that they integrated into local contexts, like the 'ideally discreet gentleman' at once 'detached from and partial to the complicated conditions' of every place.[144]

Women's dress had no equivalent core stability of appropriate wear. The ubiquitous white muslin dress was the nearest thing to international style, yet its cut and effect revealed national origins. Upon returning to London after years abroad and having obtained clothes across the Continent, Betsey Wynne found herself 'obliged to alter everything, my behaviour, my dress, my manners, all is out of fashion – and my figure into the bargain. I think I must appear perfectly ridiculous.'[145] Taste that valued the individual rather than 'socially significant decoration' – one of the hallmarks of modernity, according to Purdy – carried the day in ladies' elegance.[146]

Creating a clothed identity of Britishness in the age of Jane Austen required fluidity and the strength of mind to absorb but not be overwhelmed by extreme flourishes of dress born from the world-shaking upheavals of the French Revolution and the Napoleonic Wars. In return, English bodies clothed in the nation's woollen textiles created symbols of might at home and abroad. Equally revolutionary industrial developments sought to arrogate the power of colonial textile production to the home islands, while making the established industry ever more dominant. The nation and its nationalisms were intertwined in dress from sewing threads outwards. When Austen's gentry contemporaries donned cotton print gowns in Edinburgh, or deliberated between real and fake flowers for a cap in Cardiff, their small choices encapsulated the bigger picture of Britain's sartorial, commercial and manufacturing position on the emerging modern stage.

❋ ❋

Chapter 7

World

Such I believe are all the particulars of his Letter, that are worthy of travelling into the Regions of Wit, Elegance, fashion, Elephants and Kangaroons[.][1]

Jane Austen once avoided keeping an aunt company during genteel imprisonment when Mrs Jane Leigh Perrot was arrested for shoplifting. On the strength of this accusation, about a card of white lace, Austen could have had a convict in the family. Transportees to New South Wales (Australia)[2] found themselves not just at the ends of the earth, but at the farthest reaches of global Britain, defined by her colonies and defended by her navy. Her citizens took British clothing practices with them across the world to foreign lands and harsher environments.

What happened to British bodies outside familiar climates? Notions of respectable dressing, suited to polite society, transmitted social values but had to adapt to heat, humidity and the implacable oceans. And what did such adaptations contribute back to English dressing? This chapter explores the fashion influence of Britain's global presence and dependence on textiles through clothing worn in its major colonies in India, the Caribbean and the Antipodes, and through the bodies of the naval officers and common sailors whose maritime prowess secured trading power – legally or otherwise. For a woman who never left England, Jane Austen was in touch with the world; and the world fundamentally supported the ordinary business of Regency dress.

Maritime Networks

The sea was crucial to British identity throughout the Regency period. No other nation had the ships and efficiency to cut such a figure on the world stage, blockading ports in South America, harassing Americans in the West Indies, and ensuring the lively exchange of goods with the East Indies. Any island depends on maritime trade; a manufacturing island requires oceanic prowess to export its goods and expand its commerce. British sea power carried waves of clothed people and their textile wares around the world, facilitated infinite licit and illicit transactions, and brought back new grist for the mills of textile manufacture and fashionable dress.

Additionally, the islands represented 'an idea of hearth and home as a place of essential Englishness' during the conflict years of the revolutionary wars, just as Austen's texts and her biography are now reproduced as an 'ideal of English retirement and rural seclusion'.[3] Discussions of *Mansfield Park* suggest that Fanny Price's symbolic virtue lies partly in her domestic innocence, contrasting with the worldliness of her grasping cousins and the 'foreign' Crawfords. For her naval brother William, Fanny represents the female domestic virtues of 'giving support and solace to the imperial adventure' when the sailor finally comes home from the sea.[4] As the sister of two sailor brothers, Charles and Francis, Jane Austen knew these experiences intimately.

Austen's deep appreciation of the navy is well documented.[5] Naval service affected a large part of her life, and her personal knowledge underpins *Mansfield Park* and *Persuasion*. Her nephew James Edward Austen-Leigh pointed out that it was 'with ships and sailors' his aunt 'felt herself at home', noting her 'partiality for the Navy' and 'the readiness and accuracy with which she wrote about it'.[6] The brothers – above and below her in age – both attended the Royal Naval Academy in Portsmouth, the fictional home of Fanny Price's family. Austen knew the town well from living for three years in Southampton and visiting her brothers. Frank was made lieutenant in 1792, commander in 1798 and post-captain in 1800 (fig. 7.1). Charles progressed along the same career points in 1797, 1804 and 1810 (fig. 7.3). Sheila Johnson Kindred's biography of Charles's Bermudan wife, Fanny (fig. 7.2), considers that her experience as a naval wife influenced *Persuasion*'s depictions of how naval service and long absences at sea affected families: the novel's last sentence considers the role of the family, provider of the 'domestic virtues', as 'possibly more distinguished' 'in its national importance'.[7] Mrs Croft, the admiral's wife, who is most unusual in accompanying her husband on his voyages, recounts:

> In the fifteen years of my marriage . . . I have crossed the Atlantic four times, and have been once to the East Indies and back again, and only once; besides being in different places about home: Cork, and Lisbon, and Gibraltar. But I never went beyond the Streights, and never was in the West Indies. We do not call Bermuda or Bahama, you know, the West Indies.[8]

Fig. 7.1

Unknown artist, portrait miniature of Captain
Francis Austen, 1800–03, watercolour on ivory.
Depicted in undress uniform, the epaulette on
Frank's right shoulder indicates a captain of
fewer than three years' seniority. His shirt and
frill may have been made by Jane or Cassandra
Austen, and his unpowdered 'crop' hairstyle
is newly fashionable. Jane Austen's House
Museum, Chawton.

The brothers severally crossed the Atlantic, spent time on the North American Station
and made longer voyages to the East Indies and China, as well as fulfilling escort,
patrol or blockading duties around the Channel, the Mediterranean and the Baltic
Sea. Their expertise and exploits, and the close-knit ties formed among officers fed
Austen's imagination. Letters home to Steventon or Chawton mingled in dispatch
with those for lords, admirals and directors of the East India Company.[9]

By the end of the eighteenth century, the navy was the largest employer in Britain.
Its increasing success meant that, as the nineteenth century opened, naval officers'
status was cemented as one of newly desirable social standing. If the red coat
symbolised military might, naval uniform was the insignia of Britannia's rule of
the waves. Austen bundles together the land- and sea-based defence professions
in her characters' estimation of their members as heroes of the martial era. Frank
Austen was in Nelson's fleet before the Trafalgar action, but was away collecting
supplies when the engagement took place, and sorely regretted missing it. To be
in the king's service, as William Price (*MP*) is, elevated a man above the merchant
sailor. Naval officers fitted perfectly the post-classical image of athletic 'natural'
man, rugged yet educated, equally able to ride, box and climb rigging and to
engage in natural philosophy, mathematical navigation and estate management.

Only commissioned officers (captains, lieutenants and midshipmen) and warrant
officers (surgeons, pursers, carpenters, gunners) were required to wear a uniform.
Like military uniforms, naval dress was obtained from a tailor. An officer's body

carried an economic patriotism in fine woollen kerseymere and broadcloth coats, cut and fitted with English skill. Uniforms were required to fulfil Admiralty regulations – the 'pattern' – which decreed blue fabric; blue or white cuffs and lapels; lining colour; the distribution of epaulettes; number and type of buttons; and the position of 'distinction lace' (gold braid). Two patterns for uniforms respectively covered the years 1795–1811 and 1812–27. Within these official dictates, there was significant room for personal choice in quality, cut and even colour. Naval coats of the early nineteenth century become progressively darker, echoing fashion's embrace of sombre cloth, but the dark blue now called 'navy' was not yet standard.[10] Lord Nelson bespoke his suits from Messeldich, the latter's son Augustus Meredith of Portsmouth, and another tailor called Wright, who may have worked near Nelson's Surrey home. Uniform styles frequently echoed civilian fashion, but the naval hero was conservative in his orders: the sartorial details of his uniforms were sometimes twenty years out of date, as his clothing in the National Maritime Museum, Greenwich, demonstrates.[11]

Officers had undress and full-dress uniforms. The informal style comprised a plain blue coat with gold epaulettes to distinguish rank, introduced in 1812 for lieutenants too as a mark of consequence and distinction, with lace (braid) cuff stripes for admirals. The undress coat was close to the sober gentlemanly respectability seen on shore. Full-dress coats were a riot of gold lace and bullion (metal embroidery thread), reflecting their origin as an imitation of mid-eighteenth-century French court fashion (fig. 7.4). Lace outlined lapels, collar, cuffs, pocket-flaps and buttonholes, and coats were worn with white breeches and waistcoats. Wide lapels were popular and could be fastened double-breasted. In 1812 white facings and cuffs reappeared. There was a degree of competition between army and navy uniforms. Epaulettes were a martial imitation, and army fashion led to wearing the uniform bicorne hat front to back ('fore and aft') instead of sideways ('athwartships').[12] The uniform of marines, like Mr Price (*MP*), Fanny and William's father, provided a red note on board Royal Navy ships (see fig. 7.7).

After the 1812 revision, naval undress coats, bereft of decoration, could pass for civilian ones, as the influence of new streamlined menswear reached ever further. Officers were described as appearing 'in sober simplicity, . . . strong, noble and unassuming. Plain blue and gold coats with white lapels, hats without feathers, black neckcloths, and open breasts' (that is, not covered by the waistcoat), with 'sun-burnt countenances' and unpowdered heads, giving an idea of 'honesty and honour, of real courage and untainted manners'.[13] Tanned faces showed the seafarer, making visible Sir Walter Elliot's complaint that 'sailors do grow old betimes; I have often observed it; they soon lose the look of youth' (Pers.).[14] By the 1820s, naval full-dress uniforms were looking archaic, with breeches instead of trousers, and waistcoats ending in points instead of straight edges. Austen contrasts this sense of the 'old' navy, represented by the bickering admirals Mary Crawford encountered when she was growing up, with William Price's open, pleasant countenance and 'frank, unstudied, but feeling and respectful manners' – the new navy man.[15]

Being 'made' into a lieutenant was the highlight of a midshipman's life and the commencement of his climb up the naval career ladder. When William Price becomes second lieutenant, the new officer looks and moves 'all the taller, firmer, and more graceful' in his matching uniform set, or 'mess', got from Turner the tailor, as evoked by a caricature of 'Master Blockhead' (fig. 7.5).[16] 'All the striking parts of [William's] dress' attract familial admiration, though as wear was prohibited off-duty William can only describe his uniform's beauties to the Mansfield inhabitants. Fanny happily gets to see him in it before 'all its own freshness and all the freshness of its wearer's feelings' were worn away.[17] Austen could expect her readers to project the sort of excitement and flurry of preparation for sailing in a new appointment (conveyed by fig. 7.6) onto Sam Price, a younger brother of Fanny's, aged 11, who is 'starting his career in seamanship' on the Thrush with William. As Mrs Price distractedly exclaims, 'Sam's things . . . will never be ready in time' for the next-day sailing.[18] Complete sets of specially made new clothing would have been an exciting acquisition for a young man. The Austen family twice shared that pleasure in outfitting Francis and then Charles for beginning their lives at sea. The fictional news, 'spreading general joy through a wide circle of great people', suggests their relatives' emotions in the same circumstances.[19]

We have seen Austen and Cassandra making shirts for their brothers, but did not consider what happened next: Austen may never have travelled abroad but her stitching crossed oceans. In early 1799 Charles bought a piece of Irish linen in Basingstoke, which, as Austen warned Cassandra, was waiting to be made into shirts when she came home. Only twenty-two months later, Charles instructed Austen 'to send his shirts by half-dozens as they are finished; one set will go next week'.[20] The sisters' labour accompanied their brother on his naval adventures. Lest batches of six shirts at a time seem excessive, we may note that Charles's naval colleague Captain Thomas Fremantle (1765–1819; Betsey Wynne's husband) owned fifty-six shirts by 1810 (made in sets of fourteen in 1803, 1806 and 'new' in 1808), including fourteen 'coarse' ones, with thirty-two neckcloths and forty-eight handkerchiefs to keep him presentable at sea, where laundry opportunities were scarce.[21]

Dress in the Age of Jane Austen

Gilbert,
5th Son of Sir Wm Heathcote, 3.
Captain R.N.
Born 1779, Died 1831

Mr B. Promoted to Lieut. & first putting on his Uniform   P. 7.

"Some are born great, some atchieve greatness"   Twelfth night —

Fig. 7.5

George Cruikshank, after Frederick Marryat, 'Mr. B. Promoted to Lieut. & first putting on his Uniform', *The Progress of a Midshipman Exemplified in the Career of Master Blockhead* (1820), pl. 7, hand-coloured engraving on paper. The new lieutenant's breeches are old-fashioned by the standards of 1820, like those of his father and the footman. The tailor is arrayed in more stylish Cossack trousers. Yale Center for British Art, Paul Mellon Collection, New Haven, Conn.

Clean water was rationed, so washing clothes or bodies on board required rain, or seawater, which substituted salt for dirt. One of the concerns about women on board ship, as Captain Wentworth discusses in *Persuasion*, was their demand for higher water usage. Washing in salt water rather than fresh aged linens faster and made soaps less effective. A series of Admiralty letters in 1806 concerns Patent Marine Soap's effectiveness for salt-water laundry. The reports were favourable 'but found some prejudice from the crew'.[22] Sailors were a superstitious lot, wary of change. Another fixed opinion was that linen shirts with checks or stripes dyed blue 'tend[ed] to preserve [the wearer's] strength, as well as health', as the indigo blue dye 'is confidently said to be inimical to vermin'.[23] On account of their colour they would also require less frequent washing. Certainly, image after image of sailors shows them wearing the patterned shirts common among labouring men across the British world (fig. 7.7).

The rest of a ship's crew, the uncommissioned hands or 'ratings', had no official dress until decades later, but their idiosyncratic clothing marked them as mariners on land – 'odd-looking men', in Sir Walter Elliot's opinion, which is

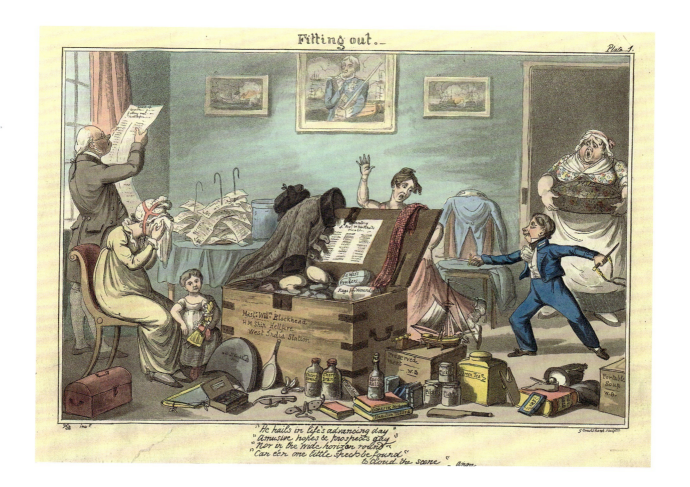

Fig. 7.6

George Cruikshank, after Frederick Marryat, 'Fitting out', *The Progress of a Midshipman Exemplified in the Career of Master Blockhead* (1820), pl. 1, hand-coloured engraving on paper. As a midshipman, Master Blockhead wears a version of mess uniform, consisting of trousers and the short jacket of a ship's rating. The crescent-shaped tin propped up against his trunk holds his dress hat. Yale Center for British Art, Paul Mellon Collection, New Haven, Conn.

all we hear from Austen of the men who operated her brothers' ships.[24] Their striped or checked shirts, blue jackets, striped trousers, and long queue clubbed with tar were identifiable miles from the sea (fig. 7.10). Trousers, in particular, were 'visual shorthand', exemplifying 'the reach of the eighteenth-century British empire, in cloth, pattern and manufacture'.[25] Loose 'petticoat breeches' and trousers enabled the young midshipman to perform his duty of climbing the rigging. Fanny's older brother Richard Price, 'midshipman on board an Indiaman' (an East India Company merchant vessel) and thus without uniform, would have worn attire similar to this, though as a trainee officer, rather than a hand, with a coat marking his more respectable status.[26] Doctors advised flannel waistcoats for seamen as well as members of militias, because, even when wet, wool held warmth to the body better than any other fibre. One of the best surviving examples is the one Nelson was wearing at his death on the *Victory* in 1805 (fig. 7.9). Perhaps Britons' being accustomed to their damp home climate contributed to their sea-going success (though, in fact, the crews of British ships were profoundly multicultural).

World

Fig. 7.7

Denis Dighton, *The Fall of Nelson, Battle of Trafalgar, 21 October 1805*, c.1825, oil on canvas. Dighton's dramatic reconstruction of shipboard action shows a number of sailors in striped trousers and jersey shirts, and others in flannel shirts; kerchiefs are worn loosely around the neck, and in one case around the head. National Maritime Museum, Greenwich, London.

In fashion, Nelson's decade of sea victories, from Genoa in 1795 to Trafalgar in 1805, were celebrated in a huge array of Nelsoniana. As Emma Hamilton boasted, you could 'dress from head to foot alla nelson', in earrings, pendants, pins, brooches, fans, ribbons, shawls and headwear (fig. 7.8).[27] Nelson's great victory at the Battle of the Nile in August 1798 inspired English ladies to dress themselves *à la Nile* the next month, so Austen's Mamalouc cap may also have been celebrating naval success.[28] The figured twill silk sarsenet of Austen's pelisse suggests another naval nod, as the pattern identified as oak leaves had strong associations with the royal navy, whose ships were made of stout English oak. From the official Royal Navy march 'Heart of Oak' (1760) to the profusion of oak-tree-laden mourning memorabilia produced for Nelson's funeral (1806), oak-leaf and acorn motifs prevalent in textile weaves, and prints expressed a patriotic Britishness invested in the navy (fig. 7.11). The leaf pattern was popular enough at the time to appear as a printed cotton cambric, the only example of the same pattern in two different textiles I have found (see fig. 3.25).[29] During the Regency period, naval gold braid acquired an oak-leaf and acorn pattern that is now traditional.

Trousers were the greatest maritime influence on Regency clothing. Long, loose male legwear, reaching below the knee or to the ankle, had existed for a long time (there is a pattern in Cook's 1787 tables of measurement for tailors),[30] worn by mariners, who took advantage of their easy availability as ready-made 'slops' in port towns worldwide, and other labouring men. As the navy rose in public estimation during the 1790s, this article of habitual informal dress among both army and navy fellows

Fig. 7.8

Silk ribbon celebrating Nelson's victory at the Battle of the Nile, 1798. The low-quality ribbon, badly printed with celebratory motifs, conveys fashionable accessories' rapid, cheap response to current events. National Maritime Museum, Greenwich, London.

Fig. 7.10

Rating's trousers, early nineteenth century, cotton. White cotton with blue stripes appears in working shirts and trousers across British areas, and the same fabric was used for government-issued slops for penal wear. National Maritime Museum, Greenwich, London.

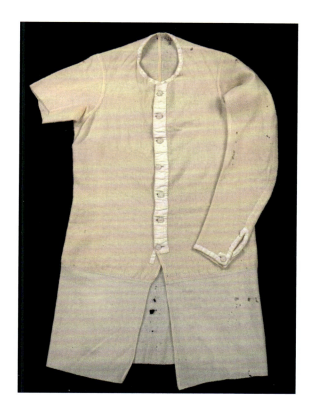

Fig. 7.9

Undershirt, 1800–04, wool. Rear-Admiral Lord Nelson's long wool flannel waistcoat, bound in silk ribbon with Dorset buttons, was worn under his uniform for warmth on board ship. National Maritime Museum, Greenwich, London.

Fig. 7.11

Handkerchief, 1806, cotton. This roller-printed handkerchief, patterned with oak-leaves and acorns to represent Britain's naval might, was produced to commemorate Nelson's funeral. Museum of London.

became recast in polite society for fashion-forward young men – a kind of youth style. 'Trowsers' were loose where pantaloons were tight. Their convenience for movement ensured their popularity among seafarers, and gentry men started to adopt them for their comfort. Museum examples all reflect easy utilitarian wear in the textiles: coloured stripes on cotton; white linen with dense twilled stripes; cream nankeen; or moleskin. By 1817 trousers were starting to be accepted as evening dress. Although loose trousers were considered effeminate on town dandies, for sailors they embodied stoic masculinity. Lord Byron preferred the new style as it disguised his club foot, and his preference no doubt helped its adoption (fig. 7.12).[31]

The difference between sea and town took some time to wash away. Dashing, charismatic Captain Thomas Cochrane (1775–1860) went to a masquerade ball in Malta in 1801 wearing 'the dress of an ordinary British seaman' and was told 'such

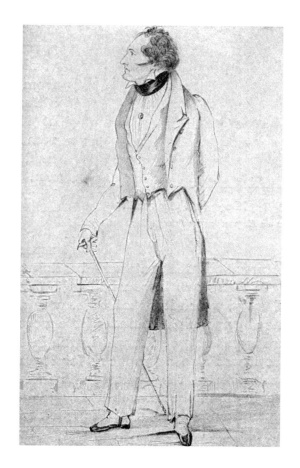

Fig. 7.12 Above Left

Alfred d'Orsay, portrait of Lord Byron, stipple engraving on paper, 1832, after a pencil sketch, 1823. Byron's 'little foot' is visible below his Cossack trousers, held under the instep. His stock is black satin, and his waistcoat has a deeper opening than was usual for men's style.

Fig. 7.13 Above Right

Charles Turner, portrait of Thomas Cochrane, 10th Earl of Dundonald, mezzotint on paper, 1809, after an oil painting by Peter Edward Stroehling, 1807. Cochrane's informal long trousers are prominent in this full-length portrait, asserting his dynamic naval presence. The captain's hat, laid on a smoky deck, also conveys his active leadership.

a dress was not admissible'. He held his ground as to the 'honourable' nature of his ensemble. His 1807 portrait epitomises 'heroic imperial masculinity' in trousers, 'a form of dress steeped in patriotism and manliness' (fig. 7.13).[32]

Blockade and Trade

Maritime men powered the transportation of textile products worldwide, through public and private channels, and they were essential for stimulating fashions. Ships were

> catalysts in this supply chain, providing clothing very different in scale and character than the . . . private infusions of clothing . . . to uphold a status quo in dress among Britons at great distance from their natal land. In contrast, the new sartorial enterprise of naval and mercantile administrations precipitated innovations evident in the look of male apparel and the scale of production . . . The massive, sustained flow of [ready-made] garments, carried to disparate locales, brought unexpected results.[33]

Thousands of yards of humble and precious textiles are hidden behind the catch-all word 'trade' in analyses of sea-borne Regency profits. Naval prize money, shared among the crew, came from capturing an enemy merchantman loaded with textiles or other traded goods. For all Napoleon's attempts at crippling trade, the war was steadily profitable for Britain. Traders and insurers in the City of London rewarded naval officers well for their protection of East India Company and private shipping through convoy escorts, no matter what some captains might feel about 'tinkers and haberdashers' presuming to reward the navy.[34] Charles Austen helped to block American trade with Europe, and intercepted slaving traffic while on his trans-Atlantic duties.

Seafarers also engaged in private trade or 'privilege', a time-honoured perquisite of maritime service.[35] 'All mariners in merchant fleets were permitted to carry goods on board to sell, barter or gift at another port or on returning home', and naval officers unofficially did the same, exploiting unique opportunities to acquire and exchange new luxuries, often embodied in textiles (such as the silk neckerchief in fig. 7.14), across Asia, the Mediterranean and the Americas.[36]

Fanny Palmer Austen reveals similar inter-familial textile transmission in a letter from Halifax, Nova Scotia, of September 1810. 'We shall send you a part of our Brother Frank's China present', she tells her sister Esther, '& hope it will prove acceptable.' That August, Francis Austen had sailed in an armed escort for thirteen East India Company ships travelling from Canton via Madras to England.[37] Evidently he sent gifts on to the Halifax connection, 'viz. . . . part of a piece of India Crape which I have had made up into a gown for you by Miss Johnson who had <u>your</u> measure and 2 pieces of Nankeen for the Boys'.[38] 'Crape' here meant silk; although it could be woven in India, Frank had started the journey in China, traditional home of silk production. London shops frequently retailed 'China Crape', and the Austen sisters owned evening gowns of this fabric. The first reference, in January 1813, is to Cassandra's China crape, and in November 1813 Austen still has not worn her own to a ball, as she planned to when staying in Godmersham.[39] In March 1814 we learn that her China crape is trimmed with ribbon at the hem, successful enough to persuade her to copy the pattern for another silk gown.[40] Fanny Austen also shared her 'piece' (9–12 yards) of crape with her sister, having it made into a gown she knew would fit Esther rather than potentially wasting fabric by estimating the cut length a gown required. It is plausible that the Austen sisters' gowns were the result of a similar gift from Frank direct from the Orient, and probably a little lovelier for his intimate kin. One Austen man could direct a textile halfway round the globe to clothe women in Hampshire, Halifax and Bermuda. The nankeen may also be of Chinese origin, as the durable buff-coloured cotton cloth took its name from Nankin (Nanjing) where it was first produced.

There was 'a strong sense of membership in a wider naval family', which 'fostered a communications network that reached out to include the wives, fiancées, and other family members of serving sea officers' (fig. 7.15).[41] Like families that shopped by proxy through military postings, the British naval network opened up alternative

Fig. 7.15

Jean Laurent Mosnier, *Margaret Callander and her Son James Kearney*, 1795, oil on canvas. The boy, a midshipman, wears the earlier cutaway or swallowtail style of coat. His mother's soft, gathered muslin gown and turban are the height of mid-1790s style, and both wear powdered natural hair. Yale Center for British Art, Paul Mellon Collection, New Haven, Conn.

World

channels of consumption for dress. Fanny Austen's mention to her sister Harriet of being told 'that there are to be had in Holland very handsome Velvets at about 4 Guineas the dress, & also Sarsenets, but I do not know the price of them' is quite casual. If Harriet and their mother 'can command the money I shall be very happy to forward your commission & am su[re] that Capt. Baldwin will have great pleasure in executing it'.[42] Although, owing to limited funds, Fanny decides to withstand the temptation of the 'Velvets' and instead to buy shift fabric for her small daughter, the incidental mention of routes of availability for Dutch textiles in 1814 suggests how common the method was, even during war. Before the birth of Fanny's child in Bermuda in 1808, her other sister, Esther, reminded Charles 'to send her twenty or thirty yards, of fine white flannel' for the baby 'as there is none to be got here fit for her use'.[43] Proxy shopping operated across distances, between the British Isles and overseas territories along acquaintance networks. Esther and Fanny bought, made and sent textiles, shoes, spencers and straw plaits for bonnets between Halifax and Bermuda, mostly out of Nova Scotia, as the shops were better and more varied there.

A side effect of the trade embargoes between Britain and France was a leap in illicit importation of textile and dress items. When direct trade to France was banned, Britain sent through Spain and Russia, and black markets operated in British seaports, especially those on the Channel; Malta and Gibraltar led the continental underground trade. Smuggling was a normal, expected and relied-upon trading method throughout the wars. Elizabeth Grant's mother developed a passion for contraband after a visit to Ramsgate and was unable to resist the 'silks, laces, gloves and other beautiful French goods so immeasurably superior to any in those days fabricated at home', that were smuggled into the country. 'Melodramatic sailors' offered the goods for sale, either profiting privately from their 'privilege', or working as part of networks of importers, who preferred to avoid customs men, taxation and the impounding of goods.[44] The Stanley family, returning from Paris, heard 'most alarming accounts of [the custom house officers'] ferocity and rapacity. They will soon, it is said, seize the very clothes you have on, if of French manufacture.'[45]

Even under official blockade, both governments sanctioned mercantile interchange. Britain issued licences to permit enemy trading within British ports – 18,000 in 1810 alone – and such trade was 'free and active' by 1812.[46] In fact, between 1810 and 1814 Napoleon supported English smuggling networks in an attempt to undermine the British economy by helping to move gold guineas, prisoners and newspapers to France. In return, he sent back French lace, leather gloves, and silk goods including fabric, shawls, bonnets and ribbons; together these goods formed 63 per cent of the total value of officially recorded shipments launched from the French 'city of smugglers', Gravelines, in these years.[47] Kent and Sussex absorbed the majority of the illicit goods – hence the Grants' encounters at Ramsgate. Owners of the smuggling vessels included shopkeepers and merchants from Deal, Dover and Folkestone, who gave the captains shopping lists of goods to obtain. In July 1813 a Mr Bushell asked Mr Motte 'Please to send me 4 dusons of plain dark sutted shalls', a similar request to another tradesman for '40 guineas worth of all plain dark shots shawls and if you can't send me the culers I send for do not send any', as previously 'you did not send the cullers that I sent for . . . Please to send them dark and good ones.'[48]

Once landed, the contraband filtered into local and London markets, laundered through private or retail channels, so that their black-market origins are whitely innocent in the history of textile retailing and consumption. Austen's Knight relatives living at Godmersham, halfway between the towns of Ashford and Canterbury, on the main routes into London from the coast, almost certainly bought smuggled goods, knowingly or not. The cheapness and quality would have marked them out, besides the word-of-mouth operating in close communities where everyone knew what fell off the back of a boat. A novel of 1814 suggests the routes that smuggled goods travelled and the widespread involvement of the population:

> Mrs. Hudson wore at church a French black mode cloak, trimmed with a very broad handsome lace. It was a piece of finery she had never sported before, and I remarked this to her. – 'It is a new Purchase,' . . . 'Lady Basilden's woman has smuggled over from France a quantity of things, which she sells very cheap. Having heard of this, I employed an acquaintance . . . to purchase me a cloak.'[49]

Naval connections helped respectable people to avoid customs duties almost as a matter of course, and Austen relatives cheerfully exploited unofficial trade channels. When Esther Palmer sent a box from Bermuda in 1814, her sister Fanny, living on HMS *Namur* at Sheerness, sent a boat to collect the gift direct from its transporting ship before it reached dock, 'as I knew the articles in it were most of them seizable' and could be impounded by customs officers. After unpacking, she redirected the parcels separately to their family in London.[50] Such domestic smuggling was common. Boats from Kentish coastal towns often met homeward-bound, textile-laden East and West India ships, or neutral merchant vessels, and purchased goods on board. The same 'neutrals' ran contraband cargoes directly onto English beaches.[51]

The list of global textile items prohibited from importation into Britain parallels records of smuggled material:

> A la modes and lustrings; . . . buttons of all sorts; printed, painted, stained, or dyed callicoes; . . . woollen cloths . . . leather gloves; East Indian, Persian, and Chinese wrought silks, Bengal stuffs mixed with silk . . . ; fringes of silk or thread; gold or silver thread, lace, fringe, or other works made thereof; . . . silk embroidered, twined silk, wrought silk mixed with gold, silver, or other materials.[52]

Local makers were keen to stem the flood of smuggling as it undercut their prices. A piece of illicit Indian bandanna could be sold in a finished state for 25s., whereas a British weaver could not compete for under 65s. – a price discrepancy that obviously made contraband attractive to retailers.[53] Contraband origins made already exotic and attractive foreign goods even more seductive. 'The [French] gloves have those qualities most tempting to the weaker sex – Mysterious & Forbidden', wrote Melesina Trench, thanking her son for a present that would have been seizable. 'They are delicacy itself, and have a peculiar and refined smell that I like much.'[54]

British manufacturers exerted considerable invention to get their wares to eager continental markets. Where Napoleon had expected his economic sanctions to undermine his enemy, 'on the contrary, the inner history of the Continental System came to consist essentially in the embittered and uninterrupted struggles against the endless stream of British goods [into the Continent]'.[55] British textiles were exported everywhere along the frontiers of the French empire. A commercial report of 1806 told how 'no sooner are [British cottons, woollens and linens] received into the French merchant's warehouse, . . . [than] evidence is procured that they are of French manufacture; . . . marks are stamped', and the textiles used as proof of superior French manufacturing.[56] Franco-American traveller Louis Simond witnessed how English goods 'are packed in small packages, fit to be carried by hand, and made to imitate the manufactures of the country to which they are sent, even to the very paper and outward wrapper, and the names of the foreign manufacturers marked on the goods'. On pieces of broadcloth in Leeds, for instance, he observed the mark of 'Journaux Frères of Sedan'.[57] By means of such counterfeiting, supposedly banned British textiles travelled as far as South America. The sea divided continents and nations but also offered them a common, highly permeable means of connection.

Global Britain

An interconnected global web of trade and settlement underpins all the shopping, making and wearing of the previous chapters of this book. British dress of the early nineteenth century cannot be separated from British imperial activity in the period, 'and must therefore be regarded . . . as constituting a *colonial discourse*'.[58] English bodies wore English clothes wherever they travelled, implicitly transmitting national values through the cut, fashion and quality of their attire. The raw materials and cheap labour of the colonies, indispensable to the emergent wealth and culture of Austen's middle classes, are absent from her fiction but obliquely present when Austen's connections are traced. Her panegyric to 'English verdure, English culture, English comfort' is a view 'seen under a sun bright, without being oppressive',[59] recalling non-English places where the sun *was* oppressive, as Austen knew at second hand.

If subscribers wished it, after the wars *La Belle Assemblée* could be sent to 'New York, Halifax, Quebec, . . . the West Indies . . . all parts of the Continent, Malta, Gibraltar, Sicily, Madeira, Brazil, Holland . . . France . . . the Cape of Good Hope and any part of the East Indies', names that map out channels of British influence, access and maritime activity.[60] The East and West Indies – the Indian subcontinent

Fig. 7.16

Fig. 7.16

Patchwork coverlet, printed cottons, made by Jane and Cassandra Austen and their mother. 'Have you remembered to collect pieces for the patchwork? We are now at a stand-still,' Austen wrote to Cassandra in the spring of 1811 (Letter 74, 31 May 1811). The cotton scraps show some of the wide selection of prints available to Regency consumers. Jane Austen's House Museum, Chawton.

and the British-run Caribbean islands – were extensions of the British Isles. As John Stuart Mill wrote, 'The trade with the West Indies is hardly to be considered an external trade, but more resembles the traffic between town and country.'[61] Both Indies were sources of highly desirable contributions to domestic dress cultures.

Beverly Lemire has expanded on the idea of 'contact zones' in colonial and imperial clothing encounters, 'social spaces where disparate cultures meet, clash, and grapple with each other'.[62] Regency bodies were implicit contact zones, 'interactive, improvisational . . . encounters', materialised in cultural cross-dressing. Many normative parts of Regency dress depended on or emerged from global contexts. All cotton came from outside the British Isles, mainly from the East Indies and the recently independent American states. Cotton's global trade role has been the subject of recent outstanding scholarship, and is a complex, far-reaching background to the history of Regency dress, hidden behind the cheerful, delicate prints cherished across society (fig. 7.16).[63] Enslaved people working cotton plantations on the other side of the Atlantic sustained Britain's booming fabric-manufacturing industry, and Austen's unease about the slave trade is present in *Emma* and *Mansfield Park*.

Conversely, new markets for exports allowed British taste and quality to spread even further. For example, ready-to-wear footwear was exported regularly to the West Indies and North American colonies. Between 1797 and 1805, 10 per cent of British shoe exports went to the Continent, 6 per cent to the East Indies and 74 per cent to the West Indies (8 per cent went to North America, and 2 per cent to the rest of the world).[64] Lancashire was one of the new industrial cotton centres of Europe, and one of the most globally connected places on earth, selling textiles to continental Europe, the Americas, Africa and Asia.[65] Cheap, ready-made or second-hand clothing was shipped from Britain to Newfoundland, Quebec, Ireland, South Carolina, Grenada, Barbados and Sydney – all places unable to produce clothes themselves or requiring inexpensive clothes in bulk.[66] Regency gentry clothing could have adventurous afterlives.

Outside England, temperatures could fluctuate dangerously, requiring those who ventured into tropical climes to dress accordingly. Readers will not be surprised by now to find that flannel underwear was recommended for Britons abroad. British wool travelled globally, hidden next to the body as often as in external trappings. Flannel in the tropics apparently helped to regulate perspiration for civilian, military and commercial travellers alike.[67] Conversely, flannel underwear helped those from warmer areas adjust to English temperatures. Colonel Brandon's waistcoat may have been helping him to re-acclimatise after a long station in India (*S&S*). Advertisements recommended garments like 'Patent Invisible Petticoats,

Opera Under Dresses, Drawers, and Waistcoats' made of Spanish lambswool, for 'Ladies returning from the East or West Indies' who 'especially suffer on their arrival in this country, at this season', as the garments were 'calculated to prevent the ill effects which is [sic] occasioned by the change of climate.'[68] Austen's future favourite aunt, Philadelphia (1730–1792), returned from India in 1765 with her husband, Tysoe Saul Hancock (1711–1775), and four-year-old daughter Eliza, and may have availed themselves of similar sartorial aids.

The East Indies

East India textiles were key for British Regency dress consumers. Through the seventeenth and eighteenth centuries, Indian fabrics set the standard against which all similar products were measured. New global histories have demonstrated that Indian cottons, in shaping markets and serving fashion, were the first consumer commodity manufactured for global markets, and the trade changed tastes and designs mutually in Europe and the East Indies.[69] Bales of printed and plain cambrics, muslins, ginghams, seersuckers, gurrahs, calicoes, palampores, chintzes and more filled the East India Company's London warehouses, before it was auctioned to retailers or distributed across Britain by other means. Many fashion images that appear to show plaid clothing or accessories in fact record Madras checks. The permanent colour, lightness and washability of Indian cottons were appealing to a public used to woollens, worsteds and silk.[70] Francis Austen, returning home in 1793 after his first five-year stint away, must have been full of tales of India, including the 'nabobs, gold mohrs, and palanquins' that Willoughby ridicules in Colonel Brandon, and accounts of Siam and Malaya.[71] It is hard not to imagine that the traveller's chests contained presents of fine, genuine Indian muslins, and perhaps a luxurious shawl or two for his mother and sisters.

Lemire's point that 'even while colonial authorities policed clothing systems, attempting to preserve a European essence in apparel, cultural cross-dressing was habitual for political and functional reasons' finds expression in army clothing.[72] For regiments like Colonel Brandon's in the East Indies, where 'the climate is hot, and the mosquitoes are troublesome', their normal woollen uniforms were tempered by a small allowance of clothing adapted to local conditions, including a lighter coat.[73] Highland corps were allowed to discontinue their Highland dress when serving in hot climates. However, by the regulations that controlled army supplies, any clothing for the armed forces had to come ready-made from Britain, and was not permitted to be sewn in India from supplied materials.[74] Under different provisioning rules, Indian-produced textiles graced manly British legs as naval uniform trousers, ready-made in the colonies.

Clothing advice for travellers to the East Indies itemises how to modify dress for the unfamiliar climate. *The East India Vade-Mecum; or Complete Guide to Gentlemen Intended for the Civil, Military, or Naval Service of the Hon. East India Company* advises taking at least forty-eight shirts, including a dozen of rather a superior quality

Fig. 7.17

Unknown artist (Lucknow school), *Four British Officers Greeted by a Young Lady*, 1800–05, gouache on paper. The lady's white muslin dress is gathered all the way round the waist, and may be of local construction. Her older companion wears what appears to be a loose, full, blue robe, a cap and a veil. The officers' uniforms make no concession to the climate. British Museum, London.

with frills, while 'Under-shirts, made of chequered calico [like sailors wore], of a moderate fineness, will . . . preserve the upper-shirts from being soiled by contact'.[75] The guide continues with a wealth of dress details. The 'whole of the supplies of clothing' recommended for a trip are prodigious, though relatives are warned against burdening travellers 'with a variety of useless apparel' that will end up as servants' perks. Essentials included 'Four dozen of neck-handkerchiefs, of very fine linen, not calico', and an equal number of a 'coarser kind' for underwear, then 'full four dozen' of 'Cotton handkerchiefs, of a small size, such as may be put into a waistcoat pocket'. 'Two good warm waistcoats of woollen must be provided, about two dozen of white waistcoats, made of fine Irish linen', accompanied by 'Breeches in the same proportion, and of the same qualities. To wear with the latter, two dozen pairs of long cotton stockings, and half a dozen pairs of short, wove, cotton drawers.' 'A dozen pairs of silk stockings' were an insurance against the scarce, expensive articles available in India. Then a 'substantial great-coat' and a light pair of shoes, 'two pairs of boots' and a stout pair of shoes would be needed. Coats to wear on board ship were recommended; two 'of broad cloth, and one of camlet, or some other light stuff', and 'a warm dressing gown of flannel, with two lighter, of printed linen, will be essentially serviceable'. Gentlemen were advised not to bother with hats as they got blown overboard.

What civilian Britons wore, once established in India, can be hard to determine
from sources that prefer to emphasise exoticism in dress. In general, both men and
women preferred English-style clothing. The danger was that they would modify
their respectable gentry clothing in response to the 'torrid clime' and 'go native', like
the European ladies living in Bengal, who 'affect, for coolness, to wear no covering on
their neck', meaning that they left off the fichus expected in daywear.[76] Men wore the
same garments as at home, but translated them into breezier fabrics: kerseymere or
some other light cloth for coats (see fig. 5.6) and white breeches; cotton fabrics like
dimity for waistcoats; nankeen for riding instead of leather, as Captain Williamson
advises; and sundry linen and cotton articles made for them upon their arrival.[77]
During the cold season, coats were worn when entering a house, for appearance, but
speedily taken off, or replaced by a lighter-sleeved waistcoat. Britons who persisted
in wearing woollen coats 'at length melted into acquiescence' with local habit.[78]

The stylistically hybrid 'Company paintings' that Indians executed for Europeans
sometimes show their patrons' outfits (fig. 7.17). As in all British areas, white gowns
ruled supreme, but here, the textiles were indigenous and traditional, reflecting what
the native population had worn for centuries. Plates in *The Costume and Customs of*

Modern India (1813) indicate that there was little to distinguish dress worn in Britain from European attire in India, except the lack of colour (fig. 7.18). Without an attribution it is rare to tell a portrait of an East India Company family member from a homeland British one (as figs 2.3 and 3.22 show). The colonial social networks ensured that the dress, taste and representations of India-dwelling Britons upheld the status quo as much as possible. The advice provided by travellers' lists really explains how to maintain oneself as a seemly British body while accommodating new climes and cultures, without ever going native. What had become familiar in domestic dress was acceptable; the visible foreign was conscious affect or suspicious duplicity.

European materials attracted steep premiums, so Company men posted for years were enjoined 'that measures be left with the tailor, the shoe and boot maker, the hatter, &c. in order that regular supplies may be sent yearly, or half-yearly', once again exploiting the proxy medium 'of some friend in London; who could get all articles of such a description shipped in the privileges of some of the officers of the Indiamen' to Calcutta, Madras or Bombay.[79] This tactic avoided the risk of the Company servant being stuck with inexpert or delayed local substitutes, and circumvented a reliance on the exorbitant prices charged by the numerous expatriate tailors, boot- and shoemakers in India, themselves trying to make Eastern fortunes. Indian tailors were more successful with soft, non-woollen clothing. The 'durzy' (tailor) or household 'sempster', who understood 'cutting out, and making, Waistcoats, small-cloaths, pantaloons', and shirts, was indispensable.[80] The British community was short of women, so 'Durzies capable of making gowns, &c. for European ladies, being scarce, and . . . much in request', could earn double the normal wage with no more than 'moderate skill in that branch'.[81]

Captain Williamson raises an interesting point when he suggests that the classic high-waisted Regency gown styles were inspired by Indian fashions. He says that 'the paishwaz' (meaning the 'peshawar shalwar' – a traditional style of dress in the north of what is now Pakistan), 'small bodi[c]ed, made extremely full, and gathering up to the bosom' and reaching the ankles, was 'the robe from which our ladies have taken their present dress'.[82] Of all the styles existing in the British-connected world in the late eighteenth century, regional Indian variations on garments with high waists or skirts starting under the bust and made of muslin are the closest match to European fashion, and may have influenced their adoption through imports and Britons returning home, like Austen's Hancock relatives. In 1792 Fanny Burney noticed the conspicuous 'Indian princess' style, 'chiefly of muslin', in the London dress of Mrs Hastings, wife of the former governor-general, just as waistlines were rising.[83] Classicism in dress may have been equally an East Indian Orientalism in dress (fig. 7.19).

From these colonial origins, muslin became the fabric uniting fashionable women's bodies worldwide. Muslin transformed life during Austen's generation, and it suffuses her personal and fictional worlds across all wardrobes. Authors often focus on the textile in Austen's work as it is inextricably entangled with perceptions of Regency England, the marker between old and new styles of dress.[84] For all the neo-classical

Fig. 7.19

Unknown artist, portrait of an Anglo-Indian girl, Delhi, c.1810–20, watercolour on ivory. The girl's white cotton dress is trimmed with a frill of nearly transparent 'clear' muslin, and pinned to her underwear at the centre front to emphasise her bosom. Victoria and Albert Museum, London.

rhetoric about white muslin's simplicity and timelessness, muslin is a fabric that tears and sullies easily, implying leisure and servants to maintain its appearance, as evidenced by Lydia Bennet directing Sally to mend a great slit in her muslin gown (P&P).[85] It was the perfect fabric for the middling sorts: delicate enough to express one's station, yet 'new every time it is clean, & new trimmed', a measure of economy appealing to the thriftiness of Austen and her peers.[86] Other complaints against muslin were that it caught fire easily, another that it was too thin for 'the inclemencies of [the British] variable climate'.[87] One young lady, stooping for a book, 'set fire to my bonnet, which being of thin muslin, was presently in a blaze, and also a lace cap I wore underneath'.[88]

The ultrafine, transparent fabric was an Indian speciality, exported to parts of Europe for millennia before the Dutch and English East India companies started shipping it in bulk among other desirable Asian textiles. Until local manufacturing took off in Europe, muslin was an investment, which elevated its suitability even to court society. It was first popularised as an elite dress fabric during the 1780s in the French court through the 'chemise gown'. While Georgiana, Duchess of Devonshire, is usually credited with introducing the style to England in 1784, the actress Mary 'Perdita' Robinson first wore the Paris fashion in 1782.[89] Muslin still undercut the price of silk and created the effect of lace's airiness for significantly less expense.

Henry Tilney (NA) famously declares that he has bought a muslin 'pronounced to be a prodigious bargain by every lady who saw it. I gave but five shillings a yard for it, and a true Indian muslin', a claim that demonstrates not only his acumen in textile shopping, but also the book's late eighteenth-century genesis, when true Indian muslins could still be bought relatively cheaply.[90] Competition between Indian and British muslins became critical in the mid-1790s, when the EIC started to be concerned about shops selling equally elegant British products for prices a quarter or a third lower than Indian ones.[91] Between 1802 and 1819, duties on imports of Indian textiles for the British market were raised nine times. By the time of the Northanger Abbey's publication in 1818, the East India Company muslin factories in the subcontinent had shut owing to increased profit-seeking and oppressive working conditions.[92]

For years, 'Indian muslins remained the benchmark against which British technical ingenuity was tested. Only when British manufacturers could equal the quality of Indian goods were British goods more secure in international markets.'[93] Striving to profit from the high consumer desire for muslins spurred industrial weavers on to new technological innovation. By the 1810s, with muslins embedded in everyone's wardrobes, they finally achieved excellence (helped by the raised tariffs). 'The yarn of the British muslins is much evener spun, by the machinery now employed', a contemporary pamphlet informs readers.[94] This is the key to distinguishing between hand-spun, hand-woven Indian muslin, with a slight undulation in its matrices, compared with smooth, straight industrial British muslins (fig. 7.20). The unevenness of Indian muslin 'gives the cloth a vitality that is lacking' in machine-made products.[95] Some charm is gone. Indian areas produced over 100 varieties of muslin, including the popular *jamdani*, muslin with the pattern woven in, and *chikan*, embroidered muslin. These names were erased in the transition to European fabrics, though the techniques remain in 'sprigged' and 'spotted' styles. The crewel spots Austen sought in a muslin (see fig. 4.23) derive from the double-sided satin-stitch dots called *do-rukha*.

Indian textiles from the late eighteenth century surviving in collections have lost one sensual aspect that made them exotically appealing to British consumers: their perfume. Packed tightly alongside spice cargoes, muslins absorbed a distinctive smell that became part of how shoppers judged a cloth's origins. A Bolton weaver used spices on his domestically produced muslin to imitate this fragrance, and a 1795 book of 'valuable secrets' cheerfully explains how to fake Indian painted silks, and add the distinctive scent of cinnamon, cloves and other spices associated with genuine imported articles.[96] British muslins were frequently sent to India to be repacked and returned to England as Indian muslins, having acquired an alluring Eastern bouquet.[97] Perhaps Tilney only smelled a bargain, his nose misleading his eye and hand.

In 1817–18 exports to India from Manchester and Glasgow of textile piece-goods overtook the reverse trade from Bengal for the first time.[98] Scotland's separate trade network sold direct from Glasgow. The value of muslin sales from these two ports to India exceeded the combined income from selling to Europe, the Americas

Fig. 7.20

Muslin gown, c.1800 (detail of the back bodice and skirt). This white muslin gown is made from two existing gowns sewn together: the fabric of the bodice is neater, straighter, English-made muslin; the skirt is of hand-woven Indian muslin. Victoria and Albert Museum, London.

and China. One of the reasons for Napoleon's Berlin Decree of November 1806 was to stop the tide of British muslins flowing into France, so that people would turn to French-made cloths. Joséphine de Beauharnais was from warm, colonial Martinique and had a passion for muslin, as her wardrobe inventories show.[99] Napoleon constantly tried to catch the empress and her daughter wearing English muslin; no matter how much they protested it was 'Saint-Quentin lawn', he always knew, and tore their gowns or burnt them.[100]

The shawl is the third defining garment of Austen women's fashion, along with bonnets and muslin gowns, and it has as complicated a trans-global history as the fabric.[101] Indian men, and some women, had worn a square or oblong piece of fine, embroidered wool since the late sixteenth century, and it possibly originated in Persia. Most prized and expensive were Kashmiri shawls of light, warm cashmere. A pale ground fabric was finished with intricately woven ends and borders incorporating the *boteh* (*buteh*, *buta*) pattern (fig. 7.21). These shawls were originally woven in pairs and worn with wrong sides together so that no construction showed. Joining two squares together end to end made the long shawl, seen in European plates and portraits from about 1795.

Europeans in India adopted the local fashion and brought back valuable shawls as presents and souvenirs – Lord Clive and Warren Hastings; Eliza de Feuillide's godfather) sent boxes of them back to their families; the East India companies started importing shawls in quantity only in the late eighteenth century via maritime routes.[102] Englishwomen appear to have adopted them as fashion first (c.1760s) and thence they spread into France. Eliza hoped her cousin Philly Walters was repelling cold with her 'new fashioned Shawl' in 1796.[103] The Egyptian campaign a couple of years later allowed men stationed there to import the luxuries personally, as Kashmiri shawls had circulated to nearer non-European cultures through land trade for centuries.[104] Here began the shawl's ascendancy in Regency dress. The unstructured shape lent itself to classical-esque styles, echoing the long *palla* that Roman matrons draped round their head and shoulders. Wearing a shawl required grace and ease, as their arrangement created – or ruined – elegance. Not all were convinced. There is a distinct note of cultural superiority in *La Belle Assemblée*'s opinion that 'nothing can be more opposite to every principle of refined taste, or carry less the appearance of that elegant simplicity at which it aims. – [The shawl] is calculated much more to conceal and vulgarise, . . . and is totally destitute of every idea of ease, elegance or dignity', turning 'any female, NOT beautiful and elegant, into an absolute *Dowdy*.' The cultural problem is the shawl's association with 'the *sickly* taste of the *tawny* Belles of the torrid zone'.[105] The shawl's supple drape complemented muslins and soft fabrics, though not stiff silks. A number of shawls survive transformed into gowns, which use the decorative borders as hems and cuffs (see fig. 6.19). A shawl's light weight and the versatile ways in which it could be worn around the torso made it a useful regulator of heat, indoors and outdoors. Women were already familiar with donning a fichu or neck-handkerchief for this purpose: a fashion magazine of 1790 introduced the shawl as 'a type of unusually ample handkerchief'.[106]

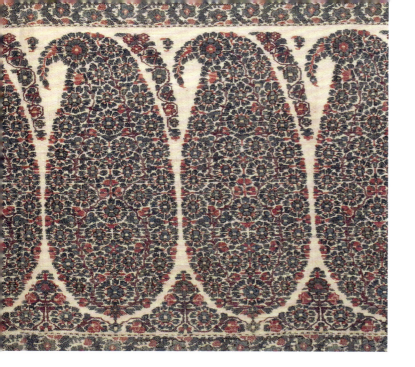

Rarity enhanced the fashion value of authentic cashmere shawls. European manufacturers' cheap copies soon flooded the market, fulfilling the demand but decreasing the fashionability by making shawls common.[107] William Price's promotion rouses Lady Bertram solely because of the prospect of his having access to the genuine Indian article. 'William must not forget my shawl if he goes to the East Indies,' she instructs Fanny, 'and I shall give him a commission for anything else that is worth having. I wish he may go to the East Indies, that I may have my shawl. I think I will have two shawls, Fanny.'[108] This is the nearest she gets to excited. The status and quality are what she lusts after, and the lower cost of private import (especially using the tax-free privilege to which William is entitled as a naval officer). The real thing cost from £50 to £100, even after EIC imports began. The opportunity to market a highly desirable accessory at one-tenth the price of the authentic version encouraged manufacturers to experiment with imitation. The first British production took place in locations that had established woollen-weaving knowledge, notably Norwich, Edinburgh and Paisley. Before consumers had regular access to genuine cashmere, British wools, or combinations including silk warps, could be made into successful copies, which sold in untold numbers.[109] Like muslin, the subtle difference between British machine-made and Indian handwoven shawls meant that the original articles retained their price and status with connoisseurs.

Adaptation to local taste soon occurred in the end designs. The *boteh* form was modified to contain patriotic oak-leaves and acorns around 1810, and Paisley-made 'Thibet' shawls came to be so synonymous with the teardrop shape used in the decoration that this entered English design as 'paisley' pattern.[110] The British shawls are probably the ones circulating in Austen's novels, suggesting their acceptance in gentry society as normal articles by the early 1810s. Local manufacture had turned

Fig. 7.22

Shawl, early nineteenth century, muslin and cotton. The shawl is made of two lengths of muslin, joined together in the centre with a strip of cotton bobbin net, then embroidered with cotton satin-stitch crosses (see detail); it is said to have been embroidered by Jane Austen. The cloth's Indian origin is revealed in the irregular texture of the threads. Jane Austen's House Museum, Chawton.

an exotic luxury into a practical yet pretty normality. In *Emma*, fussing with a shawl is twice a pretence for distraction, as is needlework elsewhere in Austen. In *Persuasion* Henrietta Musgrove uses a shawl to hide her face while sleeping in a carriage. Hilariously hypochondriac Diana Parker wraps a shawl about her shoulders as she runs about Sanditon; and shawls are a thematic garment developing *Mansfield Park*'s contemplation of national identities. Miss Bates's patter tells us that her mother's 'large new shawl', worn against the cold evening, was a present from Mrs Dixon, though its being 'bought at Weymouth' incurs some suspicion of smuggling (*Emma*).[111]

Austen's letters show shawls in a similar gift-giving yet everyday light (see chapter 3). Once shawls were established, fashion soon morphed their materials, creating wraps of all fabrics available, including silk, lace, net, muslin and gauzes (knitted versions came post-Regency). Austen's acquaintance Mary Whitby's excitement at coming out and being 'grown up & hav[ing] a fine complexion' was expressed through wearing 'great square muslin shawls.'[112] Austen owned a muslin shawl, which she may have made herself, as family tradition says she embroidered it; however, the satin-stitching is less fine than on Cassandra's handkerchief.[113] It is the perfect blend of two of her era's defining fashion trends (fig. 7.22).

The West Indies

In terms of journey time, the West Indies was the nearest major British colony. The Austens had close connections with this colonial area, and it appears as the most significant extra-English place in Austen's novels. Future suspected thief Jane Leigh

Perrot, married to Austen's maternal uncle, was born in Barbados and inherited a plantation there. George Austen was a trustee for the Antigua plantation of a schoolfriend. Cassandra's fiancé died in the West Indies of yellow fever in 1797. James Austen's father-in-law was born in Antigua, and Frank Austen served in action off its coast. Charles Austen patrolled the North American Station between 1805 and 1811. 'This surely', as Jordan says, 'makes quite an extension to the likely concerns and conversations of "three or four families in a village".'[114] Mrs Croft reminds us of the subtle difference between British Bermuda and Bahama, and the variously colonised West Indies.

West Indian influence on Regency fashion flowed into Britain in two main ways: light dress and money. A lot of scholarly attention is paid to the imperial and colonial dimensions of Austen's work, including slavery, but for our purposes the key point is that estates in the British West Indies, like Sir Thomas Bertram's in Antigua, were sources of wealth through sugar, tobacco, cotton and other commodities, supporting spending in the homeland. *Mansfield Park* is 'a novel based in England relying for the maintenance of its style on a Caribbean island'.[115] Sickly, indigent Mrs Smith in *Persuasion* is indebted to Captain Wentworth for the recovery of her husband's West Indian property, and it is valuable 'enough to make her comparatively rich'.[116]

Returnees from the West Indies were all over Britain. The rich ones' ability to spend on consumer goods, including clothing, is the influence that Austen discusses most directly. '"No people spend more freely, I believe, than West Indians,"' she says through *Sanditon*'s enthusiastic Mr Parker. However, their money reduced their class. Mr Parker's acquaintance retorts with

> 'Aye, . . . and because they have full purses [they] fancy themselves equal, may be, to your old country families. But then, they who scatter their money so freely never think of whether they may not be doing mischief by raising the price of things. And I have heard that's very much the case with your West-injines.'[117]

Sanditon is the Austen novel most concerned with material things and the availability of 'all the useless things in the world that could not be done without' in the town's shops.[118] Mr Parker assesses Sanditon's rising success by the fashionable accessories available for consumption there. Incomers, whether West Indian or Londoners, contributed to the local circulation of wealth through sartorial spending. Yet it was feared that new injections of colonial wealth would disrupt old orders, in the way that the seaside resorts Austen knew and wrote about imitated 'town' within her lifetime. Fashion might disguise unacceptable origins with seeming respectability but it was thought that a love of gewgaws and flamboyant decoration often betrayed Caribbean taste and origins. If descriptions of fashion in Austen signify vulgarity and moral uncertainty, what does that say about adornment's role in 'the wasteful expense of civilisation' so celebrated in Sanditon?[119] Who, in this situation, is 'going native' and native of where? The finished novel might have contained her most perceptive clothing critiques.

Domestic Britons considered West Indians coarse, vulgar, indolent, and lacking *ton* in their turn-out, all compounded by their anxiety to be thought the opposite. Mrs Elton (*Emma*), as a vulgar newcomer to an established social situation (and daughter of a Bristol merchant – implicitly suggesting colonial and slave-trade connections for contemporary readers), matches the scorn around creole fashion expressed throughout contemporary literature. Her overdressing implies islanders' dual shortcomings of wealth got through trade and lack of taste. Lady Bertram (*MP*) is also the model 'indolent plantocratic wife', as indifferent to managing her household and domestic estate as any satirised West Indian lady, grasping for expensive accessories to satisfy whim and pleasure.[120]

Within the West Indies, tropical discomfort was the order of the day, and there was no recourse to temperate hill stations of the kind East India Britons enjoyed as a retreat from the heat. In both the Indies, British dress, leavened with airier fabrics, created a tolerable medium. Women's clothes in those colonies followed the same light, comfortable cotton regime, and also demonstrate the ubiquity of the high waistline as a global gown template (fig. 7.23). Male planters, like their maritime colleagues, adopted casual trousers. An emigrant writing home in 1793 from the Windward Islands explained that he must now wear light, wide trousers as 'the other Cloaths I brought from england is [*sic*] of no use to me.'[121]

An attention to dress was a source of criticism of British 'dandy' planters in the islands. An anti-slavery pamphlet's description has this obvious bias, but also supplies useful details of their modified clothing:

> This pampered mortal . . . walks forth in his morning dress, which consists of a loose flowing night-gown of the finest India-chintz, . . . a cotton night cap, of the choicest texture, and over that a large beaver hat, which securely defends him from the sun, his trowsers are of fine holland, his shirt, the neck of which is open to admit the air, is equally costly, [as] are his white silk stockings and red morocco slippers . . . [He] dress[es] for dinner; his trowsers are exchanged for a pair of silk breeches, with . . . a thin coat and waistcoat, both white, and a hat lined with green; . . . A negro boy puts on his shoes and stockings, which he likewise buckles, while another dresses his hair, and the third holds his clothes or fans him, during the fatigue of dressing.[122]

The traditional black woollen clerical habits that Cassandra's doomed fiancé, the Reverend Thomas Fowle, probably wore must have been adapted for tropical wear. The rector of Allington became private chaplain to his cousin Lieutenant-Colonel Lord Craven (later Earl of Craven), to earn money for his marriage. When the 3rd Regiment of Foot went to fight the French in the Caribbean in 1795, he went too, tragically never to return. There were more British military men in the West Indies than in the East, and sartorial adaptations were vital to maintain fighting trim. Coat linings were reduced, serge waistcoats with sleeves stood in for coats, and trousers were made of Russia linen for greater comfort; naturally, 'a pair of flannel drawers' was also required, probably for its 'healthy', sweat-wicking properties.[123] Swathes of army and navy correspondence with London headquarters concerned the shortage of ready-made clothing or 'slops' in the islands, and asked for more shirts, trousers and shoes to be sent. Although the British textile machine ran on colonial products, their transformation into wearables still relied on the established production networks at home.[124]

The only character of West Indian origin in Austen is *Sanditon*'s Miss Lambe, 'about seventeen, half mulatto, chilly and tender', with 'an immense fortune'. Her English companions, the Beaufort sisters, are described as a common type of girl:

> tolerable complexions, showy figures, an upright decided carriage and an assured look . . . very accomplished and very ignorant, their time being divided between such pursuits as might attract admiration, and those labours and expedients of dexterous ingenuity by which they could dress in a style much beyond what they ought to have afforded; they were some of the first in every change of fashion. And the object of all was to captivate some man of much better fortune than their own[,][125]

as many Austen characters do. The town residents expect Miss Lambe's guardian, Mrs Griffiths, to be 'as helpless and indolent as wealth and a hot climate are apt to make us'.[126]

> [She] had preferred a small, retired place like Sanditon on Miss Lambe's account; and the Miss Beauforts, . . . having in the course of the spring been involved in the inevitable expense of six new dresses each for a three-days visit, were . . . satisfied with Sanditon also till their circumstances were retrieved.[127]

Because they have spent too much on unnecessary clothes to foster a better appearance, they must live off West Indian money for a while: 'on Miss Lambe's account' is a double entendre. All cloth in the Caribbean was imported, attracting higher prices and giving it a high social and economic value, especially for gifts. Inhabitants able to travel to England and buy direct would have found the prices delightfully low, further stimulating their spending.

The Antipodes

Francis Austen's first captain, Isaac Smith, was in 1770 the first non-native to set foot in Botany Bay. European settlement began with the arrival of the First Fleet in January 1788, sent to form the penal colony of New South Wales. Where the East Indies provided textiles to aspire to, and the West Indies raw materials and spending money, this colony was unlike any other. The indigenous people's nomadic culture was incomprehensible to British ideas of 'civilisation'. The flora and fauna were unique. Yet, the colonisers attempted to transport British culture wholesale, including the etiquettes and status of dress.

The scandal of Jane Leigh Perrot's case was the accusation of an upstanding, respectable member of Bath society. The charge was that, on 8 August 1799, Austen's aunt had deliberately slipped a packet of white lace in with her purchase of a card of black lace, then left Smith's haberdashery shop on Bath Street. This constituted not petty theft but grand larceny, a crime punishable by death.[128] The lady denied the charge vociferously, claiming that the man who sold her the legitimately purchased black lace had put the white in too, and she insisted on going to trial. If found guilty, Mrs Leigh Perrot might have faced a commuted sentence of fourteen years' transportation to New South Wales.[129] The accused spent seven months in Somerset County Gaol (albeit in the gaol-keeper's private residence) awaiting her fate, before being declared innocent in March 1800. Mrs Austen offered to send Jane or Cassandra to keep their aunt company, but she declined subjecting the 'Elegant young Women' to her own inconveniences.[130] The trial was reported in at least three newspapers and the *Lady's Magazine*, where the case was noted for its exceptionalism in that thievery was expected only of the lower classes.

The release of Austen's aunt highlights class inequalities: she probably did take the lace. One of her attorneys thought so, classing Leigh Perrot as one of those rich ladies who 'frequent bazaars and mistake other people's property for their own'.[131] Richard Austen-Leigh wrote privately that his great-great aunt did steal the material and probably meant to,[132] but she knew the mayor and magistrate socially, which accounted for the verdict in her trial. What was light-fingered eccentricity in the rich middling sorts was damning for the poor. The punishment for theft was often transportation and around 40 per cent of convicts were exiled because they had stolen clothing. Elizabeth Hayward, for example, was sentenced for stealing a linen gown, a cloak and a silk bonnet from her master, and pawning the gown. The youngest recorded convict, 9 years old, was caught at a pawnshop with stolen clothing.[133] The individual value and soft, unbreakable nature of clothes and textiles made them excellent targets for theft. A cotton handkerchief could be resold for 6*d.*, while a silk one might fetch 6*s.*, enough to buy hot food for a week.[134]

In a colony always short of material goods and with no official currency until 1813, items of clothing held a particular cachet. Dress and accessories brought from home 'found a ready market in fashion-conscious early Sydney. Bought, bartered, stolen and sold, they might allow one woman to get enough capital to start a little shop.'[135] Sarah Bird sold her petticoats at 2 guineas each, and made a tidy profit on edging, which she bought for 1*s.* 8*d.* per yard in England and sold for 5*s.* per yard in New South Wales.[136] The government even used clothing as a form of payment – when the clothing turned up. It was the Navy Board that supplied clothing for the convicts, meaning that provision for them competed with marine uniform orders, and during wartime came last. Two years could pass between orders being sent from Sydney and the goods arriving there. Delays, damage and shortfalls affected every official importation.[137]

By the nineteenth century, the clothing situation had improved, but new arrivals found dress often confounded the social orders carefully distinguished in Austen's England. Convict and settler resembled each other.[138] Even the perceived class differences between long gentlemen's coats and short labouring jackets could be disrupted when Aboriginal men adopted civilian or military coats through trade and gift-giving, in another example of cultural cross-dressing (figs 7.24 and 7.25). The customarily unclothed people often went naked in town, yet also repurposed British tailoring as complex markers of status, imitation and negotiation.[139] Clothing always has agency and reach beyond the purposes for which it was made. The class distinctions upheld by social judgement through dress, which Austen describes so nicely, became of greater importance in the colony. Dress worked differently there, and this puzzled and frustrated the early colonists, faced with vastly different, harsh environments that tore through their inadequate garment stocks. Any imported ready-made clothing, and bales of second-hand garments found an avid market in Sydney. Exporting outmoded articles from the advanced nation to less industrialised regions was a mark of emergent modern practices, and tides of gentry clothing cast-offs washed up on very distant shores.[140]

Most supply ships came from Britain, but the nascent colony soon traded directly and regularly with Bengal, Calcutta, Madras, Manila, Boston and Cork for ready-made clothing, shoes, fabric, leather and sewing accessories. Private commerce augmented government garment supplies, often relying on connections gained through colonists' previous long habitation in the East Indies. The Australian wool industry boomed

after 1815, and finally they could export fibres to the British world, adding a new power to English wool's trading might. 'Botany worsted' was used in English shawls to imitate the Indian quality.[141] Even in Australia, English women lusted after the genuine, expensive article. When Jane Williams was stationed in India, her mother wrote from Van Diemen's Land (Tasmania) requesting some Indian shawls. The reply was:

> there is really nothing at Poona that I have yet seen that is worth sending, unless it were a cashmere shawl and a decent one is not to be had under two or three hundred rupees . . . we are too much in debt for me to think of it at present.

Williams tactfully reminded her mother that English shawls were equally good, 'so much so that they may be mistaken for authentic Cashmere shawls'.[142] Still, auction advertisements carefully distinguished between 'English and Bengal prints, English and India dimities, English and Bengal shawls, fine English calico'.[143]

This longest-distance proxy shopping was common. Gentry settler women established and maintained social status by calling for supplies of exclusive fashion goods. Proxy shopping also flaunted social networks that emancipated convict women could not hope to emulate. 'Clothing and fabrics received from family and friends abroad demonstrated at least to women belonging to the New South Wales colonial gentry that they were not isolated from Britain. It signalled their membership of a transnational community, set apart from those of convict heritage' – the same elite as in the Indies, and non-English Britain.[144] One argument in favour of imports was that it was cheaper to send to England for goods than to pay premium colony prices. Elizabeth Marsden (1772–1835) ordered, via her husband, Samuel (1765–1838, a future wool magnate), precise items from a preferred seller – 'Mr. Green's Gloves, Newport St' in London. Green knew 'what sort to send' for the £5 she wished to spend, as she was an established customer. Mrs Marsden then spent a whopping £25 on ribbons.[145] Muslin, bonnets, shoes and other paraphernalia passed across the seaways just as they did along English roads. In 1807 Mary Putnam thanked her mother for sending out a new gown that she described as 'altogether different and superior to anything of the kind seen in this country'. Her sister also transmitted fashion information, writing in 1808 that Mary must notify her as to whether she wanted 'a summer or winter pelisse'.[146] The six-month journey to New South Wales was not much greater than the time it took for dress styles to become established in British non-metropolitan areas. Many surviving gowns in Australian collections were treasured items brought with settlers or sent out later (see fig. 1.2).

Fig. 7.24

Alphonse Pellion, *Sauvages de la nouvelle Galles du Sud (d'après nature dans leur Camp près de Sidney, 20 déc. 1819)*, 1819, watercolour and ink on paper. The Aboriginal warriors Tara and Peroa wear British tailored wool in the form of a blue double-breasted tail-coat and a military sleeved waistcoat, probably part of the uniform of the 76th Regiment. The men's naked lower halves were an important gender signal in their culture. State Library of New South Wales, Sydney.

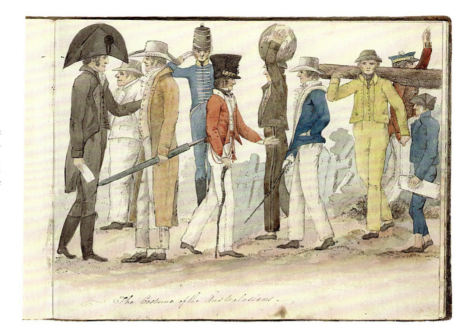

Fig. 7.25

Edward Charles Close, 'The Costume of the Australasians', 1817, *New South Wales Sketchbook*, watercolour on paper. Close records the range of ways in which dress marked position in the colony. The first man is a government official in a professional black suit, with a free settler in a duster coat; behind them is an emancipated convict in white. Next is a soldier, and then a bandsman of the 73rd Regiment greeting a settler in a blue jacket. Two labouring convicts, wearing black and yellow, another soldier, and a convict clerk in blue complete the picture. State Library of New South Wales, Sydney.

The person shopping next to Jane Austen in a London warehouse, or a country town drapers, might be sending the goods she purchased to the ends of the earth, transmitting status through a material Britishness, and comforting emigrants with their familiarity. The colonists' relatives helped to complete an informal, informed world-wide dress-consumption network. Austen's well-connected family easily spanned half the globe, and her experience was reasonably common, as naval and mercantile networks extended the possibilities for transmitting fashion. In return, these connections brought direct experience of the world's effects on bodies back into the heart of England, to whose dress colonial goods had become essential.

A contemporary observation of the cotton mills, 'seven stories high, and fill'd with inhabitants, remind[ing] me of a first rate man of war', conjures up a Britain moving its powers from the martial oceans to the manufacturing land, setting sail for the future on a sea of cotton, its labourers running both intricate factory machines and the engineering masterpieces of fighting ships.[147] The tailored coats of good English wool that shaped respectable male gentry bodies were repurposed to ends unimaginable by their makers, yet embodied the material values of home to homesick eyes. Lashed with sea spray, passed clandestinely, scented with spices, protected by the navy: dress and textiles from around the world passed into the wardrobe of British consumers, Orient blurring irrevocably into Occident and altering how Regency people fashioned their physical and cultural selves. Dress in the age of Jane Austen had come full circle.

Conclusion

People read Austen for the pleasure of how well she reads people. Her life and work encompassed a period when reading the inherent social markers of people's dressed bodies was an observation central to creating identity, itself expected to be commensurate with appearance. This book has explored the times and places of Regency Britain through the lens of clothing – a universal aspect of society and culture – taking as its guide the writings of one of the period's most incisive observers. It is about dress in the age Jane Austen has helped to define, filtered through her concerns and experiences, and about her attention as a novelist 'not upon great events, but upon private lives, not upon war but upon the characters of the warriors returned from the fray'.[1] But individual identity, like the many small details of textiles and clothing, was a microcosm that reflected macrocosms: of technology, material production, aesthetic trends, new modes of consumption and, most importantly, gentry people creating clothing systems through particular communities of acquaintance. The middle classes of society, which Sir Walter Scott considered Austen to be 'inimitable' in depicting, faithfully embedded considerable change into their clothing during the Regency, in ways that we can read now.[2] In this age of great revolutions, many smaller-scale revolutions transformed gentry dress in quiet, domestic ways, like Austen's own subtle revolutions in fiction techniques. The growing power of more people to buy and wear scraps as small as ribbons or as influential as cashmere shawls refined, defined and legitimised the rapid, tumbling shifts of changing society through dress. Austen's fiction incorporates these effects on her characters, and her letters document them on real people.

✳ ✳

On one hand, England was a small, island-bound society. On the other, Britain was a global power. Yet often 'a fantasy of total perfection is projected back onto the Regency period so that it becomes a safe haven that is completely uncontaminated by what are taken to be the vulgarities of the modern world', sweeping fashion into its prettified clutches.[3] The dress practices of Regency Britain were delightfully more vulgar and modern, more prosaic, and less romanticised than Austen heritage space of Austenland can display. Where this imaginary geography has been characterised in terms of the southern English counties, or defined by class – 'positioned both inside and outside the world of the greater gentry' – reading around Austen's life reveals connections with far larger social spheres, often at just one remove.[4] In her immediate family were people with first-hand experience of the French Revolution, court life and famous personalities in England and France, the British colonies in the East and West Indies, travel throughout Europe by land and around it by sea, the Americas, the life of a landed country gentleman, sea battle, the church, teaching, banking and prison. Regency fashion likewise reflected all these cultures in the texture of everyday gentry life. People created clothing communities of dress practices, and standards against which those of others could be judged (and often found wanting). This local Regency dress was inherently connected to global concerns, rendering British bodies visibly and materially of their nation as they moved ever further through the world, broadcasting the nation's values.

As Regency people encountered clothing through people, print and things, I have sought in the world of dress some of the breadth they knew and that informed their experience, explicitly or not. As always, Austen's missing letters are tantalising. What other details of dress solutions soothing to the economically vexed might she have recorded; what further confirmations of gentry clothing habits? And why does it matter? Because dress made people. Where Austen uses language, her compatriots used their eyes and hands to assess, scrutinize, criticize, desire or be repulsed by others' selves conveyed by their dressed appearance. Clothing was essential to determining self. As no man is an island, no garment springs fully formed from some fountainhead of 'fashion', independent of production and consumption networks. Once it exists, that garment mediates myriad factors, including the peculiar and individual body of the wearer, the cultural agreements of taste and propriety in operation, the climate, the materials and methods of its construction, the tasks and social roles to be performed in it: in short, all the values operating far beyond the fiscal. Austen, 'in delineating the manners and morals of the country gentry . . . not only puts on record what seemed too small to include in conventional history, but does so on a macro-scale'.[5] The kind of thread in a gown or a tiny piece of selvedge can expand into a view of international trade relationships in the same way as a passing word or two in Austen reveals volumes about a character – she is 'an author who wants to be "seen" to notice everything (but may not want to be caught noticing)'.[6] There are no unimportant features in either the gown or the novel, looked at with a certain eye, but it can be hard to fill in the details in the work of a woman whose genius partly lies in her lack of them.

The two threads of this book are the clothes Regency middling sorts wore, and the influences on their wearing, woven into a pattern determined by Austen's gaze. A different author's work would create a different outcome and subjects of focus. Every area is only an outline that I hope future scholars will expand in new directions. The skills of close reading a text are similar to those of close reading a garment. The more experience one brings the more one sees, and seeing changes with looking. 'A disjunction between body language and actual meaning or intention can also be seen as another manifestation of . . . Austen's irony'; so comprehending what created the Regency social body, and the disjunctions between perception and meaning in the period's clothing, is to see the world around Austen as she did, and read its unwritten expressions.[7] Considering her work through dress and textiles reveals new perspectives (and vice versa) because that starting point rearranges relationships between words, objects and meaning. The clothing practices of people who lived through Austen's age go a long way to explaining her work, her time, its histories. Dress helps us to visualize the external selves of Jane Austen's characters as clearly as she wrote their internal ones. After all, not even Lydia Bennet goes naked.

Jane Austen's Family Tree

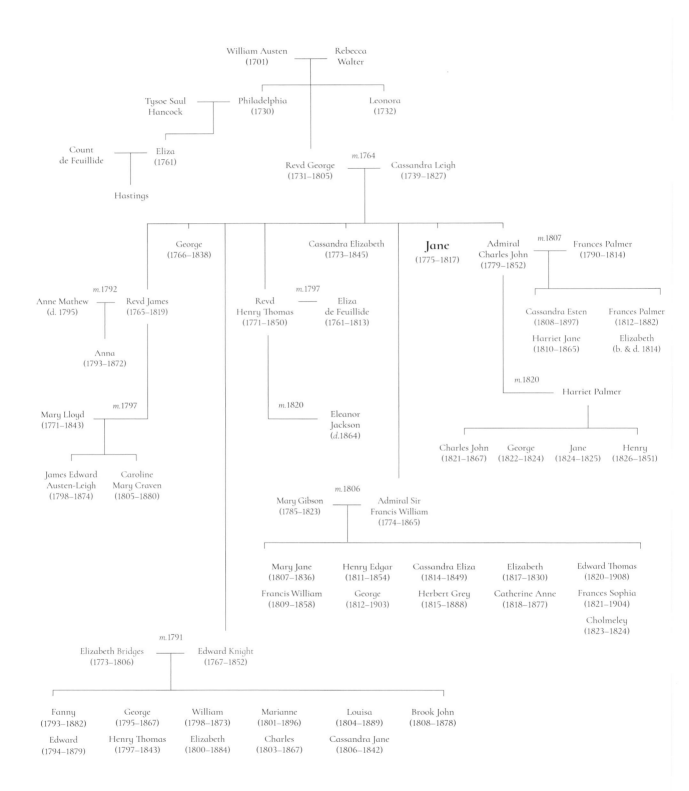

William Austen
(1701)

Rebecca
Walter

Tysoe Saul
Hancock

Philadelphia
(1730)

Leonora
(1732)

Count
de Feuillide

Eliza
(1761)

Revd George
(1731–1805)

*m.*1764

Cassandra Leigh
(1739–1827)

Hastings

George
(1766–1838)

Cassandra Elizabeth
(1773–1845)

Jane
(1775–1817)

Admiral
Charles John
(1779–1852)

*m.*1807

Frances Palmer
(1790–1814)

Anne Mathew
(d. 1795)

*m.*1792

Revd James
(1765–1819)

Revd
Henry Thomas
(1771–1850)

*m.*1797

Eliza
de Feuillide
(1761–1813)

Cassandra Esten
(1808–1897)

Frances Palmer
(1812–1882)

Anna
(1793–1872)

Harriet Jane
(1810–1865)

Elizabeth
(b. & d. 1814)

*m.*1820

Harriet Palmer

Mary Lloyd
(1771–1843)

*m.*1797

*m.*1820

Eleanor
Jackson
(*d.*1864)

Charles John
(1821–1867)

George
(1822–1824)

Jane
(1824–1825)

Henry
(1826–1851)

James Edward
Austen-Leigh
(1798–1874)

Caroline
Mary Craven
(1805–1880)

*m.*1806

Mary Gibson
(1785–1823)

Admiral Sir
Francis William
(1774–1865)

Mary Jane
(1807–1836)

Henry Edgar
(1811–1854)

Cassandra Eliza
(1814–1849)

Elizabeth
(1817–1830)

Edward Thomas
(1820–1908)

Francis William
(1809–1858)

George
(1812–1903)

Herbert Grey
(1815–1888)

Catherine Anne
(1818–1877)

Frances Sophia
(1821–1904)

Cholmeley
(1823–1824)

*m.*1791

Elizabeth Bridges
(1773–1806)

Edward Knight
(1767–1852)

Fanny
(1793–1882)

George
(1795–1867)

William
(1798–1873)

Marianne
(1801–1896)

Louisa
(1804–1889)

Brook John
(1808–1878)

Edward
(1794–1879)

Henry Thomas
(1797–1843)

Elizabeth
(1800–1884)

Charles
(1803–1867)

Cassandra Jane
(1806–1842)

List of Characters in Jane Austen's Fiction

This list records the main characters in all Jane Austen's novels, including those left unfinished. Juvenilia are omitted (see Austen, 1993, and Austen, 2006).

Emma (1815)

Henry Woodhouse, widower
Daughters of Mr Woodhouse
    Isabella Knightley
    Emma Woodhouse
John Knightley, Isabella's husband
George Knightley, a neighbour of the Woodhouses,
    brother of John Knightley
Anne Weston (née Taylor), Emma's former governess
Mr Weston, a neighbour of the Woodhouses, husband
    of Anne Weston
Frank Churchill, Mr Weston's son, raised by his aunt
    Mrs Churchill
Harriet Smith, friend of Emma
Philip Elton, vicar of Highbury
Augusta Elton, the vicar's wife
Mrs Bates, an elderly widowed friend of Mr Woodhouse
Miss Bates, spinster, daughter of Mrs Bates
Jane Fairfax, Miss Bates's niece
Robert Martin, a local farmer
Colonel and Mrs Campbell, friends of Jane Fairfax's
    late father

Mansfield Park (1814)

Sir Thomas Bertram, baronet
Lady Bertram (née Maria Ward)
Children of Sir Thomas and Lady Bertram:
    Tom Bertram
    Edmund Bertram
    Maria Bertram
    Julia Bertram
Mrs Norris, Lady Bertram's older, widowed sister
Frances (Fanny) Price, Lady Bertram's younger sister,
    and her husband, a naval marine
Children of Mr and Mrs Price:
    William Price, a naval midshipman
    Fanny Price, who goes to live with the Bertrams
    Susan Price
    Richard Price
    Samuel Price
    others
Dr Grant, parson at Mansfield Park
Mrs Grant, wife of Dr Grant
Half-siblings of Mrs Grant:
    Henry Crawford
    Mary Crawford

Northanger Abbey (1817)

Catherine Morland
James Morland, Catherine's older brother
Mrs and Mr Allen, neighbours of the Morlands
Mrs Thorpe, a friend of Mrs Allen
Children of Mrs Thorpe:
    John Thorpe
    Isabella Thorpe
General Tilney, widower, owner of Northanger Abbey
Children of General Tilney:

Captain Frederick Tilney
Henry Tilney, a clergyman
Eleanor Tilney

Persuasion (1817)

Sir Walter Elliot, baronet, widower
Daughters of Sir Walter:
    Elizabeth Elliot
    Anne Elliot
    Mary Musgrove
Mr Charles Musgrove
Mrs Musgrove, wife of Charles Musgrove
Children of Mr and Mrs Musgrove:
    Charles Musgrove, Mary's husband
    Louisa Musgrove
    Henrietta Musgrove
Admiral Croft, Sir Walter's tenant
Sophia Croft, the Admiral's wife
Captain Frederick Wentworth RN, Mrs Croft's brother
Lady Russell, a friend of the late Lady Elliot, and
    Anne's godmother
Mrs Penelope Clay, widowed daughter of Sir
    Walter's solicitor
Captain Harville RN, and Captain James Benwick RN,
    friends of Captain Wentworth
William Elliot, distant cousin and heir presumptive to
    Sir Walter
Mrs Smith, an invalid widowed friend of Anne

Pride and Prejudice (1813)

Mr and Mrs Bennet
Daughters of Mr and Mrs Bennet:
    Jane Bennet
    Elizabeth (Lizzy) Bennet
    Mary Bennet
    Catherine (Kitty) Bennet
    Lydia Bennet
Charles Bingley, neighbour of the Bennets
Sisters of Charles Bingley:
    Caroline Bingley
    Louisa Hurst
Mr Hurst, Mrs Hurst's husband
Fitzwilliam Darcy, a friend of Charles Bingley
Georgiana Darcy, Mr Darcy's younger sister
Lady Catherine de Bourgh, Mr Darcy's aunt
Anne de Bourgh, Lady Catherine's daughter
Mr William Collins, Mr Bennet's cousin, on whom Mr
    Bennet's estate is entailed; vicar of Huntsford, a
    living in Lady Catherine's gift
Edward Gardiner, Mrs Bennet's brother
Mrs M. Gardiner, Mr Gardiner's wife
George Wickham, son of the steward to
    Mr Darcy's father
Sir William and Lady Lucas, neighbours of the Bennets
Daughters of Sir William and Lady Lucas:
    Charlotte Collins
    Maria Lucas

Sanditon (1817, unfinished)

Charlotte Heywood, a visitor to Sanditon, staying
    with the Parkers
Mr Thomas Parker and Mrs Parker, residents
    of Sanditon
Siblings of Mr Parker:
    Sidney Parker, an older brother
    Diana Parker
Lady Denham, widow, resident of Sanditon
Lady Denham's nieces and nephew:
    Clara Brereton
    Sir Edward Denham
    Esther Denham, Sir Edward's sister
Mrs Griffiths, a visitor to Sanditon
Mrs Griffiths's wards:
    Miss Lambe, from the West Indies the two Misses
    Beaufort, sisters

Sense and Sensibility (1811)

Mrs Dashwood, a widow
Daughters of Mrs Dashwood:
    Elinor Dashwood
    Marianne Dashwood
    Margaret Dashwood
John Dashwood, half-brother to
    Mrs Dashwood's daughters
Mrs Fanny Dashwood [née Ferrars], John
    Dashwood's wife
Brothers to Fanny Dashwood:
    Robert Ferrars
    Edward Ferrars
Mrs Ferrars, mother of Fanny, Robert and Edward
Mrs Jennings, widow
Children of Mrs Jennings:
    Lady Middleton, Sir John Middleton's wife
    Charlotte Palmer
Sir John Middleton, cousin of Mrs Dashwood (the elder)
    and husband of Lady Middleton
Mr Thomas Palmer, Charlotte's husband
Cousins of Mrs Jennings:
    Anne Steele
    Lucy Steele
Colonel Brandon, friend of Sir John Middleton
John Willoughby
Miss Sophia Grey, Mr Willoughby's future wife

The Watsons (c.1804–5, unfinished)

Mr Watson, a widowed clergyman, father of two sons
    and four daughters
Two daughters of Mr Watson:
    Elizabeth Watson
    Emma Watson
Lord and Lady Osborne, the Watsons' neighbours
Lord and Lady Osborne's son:
    Lord Osborne
Tom Musgrave, friend of the young Lord Osborne

Changes in the Construction
of Women's Gowns, 1790–1820

1790

Bodice	The bodice is lined in linen (body lining), and pleated into shape with long vertical seams at the back. It is front opening, with straight fronts, and finishes around the natural waistline.
Skirt	The skirt is uncut, made up of straight widths of fabric, usually 3–5, depending on the width of the fabric (silk is narrow). These are pleated onto the waistline, with the bulk of the fabric at the sides and back (of front-opening gowns).
Sleeves	Gown sleeves are mostly elbow length and are usually set smoothly into the sleeve head. Straight sleeves fit to the arm through their cut.
Details	There are slits in the side seams of gowns and petticoats to give access to detachable pockets worn under the petticoats.

1795

Bodice	The bodice is lined in linen (body lining). Waistlines are rising rapidly. The 'round gown', closed at the front, is increasingly popular. Gathered necklines and waists become fashionable, adding bulk. Some gowns have pleated backs with no seam at the waist.
Skirt	The skirt is uncut, made up of straight widths of fabric, usually 2–5. These are pleated onto the waistline. The bulk of the fabric is distributed around the waist. Trains, with straight or rounded ends, are popular, and reach their maximum length c.1798–1802.
Sleeves	Gown sleeves are mostly elbow length, and are either set smoothly into the sleeve head, or have full gathers. Straight sleeves fit to the arm. If sleeves are long, on jackets or bodices, the cut is shaped to the arm with a bend at the elbow; they are cut in two pieces with the seams running down mid-back and mid-front (i.e. seams do not run down the top of the sleeve or under the arm).
Details	Necklines start to be adjustable through drawstrings. This continues until the early 1820s.

1800

Bodice	The bodice is still lined in a solid fabric. The waistline is just below the natural bust. Gathers have replaced pleats. Crossover and straight horizontal necklines are popular. Back seams become angled. Shoulder seams drop to the back, and the back neckline becomes lower. There are no side seams.
Skirt	The skirt is uncut, made up of straight widths (selvedge to selvedge) of fabric, now 2–4. Trains are still present but are becoming shorter, especially in day dress. Gathers are disappearing at the front where the skirt joins the bodice, and the top of the skirt is becoming flat. The bulk of the fabric is at the centre back.
Sleeves	Short sleeves, above the elbow, or cap sleeves are the most fashionable, with a little fullness through gathers at the sleeve head. Muslin gowns have lost the linen sleeve lining.
Details	Some gowns lose their pocket slits. The peak of tubular, straight fashion, though still with some fabric bulk.

1805

Bodice
Gowns start to have back openings. The fall front or bib fastening is popular: linen linings are pinned together over the bosom and concealed by a piece of outer gown fabric, pinned or buttoned onto the shoulder straps. The waistline is under the bust. Back seams start to curve, creating a characteristic kite shape.

Skirt
The skirt consists of 2–3 widths of straight fabric, not always using the selvedge – some pieces are cut from a length. Trains are much shorter. The skirt is flat at the centre front and the bulk of the fabric is at the back. Gathers have replaced pleats.

Sleeves
Sleeves increase slightly in fullness at the sleeve head; short cap or puffed sleeves are the most fashionable. Sometimes caps are put over longer undersleeves for day wear. Sleeves are deeply set into the bodice.

Details
Gowns of muslin and other transparent fabrics are often unlined, including the bodice. Separate, sometimes coloured, slips are worn to provide an opaque layer under the gown.

1810

Bodice
Muslin bodices are unlined, and some other gowns lose their body-lining too. Bodices are cut on the straight grain of the fabric; bust shaping is controlled through gathers or cut. The waistline begins to drop slightly. Back-opening gowns are fastened with tied tapes, or buttons. Back seams are curved.

Skirt
Triangular side gores start to increase, so skirts become slightly wider at the hem. Selvedge to selvedge widths of fabric are still used for the skirt. Trains are worn only in court dress.

Sleeves
Sleeves increase in size, with the fullness at the sleeve head towards the back. The depth of the armhole at the back decreases. Long sleeves are acceptable in evening dress, usually cut on the bias.

Details
Muslin and transparent gowns are now completely unlined. Applied surface decoration increases, especially bands of fabric. Vandyked decoration is popular.

1815

Bodice
The waistline continues to drop for daywear, but for evening wear rises to its highest, making bodices their narrowest ever c.1816–18. Bodices begin to be cut on the bias, using darts to shape the fullness for the bust. Back seams are curved.

Skirt
Skirts are increasingly triangular. Flounces and hem decorations become popular. Gown skirts are shortened so that the petticoat hem shows.

Sleeves
Sleeves continue to increase in size with gathered or pleated fullness at the sleeve head, at the top and back. The depth of the armhole at the back decreases.

Details
There is a sudden increase in the use of haberdashery to trim gowns, especially piping, cording, ribbon, fabric foliage, braids and cartisane (paper or parchment wrapped in silk floss). Gauze and net gowns worn over slips become more popular.

1820

Bodice
Gowns are now usually back opening, fastened with buttons, with hooks and eyes, or with hooks and worked eyelets. Linings are made of cotton, cut on the bias.

Skirt
Skirts are bell shaped, and always made with triangular pieces. They are flat at the front, with the bulk of the fabric gathered or pleated into the side and the back. Stiffening at the hems, using wadding and interlining, helps skirts to stand out. There is much emphasis on hem decoration.

Sleeves
Puffed sleeves are normal, and are often cut on the bias. Fullness is distributed all around the sleeve head.

Details
Cotton starts to appear in tapes and linings. Piping or cording of the bodice and sleeves seams becomes popular. Rouleaux decoration, made from the same fabric as the gown, is used increasingly, as is surface decoration.

Glossary

A

apron-front *See* *fall-front.

B

baleen *See* *whalebone.

bandanna [bandana, bamdana] A coloured silk or cotton handkerchief, with white or yellow spots made by tie-dyeing; originally from India.

bandeau [band] A headband, fillet or narrow piece of fabric or ribbon, sometimes decorated, worn on or around a woman's head.

banyan [banian, bannian; India gown] A loose, informal man's robe, nightgown or dressing-gown, originally from India, made in cotton, silk or wool; it was worn at home, before one was formally dressed.

Barcelona [Barsalona] **handkerchief** A twilled silk handkerchief, plain, checked or with fancy patterns, and usually brightly coloured; handkerchiefs of this kind were first manufactured in Spain.

batiste (Fr.) (1) *Cambric. (2) A fine linen cloth from Flanders or Picardy. Both types of cloth were popular for morning gowns.

beaver (1) [castor] A woollen felted cloth, with a heavily napped and raised surface, in imitation of beaver fur. (2) A hat made of beaver cloth or of expensive beaver skin. (3) A kind of cheap leather, dyed different colours and used for gloves.

bedgown An informal jacket or gown with loose sleeves, worn at home, or by working women.

Belcher handkerchief A patterned handkerchief, usually yellow and red, named after the prize-fighter Jem Belcher.

bib-front *See* *fall-front.

blonde [blonde lace, blonde net] Silk bobbin lace, the creamy colour of raw silk.

bobbin net [bobbinet, bobbinette] A machine-made lace, imitating fine bobbin or 'pillow' lace, plain woven in a hexagonal mesh of four sides twisted and two crossed over; it was usually made of silk and cotton. *Tulle is a kind of bobbin net.

bodice [body] (1) Any part of a woman's gown worn around the upper torso; the upper part of the gown, or the lining of that part. (2) A quilted or boned undergarment such as a corset, jumps or stays.

bombazine [bombasine, bombazin, bombazeen] A twilled fabric made of silk and wool worsted, of cotton with silk, or of worsted alone; it was often black, and in this colour was used for mourning dress.

bombazet [bombazet, bombazette] A twilled fabric of cotton and worsted, or of worsted alone, cheaper than *bombazine. It was used for mourning, and for day gowns.

bonnet (1) Structured women's headgear for outdoor wear, having a brim at the front and sides only; it was tied under the chin with 'strings' or ribbons. *See also* *cawl. (2) A soft, brimless cap made of fabric, or knitted.

book muslin [buke] A plain, very light and stiff muslin, originally shipped from India in a 'book-fold' bale.

Botany worsted A term for the finer grades of merino wool, originating in Australia, and for cloth made from it.

boteh [*buteh*, *buta*] A curved teardrop motif from Indian designs, thought to be a stylised leaf, pear, or pine cone; textiles with this pattern are now known as 'paisley' after the Scottish town where they were manufactured.

box-coat A kind of greatcoat: a heavy, loose overcoat, with one or more capes, worn by coachmen and any travellers seated outside a coach.

breeches Men's trousers reaching to just below the knee and fastened there; they were always worn with stockings, which covered the lower leg. With the advent of braces, c.1790, a slimmer silhouette replaced the earlier fuller cut. Breeches are distinct from trousers, which covered the whole leg; from c.1800 trousers began to supersede breeches, which were consigned to wear by the elderly and to evening dress and formal court dress.

broadcloth A plain- or twill-woven fabric of fine woollen yarn, highly fulled, with a slightly lustrous finish; it was used in men's coats and suits.

Brussels lace Fine-quality, expensive handmade bobbin or needlepoint lace, or sometimes these techniques combined, usually with a fine hexagonal mesh and floral patterns, and outlined by a woven edging; it was made in Brussels and the vicinity.

buckskin A fine woollen cloth, usually creamy white, with a heavily fulled finish and a distinctive twill resulting from its eight-end satin weave; its surface texture resembled the skin of the male fallow deer. Buckskin was popular for riding breeches.

bugle A straight, tubular glass bead, or decoration with such beads.

busk A smooth, straight piece of wood inserted into the front of a pair of stays or a corset between the breasts to separate them and to keep a straight centre line.

C

calash (from Fr. *calèche*: a lightweight carriage with removable, collapsible hood) [ugly] A large, folding women's hood, made of silk or satin supported by hoops of cane or whalebone, and projecting beyond the face. It was designed to protect high headwear and hairstyles out of doors.

calico [callico] Originally a plain-weave cotton cloth, imported from India in many grades, and usually printed; the term soon came to mean any cotton imported from the East, and, eventually, any cotton fabric, including those of European manufacture, and those with warps of other fibres such as linen. Printed calico could be washed without the design's colour bleeding. Calico was used in morning and day dress, and for other informal or domestic clothing. (Unbleached calico is now called 'muslin' in American English.)

calimanco [callimanco, calamanco] A highly glazed, plain or twilled woollen or worsted cloth, plain, striped, checked or figured; it was popular for waistcoats.

cambric [French lawn] A fine white linen or hard-spun cotton fabric, originally from Cambrai in France. When imported into Britain, it was known as French lawn.

cambric muslin A cotton fabric more densely woven and less transparent than muslin; it was popular for women's morning and day dress, and for small accessories.

camlet [camblet, camlette] A hard-wearing fabric woven from mixed threads of wool, especially camel or goat, and silk.

cap A general term for any close-fitting headdress of soft material and structure, worn in informal domestic settings or by members of particular trades or professions. A woman's cap could also be worn out of doors, under a bonnet.

cape An elbow-length cloak, or attached circular additional layer, falling from under the collar of a cloak or coat over the shoulders to provide extra warmth.

carmelite A fine, soft, plain-woven woollen or worsted cloth, generally of a dark colour, used for women's outer garments.

cartisane A small piece of thin cardboard, parchment or vellum, around which thread, silk, gold or silver has been wrapped to form an applied embellishment for a gown.

cashmere The soft hair of the cashmere goat and the light, warm and soft woollen cloth made from it.

cassimere *See* *kerseymere.

castor (Lat.: 'beaver') *See* beaver (1).

catgut (1) A linen canvas for embroidery. (2) Coarse corded cloth used for linings. (3) A kind of lace.

cawl [caul] (1) The soft fabric back part of a bonnet, taking the place of a structured crown, and attached to the brim or front. (2) The fabric cover applied over a bonnet foundation.

chapeau-bras *See* *opera hat.

chemise *See* *shift.

chemise gown A style of gown worn from the late eighteenth century, thought of as resembling a chemise; it was made of light, white cotton fabric, with a low, round neck gathered on a drawstring, and was cinched under the bust with a sash.

chemisette A tabard covering the upper part of the body and filling in the neck of a gown, often appearing like a false shirt front with a collar; it fastened with a drawstring at the waist or under the bust. The term appeared in the later Regency period; earlier, the garment might be called a collared neckerchief (referring to the way a woman's neck-handkerchief filled in the décolletage) or a habit-shirt.

chenille (Fr.: 'caterpillar') Soft, fluffy, silk embroidery thread.

chicken-skin A very thin yellow leather, made from the hides of unborn cows; it was used for gloves.

chintz A fabric of cotton, linen or combination-fibre calico, fast-printed or hand-painted in numerous colours with floral and other patterns, and usually glazed; it was imported from India.

chip Very thin strips of willow, plaited together to make material for hats; it was usually painted black or white.

clear muslin *Muslin of particular transparency.

cloak A loose outer garment, worn by both sexes over other clothing, usually for warmth and protection outdoors; it was like a cape, but three-quarter or full length. Women's cloaks could also be made of light, decorative textiles, worn for style.

clock The shaping at the ankle of a stocking, tapering off up the leg; the clock was often knitted decoratively or embroidered.

clogs Wooden- or leather-soled overshoes, worn out of doors, to raise the wearer above dirt and wet ground.

cording Fine cord covered with fabric, applied to a garment for decoration and to reinforce seams; it is now called 'piping'.

corduroy [corderoy] A sturdy, hard-wearing cotton fabric, with thick ridges or cords of short, velvety pile; it was used for breeches, waistcoats and coats, especially for rural and working dress. It was a type of fustian; *see* *fustian (2).

corset [corsette] (1) A close-fitting, soft undergarment, worn to support the breasts and shape the silhouette. Originally corsets were shorter and more lightly stiffened than stays, using cording or whalebone, but from the early nineteenth century onwards the terms started to converge, as corsets were more commonly worn, became longer and had more boning in them. (2) In fashion, a kind of sleeveless, decorative waistcoat or bolero, worn over, and usually contrasting with, the gown.

Cossacks Voluminous trousers, introduced in 1814, when Tsar Alexander I attended the celebrations in London of the Peace of Vienna, accompanied by Cossack soldiers wearing a similar style. They were pleated into a waistband and drawn in at the ankles with a ribbon drawstring.

court dress A form of full dress that fulfilled the regulations for appearing at court.

coutil (Fr.: 'ticking', 'drill') A strong, close-textured linen (and, later, cotton) fabric, woven in herringbone twill. The word was used increasingly in English from the Regency period.

crape A light fabric, woven from wool or gummed silk, in a plain weave with a distinctive, lightly crinkled surface achieved by extreme twisting of the fibres. Black crape was widely used for mourning dress. China crape (now called crepe de Chine) was made of fine silk with more threads in the warp than the weft; it was used in evening dress.

cravat A square of light linen, cotton or silk cloth, folded diagonally into a band, wrapped around the neck and tied in a knot or bow at the front; see also *neckcloth.

crewel [cruel] Coloured embroidery yarn made of fine, loosely twisted two-ply worsted. Hence 'crewel-work' for embroidery done with this yarn.

crop A hairstyle for men and women, in which the hair was cut short or close to the head, leaving no long hair at the back.

D

day dress See *morning dress.

dickey A man's false, detachable shirt front, like a woman's chemisette.

dimity A stout, white cotton, plain or twilled, with fine ribs or woven-in decoration on one side; it might be plain, or printed with a pattern in one or more colours. It was popular for morning dress, waistcoats, and accessories such as detachable pockets.

ditto suit [dittoes, suit of dittoes] A man's suit with breeches, waistcoat and coat made from the same fabric. The term was often used for black professional or brown sporting dress.

Dorset button Any of several types of button, made of metal rings covered in fabric, or wrapped with thread in decorative patterns.

dowlas [dowl] A heavy, coarse linen or cotton fabric, used for shirts and smocks.

drab A thick, closely woven woollen cloth, of a yellowish, grey or brown colour; also, these colours in any context.

drawers Linen, cotton or woollen underwear trousers, knee-length when worn by a man under breeches, knee- or ankle-length when worn by a woman under a gown.

dressmaker A woman engaged in the making of garments for other women; the term is synonymous with 'mantua-maker', and appeared c.1800.

drill A sturdy, twilled linen fabric, popular for men's trousers, breeches and lightweight upper garments; see also *coutil.

duck Strong, plain-woven white linen fabric, often with double warp and double weft threads; it was frequently used for trousers and summer coats.

duffel [duffil, duffield] A coarse woollen fabric with a thick nap on both sides, also an overcoat made of this fabric. It was named for the Belgian town of Duffel.

E

evening dress A form of full dress, comprising clothing and accessories suitable only for evening events (cf. *morning dress).

F

fall-front [apron front, bib-front, front fall, stomacher-front] An opening at the front of a gown consisting of a panel of fabric that pins or buttons onto the shoulder bands, covering the bust and hiding the overlapping bodice lining underneath. When unfastened it falls down onto the skirt. By extension, any opening to a garment in which a flap of cloth folds down when unfastened; see also *falls.

falls A contraction of 'fall-downs', referring to the fall-front opening of breeches or, later, pantaloons and trousers, comprising a flap of material sewn along its lower edge and buttoned to (or just below) the waistband. Whole falls extended from one side-seam to the other, while the more fashionable 'small' or 'split falls' consisted of a smaller central flap.

fan parasol A parasol with a hinged stick so that the shade could provide either vertical or horizontal protection from the sun.

ferret [ferrit] A narrow tape of silk, wool or cotton.

fichu A finished square or triangle of light linen or cotton, worn around a woman's neck, shoulders and chest for warmth and protection; it could be tucked into the gown or tied at the front.

figured Of a fabric, ornamented with patterns or designs, often achieved by means of the weave, but also by printing or needlework.

floss [silk floss] The rough, short fibres shed in the winding of silk cocoons; these fibres were carded and made into common silk fabrics, or were used, untwisted, in embroidery.

flannel A somewhat loosely woven plain-weave or twilled cloth of undyed (cream) woollen yarn, of variable fineness, with a fluffy, raised nap; historically, it was called 'Welsh cotton' after its traditional place of manufacture.

French lawn See *cambric.

French wadding A light, fluffy woollen or vegetable-fibre filling material, used for padding.

frieze A coarse, warm woollen cloth with a rough nap, used for outer garments.

frock (1) A gown with bodice and skirt in one, or one that fastens at the back before back opening became general (from the early years of the nineteenth century). (2) A frock coat: a man's double- or single-breasted coat, with large revers and full thigh- to knee-length skirts with no cutaway at the front.

front (1) A hairpiece imitating a fringe, to be worn at the front of a woman's head. (2) The brim of a bonnet, as distinct from the cawl.

full dress An ensemble or a mode of dress appropriate for formal or public occasions in the afternoon or later, such as court dress, evening dress, or dress worn to the opera or formal dinners (cf. *half-dress).

fulling A finishing process for woollen cloth that felts, compresses and thickens the fibres through scouring and pressing, raising the nap and obscuring the weave; such cloth is described as 'fulled'.

furbelow [falbela] A flounce or ruffle on a woman's petticoat, scarf, apron or sometimes gown; it was usually made of the same fabric as the item it adorned, or of lace.

fustian (1) Originally, a coarse, twilled fabric of linen warp and cotton weft, but later any textile made of mixed linen and cotton, or any coarse cotton cloth. (2) During the Regency, a thick, twilled, grey-brown cotton, with a short, velvety nap, like corduroy, but without ribs; it was used in rural and working dress.

G

gaiters [spatterdashes] Leg coverings made of leather, canvas or wool, extending from above the knee or from the calf to the front of the foot, and fastened with buttons down the outer side. Worn with breeches by men, gaiters protected the legs. Half-gaiters, or spats, extended from the ankle to the front of the foot and were worn with trousers and pantaloons.

gallaces Braces.

galloon [gallon] Narrow, close-woven ribbon or braid, made of wool, or of gold, silver or silk thread, used as trimming.

galosh (1) In the upper of a shoe, a piece of leather running round the shoe and attached to the sole; it was made of stouter material than the rest of the body of the shoe, and protected the foot from cold and wet. (2) In later use, a protective overshoe made of impermeable material. In the Regency, 'galoshes' of this kind were unknown, and other kinds of outer footwear were worn to protect the shoes from dirt and wet (see *clog, *patten).

gauze A fine, thin, transparent, open-weave fabric, usually made of silk, but sometimes of linen or cotton; the dual warp threads are twisted around the weft to give firmness. It was popular for women's evening dress.

gimp [gymp] An openwork trimming or braid, made by twisting silk or worsted yarns around wire or cord to create a sturdy texture, then plaiting or braiding the resulting threads together.

gingham A firm, medium-weight linen or (more often) cotton cloth; the yarn was dyed and woven in checks or stripes, and the fabric was sometimes glazed like chintz. Gingham originally came from India.

gipsy [gipsey, gypsy] **hat** A large-brimmed, circular straw hat, held on by a wide ribbon or sash running over the top of the hat and tied under the chin, holding down the brim on either side.

glazing A finishing process for textiles involving the application of a glossy substance to the fabric, which is then calendered, usually with rollers, to achieve a smooth, glossy surface; such cloth is described as 'glazed'.

greatcoat Any form of man's coat intended to protect the wearer and his clothes out of doors, especially when travelling. Made of heavy material, it was usually single-breasted (though could be double-breasted) and covered the wearer to the knee, calf or ankle; it was fastened in front with straps, in addition to, or instead of, buttons, and often had a cape or capes over the shoulders. See also *box-coat.

gum flowers Artificial flowers made from cambric or silk, stiffened with gum arabic and dried on glass; the use of gum resulted in a smooth, glossy finish.

gurrah Coarse, thick, plain cotton cloth made in north-eastern India; it was often printed after importation to European countries.

H

half-dress An ensemble or a mode of dress appropriate for semi-formal public events, such as daytime functions or informal evening gatherings (cf. *full dress).

half-robe A low-necked, thigh-length tunic worn over a round gown.

habit See *riding-habit.

habit-shirt A woman's linen or (later) cotton garment, usually with long sleeves like a man's shirt, worn under a waistcoat or jacket as part of a riding ensemble (hence the name 'habit'), or under a petticoat with a sleeveless bodice for informal wear at home; it might also be made of cambric or muslin, and often had ruffles at neck and wrists. A sleeveless form of habit-shirt was called a chemisette.

handkerchief A square of finished fabric, plain or decorated, worn around the head, neck or shoulders by men or women; a 'half-handkerchief' was a triangular piece of cloth used for the same purpose. A handkerchief worn around the neck was called a 'neckerchief'. A smaller piece, not worn but carried for various purposes, was called a 'pocket handkerchief'.

Hanover lace The meaning of this term is uncertain. It may refer to a variation of 'Honiton lace', a bobbin lace like *Brussels lace but coarser, and with simpler applied patterns. The use of the term in the context of poor work suggests a base of machine net with decorations of small embroidered flowers.

hard tartan Tartan cloth woven from worsted yarn.

Hessians Men's black, square-toed riding-boots, of a style first worn by the troops of Hesse, Germany; they were calf-length at the back, and, in front, curved to a point just below the knee, with a decorative tassel in the centre. Hessians sometimes had a narrow border of coloured leather bound around the upper edge.

Holland Originally, linen fabric imported from Holland, though the name became generic for many linens. When unbleached, it was called 'brown Holland'. Holland was frequently used to line coats and other outer garments, but also for shirts and gowns.

huswife [hussive, housewife, hussif] A folding case made of fabric, to hold pins, needles, scissors, thread and other sewing necessities.

Hussar boots Men's boots, resembling Hessians but without the tassel.

I

India gown See *banyan.

indispensible See *reticule.

inexpressibles A euphemism for 'breeches'.

Irish Irish linen, used for nightwear, undergarments and many miscellaneous accessories.

Isabel A name for colours of a yellowy hue, reminiscent of the coats of animals, from pale grey-yellow through to fawn and tawny browns.

J

jaconet [jacconet, jaconet muslin] A thin cotton, of a weight between muslin and cambric; it was popular for women's morning dress.

jacket Any short, close-fitting, outer coat, for men or women, sometimes called a 'spencer'. For women, such a jacket was waist-length, in accordance with the fashionable waistline. For men, it was often indistinguishable from a sleeved waistcoat.

jean (1) A stout, twilled cotton fabric, and (in the nineteenth century) also a twilled sateen. (2) A type of coarse twilled fabric of linen and cotton, used for a range of men's and women's clothing, and for linings (see also *fustian (1)).

jumps [bodies] An unboned under-bodice, worn at home by women instead of stays; jumps were often padded or quilted, with a stomacher to fill the gap where they were laced at the front. See also *bodice (2), *waistcoat (2).

K

kersey A stout, somewhat coarse twilled fabric made of wool, or of wool with a cotton warp, closely napped, and heavier than broadcloth. It was effective for repelling cold and damp, and was used in suits, coats and outerwear.

kerseymere [cassimere, cassimer] An expensive, medium-weight, twilled woollen cloth, made of densely woven, very fine yarns, finished with a close nap and having a soft texture. First patented by Francis Yerbury of Bradford in 1766, it was used in tailored clothing.

L

lamé [lama] Light, silk gauze, woven through with silver or gilt threads to create a shimmering metallic surface; it was popular for women's court and evening dress.

latchet(s) The pair of long tabs at the top front of a shoe that overlap and pass through the buckle to fasten, or tie together with a lace, without overlapping.

lawn A very fine, quite crisp, plain-weave linen or cotton, originally from Laon, France; it was widely used for undergarments, shirts, shifts and any other accessory that could be made of linen or cotton. For French lawn, *see* *cambric.

Leghorn A fine, very pliable straw from the Livorno region of Italy, plaited into strips to be made into headwear; also a hat or bonnet made from this straw.

leno A light but strong cotton or linen gauze, most often used for caps and veils but sometimes for gowns worn over slips.

Levers lace A kind of net made on the Levers machine (invented 1813), using Jacquard loom technology (1805) to form patterns, especially zig-zags and V-shapes, and to imitate handmade lace.

Limerick gloves Gloves made of chicken-skin, named for Limerick in Ireland, where such gloves were first made.

linsey-wolsey [linsey-woolsey] A coarse fabric of linen warp and wool weft.

livery The distinctive uniform, usually a suit of clothes, provided for, and worn by, a household's male retainers or servants, distinguished by colour, design and sometimes insignia.

lustre A glossy fabric, woven from silk and worsted, used for women's gowns, especially evening dress.

M

Madras check [Madras] A firm cotton fabric, woven with checks of varying proportions in dual or multiple colours that were not colourfast; it was imported from Madras in India, and used in gowns and some accessories.

mancheron In women's garments, a decorative historical-style epaulette, or a puffed upper sleeve.

mantle A loose, sleeveless, enveloping outer garment, of variable length, for outdoor wear.

mantua-maker In the eighteenth century, a maker of women's clothing; the name derives from the fashionable loose mantua gown. In the Regency, the term was synonymous with 'dressmaker'. At all periods, a mantua-maker was usually female.

marcella [marseilles] A twill cotton or linen fabric with diaper patterns woven in relief; it was used for smaller dress accessories, especially waistcoats and detachable pockets.

melton A thick, well-fulled woollen fabric with a smooth, close nap, normally with a twill weave; it was popular for riding-habits and hunting-coats.

Mechlin lace Handmade bobbin lace with the pattern outlined in flat thread on a net ground. Originating in Mechelen in the Low Countries, it began to be made by machine in 1819.

merino A fine, warm cloth made from the fleece of the merino sheep; it was used in women's dress and some tailored garments.

miser's [long, stocking, ring, string] **purse** A long, tubular purse with an access slit in the centre, closed with two metal slider rings. Such purses were often crocheted, netted or knitted, and might be decorated with beads.

mittens [mitts] Fingerless gloves that covered the arm, worn for warmth while allowing dexterity; they were often made of lightweight, openwork or knitted fabrics.

mob cap A large, soft indoor cap of lightweight linen or cotton, consisting of a rounded cawl with a ruffled brim, and drawn in at the neck with strings that tied under the chin; it covered most of the hair.

mohair A soft yarn made from the hair of the Angora goat, and the fabric made from it with a silk, wool or cotton warp.

moleskin A stout, cotton fustian, with a fine nap that was cut short before dyeing to give an even, dense texture similar to a mole's fur. It was popular for breeches, trousers and waistcoats, especially for men's sporting and labouring dress.

morning dress [day dress] An ensemble or a mode of dress for informal day wear at home or outdoors in the hours before the afternoon. For women, indoor morning dress usually consisted of a high-cut, long-sleeved round gown; when layered with a bonnet and outer garment, such as a pelisse, morning dress was also appropriate for walking, shopping, running errands and making informal visits. For men, indoor morning dress could be a loose robe such as a banyan; for outdoor wear they might wear a light-coloured or lightweight coat with plated, rather than gilt, buttons, and correspondingly light-coloured, lightweight legwear and a plain waistcoat. (*Cf.* *evening dress.)

morning gown For women, a gown worn as morning dress at home, often white with a high collar and long sleeves. For men, any unstructured robe worn at home, such as a dressing-gown or banyan.

moscheetos [moschettos, moskeetos, musquetos; gaiter pantaloons] Pantaloon-like trousers with an extension over the front of the foot, like gaiters, originally intended to give protection against mosquitoes.

mousseline (Fr.) Muslin, or a dress made of that fabric. In France, *mousseline* referred to Indian muslins, and British muslin was called *organdie*.

muffetees [muffatees, muftees] Very short mittens or small wrist muffs, often knitted; they were worn for warmth or to protect shirt cuffs.

muff A cylindrical or flat tube, made from fur, feathers or fabric, into the ends of which the hands were inserted for warmth. Muffs were padded within and often had one or more small internal pockets.

muslin A lightweight, semi-transparent, soft cotton fabric, of a plain, fairly open weave, usually white; it often had a pattern, either woven in, or applied after weaving through embroidery or tambour work ('sprigged muslin'), and came in many different weights and finishes. It originated in India and was also manufactured in Britain during the Regency. *See also* *book muslin, *calico, *cambric muslin, *clear muslin, *jaconet, *mousseline.

N

nankeen [nankin] A fabric made from a yellow variety of cotton, resulting in a yellowish brown colour. Originally made in Nankin (Nanjing), China, it was popular for men's dress, and women's shoes.

neckcloth Any fabric worn around the neck, usually by men; commonly made of white linen or cotton, it was worn over the collar and tied. *See also* *cravat, *neckerchief.

neckerchief [neck-handkerchief] A square, finished piece of cloth, worn around the neck, especially by working men. Neckerchiefs were made in a huge variety of printed or woven coloured cottons and silks. *See also* *fichu, *handkerchief.

netting A technique of looping and knotting thread into an open mesh, done with a netting needle or netting shuttle, and a netting gauge.

nightcap (1) Any soft, informal cap worn by men at home or in bed. (2) A cotton or linen cap worn by women in bed.

nightgown (1) A loose gown worn in bed, especially by women. (2) An informal robe, such as a banyan, dressing-gown or powdering-gown, worn at home, especially by men.

Norwich crape A black, twill fabric of silk warp and worsted weft; it was the official fabric for court mourning. After 1819, also a fabric plain-woven with a glossy finish, similar to *bombazine.

Norwich stuff A general term for worsted and worsted-blend fabrics manufactured in East Anglia.

O

Oldenburg bonnet A style of bonnet worn by the Grand Duchess of Oldenburg (1788–1819), with a very high crown and a wide brim that hid the face; it was popular throughout Europe after the grand duchess's tour of 1814.

open gown A gown with a skirt that opened down the centre front.

opera hat [chapeau-bras, cocked hat, military folding hat] A crescent-shaped, black hat for full dress, folded up between two brims to allow it to be carried under the arm; it was often trimmed with tassels and feathers.

P

packthread Strong twine used in sewing or to tie up packages and bundles.

palampore A mordant-painted and resist-dyed Indian cotton cloth, with floral or leaf patterns.

pantaloons (1) [tights] A type of close-fitting, calf- or ankle-length men's trousers, often strapped under the foot, with a vent on the outer side of each leg. (2) [pantalet(te)s, trowsers] A woman's undergarment, consisting of long, loose drawers, worn under the skirt.

pasteboard Rolled and compressed paper, used for bonnet fronts.

patent lace [patent net, pattinet] A general term for machine-made lace.

patten An overshoe consisting of a wooden sole attached to a tall metal ring, held onto the foot by leather straps. Pattens were worn over normal shoes when walking outside, to raise the wearer above dirt and wet ground.

pelerine A woman's small mantle or cape, made of lace, silk or fur, with the lower edges curving to meet at a point at the front.

pelisse (1) [pelisse-greatcoat] Originally a term for a cloak, and in this sense, especially in a military context, a man's cloak, trimmed or lined with fur. (2) Later, and more commonly, a woman's coat-dress, made from different kinds of material from muslin to thick wool. It might be of any length from the knee to the ankle, and have any of various styles of collar, cape and sleeve; it was usually somewhat fitted, to follow the form of the gown worn underneath.

peplum [basque skirt] A flared or gathered width of fabric forming the part of a woman's jacket that hung below the waist.

percale [perkale] A glazed, fine cotton cloth, similar to cambric muslin, but less expensive; usually white or blue or printed, it was popular for morning dress.

Persian A thin, light, soft, plain-woven silk, usually used to line garments; it was similar to, but lighter than, sarsenet.

petticoat A word with many applications. (1) Any skirt, whether visible or worn underneath a gown or other petticoats; in this sense, sometimes abbreviated to 'coat'. (2) The skirt of a dress, as distinct from the bodice, with which it could be coloured to match or contrast; it might be decorated with quilting or embroidery. (3) A skirted garment with its own bodice – usually sleeveless – to hold it up, worn under a gown (especially when made of transparent fabric), or, for informal wear, over a habit-shirt. *See also* *slip.

petticoat breeches Men's knee-length trousers, gathered at the waist and correspondingly loose about the legs, with no fastenings at the knees, and thus resembling a petticoat; they were worn for working, often over other legwear, typically by seafarers.

plaid A length of woollen cloth with a checked pattern of intersecting stripes at right-angles (tartan); the word became synonymous with the pattern.

plain weave The simplest form of weave, in which the weft threads go over one warp thread and under the next, repeatedly (*cf.* *twill).

plait (1) Pleat. (2) A braided strip of straw or very thin willow (*see* *chip) used in multiples to make hats and bonnets.

plush A kind of velvet with a long, loose pile, usually woven from wool or mohair, or sometimes from silk; it was popular for waistcoats.

pocket A pouch worn by women, usually under their skirts, and accessed through slits in the side seams of the outer garment; pockets were attached, either singly or in pairs, to a tape that was tied around the waist.

poke bonnet A bonnet with a crown fitting close to the head, and a long brim, cylindrical in shape, extending horizontally out over the face.

poplin A lightweight dress fabric with a dense silk warp and lighter worsted weft.

powdering-gown A man's informal robe, such as a banyan, dressing-gown or nightgown, originally worn in the morning while the hair was being powdered.

prunella A lightweight, twill, warp-faced worsted fabric; it was usually black, and was used so often for clerical garments that the name became a synonym for 'clergyman'.

pumps Men's and women's flat, light, close-fitting dancing- or evening shoes, open over the instep; women's pumps were sometimes laced with ribbons over the instep and ankle.

Pusher lace A kind of openwork lace made on a Pusher machine (invented 1812).

Q

quilling A thin strip of fabric or lace, wound or gathered into pleats and folds by means of stitching, and used for decoration, often as an edging.

R

redingote A man's or woman's long, double-breasted and full-skirted greatcoat, with a prominent collar. A man's redingote sometimes had a short cape, and a woman's had a fitted body. The word is a French corruption of 'riding-coat', borrowed back into English.

reticule [ridicule, indispensible] A small round, square or lozenge-shaped handbag for holding a lady's essentials. Made of a soft material, knitted or netted, it was often embellished with embroidery or beading, and was drawn closed and suspended from the hand or arm by a loop of ribbon.

ribbon [ribband] A length of narrow, fine fabric, usually of silk, used as edging or decoration on garments, millinery and soft furnishings, as a hair ornament and fastening, or to tether articles together attractively.

riding-habit [habit] A woman's garment of woollen cloth, modelled on the male riding ensemble. Made by a tailor, it consisted of a waistcoat (optional), a fitted, double-breasted jacket, and a long skirt with a train. It was also worn on other occasions than when riding, and was often simply called a 'habit'.

riding-hood A woman's large, detached hood worn when riding as protection from the elements.

robe (1) In fashion, specifically, an evening gown open in front to display a decorative petticoat and having a train behind. (2) Any loose garment (as in the modern sense).

rouleaux Narrow strips of bias-cut fabric, sewn into tubes and applied in decorative patterns to women's clothing.

round bonnet A bonnet with a flared, open brim.

round gown A gown with bodice and skirt in one; the skirt was closed all round, and not open in front to expose the petticoat. It emerged in the 1790s and continued to be worn through the Regency period.

S

sarsenet [sarcenet, sarsnet] A fine, soft silk, either plain or twilled, with a slight sheen; it was widely used for linings as well as outer garments, and could be woven with patterns.

seersucker A striped fabric of Indian origin, woven of silk and cotton, often with a rippled effect produced by weaving the cotton warps with a looser tension than the silk ones.

serge A hard-wearing, twill cloth of worsted warp and wool weft, or wholly of worsted, having a smooth face with a slight sheen.

shawl A rectangular or square piece of any textile, used as a covering for the shoulders, upper arms and torso, and sometimes worn over the head.

shift A woman's knee-length undergarment of plain linen or (especially after c.1820) cotton, worn next to the skin to protect outer clothing. The garment was also called by the older word 'smock', and in the Regency came to be called a 'chemise'.

shirt An undergarment worn on the upper body next to the skin to protect outer clothing. For men, the collar and sleeves were prominent, as these parts were visible in the openings of other clothing. *See also* *habit-shirt.

silesia A thin, twill linen cloth, used for linings, especially those of outer garments.

slip A plain silk or satin undergown, white or coloured, worn under a transparent muslin, net or gauze gown.

slops (1) Cheap clothing, ready made in set sizes, especially for seafarers and working men. (2) Petticoat breeches or other loose working garments.

small clothes [smalls, small cloths] A euphemism for 'drawers' or 'breeches'.

smock (1) A woman's undergarment of linen or (later) cotton, worn next to the skin (*see* *shift). (2) An outer, protective tunic of coarse linen worn over their clothes by agricultural workers.

spatterdashes [spats, spatts] *See* *gaiters.

spencer A short, close-fitting jacket without tails; the term is probably more common in modern usage than it was in the Regency period. Originally worn by men over a longer coat, the spencer then became popular with women and remained so throughout the Regency. The woman's spencer followed the form of the gown bodice over which it was worn.

stays A close-fitting undergarment, shaped and stiffened with whalebone, cording, canvas or a busk, and closed with lacing, which shaped the wearer's torso; women's stays also supported the breasts. Women's short stays reached from the bust to the waist; long stays consisted of a stiffened bodice, covering the hips and supporting the breasts, with a centre-front busk and shoulder straps. For men, stays reached from ribs to hips, and reduced and smoothed the waistline. The term 'stays' started to converge with 'corset' in the early nineteenth century until the two became virtually synonymous.

staylace The lace or cord with which women's stays and corsets were threaded, fastened and tightened.

stock A man's cotton, linen or silk neckwear. It commonly consisted of a yard width of linen or cotton fabric gathered into tapes or a buckled closure that fastened at the back. A structured version, inspired by military dress, consisted of black or white silk, covering a stiff canvas base, often with a whalebone or metal support inside, and buckling at the back.

stockings Leg coverings for men and women, knee-length or extending above the knee; they were held up by garters, or, in menswear, often by the knee fastening of the breeches that were worn over them.

stockinette (1) A plain, machine-knitted fabric, its name deriving from 'stocking stitch'. (2) A twill cotton cloth, similar to denim, its name deriving from the stockinette weave.

stomacher A panel covering, or inserted into the front of a woman's bodice, or into the front of jumps or stays under the lacing. *See also* *jumps.

stuff A general term for a plain- or twill-woven wool or worsted fabric, especially thin, light types of cloth, popular for women's day dress.

superfine The highest grade of woollen cloth, heavily fulled, the surface raised and cropped to produce a fabric with a soft feel and lustrous appearance; it was used in tailored garments, especially men's coats.

surtout A man's outer coat, with a skirt reaching above or below the knees, shorter than a greatcoat and looser fitting than a frock coat.

swansdown (1) The soft under-plumage of the swan, used as a trimming. (2) A cloth made of wool woven with silk or cotton; dyed in many different colours, it was popular for waistcoats. (3) *See* *swanskin.

swanskin A thick, fleecy, napped, twill cotton cloth, similar to flannel, and confusingly also referred to as 'swansdown'; it was used for undergarments, gaiters, jackets and other functional clothing.

T

taffeta A crisp, plain-weave silk, woven with highly twisted threads, having a tight finish and a somewhat glossy surface.

tambour work A form of chain-stitch embroidery, worked in silk or cotton threads with a tambour hook, usually on translucent fabrics such as muslin, net and gauze.

tete A wig or hairpiece.

thread Generally (when not otherwise qualified), a sewing thread or knitting yarn made from linen, as in 'thread stockings' or 'a skein of thread'.

thread button Any button made from a metal ring wrapped across with linen thread; *see also* *Dorset button.

tippet A woman's stole or scarf, long and narrow, or triangular; it was generally worn for warmth and often made of fur or wool, though it could also be light and decorative.

tissue A silk fabric with a satin ground and an additional weft to create ornamental patterns, usually with silver, gold or gilt-metal threads woven through – hence 'silver tissue' and 'gold tissue'; it was used in evening dress and court dress.

top boots Men's boots, reaching just below the knee, with turned-over tops in a lighter shade of leather.

tucker [chemise tucker] A separate edging of linen, lawn, muslin or some other fine material, worn around the top of a low-necked bodice and tucked into it.

tulle [tule] Machine-woven, hexagonal net, first produced in 1768 in England; *see* *bobbin net. The name derives from the French town where the net was manufactured from 1817.

tunic [tunic dress] In fashion, a knee-length gown, often sleeveless and loose, worn over an evening gown; *see also* *half-robe.

turban A round headdress, inspired by the headwear of various Eastern cultures; it consisted of a length of fabric sewn into shape or simply wound around the head. Though worn by both men and women, turbans were most common as a form of women's headwear, and were very popular for evening wear.

twill A weave in which the warp thread passes over multiple weft threads before passing under one or more (or vice versa), producing regular diagonal ridges on the fabric's surface (*cf.* *plain weave).

twist Stout silk thread, made of two or more yarns twisted round each other, used for making buttonholes and other functional but decorative parts of dress.

U

ugly *See* *calash.

undress [dishabille, negligee] Informal or ordinary dress. For women, this included morning dress, walking-dress and day dress. For men, it applied to morning wear and sporting clothing.

union cloth Any fabric woven with yarn made from cotton in one direction (either warp or weft), and another fibre, usually wool, in the other.

unmentionables A euphemism for 'drawers' or 'breeches'.

V

Vandyke Any trimming or accessory finished with V-shaped edging; the shape was inspired by the collars depicted in portraits by the seventeenth-century artist Anthony van Dyck, or possibly by the shape of his beard.

velveret A striped or ribbed fabric of cotton warp and silk weft, often ribbed; it was popular for men's dress.

W

waistcoat (1) Unless otherwise specified, a short, sleeveless, upper-body garment, worn as outer wear by men under a coat or jacket, and by women as part of a riding-habit. Working men wore sleeved waistcoats reaching to the waist. (2) As underwear, an upper-body garment, worn under or over the shirt or the shift for warmth. For men, this garment had elbow- or full-length sleeves and reached to the hips. For women, it was sleeveless and reached to the waist or hips. In this sense, the word could be used as a synonym for 'jumps'.

Wellington boots Originally, high boots covering the knee and cut away behind, like Hessians. The term was later also applied to slightly shorter boots worn under trousers, or any formal but still relatively high boots. They were named for Arthur Wellesley, 1st Duke of Wellington, and popularised by him.

whalebone [baleen] Fine keratin extrusions from the jaws of baleen whales; the material was used as flexible boning, especially in stays and corsets.

worsted The combed, long-staple fibres of a fleece, smoother, shinier and more durable than the short-staple, fluffy wool; any thread or fabric made from these fibres.

Y

York tans Leather gloves in a buff, bark or tan colour, of a slightly higher quality than tan leather, popular for riding or driving.

Notes

Notes for the Reader

1   Hume, 2014, p. 377.

Introduction

1   Souter, 1818, p. 222.
2   *Pers.*, II, v, 146.
3   Blatt, 2017.
4   Wells, 2011, p. 427.
5   Sales, 1994, p. xv.
6   Byrde, 1992, p. 22.
7   Extract from an unsigned review of Susan Ferrier's novel *The Inheritance* (1824), *Blackwood's Edinburgh Magazine*. June 1824, p. 659, quoted in Southam (ed.), 1987, p. 112.
8   The edition was released in late December 1817, but dated 1818 on the title-page.
9   Le Faye (ed.), 2011.
10   Hume, 2014, p. 377.
11   The latter four are in the collection of the Jane Austen's House Museum, Chawton, Hampshire; for the shawl see Davidson, 2017a. The pelisse is in the Hampshire Cultural Trust collection: see Davidson, 2015a; and Davidson, 2017b.
12   The controversial Rice portrait and the Byrne portrait are both known by the names of their current owners.
13   Good summaries are in Sutherland, 2005; and Wells, 2011; some of the arguments are documented in E. Butler, 2012. See also P. Byrne, 2012; Denman, 1981; C. L. Johnson, 1998; C. L. Johnson, 2013; D. Kaplan, 2012; Le Faye, 2007; Le Faye, 2012; Nigro, 2008; Ray and Wheeler, 2005; Southam, 1999; Sutherland, 2002; R. J. Wheeler, 1998; R. J. Wheeler, 1999; and Wild, 2002.
14   George Steiner, *After Babel: Aspects of Language and Translation* (1975), quoted by Vivian Jones in 'Introduction', *P&P*, p. xv.
15   Mohapatra and Nayak, 2000, p. 190.
16   M. Butler, 2003, p. xxiv.
17   Margalit, 2002.
18   Hughes, 2005, p. 34.
19   Galperin, 2003, pp. 23, 31.
20   Mrs Pole's opinion of *MP*, quoted in Southam (ed.), 1987, p. 51.
21   Extract from an unsigned review in *British Critic*, new ser., March 1818, pp. 293–301, quoted in Southam (ed.), 1987, pp. 80–81.
22   Wells, 2011, p. 427.
23   Ibid., pp. 421–2.
24   Entwistle, 2000a, p. 327.
25   Lee, 2005, p. 94.
26   Squire, 1970, p. 4.
27   Quoted in Sales, 1994, p. 19.
28   Ibid., p. 221; Lee, 2005, p. 71.
29   Mohapatra and Nayak, 2000, p. 190; see also Macdonald and Macdonald (eds), 2003.
30   Auerbach, 2005.
31   D. Kaplan, 1996.
32   The life of Austen's works in popular culture and especially film is discussed in P. Byrne, 2017; Dow and Hanson (eds), 2012; Mirmohamadi, 2014; Simons, 2009; Thompson and Pucci (eds), 2003; Wells, 2011; and Yaffe, 2013.
33   Richardson, Murdock and Merry, 2003, p. 230.
34   Baker, 1975; Baker, 1978; Pyne, 1808.
35   Arch and Marschner, 1987; Mansel, 2005.
36   Brogden, 2002; P. Jones, 2006; S. King, 2002; Richmond, 2009; Richmond, 2013; Smiles, 2002.
37   Arnold, 1968; Baumgarten, 2002; Ribeiro, 1995; Waugh, 1964; Waugh, 1968.
38   Byrde, 1992; Cunnington and Cunnington, 1957; Cunnington and Cunnington, 1970; Hart and North, 2009; Johnston, 2005; Riello, 2006.
39   Downing, 2010b; Garbett, 2018; Percoco, 2015; Swallow, 2015.
40   Byrde, 1986, repr. 2008.
41   Buck, 1971; Downing, 2010a; Forest, 2010; Hafner-Laney, 2010; Hughes, 2006; E. K. Johnson, 2011; Margalit, 2002; Nigro, 2010; Rodgers, 2011; Wagner, 2012; Wylie, 2007.
42   Le Bourhis, 1989; Leong, McNeil and Scollay, 2009; Starobinski (ed.), 1989.
43   For general studies see Le Faye, 2003; and Vickery, 1998. For material Austen see P. Byrne, 2013; S. Byrne, 2014; and Sutherland (ed.), 2017.
44   Heydt-Stevenson, 2005; C. W. Smith, 2013; Womick, 2011.
45   McNeil and Riello, 2010, p. 175.
46   Ibid., p. 174.
47   Riello, 2006, p. 6.
48   Burman and White, 2007.
49   K. Harvey, 2015, pp. 800–01.
50   Karskens, 2002, p. 41.
51   Wells, 2011, p. 105.
52   Davidson, 2015a.
53   Sutherland (ed.), 2017, p. 12.
54   Letter 146, 16–17 December 1816, Le Faye (ed.), 2011, p. 337.

1   Self

1   *NA*, I, ii, 21.
2   Entwistle, 2000a, p. 327.
3   Eighteenth-century dress before the 1790s has a comprehensive bibliography: see Arnold, 1968; Ashelford, 2000; Baumgarten, 2002; Baumgarten and Watson, 1999; Bernier, 1981; Buck, 1979; Chrisman-Campbell, 2015; Cunnington and Cunnington, 1957; Delpierre, 1997; Hart and North, 2009; Koda and Bolton, 2006; McNeil, 2018; Maeder, 1983; Martin and Willis, 1998; Ribeiro, 1983; Ribeiro, 1988; Ribeiro, 1995; and Starobinski (ed.), 1989.
4   Garbett, 2018.
5   Arnold, 1970, p. 19; Chrisman-Campbell, 2002.
6   *The Taylor's Complete Guide*, 1796, p. 110.
7   Hopkins and Hopkins, 2017.
8   Squire, 1970, p. 5.
9   Cunnington, 1935, p. 34.
10   *New Bon Ton Magazine*, April 1820, p. 57.
11   Kuchta, 2002, p. 167.
12   Ibid., p. 168.
13   Ibid., p. 177.
14   'On Modern Taste and Style', *Lady's Magazine*, quoted in Gelpi, 1997, p. 126.
15   Rauser, 2017.
16   Colville and Williams, 2016.
17   Purdy (ed.), 2004, p. 149.
18   *Dress and Address*, 1819, p. 31.
19   Rauser, 2017.
20   Arnold, 1970, p. 20.
21   Le Faye, 2002, p. 154
22   A Lady of Distinction, 1811, p. 24.
23   Honor, 1972, p. 6; Baxter and Miller, 1810, Introduction.

24 Baxter and Miller, 1810, unpaginated.

25 Hope, 1809; Hope and Moses, 1812/1973. Moses, alone, published *A Series of Twenty-Nine Designs of Modern Costume* in 1823.

26 Edwards, 1976, p. 69.

27 Honor, 1972, p. 4.

28 A Lady of Distinction, 1811, p. 21.

29 Quoted in Arnold, 1970, p. 18.

30 Austen, 1993, p. 68

31 Letter 30, 8–9 January 1801, Le Faye (ed.), 2011, p. 73.

32 Burney, 1905, vol. 5, p. 503; Edgeworth, 1971, p. 339.

33 Byrde, 1992, p. 28

34 Rousseau, 1762/1979, p. 367, 372.

35 Ibid., pp. 372–3.

36 *Emma*, II, vi, p. 333.

37 Byrde, 1992, p. 23.

38 Ibid., p. 30.

39 Austen, 2006.

40 Campbell, 2016.

41 Martin and Koda, 1994.

42 Geczy, 2013, p. 16.

43 Ibid., p. 50.

44 Quoted in Inal, 2011, p. 256.

45 Letter 17, 8–9 January 1799, Le Faye (ed.), 2011, p. 33.

46 A Lady of Distinction, 1811, p. 60.

47 Purdy (ed.), 2004, p. 145.

48 Entwistle, 2000a, pp. 7–10.

49 Scott and Taylor (eds), 1825, p. 585.

50 Styles, 2009, p. 307. For a very brief introduction to discussion of fashion through history, see Black et al. (eds) 2014; Breward, 2003; Cumming, 2004; Entwistle, 2000b; Steele, 2010; Styles, 2010; Vincent, 2009; and the journal *Fashion Theory* (1997–).

51 Riello, 2006, p. 59.

52 Ibid., p. 58.

53 Scott and Taylor (eds), 1825, p. 588.

54 *MP*, I v, p. 48.

55 Riello, 2006, p. 59.

56 Mant, 1815, p. 8.

57 *The Wanderer* (1814), quoted in Batchelor, 2005, p. 79.

58 Stewart, 1817, p. 168.

59 Ibid., p. 177.

60 Le Maistre, 1799, vol. 3, p. 102.

61 Buchan, 1811, p. 167.

62 *S&S*, I, xxi, p. 115.

63 *The Duties of a Lady's Maid*, 1825/2016, p. 56.

64 Ibid., p. 58.

65 Edgeworth, 1971, p. 59.

66 A Lady of Distinction, 1811, p. 12, quoting Philip Stanhope, 4th Earl of Chesterfield.

67 Batchelor, 2005, p. 79.

68 Cockle, 1809, p. 234.

69 Edgeworth, 1971, p. 17.

70 Ibid., p. 61.

71 Batchelor, 2005, p. 91.

72 *P&P*, I, iii, p. 12; I, viii, p. 35.

73 Batchelor, 2005, p. 92.

74 S. Byrne, 2014, p. 84.

75 Styles, 1994; Styles, 2007; Styles, 2010.

76 A Lady of Distinction, 1811, p. 12.

77 Vickery, 2013.

78 *Dress and Address*, 1819, pp. 80–81.

79 1809: Weeton, 1936/1969, vol. 1, p. 163; see also Ellen Weeton, Journals and Letters, Edward Hall Diary Collection, EHC/165a–b.

80 Batchelor, 2005, pp. 81–2.

81 Vickery, 2013.

82 Mrs Mary Topham, Lady's Account Book, 1810–25, Chawton House Library, 6641; see Davidson, 2015b.

83 Letter 89, 23–4 September 1813, Le Faye (ed.), 2011, p. 234.

84 *NA*, I, x, p. 72.

85 Letter 10, 27–8 October 1798, Le Faye (ed.), 2011, p. 17.

86 Letter 24, 1 November 1800, ibid., p. 54.

87 Vickery, 2013, p. 876.

88 Batchelor, 2005, p. 82.

89 *MP*, II, v, p. 206.

90 *S&S*, II, viii, p. 183.

91 *NA*, I, x, p. 71.

92 *P&P*, I, viii, p. 36; A Lady of Distinction, 1811, p. 61.

93 Geczy, 2013, p. 90.

94 Entwistle, 2000b, p. 325.

95 Lambert, 2010b, p. 192; see also Baumgarten, 1998.

96 Letter 27, 20–21 November 1800, Le Faye (ed.), 2011, p. 60.

97 *The Duties of a Lady's Maid*, 1825/2016, p. 164.

98 Riello, 2006, p. 38.

99 For full details see Davidson, 2015a; and Davidson, 2017b.

100 Hollander, 1994, p. 47.

101 Hope and Moses, 1812/1973.

102 Batchelor and Manushag (eds), 2018.

103 Buck and Matthews, 1984.

104 Barbara Johnson, album, 1746–1823, Victoria and Albert Museum, London, T.219-1973, containing plates and textile pieces; see Johnson, 1987. Mary White, album, 1759–1825, inscribed inside the front cover 'Mary White, 1819', Manchester City Galleries, 1987.29; the album has marbled card covers and contains fashion plates cut from magazines, starting with the *Lady's Magazine* (1759).

105 Diaries of Fanny C. Knatchbull, 1804–72, Kent History and Library Centre, U.951/F.24/1–69.

106 *MP*, I, ii, p. 21; I, v, p. 42; see also Day, 2017.

107 Vincent, 2009, pp. 65–6.

108 Ibid., p. 66; Malcolm, 1810, p. 355.

109 *NA*, I, i, p. 16.

110 Bond, 1814, vol. 2, p. 79.

111 Letter 37, 21–2 May 1801, Le Faye (ed.), 2011, p. 91.

112 *Emma*, I, v, p. 38. Wiltshire discusses the concept in Wiltshire, 1992, pp. 110–54.

113 *P&P*, I, viii, p. 39.

114 *Pers.*, II, iii, p. 132; *Emma*, II, ii, pp. 156–7.

115 Aileen Ribeiro's study of makeup throughout history covers the subject in depth: Ribeiro, 2011.

116 Cunnington and Cunnington, 1970, p. 378.

117 Letter 13, 1–2 December 1798, Le Faye (ed.), 2011, p. 24.

118 As told to Lady Charlotte Campbell in 1856: Le Faye, 2004, p. 274. Letter 13, 1–2 December, 1798, Le Faye (ed.), 2011, p. 25. Actress Susannah Harker cut off feet of her own long hair to give her character, Jane Bennet, short front curls for the BBC TV production of *Pride and Prejudice* of 1995.

119 *NA*, I, iii, p. 27.

120 *Emma*, III, ii, p. 303; I, xvi, p. 126. *The Duties of a Lady's Maid*, 1825/2016, contains 'Practical Directions for Hairdressing, including tips on hairdressing, making pomatums and hair oils, hair dyes, and depilation', pp. 233–5.

121 Letter 24, 1 November 1800, Le Faye (ed.), 2011, p. 55.

122 Letter, 12, 25 November 1798, ibid., p. 22; Letter 39, 14 September 1804, ibid., p. 99.

123 Letter 45, 24 August 1805, ibid., p. 113.

124 Edgeworth, 1971, p. 379.

125 Letter 87, 15–16 September 1813, Le Faye (ed.), 2011, p. 229.

126 Souter, 1818, p. 7.

127 Lucy, 2002, p. 17; Pinchard, 1800, p. 3.

128 Mrs Mary Topham, Lady's Account Book, 1810–25, Chawton House Library, 6641

129 Souter, 1818, pp. 189–90.

130 Letter 18, 21–23 January 1799, Le Faye (ed.), 2011, p. 40.

131 Edgeworth, 1971, p. 342.

132 Dorothea Jordan to the Duke of Clarence, 8 October 1809, D. Jordan, 1951, p. 114.

133 Vincent, 2009, p. 9.

134 Coutts's wardrobe is explored in Wilcox, 2012.

2 Home

1 Letter 80, 4 February 1813, Le Faye (ed.), 2011, p. 212.

2 Ewing, 1978, p. 52.

3 For more information on historical patterns for shirts, and patterns taken from shirts see A Lady, 1840; *Instructions for Cutting Out Apparel for the Poor*, 1789; Burnham, 1973.

4 Styles, 2009, p. 325.

5 Quoted in Cunnington and Cunnington, 1992, p. 163.

6 Le Blanc, 1828, p. 29.

7 Clabburn, 1971a, p. 21.

8 Malcolm, 1810, p. 356.

9 *Neckclothitania*, 1818.

10 Sorge-English, 2011, pp. 190–91.

11 For technical details of transitional corsets see ibid., p. 41; and Lynn, 2010, p. 82.

12 Buchan, 1811, p. 18.

13 *Emma*, I, x, 84.

14 Sinclair, 1816, p. 11.

15 For a pair of late eighteenth-century quilted jumps and a stomacher, see Sorge-English, 2011, figure 3.2; for jumps in the Victoria and Albert Museum, London, see

Lynn, 2010, p. 122 See also Mactaggart and Mactaggart, 1979, p. 41.

16 For more details see Lynn, 2010, p. 141.

17 1814, quoted in Waugh, 1954, p. 133.

18 Burney, 1905, vol. 6, p. 289.

19 'Bell's Monthly Compendium of Advertisements', *La Belle Assemblée*, December 1816, pp. 35, 34.

20 *Ipswich Journal* (1807), quoted in Cunnington and Cunnington, 1970, p. 359.

21 Gibbon, 1809, p. 46.

22 *New, General, and Complete Weekly Magazine*, 1796 vol. 1, p. 268; Le Maistre, 1799, vol. 3, p. 16.

23 In the collection of the Museum of London, A27042.

24 *Dress and Address*, 1819, p. 89.

25 Ibid., p. 59 [second page sequence].

26 Cunnington and Cunnington, 1992, p. 172.

27 A Lady, 1840, p. 83.

28 Letter 87, 15–16 September 1813, Le Faye (ed.), 2011, p. 229.

29 A Lady of Distinction, 1811, p. 96.

30 Quoted in Waugh, 1954, p. 100

31 *The Duties of a Lady's Maid*, 1825/2016, p. 176.

32 A Lady of Distinction, 1811, p. 72.

33 *Emma*, II, viii, p. 210.

34 Jervoise of Herriard Collection, Family and Estate Papers, 14 April 1800, Hampshire Record Office, 44M69/E13/11/15.

35 Letter 106, 2 September 1814, Le Faye (ed.), 2011, p. 285.

36 Letter 15, 24 December 1798, ibid., p. 31.

37 Cunnington and Cunnington, 1992, p. 178.

38 Ibid., p. 180.

39 Bill of Pains and Penalties for divorce of Queen Caroline, 15 October 1820, National Archives, Kew, London, TS 11/98/308/1/75.

40 Vincent, 2009, pp. 121–2.

41 *Dress and Address*, 1819, p. 51.

42 Fields, 2003, p. 123.

43 Baumgarten, 1992.

44 *S&S*, I, viii, p. 40.

45 For some discussion on undergarments in Coutts's wardrobe, see Baumgarten, 1992.

46 Longsdon of Little Longstone, Family and Estate Papers, 15 February 1811, Derbyshire Record Office, D3580/C161; for a history of the family see Chapman, 1970.

47 Longsdon of Little Longstone, Family and Estate Papers, 21 March 1803, Derbyshire Record Office, D3580/C32; Jervoise of Herriard Collection, Family and Estate Papers, 19 August 1799, Hampshire Record Office, 44M69/E13/11/13.

48 Letter 22, 19 June 1799, Le Faye (ed.), 2011, p. 49.

49 Letter 10, 27–8 October 1798, ibid., p. 17.

50 *The Lymiad*, 2011, pp. 103–4.

51 Kindred, 2017, p. 143.

52 Jervoise of Herriard Collection, Family and Estate Papers, Hampshire Record Office, 44M69/E13/13/1–23. The night waistcoats appear only in Mrs Jervoise's bills, not her husband's, so must have been an article of female dress.

53 Mrs Mary Topham, Lady's Account Book, 1 January 1822, Chawton House Library, 6641.

54 Gibbon, 1809, p. 43.

55 Farrell, 1992. For the history of stockings see Chapman, 2002; D. J. Cole, 2012; Croft, 1987; Gernerd, 2015; and K. Harvey, 2015.

56 *Repository of Arts*, July 1812, p. 372.

57 Mrs Mary Topham, Lady's Account Book, 22 April 1815, Chawton House Library, 6641.

58 Souter, 1818, p. 370.

59 Buchan, 1811, p. 134

60 Wilcox, 2012, p. 19.

61 Letter 23, 25–7 October 1800, Le Faye (ed.), 2011, p. 53; January 1808, Weeton, 1936/1969, vol. 1, p. 64.

62 Letter 15, 24 December 1798, Le Faye (ed.), 2011, p. 32; Letter 23, 25–7 October 1800, ibid., p. 52.

63 Mrs Mary Topham, Lady's Account Book, September 1822, Chawton House Library, 6641.

64 Letter 88, 16 September 1813, Le Faye (ed.), 2011, p. 232.

65 Sperling, 1981.

66 Cunnington and Cunnington, 1992, p. 188.

67 Longsdon of Little Longstone, Family and Estate Papers, 24 November 1811, Derbyshire Record Office, D3580/C248.

68 Edgeworth, 1971, p. 78.

69 Letter 89, 23–4 September 1813, Le Faye (ed.), 2011, p. 227; Letter 93, 21 October 1813, ibid., p. 243.

70 Tozer and Levitt, 1983, p. 67.

71 Bond, 1814, vol. 2, p. 7; September 1800, Wordsworth, 1971, p. 50.

72 J. Walker, 1810.

73 *P&P*, III, vi, p. 284.

74 Swain, 1972b; see also J. Walker, 1810.

75 For more on banyans and nightgowns see Cunningham, 1984; Fortune, 2002; Swain, 1972a.

76 Clabburn, 1971a, p. 19.

77 Ibid., p. 20.

78 *S&S*, I, xxi, p. 119.

79 Edgeworth, 1971, p. 62.

80 J. E. Austen-Leigh, 2008, p. 128; *S&S*, II, x, 206

81 Burney, 1905, vol. 5, pp. 221–2.

82 *P&P*, III, vii, p. 289.

83 February 1802, Wordsworth, 1971, p. 116.

84 Edgeworth, 1971, p. 225

85 Baumgarten, 1996, p. 16.

86 Ibid., pp. 19, 21; Fisk, 2018.

87 Letter 145, 8–9 September 1816, Le Faye (ed.), 2011, p. 320.

88 *S&S*, II iv p. 156.

89 On the dating of Mrs Weston's pregnancy, see Millard, 1983.

90 Baumgarten, 1996, p. 17

91 Letter 13. 1–2 December 1798, Le Faye (ed.), 2011, p. 25.

92 Buchan, 1811, p. 14.

93 Sorge-English, 2011, pp. 100–11.

94 Mactaggart and Mactaggart, 1979, p. 41.

95 Byrde, 1992, p. 37.

96 Cunnington and Cunnington, 1992, p. 184; Waterhouse, 2007.

97 Mactaggart and Mactaggart, 1973; Mactaggart and Mactaggart, 1979.

98 Hampshire Record Office, Jervoise of Herriard Collection, Family and Estate Papers, accounts of George Mountford [butler], 1800, 44M69/E13/11/15; 1804, 44M69/E13/11/25; 1811, 44M69/E13/11/56. Some researchers speculate that women bled directly onto their shifts. Byrde, 1992, p. 177 n. 25; Levitt, 1986; Kidd, 1994; Kidd and Farrell-Beck, 1997; Richmond, 2013, pp. 150–51.

99 March 1802, Wordsworth, 1971, p. 132

100 Fitz-Adam, 1803, pp. 223–4.

101 Weeton, 1936/1969, vol. 2, p.16.

102 Letter 13, 1–2 December 1798, Le Faye (ed.), 2011, p. 25.

103 *Repository of Arts*, December 1809, p. 405.

104 Letter 33, 25 January 1801, Le Faye (ed.), 2011, p. 81; Letter 80, 4 February 1813, ibid., p. 212.

105 Letter 94, 26 October 1813, ibid., pp. 256.

106 Sperling, 1981, pl. 49, pl. 1.

107 Letter 92, 14–15 October 1813, Le Faye (ed.), 2011, p. 249.

108 Ibid., pp. 246–7.

109 Edgeworth, 1971, p. 103.

110 *Repository of Arts*, March 1810, p. 327.

111 Letter 89, 23–4 September 1813, Le Faye (ed.), 2011, p. 238.

112 Lucy, 2002, p. 22.

113 Edgeworth, 1971 p. 393.

114 Letter 13, 1–2 December 1798, Le Faye (ed.), 2011, p. 25.

115 Letter 87, 15–16 September 1813, ibid., p. 229.

116 Vickery, 2013, p. 859.

117 Letter 32, 21–2 January 1801, Le Faye (ed.), 2011, p. 78.

118 Vickery, 2013, p. 886.

119 Mrs Mary Topham, Lady's Account Book, 1810, Chawton House Library, 6641.

120 Burman, 2003, pp. 77–99; Burman and Denbo, 2006; Burman and Fennetaux, 2019.

121 Arnold, 1970.

122 *La Belle Assemblée*, March 1806, p. 62; Cunnington and Cunnington, 1992, p. 187.

123 Mant, 1815, pp. 7–8.

124 *Repository of Arts*, November 1814, p. 256.

125 Burman, 2003, p. 81.

126 Clabburn, 1971a, p. 20.

127 Mrs Mary Topham, Lady's Account Book, 1810–25, Chawton House Library, 6641.

128 For more details see Chico, 2010; and Leuner and Boehm, 2012.

129 *P&P*, III, xiii, p. 326; *S&S*, III, x, p. 317; *P&P*, III, xvii, p. 357; Letter 67, 30 January 1809, Le Faye (ed.), 2011, p. 179.

130 Letter 35, 5–6 May 1801, ibid., p. 86.

131 Letter 87, 15–16 September 1813, ibid., p. 227.

132 Edgeworth, 1971, p. 360.

133 26 April 1813, Edgeworth, p. 25–6.

134 Ibid.

135 *S&S*, III, i, p. 242 ; *Pers.*, II, i, 119.

136 Melchior-Bonnet, 2001, pp. 84–9.

137 Tarrant, 2015, p. 161.

138 *Dress and Address*, p. v.

139 B. Hill, 1996, pp. 9–10, 253.

140 For more information on servants, see Buck, 1973; P. Cunnington, 1974; Duckenfield, 2008; Hecht, 1956; Steedman, 2009; and Styles, 2002.

141 *Emma*, I, i, p. 10.

142 *Pers.*, II, i, p. 114.

143 *S&S*, III, x, p. 318; see also *Emma*, II, xvi, p. 274.

144 *MP*, I, x, p. 99; II, v, p. 206.

145 *Pers.*, I vi 43.

146 *P&P*, III, xiii, p. 325.

147 *MP*, I i, p. 11.

148 *MP*, I, ii, p. 15.

149 Edgeworth, 1971, p. 337.

150 *P&P*, I, ix, p. 41.

151 *NA*, II, vi, p. 156; *The Watsons*, in Austen, 1974, p. 107.

152 *The Duties of a Lady's Maid*, 1825/2016, p. 113.

153 Ibid., p. 252.

154 Letter 149, 23 January 1817, Le Faye (ed.), 2011, p. 340.

155 *MP*, III, xi, p. 379.

156 J. E. Austen-Leigh, 2008, p. 35.

157 *Pers.*, II, v, p. 144.

158 *MP*, I, ii, p. 18.

159 A. Williams, 1815, p. 48.

160 *P&P*, I, xix, p. 102.

161 Letter 13, 1–2 December 1798, Le Faye (ed.), 2011, p. 26.

162 Bond, 1814, vol. 2, p. 205.

163 Garry, 2005, p. 93. Anna Larpent's diaries are in the Huntington Library, San Marino, Calif., HM 31201; microfilm of the journals may be consulted at the British Library, M1016/1–7.

164 Jervoise of Herriard Collection, Family and Estate Papers, Hampshire Record Office, 44M69/E13/13/7.

165 Ibid., 44M69/E13/13/10.

166 II, xv, p. 224.

167 Diaries of Fanny C. Knatchbull, 10 October 1805, Kent History and Library Centre, U.951/F.24/3; for a history of the diaries see Le Faye, 1986.

168 Letter 4, 1 September 1796, Le Faye (ed.), 2011, p. 7.

169 Long, 2016, p. 181. Huntington Library, San Marino, Calif., HM 31201.

170 J. E. Austen-Leigh, 2008, pp. 78–9.

171 Stewart, 1817, p. 177.

172 *P&P*, II, xvi, 212.

173 *P&P*, I, x, p. 46; I, xi, p. 53.

174 *NA*, II, xv, p. 225.

175 Long, 2016, p. 178.

176 *Pers.*, I x p. 77; , II, vii, p. 172; II, xii, p. 334.

177 J. E. Austen-Leigh, 2008, p. 32 n., p. 213.

178 Ibid., p. 32.

179 Ibid., p. 36; Letter 39, 14 September 1804, Le Faye (ed.), 2011, p. 94.

180 Garry, 2005.

181 Long, 2016, p. 178.

182 J. E. Austen-Leigh, 2008, pp. 159, 171.

183 Ibid., pp. 78–9.

184 Long, 2016, p. 178.

185 Ibid., p. 183.

186 Garry, 2005, p. 98.

187 Fry, 1825, p. 90.

188 C. Hill, 1923, p. 201.

189 *S&S*, III, xii, p. 335; *Emma*, III, xviii, p. 441.

190 *S&S*, III, xii, p. 335; *P&P*, III, xvii, p. 355.

191 Styles, 2007, pp. 80–82.

192 Letter 4, 1 September 1796, Le Faye (ed.), 2011, p. 6

193 1803, Weeton, 1936/1969, vol. 1, p. 36; October 1808, ibid., vol. 1, pp. 115–16.

194 Hume, 2013, p. 291.

3 Village

1 Letter 138D, 1 April 1816, Le Faye (ed.), 2011, p. 326.

2 Plotz, 2000, p. 165.

3 Letter 107, 9–18 September 1814, Le Faye (ed.), 2011, p. 287. Oliver MacDonagh's chapter on social traffic delves more deeply into this; MacDonagh, 1991, pp. 129–145.

4 Southam (ed.), 1987, p. 42.

5 L. Kaplan, 2010, p. 196.

6 *P&P*, I, xvii, p. 87. Jo Gardiner's novel *Longbourn* (2014) considers this rainy expedition from the servant's point of view, sent to buy the shoe-roses on behalf of her mistress.

7 Plotz, 2000, p. 165.

8 Letter 84, 20 May 1813, Le Faye (ed.), 2011, p. 218; Letter 114, 30 November 1814, ibid., p. 297.

9 Letter 27, 20–21 November 1800, ibid., p. 64.

10 Sutherland, 2014.

11 *NA*, II, ix, p. 186.

12 *Pers.*, II, v, p. 147.

13 *S&S*, II, xiv, p. 234.

14 Sutherland, 2014.

15 Styles, 2010, p.175.

16 Stewart, 1817, p. 170.

17 Ibid., p. 171.

18 *P&P*, II, ii, p. 137; II, xvi, p. 214.

19 *Dress and Address*, 1819, p. 50.

20 Burney, 1905, vol. 5, p. 199.

21 Sibbald, 1926, p. 170.

22 Letter 88, 16 September 1813, Le Faye (ed.), 2011, p. 222.

23 Edgeworth, 1971, p. 112.

24 *Pers.*, I, viii, p. 61.

25 Edgeworth, 1971, p. 357.

26 *Norfolk Chronicle*, March 1795; other, later versions of the story say a Spencer nobleman either burned off his coat-tails in front of the fire or tore one off when riding, and decided to make the truncated jacket a fashion as a way of carrying it off.

27 Letter 37, 21–2 May 1801, Le Faye (ed.), 2011, p. 92.

28 *Pers.*, II, i, p. 245.

29 Weeton. 1936/1969, vol. 1, p. 123.

30 *Dress and Address*, 1819, p. 60.

31 *MP*, I, ix, p. 86.

32 Ibid., p. 87

33 Grose, 1811.

34 *Dress and Address*, 1819, p. 54 [second page sequence].

35 *MP*, I, ix, p. 82.

36 Arch and Marschner, 1990; Ehrman, 2014; Ginsburg, 1981; Tobin, 1999.

37 *Emma*, III, xix, p. 453.

38 *MP*, II, iii, p. 188.

39 Letter 65, 17–18 January 1809, Le Faye (ed.), 2011, p. 168.

40 Hobhouse, 1910, p. 196.

41 *The Wynne Diaries*, Fremantle (ed.), 1940, vol. 3, p. 291.

42 Lucy, 2002, p. 30.

43 *NA*, I, xv, p. 115.

44 *MP*, II, v, p. 206.

45 *Repository of Arts*, July 1816, p. 361.

46 Staniland, 2000.

47 February 1815, quoted in Adkins and Adkins, 2013, p. 13.

48 *P&P*, III, viii, p. 294.

49 *P&P*, I, xviii, p. 101.

50 Letter 103, ?mid-July 1814, Le Faye (ed.), 2011, p. 278.

51 Letter 4, 1 September 1796, ibid., p. 6.

52 *Pers.*, II, ix, p. 203.

53 *S&S*, III, xiii, p. 345.

54 *P&P*, III, ix, p. 301.

55 For a fuller history see Taylor, 1983; see also Priestley, 1993.

56 Diaries of Fanny C. Knatchbull, *Polite and Fashionable Lady's Companion*, Kent History and Library Centre, U.951/F.24/2.

57 *Emma*, III, xvi, p. 430.

58 *Emma*, III, ix, p. 364.

59 Letter 152, 26 February 1817, Le Faye (ed.), 2011, p. 346.

60 Letter 155, 23–5 March 1817, ibid., p. 352.

61 Edgeworth, 1971, p. 153.

62 Letter 32, 21–2 January 1801, Le Faye (ed.), 2011 p. 80.

63 *Pers.*, I, i, p. 10; II, iv, p. 138; I, xii, p. 97.

64 Letter 19, 17 May 1799, Le Faye (ed.), 2011, p. 41.

65 Letter 57, 7–9 October 1808, ibid., p. 149; Letter 58, 13 October 1808, ibid., p. 153.

66 Letter 59, 15–16 October 1808, ibid., pp. 153–4.

67 Letter 60, 24–5 October 1808, ibid., p. 156.

68 Cunnington and Cunnington, 1970, p. 359.

69 Mrs Mary Topham, Lady's Account Book, 1810–25, Chawton House Library, 6641.

70 *P&P*, I, vii, p. 30.

71 'Classified Advertising', *Sydney Gazette and New South Wales Advertiser*, 18 December 1808.

72 *Emma*, II, ix, p. 218.

73 *Sanditon*, in Austen, 1974, ch. 6, p. 178.

74 *NA*, X, iii, p. 28.

75 Letter 10, 27–8 October 1798, Le Faye (ed.), 2011, pp. 16–17.

76 Letter 60, 24–5 October 1808, Le Faye (ed.),

2011, p. 150; Jervoise of Herriard Collection, Family and Estate Papers, Hampshire Record Office, 44M69/E13/13/5, 58.

77 Lambert, 2010a, p. 59.

78 Letter 15, 24 December 1798, Le Faye (ed.), 2011, p. 31.

79 Letter 77, 29–30 November 1812, ibid., p. 204.

80 Riello, 2006, pp. 35–7.

81 Letter 51, 25–7 October 1800, Le Faye (ed.), 2011, p. 53.

82 Cumming, 1982.

83 *Emma*, II, vi, p. 188.

84 Letter 10, 27–8 October 1798, Le Faye (ed.), 2011, p. 17.

85 *Valuable Secrets Concerning Arts and Trades*, 1795, p. 77; Foley, 2014.

86 Letter 45, 24 August 1805, Le Faye (ed.), 2011, p. 112.

87 *Pers.*, II, xi, p. 222; *The Watsons*, in Austen, 1974, p. 127.

88 *P&P*, II, xv, pp. 211–12.

89 Ibid., II, xv, p. 212.

90 Letter 14, 18–19 December 1798, Le Faye (ed.), 2011, pp. 26–7.

91 *P&P*, I, ii, p. 8.

92 Lambert, 2010a, p. 62.

93 23 November 1801, Wordsworth, 1971, p. 79; 10 March 1802, ibid., p. 129.

94 24 February 1802, ibid., p. 123.

95 Jervoise of Herriard Collection, Family and Estate Papers, 1811, Hampshire Record Office, 44M69/E13/12/45.

96 Ibid., 1802, 44M69/E13/12/28.

97 Dyer, 2016, p. 244.

98 Edgeworth, 1971, p. 252.

99 *Emma*, II, iii, p. 167.

100 *The Weird Sisters*, 1794, vol. 3, p. 79.

101 Diaries of Fanny C. Knatchbull, *Lady's Daily Companion*, Kent History and Library Centre, U.951/F.24/1.

102 Dyer, 2016, p. 249.

103 Arnold, 1973, p. 39.

104 Lazaro and Warner, 2004, p. 25.

105 Letter 25, 8–9 November 1800, Le Faye (ed.), 2011, p. 58.

106 Letter 84, 20 May 1813, ibid., p. 219.

107 Letter 19, 17 May 1799, ibid., p. 43.

108 13 May 1814, Le Faye, 2013, p. 479.

109 A Lady, 1840, p. 107.

110 4 May 1797, *The Wynne Diaries*, Fremantle (ed.), 1940, vol. 2, p. 177.

111 Fry, 1825, vol. 4, p. 94.

112 Letter 107, 9–18 September 1814, Le Faye (ed.), 2011, p. 288; McGuire, 2014, gives a history of amateur shoemaking.

113 26 July 1800, Wordsworth, 1971, p. 41.

114 Letter 72, 30 April 1811, Le Faye (ed.), 2011, p. 195.

115 Letter 57, 7–9 October 1808, ibid., 149; Letter 97, 2–3 March 1814, ibid., p. 267

116 Mrs Mary Topham, Lady's Account Book, 1810–25, Chawton House Library, 6641.

117 Letter 98, 5–8 March 1814, ibid., p. 269.

118 Styles, 2007.

119 *Emma*, II, ix, p. 219; *NA*, I, xiv, p. 110.

120 Letter 98, 5–8 March 1814, Le Faye (ed.), 2011, p. 271.

121 18–19 December 1798. Sandie Byrne notes that the similarity in sound of 'coquelicot' and 'coquette' may also be significant; S. Byrne, 2014, p. 186.

122 *NA*, I, iii, p. 26; *Emma*, II, xvii, 281; III, ii, p. 303.

123 Mrs Mary Topham, Lady's Account Book, 10 April 1810, Chawton House Library, 6641. Austen also bought bugle trimming in April 1811: Letter 70, 18–20 April 1811, Le Faye (ed.), 2011, p. 188.

124 S. Byrne, 2014, pp. 39–40; see also Lambert, 2004b.

125 Letter 56, 1–2 October 1808, Le Faye (ed.), 2011, p. 146; Diaries of Fanny C. Knatchbull, 10 June 1807, Kent History and Library Centre, U.951/F.24/1–69.

126 *Emma*, II, ii, p. 158.

127 Letter 62, 9 December 1808, Le Faye (ed.), 2011, p. 165.

128 Garry, 2005, p. 96.

129 Letter 78, 24 January 1813, Le Faye (ed.), 2011, pp. 206–7.

130 *Pers.*, II, v, p. 146.

131 *S&S*, II, xiv, p. 238.

132 Quoted in S. Byrne, 2014, p. 153.

133 *Pers.*, II, v, p. 146.

134 Batchelor, 2005; C. W. Smith, 2013.

135 Letter 49, 7–8 January 1807, Le Faye (ed.), 2011, p. 120.

136 *Henry and Eliza*, in Austen, 1993, p. 31.

137 Edgeworth, 1971, p. 162.

138 Vickery, 2009a, p. 233. For more on needlework see Dowdell, 2010; Dyer, 2016; E. K. Johnson, 2011; and Long, 2016.

139 *MP*, I, ii, p. 20.

140 13 September 1805, *The Wynne Diaries*, Fremantle (ed.), 1940, vol. 3, p. 202.

141 *NA*, I, ix, p. 59.

142 Letter 51, 20–22 February 1807, Le Faye (ed.), 2011, p. 128.

143 For more discussion of men's textile work in the nineteenth century, see Richmond, 2013, p. 117.

144 P. Byrne, 2013; Southam, 2001.

145 *NA*, I, vi, pp. 39, 167.

146 Fanny Austen's diary, *Pocket Magnet, or Elegant Picturesque Diary, for 1814*, King's College Cambridge, quoted in Kindred, 2017, p. 144.

147 Letter 10, 27–8 October 1798, Le Faye (ed.), 2011, p. 16.

148 *P&P*, I, viii, pp. 38–9.

149 Edgeworth, 1971, p. 232.

150 Mrs Mary Topham, Lady's Account Book, 1810–25, Chawton House Library, 6641.

151 *Emma*, II, xi, p. 213.

152 *The Duties of a Lady's Maid*, 1825/2016, p. 318.

153 Letter 32, 21–2 January 1801, Le Faye (ed.), 2011, p. 76.

154 Letter 20, 2 June 1799, ibid., p. 45.

155 *La Belle Assemblée*, October 1808, quoted in Arnold, 1968, p. 9.

156 *S&S*, III, xii, p. 332.

157 Clabburn, 1971a, p. 20.

158 Kerr, 1826.

159 Hafner-Laney, 2010; Holland, 1988.

160 1810, Weeton, 1936/1969, vol. 1, p. 261.

161 Batchelor and Manushag (eds), 2018.

162 Sutherland, 2014.

163 Vivienne Richmond delves into the clothing lives of the poor in the nineteenth century and the difficulties they faced in obtaining garments; Richmond, 2013.

164 *Instructions for Cutting Out Apparel for the Poor*, 1789; A Lady [Anne Streatfield], 1808.

165 Arnold, 1999, p. 224.

166 *The Wynne Diaries*, Fremantle (ed.), 1940, vol. 3, p. 84.

167 *MP*, I, vii, p. 67.

168 A Lady [Anne Streatfield], 1808, p. xi.

169 1809, Weeton, 1936/1969, vol. 1, p. 205.

170 Letter 77, 29–30 November 1812, Le Faye (ed.), 2011, p. 205.

171 Letter 78, 24 January 1813, ibid., p. 208.

172 Letter 15, 24 December 1798, ibid., p. 32.

173 Letter 23, 25–7 October 1800, ibid., p. 52.

4   Country

1 *NA*, II, ix, p. 186.

2 Nancy Armstrong, quoted in Galperin, 2003, p. 18.

3 Vickery, 2009a.

4 Raymond Williams, *The Country and the City* (1973), p. 113, quoted in Tuite, 2000, p. 98.

5 Woods, 1996, p. 311.

6 Hollander, 1994, p. 83.

7 Ibid., p. 91

8 *La Belle Assemblée*, March 1806, p. 62.

9 Riello, 2006, pp. 70–72.

10 McCormack, 2017.

11 Cockle, 1809, p. 260.

12 Le Maistre, 1799, vol. 2, p. 79.

13 To the Dowager Countess Spencer, 19 March 1810, Spencer, 1912, p. 95.

14 *Dress and Address*, 1819, pp. 23, 81.

15 Hollander, 2002, pp. 121–2.

16 *Emma*, II, xv, p. 267.

17 Pyne, 1815; Pyne, 1817; Pyne, Hill and Gray, 1806.

18 Jervoise of Herriard Collection, Family and Estate Papers, accounts of George Purefoy Jervoise, 1811, Hampshire Record Office, 44M69/E13/12/45; Godman, 1989, p. 84. *Golding's . . . Tailor's Assistant* includes patterns for drafting gaiters: Golding, 1817.

19 *Emma*, III, vi, p. 333.

20 Herbert, 1800/1930, vol. 2, p. 388.

21 *MP*, I, iv, p. 40.

22 Cunnington and Cunnington, 1992, p. 166.

23 Tarrant, 2010.

24 Mant, 1815, pp. 28, 79.

25 For a broader chronological view see De Marly, 1986; see also Cunnington and Lucas, 1967; and Lansdell, 1977. Other studies of aspects of Regency working dress can be found in Chapman, 1970; Chapman,

1993; Clabburn (ed.), 1971b; Evans, 1974; Lansdell, 1973; A. M. Scott, 1976; Spufford, 1984; Stevens, 2002; Sykas, 2009; Toplis, 2011; Vigeon, 1977; and Yates, 1973.

26 Mullan, 2012, p. 116.

27 Edgeworth, 1971, p. 93; Pyne, 1815; Pyne, 1817; Pyne, Hill and Gray, 1806. See also Pyne, 1808; and G. Walker, 1814.

28 Lambert, 2009; Stobart, 2011; Styles, 1994; Styles, 2010; Walsh, 2008.

29 Pyne, 1815, p. 4

30 December 1801, Wordsworth, 1971, p. 94.

31 P&P, I, viii, p. 36.

32 Hansen, 2017; on fustian breeches, see Sykas, 2009.

33 Godman, 1989, p. 80.

34 Jervoise of Herriard Collection, Family and Estate Papers, accounts of George Purefoy Jervoise, 1802, Hampshire Record Office, 44M69/E13/12/28.

35 Ibid., 1811, 44M69/E13/12/45.

36 Grose, 1811.

37 The Watsons, in Austen, 1974, p. 114.

38 Letter 61, 20 November 1808, Le Faye (ed.), 2011, p. 160.

39 P&P, III, ii, p. 248; Pers., I, iii, p. 22.

40 Pers., I, xii, 99.

41 To George FitzClarence, 14 March 1809, 27 March 1809, Jordan, 1951, pp. 75, 77.

42 Garry, 2005, p. 92.

43 A Lady of Distinction, 1811, p. 123; Charlotte Jane St Maur, Journal – Notes, Memoranda, 1 January 1922, Chawton House Library, 10828.

44 For fuller histories of the importance of pedlars to rural societies see Brown, 2000; Leitch, 1990; Spufford, 1984; and Toplis, 2011.

45 Sibbald, 1926, p. 183.

46 March 1802, Wordsworth, 1971, p. 128.

47 June 1802, ibid., p. 186

48 Letter 12, 25 November 1798, Le Faye (ed.), 2011, p. 22.

49 Clabburn, 1971a, p. 19.

50 Ibid., p. 21.

51 Brown, 2000, p. 4, summarises the arguments for and against in Table 6.

52 Burney, 1905, vol. 6, p. 265.

53 Mullan, 2012, pp. 101–9.

54 A Lady of Distinction, 1811, p. 56.

55 MP, I, iv, p. 35.

56 P&P, III, iii, p. 258; Dress and Address, 1819, p. 17.

57 Quoted in Vincent, 2009, p. 149, who notes that the amusement and the emphasis are Lady Elizabeth's own.

58 Sperling, 1981, pl. 22.

59 Farrell, 1985, pp. 25–37.

60 Quoted in ibid., p. 34.

61 Ibid., p. 35.

62 The New Family Receipt Book, 1818, p. 104

63 February 1802, Wordsworth, 1971, p. 113.

64 The Watsons, in Austen, 1974, p. 136.

65 Pers., II, vi, pp. 164–5.

66 Edgeworth, 1971, p. 236.

67 Mrs Mary Topham, Lady's Account Book,

1810–25, Chawton House Library, 6641.

68 J. E. Austen-Leigh, 2008, p. 36.

69 11 December 1806, Porter, 1998, p. 264.

70 Edgeworth, 1971, pp. 241, 292; Jervoise of Herriard Collection, Family and Estate Papers, 1812, Hampshire Record Office, E13/13/13, 1811, E13/12/45. Devonshire clogs were defined by the shape cut into the wooden sole (as opposed to Coburg clogs); see also Atkinson, 2008; and Vigeon, 1977.

71 Sperling, 1981, pls 38, 4.

72 Letter 107, 9–18 September 1814, Le Faye (ed.), 2011, p. 287.

73 Weeton, 1936/1969, vol. 1, p. 274.

74 Grose, 1811.

75 Emma, I, xvi, p. 131.

76 Edgeworth, 1971, p. 90.

77 S&S, III, vi, p. 286.

78 Sperling, 1981, pl. 60

79 December 1818, Weeton, 1936/1969, vol. 2, p. 314.

80 Golding, 1817, pp. 72–92; The Taylor's Complete Guide, 1796, pp. 108–63; G. Walker, 1835; Wyatt, 1822, pp. 89–114.

81 Blackman, 2001, p. 47.

82 December 1801, Wordsworth, 1971, p. 93.

83 Ferrier, 1929, p. 49.

84 Porter, 1998, pp. 154–5.

85 Lady's Magazine, April 1789, quoted in Blackman, 2001, p. 49.

86 Walker, 1838, p. 10.

87 Sperling, 1981, pl. 7. The donkey cart mentioned in Letter 153, 13 March 1817, Le Faye (ed.), 2011, p. 348, survives today at the Jane Austen's House Museum.

88 Sperling, 1981, pl. 40.

89 The Watsons, in Austen, 1974, p. 136. For the role of riding in health and in the making of gentlewomen see Landry, 2000.

90 Blackman, 2001, p. 47. Sperling, 1981, pl. 36, shows the Sperling girls in riding-habits for hunting.

91 Edgeworth, 1971, p. 202.

92 Letter 70, 18–20 April 1811, Le Faye (ed.), 2011, p. 188.

93 Byrde, 1987, p. 52; see also D. Wheeler, 2004.

94 R. A. Austen-Leigh, 1949; Selwyn (ed.), 2003.

95 Byrde, 1987, p. 52.

96 Ibid., p. 56 n. 33. Detailed instructions for making a bathing-gown of 'blue or white flannel, stuff, calimanco, or blue linen' and a bathing cap of 'oil-silk' or plain linen are given in A Lady, 1840, pp. 61, 68.

97 Papworth, Wrangham and Combe, 1813, p. 111.

98 May 1809, Weeton, 1936/1969, vol. 1, p. 166; 11 May 1810, vol. 1, p. 261.

99 8 June 1802, Wordsworth, 1971, p. 174.

100 Emma, II, i, p. 150.

101 Sperling, 1981, pl. 2 (shuttlecock), pl. 13 (bowls), pl. 17 (fishing).

102 9 July 1793, Clabburn, 1971a, p. 21.

103 5–11 September 1810, Weeton, 1936/1969, vol. 1, p. 284.

104 Diary of Harriet Wynne, 24 June 1803, The Wynne Diaries, Fremantle (ed.), 1940, vol. 3, p. 81.

105 For the pugilist's life see Belcher, 1809/2006. Many of the street people John Dempsey painted wear belchers.

106 Sibbald, 1926, p. 232.

107 Purdy, 1998, p. 121.

108 Edgeworth, 1971, p. 303.

109 Vickery, 1998, passim.

110 H. Jones, 2014; Skillen, 2012.

111 Letter 9, 24 October 1798, Le Faye (ed.), 2011, p. 15.

112 The Watsons, in Austen, 1974, p. 145.

113 'The box or driving coat'; Golding, 1817, has a pattern for such a coat.

114 NA, I, xi, p. 81.

115 NA, II, v, p. 147; Pers., I, xii, p. 99.

116 J. Walker, 1810.

117 NA, II, v, p. 149.

118 Sperling, 1981, pl. 44; pl. 70 shows Diana wearing the same greatcoat in an open carriage.

119 Clabburn, 1971a, p. 20.

120 Engel, 2009; Engel, 2015.

121 Bond, 1814, vol. 2, pp. 66–7, 69.

122 Letter 60, 24–5 October 1808, Le Faye (ed.), 2011, p. 156. The New Family Receipt Book, 1818, pp. 113–14.

123 Edgeworth, 1971 p. 258.

124 Ibid., p. 381

125 NA, I, xiii, p. 99.

126 Letter 6, 15 September 1796, Le Faye (ed.), 2011, p. 10.

127 A Lady of Distinction, 1811, p. 45.

128 Sibbald, 1926, p. 112.

129 The Clairmont Correspondence, 1995, p. 87.

130 6 March 1805, Porter, 1998, p. 250.

131 13 April 1803, ibid., p. 224.

132 'The Universal Advertiser', La Belle Assemblée, February 1816.

133 Edgeworth, 1971, p. 381.

134 Letter 85, 24 May, Le Faye (ed.), 2011, pp. 221–2.

135 Letter 97, 2–3 March 1814, ibid., pp. 267–8.

136 NA, II, vi, p. 155.

137 P&P, II, xiv, p. 207.

138 Edgeworth, 1971, p. 62.

139 Poem by the Rev. B—C—, Diaries of Fanny C. Knatchbull, pocket-book, 1810, p. 7, Kent History and Library Centre, U.951/F.24/1–69.

140 Jervoise of Herriard Collection, Family and Estate Papers, accounts of George Mountford (butler), 1804, Hampshire Record Office, 44M69/E13/11/25; 1811, 44M69/E13/11/56.

141 Letter 33, 25 January 1801, Le Faye (ed.), 2011, p. 81. Eliza de Feuillide relates her proxy shopping endeavours in 1795, Le Faye, 2002, pp. 149–50.

142 Lambert, 2009, p. 67.

143 Letter 95, 3 November 1813, Le Faye (ed.), 2011, p. 259.

144 Quoted in Lambert, 2009, p. 84 n. 31.

145 NA, I, ii, p. 28.

146 Lambert, 2009, p. 67.

147 *Emma*, II, x, p. 228.

148 Lambert, 2009, p. 75.

149 Walsh, 2008; see also Walsh, 2006.

150 To Lady Mary Talbot, 7 June 1813, Porter, 1998, p. 327.

151 Lambert, 2009, p. 75.

152 Edgeworth, 1971, p. 181.

153 Ibid., pp. 299, 323, 356.

154 Letter 105, 23–4 August 1814, Le Faye (ed.), 2011, p. 283; see also Letter 139, 1 April 1816, ibid., p. 327. The pelisse Austen mentions could well be the surviving garment (see fig. 1.15).

155 Letter 89, 23–4 September 1813, ibid., pp. 236–7.

156 7 November 1812, Porter, 1998, p. 322.

157 2 June 1802, Clabburn, 1971a, p. 21.

158 1810, Weeton, 1936/1969, vol. 1, p. 261.

159 Longsdon of Little Longstone, Family and Estate Papers, 21 March 1803, Derbyshire Record Office, D3580/C32.

160 Ibid., 18 April 1803, D3580/C38.

161 Ibid., 29 May 1811, D3580/C208.

5 City

1 Letter 3, 23 August 1796, Le Faye (ed.), 2011, p. 5.

2 *NA*, I, x, p. 75.

3 Woods, 1996, p. 311.

4 Riello, 2006, p. 18.

5 Easton, 2004, p. 128; see also Greig, 2013; and Murray, 1998.

6 *NA*, I, x, p. 75.

7 Emsley, Hitchcock and Shoemaker, 'London History'.

8 L. Kaplan, 2010, p. 203.

9 Riello, 2006, p. 59; see also Rendell, 2002.

10 Riello, 2006, p. 64.

11 *Pers.*, II, vi, p. 154.

12 Lane, 1986, p. 177.

13 Adkins and Adkins, 2013; Allen, 2013; P. Byrne, 2017; Easton, 2004; L. Kaplan, 2011; Lane, 1986; Sales, 1994; Selwyn, 1999.

14 E. Austen-Leigh, 1976; P. Byrne, 2004b; Freeman, 2002; Lane, 1988; K. Parker, 2001; Ragg, 1972.

15 Sutherland, 2014.

16 Riello, 2006, pp. 60–61.

17 Letter 85, 24 May 1813, Le Faye (ed.), 2011, p. 222.

18 Powys, 1899, pp. 280, 283.

19 Letter 52, 15–17 June 1808, Le Faye (ed.), 2011, p. 133.

20 P. Byrne, 2013.

21 Erwin, 2012, p. 202; see also Bills, 2006; Donald, 1996; Heard, 2013; and Phagan and Gatrell, 2011.

22 *NA*, I, ii, p. 23.

23 Letter 106, 2 September 1814, Le Faye (ed.), 2011, p. 285.

24 Letter 97, 2–3 March 1814, ibid., p. 266.

25 *NA*, I, ii, p. 21.

26 *NA*, I, v, p. 32.

27 See summary in Riello, 2006, p. 16; see also Berg, 2004; Berg and Clifford, 1999; Lemire, 1991; and Vickery, 1993.

28 Riello, 2006, p. 9.

29 Dyer, 2016, p. 261; K. Smith, 2012.

30 Letter 128, 26 November 1815, Le Faye (ed.), 2011, p. 313.

31 26 July 1798, Powys, 1899, p. 300.

32 Adburgham, 1964, p. 12.

33 Lambert, 2009, p. 71.

34 Letter 70, 18–20 April 1811, Le Faye (ed.), 2011, pp. 187–8.

35 *The Picture of London* (1803), quoted in Adburgham, 1964, p. 5.

36 Ibid., p. 14; Fawcett, 1992.

37 Lane, 1988, p. 55.

38 Simond, 1815–17, vol. 1, p. 15.

39 Fawcett, 1992, pp. 37–8; see also Fawcett, 1990.

40 Adburgham, 1964, p. 14.

41 Dyer, 2016; Lemire, 1984; Lemire, 1988; Lemire, 1994; Lemire, 1999; Lambert, 2004a; Lambert, 2010a; Walsh, 2006.

42 Letter 98, 5–8 March 1814, Le Faye (ed.), 2011, p. 271.

43 Lemire, 1988, p. 3; Lemire gives a fuller account of second-hand clothing distribution.

44 Ginsburg, 1980; see also Sanderson, 1997; and Tebbutt, 1984.

45 Lemire, 1988, p. 4.

46 R. Walker, 1989.

47 Hollander, 1994.

48 *Almanach des Modes et Annuaires des Modes*, 1815, p. 136, quoted and trans. by Riello, 2006, p. 57.

49 *The Whole Art of Dress!*, 1830, p. 9.

50 *S&S*, I, x, p. 53.

51 Letter 6, 15 September 1796, Le Faye (ed.), 2011, p. 10.

52 For details of Werther's sartorial influence see Purdy, 1996; and Purdy, 1998.

53 Letter 1, 9–10 January 1796, Le Faye (ed.), 2011, p. 2; see also Solinger, 2012.

54 *The Whole Art of Dress!*, 1830, p. 13.

55 R. Walker, 1985. The National Portrait Gallery and the Victoria and Albert Museum have sets of the pictures.

56 Bazalgette, 2015.

57 *The Taylor's Complete Guide*, 1796, pp. vi–vii, 82.

58 Letter 17, 8–9 January 1799, Le Faye (ed.), 2011, p. 34.

59 Collins, 2013.

60 16 May 1813, Edgeworth, 1971, p. 59.

61 Letter 35, 5–6 May 1801, Le Faye (ed.), 2011, pp. 86–7.

62 For more on professional women dressmakers, milliners and fashion workers see Arnold, 1973; Batchelor, 2005; Collins, 2013; Dowdell, 2010; Ginsburg, 1972; and C. W. Smith, 2013.

63 Letter 38, 26–7 May 1801, Le Faye (ed.), 2011, pp. 95–6.

64 8 January 1822, Edgeworth, 1971, p. 315.

65 Dyer, 2016, p. 237.

66 Place, 1972, p. 13.

67 *NA*, I, x, p. 68.

68 Edgeworth, 1971, p. 78.

69 15 Park Street, Grosvenor Square, then 36 Somerset Street, Portman Square.

70 Letter 15, 24 December 1798, Le Faye (ed.), 2011, p. 32.

71 Letter 70, 18–20 April 1811, Le Faye (ed.), 2011, p. 188.

72 Jervoise of Herriard Collection, Family and Estate Papers, Hampshire Record Office, 44M69/E13/13/3, 4, 8, 20.

73 Letter 13, 1–2 December 1798, Le Faye (ed.), 2011, p. 24.

74 Souter, 1818, p. 225.

75 Fawcett, 1992, p. 35.

76 *Lady's Magazine*, 1811, p. 306, quoted in Vincent, 2009, p. 146.

77 *P&P*, I, viii, p. 37.

78 Letter 92, 14–15 October 1813, Le Faye (ed.), 2011, p. 247.

79 *P&P*, III, ii, p. 252.

80 *NA*, II, ix, p. 184.

81 *NA*, II, v, p. 154.

82 *The Watsons*, in Austen, 1974, p. 119.

83 1801, *The Wynne Diaries*, Fremantle (ed.), 1940, vol. 2, p. 111.

84 Ferrier, 1929, p. 53.

85 Jones and Westmacott, 1807, p. 97.

86 Letter 36, 12–13 May 1801, Le Faye (ed.), 2011, p. 89.

87 Letter 99, 9 March 1814, ibid., pp. 272–3.

88 *P&P*, II, ii, p. 138.

89 29 March 1803, Porter, 1998, p. 222.

90 *Dress and Address*, 1819, p. 39; see also Day, 2017, pp. 607–14. There are no known instances of British Regency authors using the term 'muslin disease', a name for an illness caused by underdressing; it was apparently first mentioned in Wilhelm Harcken, 'Die Mousselin-Krankheit: Ein Wort zur Beherzigung für junge Damen', *Journal des Luxus und der Moden*, 22 (1807), pp. 164–8, quoted by Max von Boehn in *Die Mode: Menschen und Moden in neunzehnten Jahrhundert nach Bildern und Kupfern*, Eng. trans. as *Modes and Manners of the Nineteenth Century*, vol. 2 (1909), and requoted ever since.

91 Burney, 1905, vol. 6, p. 7.

92 *The Whole Art of Dress!*, 1830, p. 14.

93 J. R. Harvey, 1995, p. 30.

94 *Emma*, III, ii, p. 305.

95 C. W. Cunnington, 1937, p. 13.

96 *La Belle Assemblée*, February 1806, p. 61.

97 Edgeworth, 1971, p. 63.

98 Thursday, 11 November 1813. I thank Deirdre Le Faye for this reference (personal communication, 22 March 2018).

99 Edgeworth, 1971, p. 225; Sibbald, 1926, pp. 60, 270.

100 Ferrier, 1929, p. 53.

101 3 February 1804, *The Wynne Diaries*, Fremantle (ed.), 1940, vol. 2, p. 105.

102 Letter 44, 21–3 April 1805, Le Faye (ed.), 2011, p. 107.

103 Letter 87, 15–16 September 1813, ibid., p. 229.

104 Byrde and Saunders, 2000; D. Miller, 2005.

105 Copeland and McMaster (eds), 2011; Engelhardt, 2009; Fullerton, 2012; Hearn, 2010; Marsh, 2005; Millard, 1983; Johnson and Tuite (eds), 2009; E. Smith, 2010; A. Thompson, 2000; A. Thompson, 2010; C. A. Wilson, 2009. Period texts include R. Hill, 1807; T. Wilson, 1808; T. Wilson, 1816.

106 Deirdre Le Faye, 'Foreword', in Fullerton, 2012.

107 *P&P*, I, vi, p. 26

108 Sutherland, 2014.

109 Sibbald, 1926, p. 248.

110 Sperling, 1981, pl. 29.

111 The average height for women in the Regency was 5 feet 2 inches, for men, 5 feet 7 inches: Roberts and Cox, 2003, Table 6.7, p. 308.

112 Edgeworth, 1971, p. 297.

113 Diaries of Fanny C. Knatchbull, *The Lady's Daily Companion*, 13 August 1811, Kent History and Library Centre, U.951/F.24/1–69.

114 A. Thompson, 2010.

115 3 April 1822, Edgeworth, 1971, p. 379.

116 4 April 1822, ibid., p. 380.

117 W. Scott, 1985, p. 34.

118 Greig, 2013, pp. 15, 19.

119 E. Wilson, 2007, p. 97.

120 Byrde, 1992, p. 94; see also Barbey d'Aurevilly, 2002; Svelte, 2017; R. Walker, 1989.

121 Hollander, 1993, p. 348.

122 Lambert, 1988, p. 60.

123 D. L. Moore, 1971.

124 Kelly, 2005, p. 164; see also Barbey d'Aurevilly, 2002; S. Cole, 2012; Lambert, 1988; Hazlitt, 1998.

125 E. Wilson, 2007, p. 98.

126 Sales, 1994, p. 176.

127 *NA*, II, xii, p. 203.

128 *S&S*, II, ii, p. 142.

129 *S&S*, II, xiv, p. 235; Grose, 1811.

130 *S&S*, II, xiv, p. 135.

131 *Emma*, II, vii, p. 192.

132 Grose, 1811.

133 *NA*, I, iv, p. 32.

134 *NA*, I, vii, p. 48.

135 Vincent, 2018b, p. 6.

136 *Emma*, II, ii, p. 301.

137 11 February 1822, Edgeworth, 1971, p. 348.

138 *Dress and Address*, 1819, p. v.

139 Ibid., p. 3.

140 Ibid., p. 125.

141 Sales, 1994, p. 108.

142 Hollander, 1993, p. 92.

143 *Emma*, II, xvii, p. 281.

144 *Dress and Address*, 1819, p. 47.

145 *Emma*, III, vi, p. 336.

146 *Emma*, II, xiv, pp. 251, 253, 261.

147 *Dress and Address*, 1819, p. 120.

148 18 June 1814, Stanley, 1907, p. 91. There follows a lot of discussion of the emperor's visit to England.

149 Williams, 1815, pp. 71–2.

150 Ibid., p. 48.

151 Mansel, 2005, p. 60. Samples of her gown fabrics can be seen in Lister, 2003.

152 Edgeworth, 1971, p. 348.

153 Jordan, 1951, p. 190.

154 Papworth, Wrangham and Combe, 1813, p. 173; Sibbald, 1926, p. 306. Austen's 'new Regency walking dress' in her juvenilia was inspired by the first Regency crisis in 1788; *Catharine, or The Bower*, in Austen, 1993, p. 203.

155 Bazalgette, 2015, p. 27.

156 Lambert, 1988, p. 61; Ribeiro, 1995, p. 99.

157 Staniland, 2000; Staniland, 1997. See Charlotte, 1949.

158 E. C. Knight, 1861, p. 235.

159 Letter 47, 30 August 1805, Le Faye (ed.), 2011, p. 117.

160 Behrendt, 1997.

161 Letter 75, 6 June 1811, Le Faye (ed.), 2011, p. 202. ; Austen, Mrs. Cassandra, 'To Mary Austen', June 1811, 23M93/62/2/3, Hampshire Record Office.

162 Edwards, 1976, p. 70.

163 Mrs Mary Topham, Lady's Account Book, 1820, Chawton House Library, 6641.

164 Jervoise of Herriard Collection, Family and Estate Papers, 11 February 1820, Hampshire Record Office, 44M69/E13/13/23 .

165 Galt, 1822, p. 194.

166 Letter 14, 18–19 December 1798, Le Faye (ed.), 2011, p. 28.

167 Letter 35, 5–6 May 1801, ibid., p. 87.

168 *A Book Explaining the Ranks and Dignities of British Society*, 1809, p. 110. For more on court wear generally see Mansel, 2005; and Arch and Marschner, 1987.

169 *A Book Explaining the Ranks and Dignities of British Society*, 1809, p. 111.

170 Letter to Philadelphia Walter, 9 April 1787, Le Faye, 2002, p. 76.

171 *A Book Explaining the Ranks and Dignities of British Society*, 1809, p. 109.

172 *Dress and Address*, 1819, p. 120.

6 Nation

1 Diaries of Fanny C. Knatchbull, *Annually La Belle Assemblée, or Lady's Fashionable Companion*, 3–10 April 1814, Kent History and Library Centre, U.951/F.24/1–69.

2 Letter 101, 14 June 1814, Le Faye (ed.), 2011, p. 275.

3 'Documents upon the Continental System', The Napoleon Series, https://www.napoleon-series.org/research/government/diplomatic/c_continental.html (accessed 9 April 2018).

4 Colley, 2005, pp. 5–7.

5 *Sanditon*, in Austen, 1974, p. 172.

6 Riello, 2006, p. 30.

7 Sanderson, 1986; Sanderson, 1997; Sanderson, 2001.

8 Jon Stobart summarised in Lambert, 2009, p. 70.

9 Edgeworth, 1971, p. 347; see Baudis, 2014.

10 Edwards, 1976, pp. 72–3.

11 Stevens, 2002, pp. 67–8.

12 Buck, 1979, p. 151.

13 E. G. Smith, 1911, p. 79.

14 Tartan has benefited from recent scholarship: Coltman, 2010; Dziennik, 2012; Faiers, 2008, pp. 31–50; Nicholson, 2005.

15 Nicholson, 2005, p. 165.

16 Ibid., p. 162.

17 Coltman, 2010, p. 207.

18 Ibid., p. 183.

19 Dzienneik, 2012, p. 136.

20 Dunleavy, 1989; Dunleavy, 2011.

21 Letter 12, 25 November 1798, Le Faye (ed.), 2011, p. 22.

22 Mortimer, 1810, 'Europe: Manufactures', n.p.

23 Letter 95, 3 November 1813, Le Faye (ed.), 2011, p. 260.

24 22 July 1800, Powys, 1899, pp. 335–6.

25 Jervoise of Herriard Collection, Family and Estate Papers, Hampshire Record Office, 44M69/E13/12/47; Sykas, 2009.

26 Adburgham, 1964, p. 11.

27 Levey, 2003.

28 Letter 12, 25 November 1798, Le Faye (ed.), 2011, p. 21.

29 22 July 1806, *The Wynne Diaries*, Fremantle (ed.), 1940, vol. 3, p. 291.

30 Levey, 2003, p. 846; *Instructions for Cutting Out Apparel for the Poor*, 1789.

31 Letter 21, 11 June 1799, Le Faye (ed.), 2011, pp. 45–6; Letter 88, 16 September 1813, ibid., p. 224; Letter 24, 1 November 1800, ibid., p. 52; Letter 88, 16 September 1813, ibid., p. 222.

32 Letter 88, 16 September 1813, ibid., p. 233.

33 *NA*, I, iv, p. 31; *Pers.*, II, v, p. 147.

34 *Emma*, II, xix, p. 453.

35 Le Faye, 2013, p. 431.

36 Letter 30, 8–9 January 1801, Le Faye (ed.), 2011, p. 73.

37 *P&P*, I, iii, p. 15.

38 Mrs Mary Topham, Lady's Account Book, 10 April 1814, 23 March(?) 1815, Chawton House Library, 6641.

39 Le Faye, 2002, p. 137.

40 Edgeworth, 1971, p. 89.

41 *S&S*, III, xi, p. 329.

42 Mortimer, 1810, 'Hat', n.p. 'Castor' (from Latin: 'beaver') was an imitation of the genuine fur, made from wool. 'Drab' is a dull light brown or yellowish brown colour.

43 Sleeper-Smith (ed.), 2009, p. xvii; Matthews David, 2015.

44 Letter 31, 14–16 January 1801, Le Faye (ed.), 2011, p. 77.

45 Papworth, Wrangham and Combe, 1813, pp. 178–80.

46 *The Whole Art of Dress!*, 1830, p. 43.

47 *Emma*, II, iv, p. 173.

48 R. Lloyd, 1819, p. 4.

49 Ibid., *passim*.

50 See, for example, S. Byrne, 2013; Rodi, 2012; and Sutherland, 2002.

51 Letter 35, 5–6 May 1801; Letter 50, 8–9 February 1807, Le Faye (ed.), 2011, pp. 87, 126.
52 Letter 20, 2 June 1799, ibid., p. 44; see also Nichols, 1996; and Dony, 1942.
53 Letter 70, 18–20 April 1811, Le Faye (ed.), 2011, p. 188; Letter 50, 8–9 February 1807, ibid., p. 126.
54 Letter 97, 2–3 March 1814, ibid., p. 267.
55 *Lady's Monthly Museum*, vol. 6, 1801, p. 156.
56 *Captain Rock in London*, 1825, p. 276.
57 Summarised in McGuigan and Burnham, 2005; and Mosher, 2006.
58 See publications such as the comprehensively illustrated *The Military Costume of Europe*, 1812.
59 Arch, 2007, p. 99.
60 Ibid., p. 104.
61 Ibid., p. 102; Grose, 1811.
62 *P&P*, I, vii, p. 30.
63 *P&P*, II, xviii, p. 224.
64 L. Carter, 2014.
65 *MP*, I, ix, p. 102.
66 Sibbald, 1926, p. 260.
67 1801, *The Wynne Diaries*, Fremantle (ed.), 1940, p. 111.
68 Arch, 2007, p. 99.
69 Edward Stanley to Lucy Stanley, 24 June 1816, Stanley, 1907, p. 269.
70 *P&P*, I, vii, p. 30.
71 Jervoise of Herriard Collection, Family and Estate Papers, June–December 1805, Hampshire Record Office, 44M69/E13/12/32.
72 Scott and Taylor (eds), 1825.
73 *New Bon Ton Magazine*, May–October 1819, p. 138.
74 *S&S*, I, xix, p. 100.
75 Sales, 1994, pp. 118–31, 222–6.
76 Dziennik, 2012, p. 130.
77 Buchan, 1811, p. 179.
78 Blair, 1803, p. 104.
79 There are many more specific studies on military clothing of this period: Abler, 1999; Buckley, 1979; Carman, 1967; Hughes Myerly, 1996; D. J. Smith, 1983; Thorburn, 1976.
80 Blair, 1803, p. 114.
81 Duke of Clarence to George FitzClarence, 6 April 1809, Jordan, 1951, p. 78.
82 *S&S*, I, viii, p. 40. Austen slyly connotes a third trope of the flannel waistcoat, that an old man should wear such a garment to keep him warm instead of seeking a young wife for the task. 'We should not then see... old debauchees taking a blooming beauty to their bosom, when an additional flannel waistcoat would have been a bedfellow much more salutary and appropriate', Colton, 1813, p. 224.
83 *Dress and Address*, 1819, p. 83.
84 Golding, 1817, p. 50.
85 Jervoise of Herriard Collection, Family and Estate Papers, 27 December 1802, Hampshire Record Office, 44M69/E13/12/28.
86 Matthews David, 2006, p. 133.

87 16 February 1798, Le Faye, 2002, p. 153.
88 E. G. Smith, 1911, p. 287
89 Edwards, 1976, p. 71.
90 Lambert, 2010a, pp. 61–2; Riello, 2006, pp. 45–7.
91 Lemire, 2016, p. 1.
92 Hollander, 1994, p. 74.
93 C. W. Cunnington, 1937, p. 13.
94 E. G. Smith, 1911, p. 72.
95 *NA*, II, xii, p. 203.
96 *Repository of Arts*, April 1809, p. 250.
97 Adburgham, 1964, p. 10; Letter 98, 5–8 March 1814, Le Faye (ed.), 2011, p. 271.
98 Melesina Trench to Charles St George, February 1814, Hampshire Record Office, 23M93/30/1/38.
99 Daly, 2013.
100 *MP*, II, vi, p. 217.
101 *S&S*, I, xiv, p. 71.
102 Alexander, 1805; Alexander, 1811; Alexander, 1814a; Alexander, 1814b; Alexander, 1814c; Alexander, 1814d; Baxter and Miller, 1810; Bradford, 1809; L'Évêque, 1814; Semple, 1809.
103 The idea is Bernard Smith's in *European Vision and the South Pacific* (1960), quoted in Geczy, 2013, p. 16.
104 For French pre-and post-Revolutionary dress see Cage, 2009; Chrisman, 1997; Chrisman-Campbell, 2002; Chrisman-Campbell, 2015; Delpierre, 1997; Donaghay, 1982; Hunt, 2009; Ribeiro, 1988; Ribeiro, 1991; Ribeiro, 1995; and Sewell, 2010.
105 Ribeiro, 1991, p. 329.
106 Letter 145, 8–9 September 1816, Le Faye (ed.), 2011, p. 335; see also E. Knight, 2005.
107 Other popular French magazines included *Le Suprême Bon Ton, ou Étrennes de la Mode*; *Le Goût du Jour*; *L'Ami de la Mode*; *Les Costumes des Dames Parisiennes, ou L'Ami de la Mode*; *Les Délices de Paris*; *L'Annuaire des Modes de Paris*; *L'Almanach des Modes*.
108 Letter 106, 2 September 1814, Le Faye (ed.), 2011, p. 285.
109 28 January 1819, Edgeworth, 1971, p. 165.
110 *MP*, I, v, pp. 42–3; see also P. Byrne, 2017.
111 W. Roberts, 1980, p. 34; Auerbach, 2004, pp. 181–3. Austen's founding editor, R. W. Chapman, dismissed the idea but it has lately been reiterated: Southam, 2006, pp. 145–50.
112 *MP*, I, v, p. 42; see also Moores, 2015.
113 *MP*, I, iv, p. 41.
114 *P&P*, I, viii, p. 39.
115 *The Duties of a Lady's Maid*, 1825/2016, p. 215.
116 Edward Stanley to Louisa Stanley, 13 July 1816, Stanley, 1907, p. 301.
117 'The Universal Advertising Sheet', *La Belle Assemblée*, August 1817, p. 1.
118 A Lady of Distinction, 1811; Charlotte Bury, *Diary of a Lady in Waiting* (1814), quoted in Waugh, 1954, p. 133.
119 Edgeworth, 1971, p. 251.
120 To Sophy Ruxton, 9 September 1818, Edgeworth, 1971, p. 103.

121 Ribeiro, 1991, pp. 331. For details of how post-Revolutionary dress struck the English eye see A Lady, 1798.
122 Arnold, 1970, p. 19.
123 Le Bourhis, 1989, p. 234.
124 Edward Stanley to his father, Sir John T. Stanley, 17 June 1802, Stanley, 1907, p. 34.
125 Edgeworth, 1971, p. 306.
126 Edward Stanley to Mrs Stanley, 26 June 1814, Stanley, 1907, p. 101.
127 Edward Stanley to Mrs Stanley, 30 June 1814, ibid., p. 115.
128 Edward Stanley to [his daughter?] Louisa Stanley, 13 July 1816, ibid., p. 297.
129 *The Duties of a Lady's Maid*, 1825/2016, p. 125.
130 Letter 20, 2 June 1799, Le Faye (ed.), 2011, p. 44.
131 Letter 21, 11 June 1799, ibid., p. 44.
132 Mackrell, 1998.
133 Burney, 1905, vol. 6, p. 222.
134 Ribeiro, 1991, p. 331.
135 *Repository of Arts*, June 1810, p. 389.
136 For more information on the relationship between queen and milliner, see Chrisman-Campbell, 2002; and Chrisman-Campbell, 2015.
137 Chrisman, 1997
138 Le Faye, 2002, pp. 133, 168. For more on relations between Austen and the French see W. Roberts, 1980.
139 *Dress and Address*, 1819, p. 57.
140 Riello, 2006, p. 15.
141 Edgeworth, 1971, p. 253.
142 Purdy, 1998, pp. 130, 122.
143 5 May 1798, *The Wynne Diaries*, Fremantle (ed.), 1940, p. 225.
144 Quoted in Purdy, 1998, p. 212.
145 31 May 1798, *The Wynne Diaries*, Fremantle (ed.), 1937, p. 229.
146 Purdy, 1998, p. 187.

7 World

1 Letter 34, 11 February 1801, Le Faye (ed.), 2011, p. 84.
2 New South Wales, the first British colony in Australia, was founded as a penal colony in 1788. 'Australia' originally applied to all territory on the continent to the east of longitude 135° East; the name began to be used in the late 1810s.
3 Landry, 2000, p. 86; Pidduck, 2000, p. 126.
4 Landry, 2000, p. 86.
5 Fulford, 1999; Harris, 2007; Hubback and Hubback, 1906; Kindred, 2004; Kindred, 2009; Southam, 2001; Southam, 2003.
6 J. E. Austen-Leigh, 2008, p. 18.
7 Kindred, 2017; *Pers.*, II, xii, p. 236.
8 *Pers.*, I, viii, pp. 65–6.
9 Letter 13, 1–2 December 1798, Le Faye (ed.), 2011, p. 24.
10 A. Miller, 2007, p. 44.
11 Hart, 2006, p. 10; A. Miller, 2007.
12 Annis, 1970, p. 32.
13 *Pers.*, I, iii, p. 21.

14 *New Bon Ton Magazine*, vol. 1, 1818, p. 139.

15 *MP*, II, vi, p. 216; see also A. Miller, 2007, p. 60.

16 *MP*, III, viii, pp. 352, 356.

17 Ibid., III, vi, p. 341.

18 Ibid., III, vii, p. 351.

19 Ibid., II, xiii, p. 276.

20 Letter 18, 21–3 January 1799, Le Faye (ed.), 2011, p. 39; Letter 24, 1 November 1800, ibid., p. 55.

21 2 August 1810, *The Wynne Diaries*, Fremantle (ed.), 1940, vol. 3, p. 324.

22 Board of Admiralty, In-Letters from the Navy Board, National Maritime Museum, Caird Library, Manuscripts Section, 9 April 1806, ADM 354/222/76; 14 April 1806, ADM 354/222/75; 15 April 1806, ADM 354/222/74; 19 April 1806, ADM 354/222/240.

23 Blair, 1803, p. 106.

24 *Pers.*, II, vi, p. 156.

25 Lemire, 2016, p. 10.

26 *MP*, III, vii, p. 354.

27 Quoted in Southam, 2001, p. 229.

28 Letter 17, 8–9 January 1799, Le Faye (ed.), 2011, p. 34.

29 Davidson, 2015a, pp. 206–7.

30 Cook, 1787, p. xiii.

31 D. L. Moore, 1971.

32 Lemire, 2016, pp. 17–18.

33 Ibid., pp. 4–5.

34 Captain Francis Beaufort, 1805, quoted in Southam, 2001, p. 118.

35 *MP*, II, vi, p. 218.

36 Lemire, 2015, p. 298.

37 Southam, 2001, p. 103.

38 Kindred, 2017, p. 68.

39 Letter 79, 29 January 1813, Le Faye (ed.), 2011, p. 211; Letter 80, 4 February 1813, ibid., p. 212; Letter 96, 6–7 November 1813, ibid., p. 262.

40 Letter 98, 5–8 March 1814, ibid., p. 269.

41 Kindred, 2017, p. 63.

42 5 February 1814, Kindred, 2017, p. 148.

43 26 July 1808, Kindred, 2017, p. 30.

44 E. G. Smith, 1911, p. 154.

45 Edward Stanley to Louisa Stanley, 13 July 1816, Stanley, 1907, p. 297.

46 Southam, 2001, p. 120.

47 Daly, 2007b, p. 350.

48 Ibid., p. 344.

49 Hervey, 1814, vol. 1, pp. 25–6.

50 Kindred, 2017, p. 154.

51 Daly, 2007a, p. 39.

52 Mortimer, 1810, 'Contraband', n.p.

53 Parliament of Great Britain, 1818, p. 84.

54 Melesina Trench, letter to Charles St George, September 1820, Hampshire Record Office, 23M93/30/1/70.

55 Heckscher, 1922, p. 191.

56 *Monthly Magazine*, December 1806, p. 514.

57 Simond, 1815–17, vol. 1, p. 241.

58 Rajan, 2000, p. 8.

59 *Emma*, II, vi, p. 338.

60 *La Belle Assemblée*, July 1816, p. 2.

61 Tuite, 2000, p. 95.

62 Lemire, 2015, p. 295.

63 Sykas, 2001.

64 Riello, 2006, p. 50.

65 Riello, 2009, pp. 286–7.

66 Lemire, 1988, p. 5 n. 7.

67 Blair, 1803, pp. 113–14.

68 'Compendium of Advertisements', *La Belle Assemblée*, February 1816, p. 356.

69 Berg, 2007; King, 2009; Lemire, 1991; Lemire, 2010; Lemire, 2013; Riello, 2013; Riello and Parthasarathi, 2009; Riello and Roy, 2009.

70 Riello, 2009, p. 266; Styles, 2007.

71 Southam, 2001, p. 46; *S&S*, I, x, p. 52.

72 Lemire, 2016, p. 8.

73 *S&S*, I, x, p. 52.

74 *Treatise on Military Finance*, 1809. For the experiences of British troops in both Indies see Buckley, 1979; and Holmes, 2006.

75 Williamson, 1810, vol. 1, pp. 8–9.

76 Stavorinus and Wilcocke, 1798, p. 524.

77 Williamson, 1810, pp. 10–12.

78 Williamson and Doyley, 1813, p. xv.

79 Williamson, 1810, p. 8.

80 Ibid., p. 242.

81 Ibid., p. 243.

82 Williamson and Doyley, 1813, p. 375.

83 Burney, 1905, vol. 5, p. 495.

84 Hafner-Laney, 2010; Hughes, 2005; Nigro, 2010; Wylie, 2007.

85 *P&P*, III, v, p. 277.

86 Lazaro and Warner, 2004, p. 22.

87 Aikin, 1802, p. 122.

88 Charlotte Jane St Maur, Journal – Notes, Memoranda, 21 May 1820, Chawton House Library, 10828.

89 P. Byrne, 2004a, pp. 203–6.

90 *NA*, I, ii, p. 28.

91 Ashmore, 2012, p. 38.

92 Ashmore, 2012, p. 31.

93 Lemire, 2009, pp. 224–5.

94 Cochrane, 1806, p. 6.

95 Ashmore, 2012, p. 16.

96 *Valuable Secrets Concerning Arts and Trades*, 1795, p. 50.

97 Ashmore, 2012, p. 38.

98 Ibid., p. 34.

99 Papers relating to the Empress Josephine's wardrobe, 1809, Victoria and Albert Museum, National Art Library, MSL/1978/3587–3588; see also Meunier, 2016.

100 Recollections of Hortense de Beauharnais, quoted in Ashmore, 2012, p. 64.

101 Clabburn, 1996; Clabburn, 2002; Lévi-Strauss, 1988; Mackrell, 1986; Maskiell, 2009; Rizvi. Ahmed (India) 2009; Whyte, 1970; Whyte, 1976.

102 Whyte, 1970, pp. 32–6.

103 17 October 1796, Le Faye, Deirdre, 2002, p. 126.

104 Maskiell, 2009, pp. 211–12.

105 *La Belle Assemblée*, March 1806, p. 63.

106 *Journal de la Mode et du Goût*, 5 June 1790, quoted in Mackrell, 1986, p. 38.

107 Hiner, 2010, pp. 83–6, 90, 103.

108 *MP*, II, xiii, p. 282.

109 Whyte, 1970; Whyte, 1976.

110 Irwin, 1981.

111 *Emma*, III, ii, p. 302.

112 Letter 44, 21–3 April 1805, Le Faye (ed.), 2011, p. 103.

113 Davidson, 2017a.

114 E. Jordan, 2000, p. 40.

115 Saïd, 1994, p. 115.

116 *Pers.*, II, ix, pp. 197, 235.

117 *Sanditon*, in Austen, 1974, p. 180.

118 Ibid., p. 178.

119 E. Jordan, 2000, p. 48.

120 Moira Ferguson, 1993, quoted in Landry, 2000, p. 56.

121 Lemire, 2016, p. 14.

122 *Authentic History of the English West Indies*, 1810, p. 57.

123 *Treatise on Military Finance*, 1809, p. 354.

124 For example, Board of Admiralty, In-Letters from the Navy Board, National Maritime Museum, Caird Library, Manuscripts Section, 21 January 1802, ADM 354/203/263.

125 *Sanditon*, in Austen, 1974, p. 206.

126 Ibid., pp. 195.

127 Ibid., pp. 181.

128 Galperin, 2003, p. 37; see also MacKinnon, 1937; and Le Faye, 2004, pp. 120–24.

129 MacKinnon, 1937, p. 45.

130 J. E. Austen-Leigh, 2008, p. 122.

131 Galperin, 2003, p. 39

132 Ibid.

133 Riley, 2005, p. 50.

134 Emsley, Hitchcock and Shoemaker, 'London History'.

135 Karskens, 2002, p. 44.

136 Sarah Bird, letter to her father, c.1798, in *Dear Fanny*, Heney (ed.), 1985, pp. 16–17.

137 Maynard, 1990; Maynard, 1994, pp. 27–32.

138 Elliott, 1995.

139 Karskens, 2011.

140 Lemire, 1988, p. 18.

141 Yale Center for British Art, 1975, p. 19.

142 Butterfield, 2012, pp. 21–2.

143 'Classified Advertising', 23 October 1808, 18 December 1808.

144 Butterfield, 2012, p. 60.

145 Ibid., pp. 18–19.

146 Ibid., p. 16.

147 1790, Adkins and Adkins, 2013, p. 190.

Conclusion

1 Southam, 2000, p. 3.

2 Sir Walter Scott, diary entry, 18 September 1827, quoted in Southam (ed.), 1987, p. 106.

3 Sales, 1994, p. 20.

4 Ibid., p. 23.

5 Fulford, 2002, p. 163.

6 Nigro, 2008.

7 Hudelet, 2009, p. 65.

Bibliography

Manuscripts

Chawton House Library, Hampshire

Charlotte Jane St Maur, Journal – Notes, Memoranda, 1819–21, 10828
Mrs Mary Topham, Lady's Account Book, 1810–25, 6641

Derbyshire Record Office, Matlock

Longsdon of Little Longstone, Family and Estate Papers: 21 March 1803, D3580/C32; 18 April 1803, D3580/C38; 11 February 1810, D3580/C94; 15 February 1811, D3580/C161; 29 May 1811, D3580/C208; 24 November 1811, D3580/C248

Hampshire Record Office, Winchester

Mrs Cassandra Austen, 'To Mary Austen', June 1811, 23M93/62/2/3
Jervoise of Herriard Collection, Family and Estate Papers: 44M69/E13/11/8–95; 44M69/E13/12/27–158; 44M69/E13/13/1–23
Melesina Trench 'To Charles St George', 1814–20, 23M93/30/1/38, 42, 46, 70, 152

Huntington Library, San Marino, Calif.

Anna Larpent's diaries, HM 31201; microfilm of the journals may be consulted at the British Library, M1016/1–7

Kent History and Library Centre, Maidstone

Fanny Knight (née Austen, married name Knatchbull), Diaries of Fanny C. Knatchbull, 1804–72, U.951/F.24/1–69

King's College Cambridge

Fanny Austen's diary, *Pocket Magnet, or Elegant Picturesque Diary, for 1814*

Manchester City Galleries

Mary White, album, 1759–1825, inscribed inside the front cover 'Mary White, 1819', 1987.29

National Maritime Museum, Greenwich, London

Board of Admiralty, In-Letters from the Navy Board, Caird Library, Manuscripts Section, 21 January 1802, ADM 354/203/263; 9 April 1806, ADM 354/222/76; 14 April 1806, ADM 354/222/75; 15 April 1806, ADM 354/222/74; 19 April 1806 ADM 354/222/240
Charles Austen, Private journals and pocket-books, 1815, AUS/101–3; 1816, AUS/105; 1817, AUS/109; 1820, AUS/111

The National Archives, Kew, London

Will of Catherine Peyton, 6 November 1823, PROB 11/1677/138
Will of Mary Topham, 10 February 1825, PROB 11/1695/186
Bill of Pains and Penalties for divorce of Queen Caroline, 15 October 1820, TS 11/98/308/1/75, fol. 38

Victoria and Albert Museum, London

Barbara Johnson, album, 1746–1823, T.219-1973
Papers relating to the Empress Josephine's wardrobe at St Cloud, the Tuileries, Malmaison and other places, 1809, National Art Library, MSL/1978/3587–3588

Wigan and Leigh Archives

Ellen Weeton, Journals and Letters, Edward Hall Diary Collection, EHC/165a–b <archives.wigan.gov.uk/archive/the-edward-hall-diary-collection/ellen-weeton> (accessed 18 October 2018)

Primary Sources and Editions

MP   Mansfield Park
NA   Northanger Abbey
P&P   Pride and Prejudice
Pers. Persuasion
S&S   Sense and Sensibility

A

A Book Explaining the Ranks and Dignities of British Society. Intended Chiefly for the Instruction of Young Persons, 1809 (London: Tabart & Co.; Heney & Haddon)

Aikin, John, 1802, The Arts of Life: I. Of Providing Food, II. Of Providing Cloathing, III. Of Providing Shelter: Described in a Series of Letters: For the Instruction of Young Persons (London: Printed for J. Johnson, St Paul's Church-Yard)

A Lady, 1798, A Sketch of Modern France; In a Series of Letters to a Lady of Fashion. Written in the Years 1796 and 1797, during a Tour Through France, C. L. Moody (ed.) (London: Cadell, and Davies)

A Lady [Anne Streatfield], 1808, The Lady's Economical Assistant: or, The Art of Cutting Out, and Making, the Most Useful Articles of Wearing Apparel, without Waste; Explained by the Clearest Directions, and Numerous Engravings, of Appropriate and Tasteful Patterns (London: John Murray)

A Lady, 1840, The Workwoman's Guide, Containing Instructions in Cutting Out and Completing Articles of Wearing Apparel, by a Lady (London: Simpkin, Marshall and Co.)

A Lady of Distinction [Mary Hill], 1811, The Mirror of the Graces; or, The English Lady's Costume, 2nd edn (London: Printed for B. Crosby and Co.)

Alexander, William, 1805, The Costume of China: Illustrated in Forty-Eight Coloured Engravings (London: William Miller)

Alexander, William, 1811, The Costume of the Russian Empire: Illustrated by Engravings (London: T. Bensley for J. Stockdale)

Alexander, William, 1814a, Picturesque Representations of the Dress and Manners of the Austrians (London: Thomas McLean)

Alexander, William, 1814b, Picturesque Representations of the Dress and Manners of the Chinese: Illustrated in Fifty Coloured Engravings, with Descriptions (London: John Murray)

Alexander, William, 1814c, Picturesque Representations of the Dress and Manners of the English (London: Printed for John Murray by W. Bulmer and Co.)

Alexander, William, 1814d, Picturesque Representations of the Dress and Manners of the Russians: Illustrated in Sixty-Four Coloured Engravings, with Descriptions (London: Printed for John Murray by W. Bulmer and Co.)

Austen, Jane, 1811/2003, Sense and Sensibility, Ros Ballaster (ed.), Penguin Classics (London: Penguin)

Austen, Jane, 1813/2003, Pride and Prejudice, Vivian Jones (ed.), Penguin Classics (London: Penguin)

Austen, Jane, 1814/2003, Mansfield Park, Kathryn Sutherland (ed.), Penguin Classics (London: Penguin)

Austen, Jane, 1815/2003, Emma, Fiona Stafford (ed.), Penguin Classics (London: Penguin)

Austen, Jane, 1817/2003, Northanger Abbey , Marilyn Butler (ed.), Penguin Classics (London: Penguin)

Austen, Jane, 1817/2003, Persuasion, Marilyn Butler (ed.), Penguin Classics (London: Penguin)

Austen, Jane, 1974, Lady Susan / The Watsons / Sanditon, Margaret Drabble (ed.), Penguin Classics (London: Penguin)

Austen, Jane, 1993, Catharine and Other Writings, Margaret Anne Doody and Douglas Murray (eds), Oxford World's Classics (Oxford: Oxford University Press)

Austen, Jane, 2006, Juvenilia, Peter Sabor (ed.) (Cambridge: Cambridge University Press)

Austen, Jane, 2011, Jane Austen's Letters, Deirdre Le Faye (ed.), 4th edn (Oxford: Oxford University Press)

Austen-Leigh, J. E., 2008, A Memoir of Jane Austen and Other Family Recollections, Kathryn Sutherland (ed.), Oxford World's Classics (Oxford: Oxford University Press)

Authentic History of the English West Indies: With the Manners and Customs of the Free Inhabitants, Including Their Civil and Criminal Laws, Establishments, &c.: A Description of the Climate, Buildings, Towns, & Sea Ports: With the Condition and Treatment of the Negroes: An Account of the Lands in Cultivation, and the Natural & Vegetable Productions, Exports, &c., 1810 (London: Printed and sold for the author by Dean and Munday)

B

Baxter, Thomas, and William Miller, 1810, An Illustration of the Egyptian, Grecian, and Roman Costume: In Forty Outlines, with Descriptions (London: Printed for William Miller by J. & E. Hodson)

Belcher, James, 1809/2006, Jem Belcher: Champion Prizefighter and His Historic Belcher Handkerchief: Including Jem Belcher's Treatise on Boxing (Belcher, Ky.: Belcher Foundation)

Blair, William, 1803, The Soldier's Friend, Containing Familiar Instructions to the Military Men in General on the Preservation and Recovery of Their Health (London: John Murray)

Bond, Elizabeth, 1814, Letters of a Village Governess, 2 vols (London: E. Blackader)

Bradford, William, 1809, Sketches of the Country, Character, and Costume, in Portugal and Spain, Made during the Campaign, and on the Route of the British Army, in 1808 and 1809 (London: J. Booth)

Buchan, William, 1811, Advice to Mothers, on the Subject of Their Own Health; and on the Means of Promoting the Health, Strength, and Beauty, of Their Offspring, 2nd edn (London: Cadell and Davies)

Burney, Fanny, 1905, Diary and Letters of Madame D'Arblay, Charlotte Barrett and Austin Dobson (eds), 6 vols (London: Macmillan), vols 5–6

Busby, T. L., 1820, Costume of the Lower Orders of London (London: Baldwin, Craddock and Joy)

C

Captain Rock in London: or, The Chieftain's Gazette (London: J. Robins and Co.)

Chalon, John James, 1822, Twenty-Four Subjects Exhibiting the Costume of Paris. The Incidents Taken from Nature (London: Rodwell and Martin)

Charlotte, 1949, Letters of the Princess Charlotte, 1811–1817, A. Aspinall (ed.) (London: Home and Van Thal)

Chubb, W. P., 1820, A Complete Treatise on the Arts of Dying and Scouring Every Artcle [sic] of Dress, Linen, Silks, Bonnets, Feathers, & c. & c. (London: by W. P. Chubb)

'Classified Advertising', Sydney Gazette and New South Wales Advertiser (Sydney: G. Howe), 5 March 1803–14 April 1821 [79 issues]

Cochrane, Archibald, Earl of Dundonald, 1806, Introduction to and Contents of an Intended Publication (London: Thomas Burton)

Cockle, Mrs, 1809, Important Studies, for the Female Sex, in Reference to Modern Manners; Addressed to a Young Lady of Distinction (London: Printed for C. Chapple)

Colton, Charles Caleb, 1813, Lacon: or, Many Things in Few Words; Addressed to Those Who Think (London: Longman, Hurst, Rees, Orme and Brown), vol. 2

Cook, M., 1787, A Sure Guide Against Waste in Dress; or The Woollen Draper's, Man's Mercer's, and Tailor's Assistant (London: Printed for the author)

D

Dear Fanny: Women's Letters to and from New South Wales, 1788–1857, 1985, Helen Heney (ed.) (Canberra: Australian National University Press)

Dress and Address, 1819, 2nd edn (London: Printed for J. J. Stockdale)

E

Edgeworth, Maria, 1971, *Maria Edgeworth, Letters from England, 1813–1844*, Christina Colvin (ed.) (Oxford: Clarendon Press)

F

Feltham, John, 1802, *The Picture of London, for 1803: Being a Correct Guide to All the Curiosities, Amusements, Exhibitions, Public Establishments, and Remarkable Objects, In and Near London; with a Collection of Appropriate Tables. For the Use of Strangers, Foreigners, and All Persons Who Are Not Intimately Acquainted with the British Metropolis* (London: Printed by Lewis & Co. for R. Phillips)

Ferrier, Susan, 1929, *Memoir and Correspondence of Susan Ferrier, 1782–1854: Based on Her Private Correspondence in the Possession of, and Collected by, Her Grand-Nephew John Ferrier*, John Andrew Doyle and John Ferrier (eds), The Works of Susan Ferrier: Holyrood Edition (London: Eveleigh Nash & Grayson), vol. 4

Fiske, Mrs [Elizabeth], 1808, *Records of Fashion and Court Elegance, 1807* (London: Published under the direction of Mrs Fiske by J. Shaw)

Fitz-Adam, Adam, 1803, *The World* (Philadelphia: Samuel F. Bradford)

Fry, Caroline, 1825, *The Assistant of Education: Religious and Literary* (London: Baker and Fletcher), vol. 4

G

Galt, John, 1822, The *Steam-Boat* (London: W. Blackwood)

Gibbon, Mrs Lloyd, 1809, *A Treatise on the Use and Effects of Anatomical Stays* (Brentford: P. Norbury)

Golding, J., 1817, *Golding's New Edition of the Tailor's Assistant, or, Improved Instructor, Containing a Synthesis of the Art of Cutting to Fit the Human Form* (London: Printed for the author)

Gronow, Captain, 1892, *The Reminiscences and Recollections of Captain Gronow*, 2 vols (London: John C. Nimmo)

Grose, Francis, 1811, *A Classical Dictionary of the Vulgar Tongue* (London: n.pub.)

H

Hamilton, Alexander, 1791, *Outlines of the Theory and Practice of Midwifery*, 3rd edn (London: Printed for T. Kay)

Hamilton, Alexander, 1797, *A Treatise on the Management of Female Complaints, and of Children in Early Infancy*, 4th edn (Edinburgh: Printed for Peter Hill)

Havell, Robert, A. D. Peake and Richard Brinsley Peake (eds), 1819, *The Characteristic Costume of France: From Drawings Made on the Spot, with Appropriate Descriptions* (London: Published by William Sams)

Hazlitt, William, 1998, 'Brummelliana', in *Selected Writings*, Jon Cook (ed.), Oxford World's Classics (Oxford: Oxford University Press)

Herbert, Dorothea, 1800/1930, *Retrospections of Dorothea Herbert*, 2 vols (London: Gerald Howe)

Hervey, Mrs [Elizabeth], 1814, *Amabel; or, Memoirs of a Woman of Fashion*, 4 vols (London: Henry Colburn)

Hill, Richard, 1807, *An Address to Persons of Fashion Relating to Balls: With a Few Occasional Hints Concerning Play-Houses, Card-Tables, &c. in which is Introduced the Character of Lucinda, a Lady of the Very Best Fashion, and of the Most Extraordinary Piety, with an Appendix Containing Some Extracts from the Writings of Chief Justice Hale, the Prince of Conti, Mr. Wilburforce, and Other Eminent Pious Men* (Baltimore: Printed by J. Robinson for Cole and I. Bonsal, Warner and Hanna, and George Hill)

Hobhouse, John Cam, 1910, *Recollections of a Long Life*, vol. 1: *1786–1816*, Charlotte Hobhouse Carleton (ed.) (London: John Murray)

Hope, Thomas, 1809, *Costume of the Ancients* (London: Printed for W. Miller by W. Bulmer and Co.)

Hope, Thomas, and Henry Moses, 1812/1973, *Designs of Modern Costume Engraved for Thomas Hope of Deepdene*, Costume Society Extra Series, no. 4 (London: Costume Society)

I

Instructions for Cutting Out Apparel for the Poor; Principally Intended for the Assistance of the Patronesses of Sunday Schools, . . . Containing Patterns, Directions, and Calculations, 1789 (London: J. Walter)

J

Jackson, Seguin Henry, 1798, *Cautions to Women, Respecting the State of Pregnancy; the Progress of Labour and Delivery; the Confinement of Child-Bed; and Some Constitutional Diseases: Including Directions to Midwives and Nurses* (London: G. G. and J. Robinson)

Johnson, Barbara, 1987, *Barbara Johnson's Album of Fashions and Fabrics*, Natalie Rothstein (ed.) (London: Thames & Hudson)

Jones, Stephen, and Charles Molloy Westmacott, 1807, *Spirit of the Public Journals* (London: James Ridgway)

Jones, William, 1808, *The Trial of Charles Angus . . . for the Wilful Murder of Margaret Burns . . . Taken in Short Hand by William Jones, Jun.* (Liverpool: Printed by William Jones)

Jordan, Dorothea, 1951, *Mrs. Jordan and Her Family: Being the Unpublished Correspondence of Mrs. Jordan and the Duke of Clarence, Later William IV*, A. Aspinall (ed.) (London: Arthur Barker)

K

Kerr, Letitia Louisa, 1826, *Book of Patterns for Work of Different Kinds*, Winterthur Library, Joseph Downs Collection of Manuscripts and Printed Ephemera, DE 19735, Doc. 36 <library.winterthur.org:8001/lib/item?id=chamo:25866> (accessed 17 June 2017)

Knight, Edward, 2005, *Jane Austen's Brother Abroad: The Grand Tour Journals by Edward Austen*, Jon Spence (ed.) (Lindfield, NSW: Jane Austen Society of Australia)

Knight, Ellis Cornelia, 1861, *Autobiography of Miss Cornelia Knight, Lady Companion to the Princess Charlotte of Wales: With Extracts from Her Journals and Anecdote Books* (London: W. H. Allen and Co.)

Knight, Richard Payne, 1805, *An Analytical Inquiry into the Principles of Taste*, 2nd edn (London: Printed by Luke Hansard for T. Payne and J. White)

L

La Belle Assemblée (London: J. Bell)

Lady's Monthly Museum (London: Vernor & Hood)

Le Blanc, H., 1828, *The Art of Tying the Cravat: Demonstrated in Sixteen Lessons, Including Thirty-Two Different Styles, Forming a Pocket Manual; and Exemplifying the Advantage Arising from an Elegant Arrangement of this Important Part of the Costume; Preceded by a History of the Cravat, from Its Origin to the Present Time; and Remarks on Its Influence on Society in General* (London: Effingham Wilson and Ingrey & Madeley)

Le Maistre, J. G., 1799, *Frederic Latimer: or, The History of a Young Man of Fashion*, 3 vols (London: Cadell and Davies)

L'Évêque, Henri, 1814, *Costume of Portugal* (London: Colnaghi & Co.)

Lloyd, Robert, 1819, *Lloyd's Treatise on Hats with Twenty-Four Engravings: Containing Novel Delineations of His Various Shapes, Shewing the Manner in which They Should be Worn, the Sort of Face and Person Best Suited to Each Particular Hat, and Rules for Their Preservation* (London: Printed for the author by F. Thorowgood)

Lucy, Mary Elizabeth, 2002, *Mistress of Charlecote: The Memoirs of Mary Elizabeth Lucy, 1803–1889*, Elsie Burch Donald (ed.) (London: Orion Books)

M

Malcolm, James Peller, 1810, *Anecdotes of the Manners and Customs of London during the Eighteenth Century: Including the Charities, Depravities, Dresses, and Amusements, of the Citizens of London, during that Period: With a Review of the State of Society in 1807: To which is Added, a Sketch of the Domestic Architecture, and of the Various Improvements in the Metropolis: Illustrated by Forty-Five Engravings*, 2nd edn (London: Longman, Hurst, Rees and Orme)

Mann, David Dickinson, 1811, *The Present Picture of New South Wales: Illustrated with Four Large Coloured Views, from Drawings Taken on the Spot, of Sydney, the Seat of Government. With a Plan of the Colony Taken from Actual Survey by Public Authority . . . with Hints for the Further Improvement of the Settlement* (London: J. Booth)

Mant, Alicia Catherine, 1815, *Caroline Lismore: or, The Errors of Fashion* (London: Law and Whittaker)

Mears, Martha, 1797, *The Pupil of Nature; or Candid Advice to the Fair Sex, on the Subjects of Pregnancy; Childbirth; the Diseases Incident to Both; the Fatal Effects of Ignorance and Quackery; and the Most Approved Means of Promoting the Health, Strength, and Beauty of Their Offspring* (London: Printed for the authoress)

Moore, Thomas, 1818, *The Fudge Family in Paris* (London: Longman, Hurst, Rees, Orme and Brown)

More, Hannah, 1799, *Strictures on the Modern System of Female Education: With a View of the Principles and Conduct Prevalent among Women of Rank and Fortune* (Dublin: Printed by William Porter, for Patrick Wogan and William Porter)

Mortimer, Thomas, 1810, *A General Dictionary of Commerce, Trade, and Manufactures: Exhibiting Their Present State in Every Part of the World; and Carefully Comp. from the Latest and Best Authorities* (London: R. Phillips)

Moses, Henry, 1823, *A Series of Twenty-Nine Designs of Modern Costume* (London: James Appleton)

N

Neckclothitania; or, Tietania, an Essay on Starchers, by One of the Cloth, 1818 (London: J. J. Stockdale)

New Bon Ton Magazine; or, Telescope of the Times (London: J. Johnston)

New, General, and Complete Weekly Magazine; or, Entertaining Miscellany (London: Printed for Alex Hogg)

Norfolk Chronicle (Norwich: Printed by J. Crouse)

P

Papworth, John Buonarotti, Francis Wrangham and William Combe, 1813, *Poetical Sketches of Scarborough: Illustrated by Twenty-One Engravings of Humorous Subjects* (London: Printed for R. Ackermann, by J. Diggens)

Parliament of Great Britain, 1818, *Report from the Select Committee on Silk Ribbon Weavers Petition*, Parliamentary Papers (London: H. M. Stationery Office, 1818), vol. 9

Pinchard, John, 1800, *The Trial of Jane Leigh Perrot, Wife of James Leigh Perrot, Esq; Charged with Stealing a Card of Lace, in the Shop of Elizabeth Gregory, Haberdasher and Milliner, at Bath, before Sir Soulden Lawrence, Knight, One of the Justices of His Majesty's Court of King's Bench. At Taunton Assizes, on Saturday the 29th Day of March, 1800. Taken in Court by John Pinchard, Attorney, of Taunton* (Taunton: Printed by and for Thomas Norris)

Place, Francis, 1972, *The Autobiography of Francis Place (1771–1854)*, Mary Thale (ed.) (Cambridge: Cambridge University Press)

Porter, Agnes, 1998, *A Governess in the Age of Jane Austen: The Journals and Letters of Agnes Porter*, Joanna Martin (ed.) (London: Hambledon Press)

Powys, Mrs Philip Lybbe, 1899, *Passages from the Diaries of Mrs. Philip Lybbe Powys of Hardwick House, Oxon: A.D. 1756–1808*, Emily J. Climenson (ed.) (London: Longmans, Green, and Co.)

Pyne, W. H., 1808, *The Costume of Great Britain* (London: William Miller)

Pyne, W. H., 1815, *Etchings of Rustic Figures: For the Embellishment of Landscape* (London: R. Ackermann)

Pyne, W. H., 1817, *W. H. Pyne on Rustic Figures: In Imitation of Chalk* (London: R. Ackermann)

Pyne, W. H., 1827, *The World in Miniature: England, Scotland, and Ireland. Containing a Description of the Character, Manners, Customs, Dress, Diversions, and Other Peculiarities of the Inhabitants of Great Britain* (London: Printed for R. Ackermann)

Pyne, W. H., and William Combe, 1808, *The Microcosm of London; or, London in Miniature* (London: R. Ackermann)

Pyne, W. H., John Hill and Charles Gray, 1806, *Microcosm: or, A Picturesque Delineation of the Arts, Agriculture, Manufactures, &c. of Great Britain. In a Series of above Six Hundred Groups of Small Figures for the Embellishment of Landscape . . . the Whole Accurately Drawn from Nature, and Etched*, 2nd edn (London: W. H. Pyne and J. C. Nattes)

R

Repository of Arts, Literature, Fashions, Etc. (London: Published by R. Ackermann)

Rousseau, Jean-Jacques, 1762/1979, *Emile: or, On Education* (New York: Basic Books)

S

Sawyer, Benjamin, 1818, 'Dye Book by Benjamin Sawyer of Reading' <archive.org/details/MAB.31962000742092Images> (accessed 13 June 2017)

Semple, Robert, 1809, *A Second Journey in Spain, in the Spring of 1809 . . . with Plates, Containing 24 Figures Illustrative of the Costume and Manners of the Inhabitants of Several of the Spanish Provinces* (London: C. & R. Baldwin)

Scott, John, and John Taylor (eds), 1825, 'On Fashions', *London Magazine*, vol. 12, p. 585

Scott, Walter, 1814/1985, *Waverley*, Claire Lamont (ed.), Penguin Classics (London: Penguin)

Sibbald, Susan Mein, 1926, *The Memoirs of Susan Sibbald (1783–1812)*, Francis Paget Hett (ed.) (London: John Lane)

Simond, Louis, 1815–17, *Journal of a Tour and Residence in Great Britain, during the Years 1810 and 1811*, 2 vols (London: J. Ballantyne and Company)

Sinclair, John, 1816, *The Code of Health and Longevity; or, A Concise View of the Principles Calculated for the Preservation of Health, and the Attainment of Long Life*, 3rd edn (London: Printed for the author by B. McMillan)

Smith, Elizabeth Grant, 1911, *Memoirs of a Highland Lady* (London: John Murray)

Solvyns, Balt, 1799, *A Collection of Two Hundred and Fifty Colored Etchings: Descriptive of the Manners, Customs, Character, Dress, and Religious Ceremonies of the Hindoos* (Calcutta: Mirror Press)

Souter, John, 1818, *The Book of English Trades and Library of the Useful Arts: With Seventy Engravings*, new enlarged edn (London: John Souter)

Spencer, Sarah, Lady Lyttelton, 1912, *Correspondence of Sarah Spencer, Lady Lyttelton, 1787–1870*, the Hon. Mrs Hugh Wyndham (ed.) (New York: Charles Scribner's Sons)

Sperling, Diana, 1981, *Mrs Hurst Dancing and Other Scenes from Regency Life, 1812–23*, Gordon Mingay (ed.) (London: Victor Gollancz)

Stanley, Edward, 1907, *Before and After Waterloo: Letters from Edward Stanley, Sometime Bishop of Norwich (1802; 1814; 1816)*, Jane H. Adeane and Maud Grenfell (eds) (London: T. Fisher Unwin)

Stavorinus, Johan Splinter, and Samuel Hull Wilcocke, 1798, *Voyages to the East-Indies* (London: G. G. and J. Robinson)

Stewart, J. A., 1817, *The Female Instructor; or, Young Woman's Companion: Being a Guide to All the Accomplishments which Adorn the Female Character* (Liverpool: Nuttall, Fisher and Dixon)

Strutt, Joseph, 1796, *A Complete View of the Dress and Habits of the People of England: From the Establishment of the Saxons in Britain to the Present Time, Illustrated by Engravings Taken from the Most Authentic Remains of Antiquity: To which is Prefixed an Introduction, Containing a General Description of the Ancient Habits in Use among Mankind, from the Earliest Period of Time to the Conclusion of the Seventh Century* (London: Printed by J. Nichols for J. Edwards)

T

Taylor, Mrs, 1815, *Practical Hints to Young Females, on the Duties of a Wife, a*

Mother, and a Mistress of a Family, 5th edn (London: Taylor & Hessey)

Taylor, Mrs Ann, 1817, Correspondence between a Mother and Her Daughter at School, 5th edn (London: Taylor & Hessey)

The Clairmont Correspondence: Letters of Claire Clairmont, Charles Clairmont, and Fanny Imlay Godwin, 1995, Marion Kingston Stocking (ed.), vol. 1: 1808–1834 (Baltimore, London: Johns Hopkins University Press)

The Duties of a Lady's Maid: With Directions for Conduct, and Numerous Receipts for the Toilette, 1825/2016 (London: James Bulcock; repr. Chawton, Hampshire: Chawton House Library)

The Footman's Directory, and Butler's Remembrancer, or The Advice of Onesimus to His Young Friends: Comprising, Hints on the Arrangement and Performance of Their Work, Rules for Setting out Tables and Sideboards, the Art of Waiting at Table, and Conducting Large and Small Parties, Directions for Cleaning Plate, Glass, Furniture, Clothes, and All Other Things which Come within the Care of a Man-Servant, and Advice Respecting Behaviour to Superiors, Tradespeople and Fellow-Servants: With an Appendix, Comprising Various Useful Receipts and Tables, 1823 (London: Printed for the author and sold by J. Hatchard and Son)

The Lymiad: A Poem in the Form of Letters from Lyme to a Friend at Bath Written during the Autumn of 1818, 2011, John Fowles and John Constable (eds) (Lyme Regis: Philpot Museum)

The Military Costume of Europe: Exhibited in a Series of Highly Finished Military Figures in the Uniform of Their Several Corps: With a Concise Description, and Historical Anecdotes: Forming Memoirs of the Various Armies of the Present Time, 1812 (London: T. Goddard & J. Booth)

The New Bath Guide: or, Memoirs of the B-n-r-d family. In a Series of Poetical Epistles, 1797, new edn (London: Printed for the Associated Booksellers)

The New Family Receipt Book, Containing Eight Hundred Truly Valuable Receipts in Various Branches of Domestic Economy, Selected from the Works of British and Foreign Writers of Unquestionable Authority and Experience, and from the Attested Communications of Scientific Friends, 1818 (Philadelphia, Pa.: Collins & Croft)

The Taylor's Complete Guide; or, A Comprehensive Analysis of Beauty and Elegance in Dress. Containing Rules for Cutting out Garments of Every Kind. With Copper-Plates, 1796 (London: Printed for Allen and West)

The Weird Sisters: A Novel, in Three Volumes, 1794 (London: Printed for William Lane at the Minerva Press)

The Whole Art of Dress! Or, the Road to Elegance and Fashion, at the Enormous Saving of Thirty Per Cent!!! Being a Treatise upon that Essential and Much-Cultivated Requisite of the Present Day, Gentlemen's Costume . . . by a Cavalry Officer, 1830 (London: Effingham Wilson)

The Wynne Diaries, 1940, Anne Fremantle (ed.), 3 vols (London: Oxford University Press)

Thicknesse, Mrs [Ann], 1800, The School for Fashion (London: Debrett & Fores and Robinsons), vol. 1

Treatise on Military Finance Containing the Pay and Allowances in Camp, Garrison and Quarters of the British Army; with All the Official Documents for the Guidance of Officers in Every Military Department, 1809, 10th edn (London: T. Egerton Military Library)

U

Upright, Solomon, 1809, Hints to the Bearers of Walking-Sticks and Umbrellas, 3rd edn (London: John Murray)

V

Valuable Secrets Concerning Arts and Trades: or, Approved Directions, from the Best Artists: for the Various Methods of Engraving on Brass, Copper, or Steel . . ., 1795 (Norwich, CT: Thomas Hubbard)

W

Walker, George, 1814, The Costume of Yorkshire, Illustrated by a Series of Forty Engravings, Being Fac-Similes of Original Drawings. With Descriptions in English and French (London: Longman, Hurst, Rees, Orme and Brown)

Walker, George, 1835, The Tailor's Ready Assistant, or Walker's Tables; of Quantities and Positions for Dress Coats, Great Coats, Frock Coats, Hussar Suits, Skeleton and Tunic Dresses; also Habits and Pelisses, 5th edn (London: G. Walker)

Walker, George, 1836, The Art of Cutting Breeches, Trowsers, Pantaloons, etc. etc. of Every Description with Instructions for Making-Up the Same (London: G. Walker)

Walker, George, 1837, The Art of Cutting Ladies' Riding Habits, Pelisses, Gowns, Frocks, Etc. Also Ladies' Chaise or Phaeton Coats, 7th edn (London: G. Walker)

Walker, George, 1838, The Tailor's Masterpiece: Containing the Art of Cutting All Kinds of Coats, Waistcoats, Children's Dresses; Military Hussar and Other Jackets; Gaiters, Gentlemen's and Ladies' Cloaks, Etc. Etc. With Instructions on the Most Approved Method of Making-up the Same (London: Richardson and Sons)

Walker, John, 1810, A Critical Pronouncing Dictionary and Expositor of the English Language (London: T. Cadell and W. Davies)

Weeton, Ellen, 1936/1969, Miss Weeton's Journal of a Governess, vol. 1: 1807–1811; vol. 2: 1811–1825 (London: Oxford University Press; repr. Newton Abbot: David & Charles)

Williams, Anna, 1815, Hints from an Invalid Mother to Her Daughter, on Subjects Connected with Moral and Religious Improvement in the Conduct of Life, in Various Relations (London: J. Hatchard and Williams and Son)

Williamson, Thomas, 1810, The East India Vade-Mecum; or Complete Guide to Gentlemen Intended for the Civil, Military, or Naval Service of the Hon. East India Company, 2 vols (London: Black, Parry and Kingsbury)

Williamson, Thomas, and Charles Doyley, 1813, The Costume and Customs of Modern India (London: Published and sold by Edward Orme)

Wilson, Thomas, 1808, An Analysis of Country Dancing: Wherein are Displayed All the Figures Ever Used in Country Dances, in a Way so Easy and Familiar, that Persons of the Meanest Capacity May in a Short Time Acquire (without the Aid of a Master) a Complete Knowledge of that Rational and Polite Amusement. To which are Added, Instructions for Dancing some Entire New Reels; Together with the Rules, Regulations, and Complete Etiquette of the Ball Room (London: Printed by W. Calvert)

Wilson, Thomas, 1816, A Description of the Correct Method of Waltzing: The Truly Fashionable Species of Dancing (London: Printed for the author, published by Sherwood, Neely and Jones)

Wordsworth, Dorothy, 1971, Journals of Dorothy Wordsworth: The Alfoxden Journal, 1798; The Grasmere Journals, 1800–1803, Mary Moorman and Helen Darbishire (eds) (Oxford: Oxford University Press)

Wyatt, James, 1822, The Tailor's Friendly Instructor, Being an Easy Guide for Finding the Principal and Leading Points Essential to the Art of Filling the Human Shape . . . Illustrated with Twenty-Four Engraved Models of Different Garments (London: Printed by J. Harris for, and sold by, the author)

Secondary Sources

A

Abler, Thomas S., 1999, Hinterland Warriors and Military Dress: European Empires and Exotic Uniforms (Oxford, New York: Berg)

Adburgham, Alison, 1964, Shops and Shopping, 1800–1914: Where, and in What Manner the Well-Dressed Englishwoman Bought Her Clothes (London: Allen and Unwin)

Adburgham, Alison, 1965, 'Shopping for Clothes in the 19th Century', Costume, vol. 1, pp. 3–10

Adburgham, Alison, 2012, Women in Print: Writing Women and Women's Magazines from the Restoration to the Accession of Victoria (London: Faber and Faber)

Adkins, Roy, and Lesley Adkins, 2013, *Jane Austen's England* (New York: Viking)

Allen, Louise, 2013, *Walking Jane Austen's London: A Tour Guide for the Modern Traveller* (Oxford: Shire Publications)

Annis, P. G. W., 1970, 'The Royal Navy', *Costume*, vol. 4, Supplement no. 1, pp. 29–35

Arch, Nigel, 2007, 'The Wearing of the Red: The Redcoat and the British Brand', *Costume*, vol. 41, pp. 99–104

Arch, Nigel, and Joanna Marschner, 1987, *Splendour at Court: Dressing for Royal Occasions since 1700* (London: Unwin Hyman)

Arch, Nigel, and Joanna Marschner, 1990, *The Royal Wedding Dresses* (London: Sidgwick & Jackson)

Arnold, Janet, 1968, *Patterns of Fashion*, vol. 1: *Englishwomen's Dresses and Their Construction c.1660–1860* (London: Macmillan)

Arnold, Janet, 1970, 'The Classical Influence on the Cut, Construction and Decoration of Women's Dress c.1785–1820', *Costume*, vol. 4, Supplement no. 1, pp. 17–23

Arnold, Janet, 1973, 'The Dressmaker's Craft', *Costume*, vol. 7, pp. 29–40

Arnold, Janet, 1989, 'The Cut and Construction of Women's Clothes in the Eighteenth Century', in *Revolution in Fashion: European Clothing, 1715–1815*, Jean Starobinski (ed.) (New York: Abbeville Press), pp. 126–34

Arnold, Janet, 1999, '"The Lady's Economical Assistant" of 1808', in *The Culture of Sewing: Gender, Consumption, and Home Dressmaking*, Barbara Burman (ed.) (Oxford: Berg), pp. 223–33

Ashelford, Jane, 2000, *The Art of Dress: Clothes and Society, 1500–1914* (London: National Trust)

Ashmore, Sonia, 2012, *Muslin* (London: V&A Publishing)

Atkinson, Jeremy, 2008, *Clogs and Clogmaking* (Botley: Shire Publications)

Auerbach, Emily, 2004, *Searching for Jane Austen* (Madison, Wis.: University of Wisconsin Press)

Auerbach, Emily, 2005, 'Searching for Jane Austen: Restoring the "Fleas" and "Bad Breath"', *Persuasions*, vol. 27, pp. 31–8

Austen-Leigh, Emma, 1976, *Jane Austen and Bath* (Folcroft, Pa.: Folcroft Library Editions)

Austen-Leigh, Richard Arthur, 1949, *Jane Austen at Southampton* (London: Spottiswoode, Ballantyne)

B

Baker, J. H., 1975, 'History of the Gowns Worn at the English Bar', *Costume*, vol. 9, pp. 15–21

Baker, J. H., 1978, 'A History of English Judges' Robes', *Costume*, vol. 12, pp. 27–39

Barbey d'Aurevilly, J., 2002, *Who Is a Dandy? Dandyism and Beau Brummell*, trans. George Walden (London: Gibson Square)

Batchelor, Jennie, 2005, *Dress, Distress and Desire: Clothing and the Female Body in Eighteenth-Century Literature* (Basingstoke: Palgrave Macmillan)

Batchelor, Jennie, and N. Powell Manushag (eds), 2018, *Women's Periodicals and Print Culture in Britain, 1690–1820s: The Long Eighteenth Century* (Edinburgh: Edinburgh University Press)

Baudis, Macushla, 2014, '"Smoking Hot with Fashion from Paris": The Consumption of French Fashion in Eighteenth-Century Ireland', *Costume*, vol. 48, pp. 141–59

Baumgarten, Linda, 1992, 'Under Waistcoats and Drawers', *Dress*, vol. 19, pp. 5–16

Baumgarten, Linda, 1996, 'Dressing for Pregnancy: A Maternity Gown of 1780–1795', *Dress*, vol. 23, pp. 16–24

Baumgarten, Linda, 1998, 'Altered Historical Clothing', *Dress*, vol. 25, pp. 42–57

Baumgarten, Linda, 2002, *What Clothes Reveal: The Language of Clothing in Colonial and Federal America* (Williamsburg, Va.: Colonial Williamsburg Foundation in association with Yale University Press)

Baumgarten, Linda, and John Watson, 1999, *Costume Close-up: Clothing Construction and Pattern, 1750–1790* (Williamsburg, Va.: Colonial Williamsburg Foundation, in association with Quite Specific Media Group, New York)

Bazalgette, Charles, 2015, *Prinny's Taylor: The Life and Times of Louis Bazalgette (1750–1830)* (Chennai: Tara Books)

Beetham, Margaret, 1996, *A Magazine of Her Own? Domesticity and Desire in the Woman's Magazine, 1800–1914* (London, New York: Routledge)

Behrendt, S., 1997, *Royal Mourning and Regency Culture: Elegies and Memorials of Princess Charlotte* (Basingstoke: Macmillan)

Berg, Maxine, 1994, *The Age of Manufactures, 1700–1820: Industry, Innovation, and Work in Britain* (London, New York: Routledge)

Berg, Maxine, 2004, 'In Pursuit of Luxury: Global History and British Consumer Goods in the Eighteenth Century', *Past & Present*, vol. 182, pp. 85–142

Berg, Maxine, 2007, 'From Globalization to Global History', *History Workshop Journal*, vol. 64, pp. 335–40

Berg, Maxine, and Helen Clifford, 1999, *Consumers and Luxury: Consumer Culture in Europe, 1650–1850* (Manchester: Manchester University Press)

Bernier, Olivier, 1981, *The Eighteenth-Century Woman* (Garden City, NY: Doubleday in association with the Metropolitan Museum of Art)

Bills, Mark, 2006, *The Art of Satire: London in Caricature* (London: Philip Wilson Publications)

Black, Sandy, Amy De la Haye, Joanne Entwistle, Agnes Rocamora, Regina A. Root and Helen Thomas (eds), 2014, *The Handbook of Fashion Studies* (London: Bloomsbury Publishing)

Blackman, Cally, 2001, 'Walking Amazons: The Development of the Riding Habit in England during the Eighteenth Century', *Costume*, vol. 35, pp. 47–58

Blank, Antje, 2005, 'Dress', in *Jane Austen in Context*, Janet Todd (ed.), Cambridge Edition of the Works of Jane Austen (Cambridge: Cambridge University Press), pp. 234–51

Blatt, Ben, 2017, 'From "Alibi" to "Mauve": What Famous Writers' Most Used Words Say about Them', *The Guardian*, 10 March

Blum, Dilys E., 1983, 'Englishwomen's Dress in Eighteenth-Century India: The Margaret Fowke Correspondence (1776–1786)', *Costume*, vol. 17, pp. 47–58

Blum, Stella (ed.), *Ackermann's Costume Plates: Women's Fashions in England, 1818–1828* (New York: Dover Publications, 1978)

Bogansky, Amy Elizabeth, 2013, *Interwoven Globe: The Worldwide Textile Trade, 1500–1800* (New York: Metropolitan Museum of Art)

Bohleke, Karin J., 2010, 'Nile Style: Nineteenth-Century Women Travelers in Egypt and the Dilemma of Dress, 1815–1875', *Dress*, vol. 36, pp. 63–86

Bradfield, Nancy, 1973, 'Studies of an 1814 Pelisse and Bonnet', *Costume*, vol. 7, pp. 60–61

Breward, Christopher, 1995, *The Culture of Fashion: A New History of Fashionable Dress* (Manchester: Manchester University Press)

Breward, Christopher, 2003, *Fashion* (Oxford: Oxford University Press)

Broadbent, James, Margaret Steven and Suzanne Rickard, 2003, *India, China, Australia: Trade and Society, 1788–1850* (Glebe, NSW: Historic Houses Trust of New South Wales)

Brogden, Anne, 2002, 'Clothing Provision by the Liverpool Workhouse', *Costume*, vol. 36, pp. 50–55.

Brown, David, 2000, '"Persons of Infamous Character" or "an Honest, Industrious and Useful Description of People"? The Textile Pedlars of Alstonfield and the Role of Peddling in Industrialization', *Costume*, vol. 31, pp. 1–26

Buck, Anne, 1971, 'The Costume of Jane Austen and Her Characters', in *Proceedings of the Fourth Annual Conference of the Costume Society, 1970* (London: Costume Society), pp. 36–45

Buck, Anne, 1973, 'The Dress of Domestic Servants in the Eighteenth Century', *Costume*, vol. 7, pp. 10–16

Buck, Anne, 1979, *Dress in Eighteenth-Century England* (New York: Holmes & Meier)

Buck, Anne, 1991, 'Buying Clothes in Bedfordshire: Customers and Tradesmen, 1700–1800', *Costume*, vol. 22, pp. 211–37

Buck, Anne, and Harry Matthews, 1984, 'Pocket Guides to Fashion: Ladies' Pocket Books Published in England, 1760–1830', *Costume*, vol. 18, pp. 35–58

Buckley, Roger Norman, 1979, *Slaves in Red Coats: The British West India*

Regiments, 1795–1815 (New Haven and London: Yale University Press)

Burman, Barbara, 2003, 'Pocketing the Difference: Gender and Pockets in Nineteenth-Century Britain', in Material Strategies: Dress and Gender in Historical Perspective, Barbara Burman and Carole Turbin (eds) (Malden, Mass.: Blackwell Publishers), pp. 77–99

Burman, Barbara, and Seth Denbo, 2006, Pockets of History: The Secret Life of an Everyday Object (Bath: Museum of Costume)

Burman, Barbara, and Ariane Fennetaux, 2019, The Pocket: A Hidden History of Women's Lives, 1660–1900 (London: Yale University Press)

Burman, Barbara, and Jonathan White, 2007, 'Fanny's Pockets: Cotton, Consumption and Domestic Economy, 1780–1850', in Women and Material Culture, 1660–1830, Jennie Batchelor and Cora Kaplan (eds) (Basingstoke, New York: Palgrave Macmillan), pp. 46–7

Burnham, Dorothy K., 1973, Cut My Cote (Toronto: Royal Ontario Museum)

Butler, Ed, 2012, 'Jane Austen: A Portrait of the Artist as a Young Girl?', Guardian Online <www.theguardian.com/books/2012/jun/08/jane-austen-portrait-as-young-girl> (accessed 28 February 2014)

Butler, Marilyn, 1975, Jane Austen and the War of Ideas (Oxford: Clarendon Press)

Butler, Marilyn, 2003, 'Introduction', in Jane Austen, Northanger Abbey, Marilyn Butler (ed.), Penguin Classics (London: Penguin)

Butler, Marilyn, 2007, Jane Austen (Oxford: Oxford University Press)

Butterfield, Amy, 2012, '"SEND ME A BONNET": Colonial Connections, Class Consciousness and Sartorial Display in Colonial Australia, 1788–1850' (unpublished BA Honours thesis, University of Sydney)

Byrde, Penelope, 1979, The Male Image: Men's Fashion in Britain, 1300–1970 (London: B. T. Batsford)

Byrde, Penelope, 1986, A Frivolous Distinction: Fashion and Needlework in the Works of Jane Austen (Bath: Bath City Council); repr. with a new Introduction as Jane Austen Fashion: Fashion and Needlework in the Works of Jane Austen (Ludlow: Moonrise Press, 2008)

Byrde, Penelope, 1987, '"That Frightful Unbecoming Dress": Clothes for Spa Bathing at Bath', Costume, vol. 21, pp. 44–56

Byrde, Penelope, 1992, Nineteenth Century Fashion (London: Batsford)

Byrde, Penelope, 2008, Jane Austen Fashion: Fashion and Needlework in the Works of Jane Austen (Ludlow: Moonrise Press)

Byrde, Penelope, and Ann Saunders, 2000, 'The "Waterloo Ball" Dresses at the Museum of Costume, Bath', Costume, vol. 34, pp. 64–9

Byrne, Paula, 2004a, Perdita: The Life of Mary Robinson (London: HarperCollins)

Byrne, Paula, 2004b, '"The Unmeaning Luxuries of Bath": Urban Pleasures in Jane Austen's World', Persuasions, vol. 26, pp. 13–26

Byrne, Paula, 2012, 'Who Was Miss Jane Austin?', Times Literary Supplement, 13 April, pp. 15–17

Byrne, Paula, 2013, The Real Jane Austen: A Life in Small Things (London: HarperPress)

Byrne, Paula, 2017, The Genius of Jane Austen: Her Love of Theatre and Why She Works in Hollywood (London: HarperPerennial)

Byrne, Sandie, 2013, What's so Great about Austen? Isn't She Just Bonnets and Balls? (Oxford: University Department for Continuing Education) <www.youtube.com/watch?v=Tmdi6m84AaQ> (accessed 20 March 2018)

Byrne, Sandie, 2014, Jane Austen's Possessions and Dispossessions: The Significance of Objects (Basingstoke: Palgrave Macmillan)

C

Cage, Claire E., 2009, 'The Sartorial Self: Neoclassical Fashion and Gender Identity in France, 1797–1804', Eighteenth-Century Studies, vol. 42, pp. 193–215

Cameron, Judith, 2014, 'Textile Symbolism and Social Mobility during the Colonial Period in Sydney Cove', in Global Textile Encounters, Marie-Louise Nosch, Feng Zhao and Lotika Varadarajan (eds) (Oxford: Oxbow Books), pp. 189–99

Campbell, Timothy, 2016, Historical Style: Fashion and the New Mode of History, 1740–1830 (Philadelphia: University of Pennsylvania Press)

Carman, W. Y., 1967, 'Bibliographies and Book Lists: British Military Uniform', Costume, vol. 1, no. 3, pp. 18–32

Carter, Alison J., 1992, Underwear: The Fashion History (New York: Drama Book Publishers)

Carter, Alison J., 2012, 'From Revolution to Frivolity', in Fashion: The Ultimate Book of Costume and Style, Anna Fischel (ed.) (London: Dorling Kindersley), pp. 166–216

Carter, Louise, 2014, 'Scarlet Fever: Female Enthusiasm for Men in Uniform, 1780–1815', in Britain's Soldiers: Rethinking War and Society, 1715–1815, Kevin Linch and Matthew McCormack (eds) (Liverpool: Liverpool University Press), vol. 5, pp. 155–80

Cavell, S. A., 2012, Midshipmen and Quarterdeck Boys in the British Navy, 1771–1831 (Woodbridge: Boydell and Brewer)

Chapman, S. D., 1970, 'James Longsdon (1745–1821), Farmer and Fustian Manufacturer: The Small Firm in the Early English Cotton Industry', Textile History, vol. 1, pp. 265–92

Chapman, Stanley, 1993, 'The Innovating Entrepreneurs in the British Ready-Made Clothing Industry', Textile History, vol. 24, pp. 5–25

Chapman, Stanley, 2002, Hosiery and Knitwear: Four Centuries of Small-Scale Industry in Britain, c.1589–2000 (Oxford: Oxford University Press)

Chazin-Bennahum, Judith, 2002, 'A Longing for Perfection: Neoclassic Fashion and Ballet', Fashion Theory, vol. 6, pp. 369–86

Chico, Tita, 2010, Designing Women: The Dressing Room in Eighteenth-Century English Literature and Culture (Cranbury, NJ: Associated University Presses)

Chrisman, Kimberly, 1997, 'L'émigration à la mode: Clothing Worn and Produced by the French Émigré Community in England from the Revolution to the Restoration' (unpublished MA thesis, Courtauld Institute of Art, University of London)

Chrisman-Campbell, Kimberly, 2002, 'Minister of Fashion: Marie-Jeanne "Rose" Bertin, 1747–1813' (unpublished PhD thesis, University of Aberdeen)

Chrisman-Campbell, Kimberly, 2015, Fashion Victims: Dress at the Court of Louis XVI and Marie-Antoinette (London, New Haven: Yale University Press)

Clabburn, Pamela, 1971a, 'Parson Woodforde's View of Fashion', Costume, vol. 5, pp. 19–21

Clabburn, Pamela (ed.), 1971b, Working Class Costume 1818, Costume Society Extra Series, 3 (London: Costume Society)

Clabburn, Pamela, 1977, 'A Provincial Milliner's Shop in 1785', Costume, vol. 11, pp. 100–12

Clabburn, Pamela, 1996, The Norwich Shawl: Its History and a Catalogue of the Collection at Strangers' Hall Museum, Norwich (London: HMSO)

Clabburn, Pamela, 2002, Shawls (Princes Risborough: Shire Publications)

Clark, Hazel, 1984, 'The Design and Designing of Lancashire Printed Calicoes during the First Half of the 19th Century', Costume, vol. 15, pp. 101–18

Cliff, Kenneth, 1999, 'Mr Lock, Hatter to Admiral Lord Nelson', Costume, vol. 33, pp. 98–104

Cliff, Kenneth, 2001, 'Mr Lock, Hatter to the Ladies, 1783–1805', Costume, vol. 35, pp. 59–66

Cole, Daniel James, 2012, 'Hierarchy and Seduction in Regency Fashion', Persuasions On-Line, vol. 33 <www.jasna.org/persuasions/on-line/vol33no1/cole.html> (accessed 20 February 2014)

Cole, Hubert, 1977, Beau Brummell (London, Toronto: Granada Publishing)

Cole, Shaun, 2012, The Story of Men's Underwear (New York: Parkstone International)

Colley, Linda, 2005, Britons: Forging the Nation, 1707–1837, 2nd edn (New Haven: Yale University Press)

Collins, Jessica, 2013, 'Jane Holt, Milliner, and Other Women in Business: Apprentices, Freewomen and Mistresses in the Clothworkers' Company, 1606–1800', Textile History, vol. 44, pp. 72–94

Coltman, Viccy, 2010, 'Party-Coloured Plaid? Portraits of Eighteenth-Century Scots in Tartan', Textile History, vol. 41, pp. 182–216

Colville, Quintin, and Kate Williams, 2016, Emma Hamilton: Seduction and Celebrity (London: National Maritime Museum)

Copeland, Edward, and Juliet McMaster (eds), 2011, The Cambridge

Companion to Jane Austen, 2nd edn, Cambridge Companions to Literature (Cambridge: Cambridge University Press)

Croft, Pauline, 1987, 'The Rise of the English Stocking Export Trade', *Textile History*, vol. 18, pp. 3–16

Cumming, Valerie, 1982, *Gloves* (London: Batsford)

Cumming, Valerie, 2004, *Understanding Fashion History* (New York: Costume and Fashion Press)

Cunningham, Patricia A., 1984, 'Eighteenth Century Nightgowns: The Gentleman's Robe in Art and Fashion', *Dress*, vol. 10, pp. 2–11

Cunnington, C. Willett, 1935, *Feminine Attitudes in the Nineteenth Century* (London: William Heinemann)

Cunnington, C. Willett, 1937, *English Women's Clothing in the Nineteenth Century* (London: Faber and Faber)

Cunnington, C. Willett, and Phillis Cunnington, 1957, *Handbook of English Costume in the Eighteenth Century* (London: Faber and Faber)

Cunnington, C. Willett, and Phillis Cunnington, 1970, *Handbook of English Costume in the Nineteenth Century* (London: Faber and Faber)

Cunnington, C. Willett, and Phillis Cunnington, 1992, *The History of Underclothes* (New York: Dover Publications Inc.)

Cunnington, C. W., P. E. Cunnington and Charles Beard, 1976, *A Dictionary of English Costume, 900–1900* (London: A. and C. Black)

Cunnington, Phillis, 1974, *Costume of Household Servants, from the Middle Ages to 1900* (London: A. and C. Black)

Cunnington, Phillis, and Catherine Lucas, 1967, *Occupational Costume in England: From the Eleventh Century to 1914* (London: A. and C. Black)

Curry, Mary Jane, 2000, '"Not a day went by without a solitary walk": Elizabeth Bennet's Pastoral World', *Persuasions*, vol. 22, pp. 175–86

D

Daly, Gavin, 2007a, 'English Smugglers, the Channel, and the Napoleonic Wars, 1800–1814', *Journal of British Studies*, vol. 46, pp. 30–46

Daly, Gavin, 2007b, 'Napoleon and the "City of Smugglers", 1810–1814', *Historical Journal*, vol. 50, pp. 333–52

Daly, Gavin, 2013, *The British Soldier in the Peninsular War: Encounters with Spain and Portugal, 1808–1814* (New York: Palgrave Macmillan)

Davidson, Hilary, 2015a, 'Reconstructing Jane Austen's Silk Pelisse, 1812–14', *Costume*, vol. 49, pp. 198–223

Davidson, Hilary, 2015b, 'The Unknown Lady's Account Book: or, Mrs. Topham's Treasure, Being a Tale of Historical Deduction, True in All Particulars', *Female Spectator*, vol. 1, no. 2, pp. 6–9

Davidson, Hilary, 2017a, 'Jane Austen's Muslin Shawl', *Jane Austen in 41 Objects* <www.jane-austens-house-museum.org.uk/6-muslin-shawl> (accessed 22 June 2018)

Davidson, Hilary, 2017b, 'Jane Austen's Pelisse', in *Jane Austen: A Novelist in the World*, Kathryn Sutherland (ed.) (Oxford: Bodleian Publications), pp. 56–75

Day, Carolyn, 2017, *Consumptive Chic: A History of Beauty, Fashion, and Disease* (London: Bloomsbury Academic)

Deforest, Mary, 1987, 'Mrs. Elton and the Slave Trade', *Persuasions*, vol. 9, pp. 11–12

Delpierre, Madeleine, 1997, *Dress in France in the Eighteenth Century*, trans. Caroline Beamish (London, New Haven: Yale University Press)

De Marly, Diana, 1986, *Working Dress: A History of Occupational Clothing* (New York: Holmes & Meier)

Denman, Helen C., 1981, 'Portraits of Jane Austen', *Persuasions*, vol. 3, pp. 12–13

Dolan, Alice, 2016, 'The Fabric of Life: Linen and Life Cycle in England, 1678–1810' (unpublished PhD thesis, University of Hertfordshire)

Donaghay, Marie, 1982, 'Textiles and the Anglo-French Commercial Treaty of 1786', *Textile History*, vol. 13, pp. 205–24

Donald, Diana, 1996, *The Age of Caricature: Satirical Prints in the Reign of George III* (New Haven: Published for the Paul Mellon Centre for Studies in British Art by Yale University Press)

Dony, John S., 1942, *A History of the Straw Hat Industry* (Luton: Gibbs, Bamforth & Co.)

Dow, Gillian, and Clare Hanson (eds), 2012, *Uses of Austen: Jane's Afterlives* (Basingstoke: Palgrave Macmillan)

Dowdell, Carolyn, 2010, 'The Fruits of Nimble Fingers: Garment Construction and the Working Lives of Eighteenth-Century English Needlewomen' (unpublished MA thesis, University of Alberta)

Downing, Sarah Jane, 2010a, 'Detailed Statements: Fashion and Needlework in Jane Austen's Letters', *Selvedge*, vol. 34, pp. 34–5

Downing, Sarah Jane, 2010b, *Fashion in the Time of Jane Austen* (Oxford: Shire Publications)

Duckenfield, Bridget, 2008, 'Jane Austen behind the Green Baize: Servants in Jane Austen's Novels', *Austentations*, no. 8, pp. 48–57

Du Mortier, Bianca M., 1988, 'Men's Fashion in the Netherlands (1790–1830), Caught between France and England', *Costume*, vol. 22, pp. 51–9

Dunleavy, Mairead, 1989, *Dress in Ireland* (New York: Holmes & Meier)

Dunleavy, Mairead, 2011, *Pomp and Poverty: A History of Irish Silk* (New Haven and London: Yale University Press)

DuPlessis, Robert S., 2015, *The Material Atlantic: Clothing, Commerce, and Colonization in the Atlantic World, 1650–1800* (Cambridge: Cambridge University Press)

Dyer, Serena, 2016, 'Trained to Consume: Dress and the Female Consumer in England, 1720–1820' (unpublished PhD thesis, University of Warwick)

Dziennik, Matthew P., 2012, 'Whig Tartan: Material Culture and Its Use in the Scottish Highlands, 1746–1815', *Past & Present*, vol. 217, pp. 117–47

E

Eacott, Jonathan, 2016, *Selling Empire: India in the Making of Britain and America, 1600–1830* (Chapel Hill, NC: University of North Carolina Press)

Earnshaw, Pat, 1985, *Lace in Fashion: From the Sixteenth to the Twentieth Centuries* (London: B. T. Batsford)

Earnshaw, Pat, 1986, *Lace Machines and Machine Laces* (London: B. T. Batsford)

Easton, Celia A., 2004, 'Austen's Urban Redemption: Rejecting Richardson's View of the City', *Persuasions*, vol. 26, pp. 121–35

Edwards, Joan, 1976, 'Elizabeth Grant of Rothiemurchus', *Costume*, vol. 10, pp. 68–73

Ehrman, Edwina, 2014, *The Wedding Dress: 300 Years of Bridal Fashions* (London: V&A Publishing)

Elliott, Jane, 1995, '"Was there a convict dandy?" Convict Consumer Interests in Sydney, 1788–1815', *Australian Historical Studies*, vol. 26, pp. 382–3

Ellis, Lorna, 1999, 'Seeing and "Fit to Be Seen": Emma Woodhouse and Elizabeth Bennet', in *Appearing to Diminish: Female Development and the British Bildungsroman, 1750–1850* (Cranbury, NJ: Associated University Presses), pp. 114–37

Emsley, Clive, Tim Hitchcock and Robert Shoemaker, 'London History: A Population History of London', *Old Bailey Proceedings Online* <www.oldbaileyonline.org>, version 7.0 (accessed 4 February 2019)

Engel, Laura, 2009, 'The Muff Affair: Fashioning Celebrity in the Portraits of Late-Eighteenth-Century British Actresses', *Fashion Theory*, vol. 13, pp. 279–98

Engel, Laura, 2015, *Austen, Actresses and Accessories* (London: Palgrave Macmillan)

Engelhardt, Molly, 2009, 'Jane Austen and the Semiotics of Dance: The Manner of Reading', *Dancing Out of Line: Ballrooms, Ballets, and Mobility in Victorian Fiction and Culture* (Athens: Ohio University Press), pp. 24–50

Entwistle, Joanne, 2000a, 'Fashion and the Fleshy Body: Dress as Embodied Practice', *Fashion Theory*, vol. 4, pp. 323–47

Entwistle, Joanne, 2000b, *The Fashioned Body: Fashion, Dress and Modern Social Theory* (Cambridge: Polity Press)

Erwin, Timothy, 2012, 'Comic Prints, the Picturesque and Fashion: Seeing and Being Seen in Jane Austen's Northanger Abbey', in *Women, Popular Culture, and the Eighteenth Century*, Tiffany Potter (ed.) (Toronto: University of Toronto), pp. 202–22

Evans, George Ewart, 1974, 'Dress and the Rural Historian', *Costume*, vol. 8, pp. 38–40

Ewing, Elizabeth, 1978, *Dress and Undress: A History of Women's Underwear* (London: B. T. Batsford)

F

Faiers, Jonathan, 2008, *Tartan* (Oxford: Berg)

Farrell, Jeremy, 1985, *Umbrellas & Parasols* (London: B. T. Batsford)

Farrell, Jeremy, 1992, *Socks & Stockings* (London: B. T. Batsford)

Fawcett, Trevor, 1990, 'Retailing Norwich Textiles at Bath, 1750–1800', *Norfolk Archaeology*, vol. 41, no. 1, pp. 67–70

Fawcett, Trevor, 1992, 'Bath's Georgian Warehouses', *Costume*, vol. 26, pp. 32–9

Fergus, Jan, 2005, 'Biography', in *Jane Austen in Context*, Janet Todd (ed.), Cambridge Edition of the Works of Jane Austen (Cambridge: Cambridge University Press), pp. 3–10

Fields, Jill, 'Erotic Modesty: (Ad)dressing Female Sexuality and Propriety in Open and Closed Drawers, USA, 1800–1930', in *Material Strategies: Dress and Gender in Historical Perspective*, Barbara Burman and Carole Turbin (eds) (Malden, Mass.: Blackwell Publishers, 2003), pp. 122–32

Fisk, Catriona, 2018, 'Confined by History: Dress and Pregnancy, 1750–1900' (unpublished PhD thesis, University of Technology, Sydney)

Flower, Cedric, 1968, *Duck & Cabbage Tree: A Pictorial History of Clothes in Australia, 1788–1914* (Sydney: Angus and Robertson)

Foley, Liza, 2014, '"An Entirely Fictitious Importance"? Reconsidering the Significance of the Irish Glove Trade: A Study of Limerick Gloves, 1778–1840', *Costume*, vol. 48, pp. 160–71

Forest, Jennifer, 2010, 'Jane Austen's Women and Their Crafts.' *Piecework*, September–October, pp. 14–18

Fortune, Brandon Brame, 2002, '" Studious men are always painted in gowns": Charles Willson Peale's *Benjamin Rush* and the Question of Banyans in Eighteenth-Century Anglo-American Portraiture', *Dress*, vol. 29, pp. 27–40

Freeman, Jean, 2002, *Jane Austen in Bath*, rev. edn (Chawton: Jane Austen Society)

Fulford, Tim, 1999, 'Romanticizing the Empire: The Naval Heroes of Southey, Coleridge, Austen, and Marryat', *Modern Language Quarterly*, no. 60, pp. 161–96

Fulford, Tim, 2002, 'Sighing for a Soldier: Jane Austen and Military Pride and Prejudice', *Nineteenth-Century Literature*, vol. 57, pp. 153–78

Fullerton, Susannah, 2012, *A Dance with Jane Austen: How a Novelist and Her Characters Went to the Ball* (London: Frances Lincoln)

G

Galperin, William H., 2003, *The Historical Austen* (Philadelphia, Pa.: University of Pennsylvania Press)

Garbett, Natalie, 2018, *A History of Women's Fashion from 1790 to 1820* (Havertown, Pa.: Pen and Sword)

Garry, Mary Anne, 2005, '"After they went I worked": Mrs Larpent and Her Needlework, 1790–1800', *Costume*, vol. 39, pp. 91–9

Gau, Colleen, 1999, 'Physiologic Effects of Wearing Corsets: Studies with Reenactors', *Dress*, vol. 26, pp. 63–70

Gayle, Jody, 2012, *Fashions in the Era of Jane Austen* (Columbia, Mo.: Publications of the Past)

Gayle, Jody, 2015, *Needlework Patterns after the Era of Jane Austen: Ackermann's Repository of Arts, Literature, Commerce, Manufactures, Fashions and Politics, 1821–1828* (Columbia, Mo.: Publications of the Past)

Geczy, Adam, 2013, *Fashion and Orientalism: Dress, Textiles and Culture from the 17th to the 21st Century* (London: Bloomsbury)

Gelpi, Barbara C., 1997, 'Significant Exposure: The Turn-of-the-Century Breast', *Nineteenth-Century Contexts*, vol. 20, pp. 125–45

Gernerd, Elisabeth, 2015, 'Pulled Tight and Gleaming: The Stocking's Position within Eighteenth-Century Masculinity', *Textile History*, vol. 46, pp. 3–27

Ginsburg, Madeleine, 1972, 'The Tailoring and Dressmaking Trades, 1700–1850', *Costume*, vol. 6, pp. 64–71

Ginsburg, Madeleine, 1980, 'Rags to Riches: The Second-Hand Clothes Trade, 1700–1978', *Costume*, vol. 14, pp. 121–35

Ginsburg, Madeleine, 1981, *Wedding Dress: 1740–1970* (London: HMSO)

Godman, Melina, 1989, 'Everyday Tailoring in the 1820s', *Costume*, vol. 23, pp. 80–85

Greig, Hannah, 2013, *The Beau Monde* (Oxford: Oxford University Press)

H

Hafner-Laney, Mary. 2010, '"I was tempted by a pretty coloured muslin": Jane Austen and the Art of Being Fashionable', *Persuasions*, vol. 32, pp. 135–43

Hansen, David, 2017, *Dempsey's People: A Folio of British Street Portraits, 1824–1844* (Canberra: National Portrait Gallery)

Harris, Jocelyn, 2007, *A Revolution Almost Beyond Expression: Jane Austen's Persuasion* (Newark: University of Delaware Press)

Hart, Avril, 2006, 'Nelson Remembered: Reproductions of Historical Naval Uniforms', *Costume*, vol. 40, pp. 8–12

Hart, Avril, and Susan North, 2009, *Seventeenth and Eighteenth-Century Fashion in Detail* (London: V&A Publishing)

Harvey, John R., 1995, *Men in Black* (Chicago: University of Chicago Press)

Harvey, Karen, 2015, 'Men of Parts: Masculine Embodiment and the Male Leg in Eighteenth-Century England', *Journal of British Studies*, vol. 54, pp. 797–821

Harvey, Karen, 2017, *History and Material Culture: A Student's Guide to Approaching Alternative Sources* (Abingdon, New York: Routledge)

Heard, Kate, 2013, *High Spirits: The Comic Art of Thomas Rowlandson* (London: Royal Collection Trust)

Hearn, Colleen Porter, 2010, 'Jane Austen's Views on Dance, Physical Activity, and Gender as an Interdisciplinary Topic', *Journal of Physical Education, Recreation and Dance*, vol. 81, no. 2, pp. 6–8

Hecht, J. Jean, 1956, *Domestic Servant Class in Eighteenth-Century England* (London: Routledge & Paul)

Heckscher, Eli F., 1922, *The Continental System: An Economic Interpretation* [1918], Harald Westergaard (ed.) (Oxford: Clarendon Press)

Heydt-Stevenson, Jillian, 2005, *Austen's Unbecoming Conjunctions: Subversive Laughter, Embodied History* (New York: Palgrave Macmillan)

Hill, Bridget, 1996, *Servants: English Domestics in the Eighteenth Century* (Oxford: Oxford University Press)

Hill, Constance, 1923, *Jane Austen: Her Homes and Her Friends* (London, New York: John Lane)

Hiner, Susan, 2010, *Accessories to Modernity: Fashion and the Feminine in Nineteenth-Century France* (Philadelphia, Pa.: University of Pennsylvania Press)

Holland, Vyvyan Beresford, 1988, *Hand Coloured Fashion Plates, 1770 to 1899* (London: B. T. Batsford)

Hollander, Anne, 1993, *Seeing through Clothes* (Berkeley: University of California Press)

Hollander, Anne, 1994, *Sex and Suits* (New York: Knopf)

Hollander, Anne, 2002, *Fabric of Vision: Dress and Drapery in Painting* (London: National Gallery)

Holmes, Richard, 2001, *The Oxford Companion to Military History* (Oxford: Oxford University Press)

Holmes, Richard, 2006, *The British Soldier in India, 1750–1914* (London: HarperPerennial)

Honan, Park, 1987, *Jane Austen, Her Life* (London: Weidenfeld & Nicolson)

Honor, Hugh, 1972, 'Neo-Classicism', in *The Age of Neo-Classicism: The Fourteenth Exhibition of the Council of Europe: The Royal Academy and the Victoria and Albert Museum, London, 9 September – 19 November 1972* (London: Arts Council of Great Britain), pp. 3–11

Hopkins, Vanessa, and Alan Hopkins, 2015, *Footwear: Shoes and Boots from the Hopkins Collection, c.1730–1950* (London: School of Historical Dress)

Hopkins, Vanessa, and Alan Hopkins, 2017, *Waistcoats from the Hopkins Collection, c.1720–1950* (London: School of Historical Dress)

Hubback, John Henry, and Edith Charlotte Hubback, 1906, *Jane Austen's Sailor Brothers: Being the Adventures of Sir Francis Austen and Charles Austen* (London: John Lane)

Hudelet, Ariane, 2009, 'Beyond Words, Beyond Images: Jane Austen and the Art of Mise en Scene', in *The Cinematic Jane Austen: Essays on the Filmic Sensibility of the Novels*, David Monaghan, Ariane Hudelet and

John Wiltshire (eds) (Jefferson, NC: McFarland), pp. 76–93

Hughes, Clair, 2005, 'Talk about Muslin: Jane Austen's Northanger Abbey', in *Dressed in Fiction* (London: Berg), pp. 33–46

Hughes Myerly, Scott, 1996, *British Military Spectacle: From the Napoleonic Wars through the Crimea* (Cambridge, Mass.: Harvard University Press)

Hume, Robert D., 2013, 'Money in Jane Austen', *Review of English Studies*, vol. 64, pp. 289–310

Hume, Robert D., 2014, 'The Value of Money in Eighteenth-Century England: Incomes, Prices, Buying Power – and Some Problems in Cultural Economics', *Huntington Library Quarterly*, vol. 77, pp. 373–416

Hunt, Lynn, 2009, 'Freedom of Dress in Revolutionary France', in *Fashion: Critical and Primary Sources*, vol. 2: *The Eighteenth Century*, Peter McNeil (ed.) (Oxford, New York: Berg), pp. 42–58

I

Inal, Onur, 2011, 'Women's Fashions in Transition: Ottoman Borderlands and the Anglo-Ottoman Exchange of Costumes', *Journal of World History*, vol. 22, pp. 243–72

Irwin, Francina, 1981, 'The Printed Shawl in Scotland, 1785–1870', *Costume*, vol. 15, pp. 24–39

J

Jenkins, D. T. (ed.), *The Cambridge History of Western Textiles* (Cambridge: Cambridge University Press, 2003)

Jocic, Laura, 2017, 'Anna King's Dress: Trade and Society in Early Colonial Sydney', in *Cosmopolitan Moments: Instances of Exchange in the Long Eighteenth Century*, Jennifer Milam (ed.), *emaj* [special issue 9.1] <emajartjournal.com/special-editions/cosmopolitan-moments/laura-jocic-anna-kings-dress-trade-and-society-in-early-colonial-sydney/> (accessed 9 April 2018)

Johnson, Claudia L., 1998, 'Fair Maid of Kent? The Arguments For (and Against) the Rice Portrait of Jane Austen', *Times Literary Supplement*, 13 March, pp. 14–15

Johnson, Claudia L., 2013, 'Jane Austen to the Life?' *Times Literary Supplement*, 23 August, online edn <www.the-tls.co.uk/tls/public/article1305725.ece>

Johnson, Claudia L., and Clara Tuite (eds), 2009, *A Companion to Jane Austen*, Blackwell Companions to Literature and Culture, 57 (Oxford: Wiley-Blackwell)

Johnson, Ellen Kennedy, 2011, 'The Contradictory Rhetoric of Needlework in Jane Austen's Letters and Novels', *Female Spectator*, vol. 15, no. 4, pp. 4–5

Johnston, Lucy, 2005, *Nineteenth-Century Fashion in Detail* (London: V&A Publications)

Jones, Hazel, 2014, *Jane Austen's Journeys* (London: Robert Hale)

Jones, Peter, 2006, 'Clothing the Poor in Early-Nineteenth-Century England', *Textile History*, vol. 37, pp. 17–37

Jordan, Elaine, 2000, 'Jane Austen Goes to the Seaside: Sanditon, English Identity, and the "West Indian" Schoolgirl', in *The Postcolonial Jane Austen*, You-me Park and Rajeswari Sunder Rajan (eds) (London, New York: Routledge), pp. 29–55

K

Kaplan, Deborah, 1996, 'Mass Marketing Jane Austen: Men, Women, and Courtship in Two of the Recent Films', *Persuasions*, vol. 18, pp. 171–81

Kaplan, Deborah, 2012, '"There she is at last": The Byrne Portrait Controversy', *Persuasions*, vol. 34, pp. 121–33

Kaplan, Laurie, 2010, 'Sense and Sensibility: 3 or 4 Country Families in an Urban Village', *Persuasions*, vol. 32, pp. 196–209

Kaplan, Laurie, 2011, 'London as Text: Teaching Jane Austen's "London" Novels In Situ', *Persuasions On-Line*, vol. 32 <jasna.org/persuasions/on-line/vol32no1/kaplan.html> (accessed 20 February 2014)

Karskens, Grace, 2002, 'Engaging Artefacts: Urban Archaeology, Museums and the Origins of Sydney', *Humanities Research*, vol. 9, pp. 36–56

Karskens, Grace, 2010, *The Colony: A History of Early Sydney* (Crows Nest, NSW: Allen & Unwin)

Karskens, Grace, 2011, 'Red Coat, Blue Jacket, Black Skin: Aboriginal Men and Clothing in Early New South Wales,' *Aboriginal History*, vol. 35, pp. 1–36.

Kelly, Ian, 2005, *Beau Brummell: The Ultimate Dandy* (London: Hodder and Stoughton)

Kidd, Laura K., and Jane Farrell-Beck, 1997, 'Menstrual Products Patented in the United States, 1854–1921', *Dress*, vol. 24, pp. 27–42

Kidd, Laura Klosterman, 1994, 'Menstrual Technology in the United States, 1854 to 1921' (unpublished PhD thesis, Iowa State University)

Kidwell, Claudia B., 1968, *Women's Bathing and Swimming Costume in the United States* (Washington DC: Smithsonian Institution Press)

Kindred, Sheila Johnson, 2004, 'Charles Austen: Prize Chaser and Prize Taker on the North American Station, 1805–1808', *Persuasions*, vol. 26, pp. 188–94

Kindred, Sheila Johnson, 2009, 'The Influence of Naval Captain Charles Austen's North American Experiences on *Persuasion* and *Mansfield Park*', *Persuasions*, vol. 31, pp. 115–29

Kindred, Sheila Johnson, 2017, *Jane Austen's Transatlantic Sister: The Life and Letters of Fanny Palmer Austen* (Toronto: McGill-Queen's University Press)

King, Brenda M., 2009, *Silk and Empire*, Studies in Imperialism (Manchester: Manchester University Press)

King, Steven, 2002, 'Reclothing the English Poor, 1750–1840', *Textile History*, vol. 33, pp. 37–47

Kittredge, Katharine, 2012, 'No Shame in Patchwork: Lessons Found in the Fiction for Labouring-Class Girls', unpublished paper presented at the 43rd Annual Meeting of the East-Central American Society for Eighteenth-Century Studies, Baltimore, 1–3 November

Koda, Harold, and Andrew Bolton, 2006, *Dangerous Liaisons: Fashion and Furniture in the Eighteenth Century* (New York: Metropolitan Museum of Art; New Haven: Yale University Press)

Küchler, Susanne, and Daniel Miller, 2005, *Clothing as Material Culture* (Oxford: Berg)

Kuchta, David, 2002, *The Three-Piece Suit and Modern Masculinity England, 1550–1850* (Berkeley: University of California Press)

L

Lambert, Miles, 1988, 'The Dandy in Thackeray's "Vanity Fair" and "Pendennis": An Early Victorian View of the Regency Dandy', *Costume*, vol. 22, pp. 60–69

Lambert, Miles, 2004a, 'Drapers, Tailors, Salesmen and Brokers: The Retailing of Woollen Clothing in Modern England, c.1660–1830', in *Wool Products and Markets: 13th–20th Century*, G. L. Fontana and G. Gayot (eds) (Padua: Cleup), pp. 1083–1101

Lambert, Miles, 2004b, 'Small Presents Confirm Friendship: The "Gifting" of Clothing and Textiles in England from the Late Seventeenth to the Early Nineteenth Centuries', *Text Journal* [Textile Society of Great Britain], vol. 32, pp. 24–32

Lambert, Miles, 2009, 'Sent from Town: Commissioning Clothing in Britain during the Long Eighteenth Century', *Costume*, vol. 43, pp. 66–84

Lambert, Miles, 2010a, 'Bespoke Versus Ready-Made: The Work of the Tailor in Eighteenth-Century Britain', *Costume*, vol. 44, pp. 56–65

Lambert, Miles, 2010b, 'Fashion in the Museum: The Material Culture of Artefacts', in *The Fashion History Reader: Global Perspectives*, Peter McNeil and Giorgio Riello (eds) (Abingdon, New York: Routledge), pp. 191–3

Lambert, Miles, 2014, 'Death and Memory: Clothing Bequests in English Wills 1650–1830', *Costume*, vol. 48, pp. 46–59

Landry, Donna, 2000, 'Learning to Ride at Mansfield Park', in *The Postcolonial Jane Austen*, You-me Park and Rajeswari Sunder Rajan (eds) (London, New York: Routledge), pp. 56–73

Lane, Maggie, 1986, *Jane Austen's England* (London: Hale)

Lane, Maggie, 1988, *A Charming Place: Bath in the Life and Times of Jane Austen* (Bath: Millstream Books)

Lansdell, Avril, 1973, 'A Guide to the Study of Occupational Costume in the Museums of England and Wales', *Costume*, vol. 7, pp. 41–55

Lansdell, Avril, 1977, *Occupational Costume and Working Clothes, 1776–1976* (Aylesbury: Shire Publications)

Laver, James, 1943, *Fashions and Fashion Plates, 1800–1900* (Harmondsworth: Penguin)

Lazaro, David E., and Patricia Campbell Warner, 2004, 'All-Over Pleated Bodice: Dressmaking in Transition, 1780–1805', *Dress*, vol. 31, pp. 15–24

Le Bourhis, Katell, 1989, *The Age of Napoleon: Costume from Revolution to Empire, 1789–1815* (New York: Metropolitan Museum of Art)

Lee, Hermione, 2005, *Virginia Woolf's Nose: Essays on Biography* (Princeton, NJ: Princeton University Press)

Le Faye, Deirdre, 1986, 'Fanny Knight's Diaries: Jane Austen through Her Niece's Eyes', *Persuasions*, Occasional Paper no. 2, pp. 5–27

Le Faye, Deirdre, 2002, *Jane Austen's 'Outlandish Cousin': The Life and Letters of Eliza de Feuillide* (London: British Library)

Le Faye, Deirdre, 2003, *Jane Austen: The World of Her Novels* (London: Frances Lincoln)

Le Faye, Deirdre, 2004, *Jane Austen: A Family Record* (Cambridge: Cambridge University Press)

Le Faye, Deirdre, 2007, 'Imaginary Portraits of Jane Austen', *Jane Austen Society Report*, pp. 42–52

Le Faye, Deirdre, 2012, 'Black Ink and Three Telltale Words: or, Not Jane Austen's Portrait', *Sensibilities*, no. 44, pp. 18–30

Le Faye, Deirdre, 2013, *A Chronology of Jane Austen and Her Family: 1600–2000* (Cambridge: Cambridge University Press)

Leitch, R., 1990, '"Here chapman billies tak their stand": A Pilot Study of Scottish Chapmen, Packmen and Pedlars', *Proceedings of the Society of Antiquaries of Scotland*, no. 120, pp. 173–88

Le Menn, Richard, 2015, *Les Petits-Maîtres de la mode: XIIe–XXIe siècles* (Paris: Éditions Richard Le Menn)

Lemire, Beverly, 1984, 'Developing Consumerism and the Ready-Made Clothing Trade in Britain, 1750–1800', *Textile History*, vol. 15, pp. 21–44

Lemire, Beverly, 1988, 'Consumerism in Pre-Industrial and Early Industrial England: The Trade in Secondhand Clothes', *Journal of British Studies*, vol. 27, pp. 1–24

Lemire, Beverly, 1991, *Fashion's Favourite: The Cotton Trade and the Consumer in Britain, 1660–1800* (Oxford, New York: Pasold Research Fund, Oxford University Press)

Lemire, Beverly, 1994, 'Redressing the History of the Clothing Trade in England: Ready-Made Clothing, Guilds, and Women Workers, 1650–1800', *Dress*, vol. 21, pp. 61–74

Lemire, Beverly, 1999, '"In the Hands of Work Women": English Markets, Cheap Clothing and Female Labour, 1650–1800', *Costume*, vol. 33, pp. 23–35

Lemire, Beverly, 2003, 'Domesticating the Exotic: Floral Culture and the East India Calico Trade with England, c. 1600–1800', *Textile: Cloth and Culture*, vol. 1, pp. 64–85

Lemire, Beverly, 2009, 'Revising the Historical Narrative: India, Europe, and the Cotton Trade, c. 1300–1800', in *The Spinning World: A Global History of Cotton Textiles, 1200–1850*, Giorgio Riello and Prasannan Parthasarathi (eds) (Oxford: Oxford University Press, Pasold Research Fund), pp. 205–25

Lemire, Beverly, 2010, *The British Cotton Trade, 1660–1815* (London: Pickering & Chatto)

Lemire, Beverly, 2013, *Cotton* (London: Bloomsbury)

Lemire, Beverly, 2015, '"Men of the World": British Mariners, Consumer Practice, and Material Culture in an Era of Global Trade, c. 1660–1800', *Journal of British Studies*, vol. 54, pp. 288–319

Lemire, Beverly, 2016, 'A Question of Trousers: Seafarers, Masculinity and Empire in the Shaping of British Male Dress, c. 1600–1800', *Cultural and Social History*, vol. 13, pp. 1–22

Leong, Roger, Peter McNeil and Susan Scollay, 2009, *Persuasion: Fashion in the Age of Jane Austen. Exhibition: 22 May to 8 November 2009* (Melbourne: National Gallery of Victoria)

Leuner, Kirstyn, and Katharina Boehm, 2012, '"The End of All the Privacy and Propriety": Fanny's Dressing Room in Mansfield Park', in *Bodies and Things in Nineteenth-Century Literature and Culture*, Katharina Boehm (ed.) (New York: Palgrave Macmillan), pp. 45–65.

Levey, Santina M, 2003, 'Machine-Made Lace: The Industrial Revolution and After', in *The Cambridge History of Western Textiles*, D. T. Jenkins (ed.), 2 vols (Cambridge: Cambridge University Press), vol. 2, pp. 846–52

Lévi-Strauss, Monique, 1988, *The Cashmere Shawl* (New York: Abrams)

Levitt, Sarah, 1986, *Victorians Unbuttoned: Registered Designs for Clothing, Their Makers and Wearers, 1839–1900* (London: Allen & Unwin)

Liscombe, Rhodri Windsor, 2008, 'From the Polar Seas to Australasia: Jane Austen, "English Culture," and Regency Orientalism', *Persuasions On-Line*, vol. 28 <http://www.jasna.org/persuasions/on-line/vol28no2/windsor-liscombe.htm> (accessed 20 February 2014)

Lister, Jenny, 2003, 'Twenty-Three Samples of Silk: Silks Worn by Queen Charlotte and the Princesses at Royal Birthday Balls, 1791–1794', *Costume*, vol. 37, pp. 51–65

Lloyd, Trevor, 1999, 'Myths of the Indies: Jane Austen and the British Empire', *Comparative Criticism*, no. 21, pp. 59–78

Long, Bridget, 2016, '"Regular progressive work occupies my mind best": Needlework as a Source of Entertainment, Consolation and Reflection', *Textile: Cloth and Culture*, vol. 14, pp. 176–87

Lynn, Eleri, 2010, *Underwear: Fashion in Detail* (London: V&A Publishing)

M

McCormack, Matthew, 2017, 'Boots, Material Culture and Georgian Masculinities', *Social History*, vol. 42, pp. 461–79

MacDonagh, Oliver, 1991, *Jane Austen: Real and Imagined Worlds* (New Haven: Yale University Press)

Macdonald, Gina, and Andrew Macdonald (eds), 2003, *Jane Austen on Screen* (Cambridge: Cambridge University Press)

McGuigan, Ron, and Robert Burnham, 2005, 'Sources on British Uniforms of the Napoleonic Period', *The Napoleon Series* <http://www.napoleon-series.org/research/bibliographic/c_brituniforms.html> (accessed 9 April 2018)

McGuire, Noreen, 'The Genteel Craft of Subversion: Amateur Female Shoemaking in the Late Eighteenth and Early Nineteenth Centuries', in *Love Objects: Emotion, Design and Material Culture*, Anna Moran and Sorcha O'Brien (eds) (London: Bloomsbury Academic, 2014), pp. 53–62

MacKinnon, Frank Douglas, 1937, *Grand Larceny: Being the Trial of Jane Leigh Perrot, Aunt of Jane Austen* (London: Oxford University Press)

Mackrell, Alice, 1986, *Shawls, Stoles, and Scarves* (London, New York: Batsford)

Mackrell, Alice, 1998, 'Dress in Le Style Troubadour', *Costume*, vol. 32, pp. 33–44

Mackrell, Alice, 2005, *Art and Fashion: The Impact of Art on Fashion and Fashion on Art* (London: Batsford)

McNeil, Peter, *Pretty Gentlemen: Macaroni Men and the Eighteenth-Century Fashion World* (London, New Haven: Yale University Press, 2018)

McNeil, Peter, and Giorgio Riello, 2010, 'The Fashion Revolution: The "Long" Eighteenth Century', in *The Fashion History Reader: Global Perspectives*, Peter McNeil and Giorgio Riello (eds) (Abingdon, New York: Routledge), pp. 173–8

Mactaggart, P., and R. A. Mactaggart, 1973, 'Some Aspects of the Use of Non-Fashionable Stays', *Costume*, vol. 7, pp. 20–28

Mactaggart, Peter, and Ann Mactaggart, 1979, 'Ease, Convenience and Stays, 1750–1850', *Costume*, vol. 13, pp. 41–51

Maeder, Edward, 1983, *An Elegant Art: Fashion & Fantasy in the Eighteenth Century. Los Angeles County Museum of Art Collection of Costumes and Textiles* (Los Angeles: Los Angeles County Museum of Art)

Mansel, Philip, 2005, *Dressed to Rule: Royal and Court Costume from Louis XIV to Elizabeth II* (London, New Haven: Yale University Press)

Margalit, Efrat, 2002, 'On Pettiness and Petticoats: The Significance of the Petticoat in Pride and Prejudice' *Persuasions On-Line*, vol. 23 <http://www.jasna.org/persuasions/on-line/vol23no1/margalit.html> (accessed 20 February 2014)

Marsh, Maggie, 2005, *Mr Noverre's Academy: A Georgian Dancing Master in Norwich* (Norwich: Norwich Early Dance Group / Running Angel)

Martin, Richard, and Harold Koda, 1994, *Orientalism: Visions of the East in Western Dress* (New York: Metropolitan Museum of Art)

Martin, Richard, and Karin L Willis, 1998, *The Ceaseless Century: 300 Years of Eighteenth-Century Costume* (New York: Metropolitan Museum of Art)

Maskiell, Michelle, 2009, 'Consuming Kashmir: Shawls and Empires, 1500–2000', in *Fashion: Critical and Primary Sources*, vol. 3: *The Nineteenth Century*, Peter McNeil (ed.) (Oxford, New York: Berg), pp. 207–40

Matthews David, Alison, 2006, 'War and Wellingtons: Military Footwear in the Age of Empire', in *Shoes: A History from Sandals to Sneakers*, Giorgio Riello and Peter McNeil (eds) (Oxford: Berg), pp. 116–37

Matthews David, Alison, 2015, *Fashion Victims* (London: Bloomsbury)

Maynard, Margaret, 1987, 'A Form of Humiliation: Early Transportation Uniforms in Australia', *Costume*, vol. 21, pp. 57–66

Maynard, Margaret, 1990, 'Civilian Clothing and Fabric Supplies: The Development of Fashionable Dressing in Sydney, 1790–1830', *Textile History*, vol. 21, pp. 87–100

Maynard, Margaret, 1994, *Fashioned from Penury: Dress as Cultural Practice in Colonial Australia* (Cambridge: Cambridge University Press)

Mee, Jon, 2000, 'Austen's Treacherous Ivory: Female Patriotism, Domestic Ideology, and Empire', in *The Postcolonial Jane Austen*, You-me Park and Rajeswari Sunder Rajan (eds) (London, New York: Routledge), pp. 74–92

Melchior-Bonnet, Sabine, 2001, *The Mirror: A History* (New York: Routledge)

Meunier, Céline, 2016, *Dans les armoires de l'impératrice Joséphine: La Collection de costumes féminins du château de Malmaison* (Versailles: Éditions Art Lys)

Miles, Adrian, Natasha Powers, Robin Wroe-Brown and Don Walker, 2008, *St Marylebone Church and Burial Ground in the 18th to 19th Centuries: Excavations at St Marylebone School, 1992 and 2004–6*, MOLAS Archaeology Studies, 46 (London: Museum of London Archaeology Service)

Milhous, Judith, and R. T. C. Hume, 2001, 'The Tailor's Shop at the Pantheon Opera, 1790–1792', *Costume*, vol. 35, pp. 24–46

Millard, Mary, 1983, '"Do you not dance, Mr. Elton?"', *Persuasions*, vol. 5, p. 14

Miller, Amy, 2007, *Dressed to Kill: British Naval Uniform, Masculinity and Contemporary Fashions, 1748–1857* (London: National Maritime Museum)

Miller, David, 2005, *The Duchess of Richmond's Ball, 15 June 1815* (Staplehurst, Kent: Spellmount)

Mirmohamadi, Kylie, 2014, *The Digital Afterlives of Jane Austen: Janeites at the Keyboard* (Basingstoke: Palgrave Macmillan)

Mohapatra, Himansu S., and Jatindra K. Nayak, 2000, 'Farewell to Jane Austen: Uses of Realism in Vikram Seth's *A Suitable Boy*', in *The Postcolonial Jane Austen*, You-me Park and Rajeswari Sunder Rajan (eds) (London, New York: Routledge), pp. 189–204

Monaghan, David, Ariane Hudelet and John Wiltshire (eds), 2009, *The Cinematic Jane Austen: Essays on the Filmic Sensibility of the Novels* (Jefferson, NC: McFarland)

Moore, Doris Langley, 1971, 'Byronic Dress', *Costume*, vol. 5, pp. 1–13

Moores, John Richard, 2015, *Representations of France in English Satirical Prints, 1740–1832* (London, New York: Palgrave Macmillan)

Morison, Stanley, 2009, *John Bell, 1745–1831: A Memoir* (Cambridge: Cambridge University Press)

Morley, Geoffrey, 1994, *The Smuggling War: The Government's Fight against Smuggling in the 18th and 19th Centuries* (Stroud: Alan Sutton)

Mosher, Robert, 2006, 'An Annotated Bibliography of Books on Napoleonic Period Uniforms', *The Napoleon Series* <www.napoleon-series.org/research/bibliographic/c_uniformology.html> (accessed 9 April 2018)

Mullan, John, 2012, *What Matters in Jane Austen?: Twenty Crucial Puzzles Solved* (London: Bloomsbury)

Murray, Venetia, 1998, *High Society: A Social History of the Regency Period, 1788–1830* (London: Viking)

N

Nichols, Marian J., 1996, 'Straw Plaiting and the Straw Hat Industry in Britain', *Costume*, vol. 30, pp. 112–24

Nicholson, Robin, 2005, 'From Ramsay's Flora MacDonald to Raeburn's MacNab: The Use of Tartan as a Symbol of Identity', *Textile History*, vol. 36, pp. 146–67

Nigro, Jeffrey, 2008, 'Visualizing Jane Austen and Jane Austen Visualizing', *Persuasions On-Line*, vol. 29 <http://www.jasna.org/persuasions/on-line/vol29no1/nigro.html>

Nigro, Jeffrey, 2010, 'Mystery Meets Muslin: Regency Gothic Dress in Art, Fashion, and the Theater', *Persuasions On-Line*, vol. 31 <www.jasna.org/persuasions/on-line/vol31no1/nigro.html> (accessed 20 February 2014)

Nigro, Jeffrey A., and William A. Phillips, 2015, 'A Revolution in Masculine Style: How Beau Brummell Changed Jane Austen's World', *Persuasions On-Line*, vol. 36 <www.jasna.org/publications/persuasions-online/vol36no1/nigro-phillips/> (accessed 20 February 2014)

P

Park, You-me, and Rajeswari Sunder Rajan (eds), 2000, *The Postcolonial Jane Austen* (London, New York: Routledge)

Parker, Geoffrey (ed.), 2005, *The Cambridge History of Warfare* (Cambridge, New York: Cambridge University Press)

Parker, Keiko, 2001, '"What part of Bath do you think they will settle in?": Jane Austen's Use of Bath in *Persuasion*', *Persuasions*, vol. 23, pp. 166–76

Percoco, Cassidy, 2015, *Regency Women's Dress: Techniques and Patterns, 1800–1830* (London: Batsford)

Perkins, Moreland, 2005, '*Mansfield Park* and Austen's Reading on Slavery and Imperial Warfare', *Persuasions On-Line*, vol. 26 <www.jasna.org/persuasions/on-line/vol26no1/perkins.htm> (accessed 20 February 2014)

Phagan, Patricia, and Vic Gatrell, 2011, *Thomas Rowlandson: Pleasures and Pursuits in Georgian England* (London: Giles)

Plotz, Judith, 2000, 'Jane Austen Goes to India: Emily Eden's Semi-Detached Home Thoughts from Abroad', in *The Postcolonial Jane Austen*, You-me Park and Rajeswari Sunder Rajan (eds) (London, New York: Routledge), pp. 163–88

Priestley, Ursula, 1993, 'Norwich and the Mourning Trade', *Costume*, vol. 27, pp. 47–56

Purdy, Daniel L., 1996, 'The Veil of Masculinity: Clothing and Identity via Goethe's "Die Leiden des jungen Werthers"', in *Lessing Yearbook XXVII* (Detroit: Wayne State University Press), pp. 103–29

Purdy, Daniel L., 1998, *The Tyranny of Elegance: Consumer Cosmopolitanism in the Era of Goethe* (Baltimore: Johns Hopkins University Press)

Purdy, Daniel L. (ed.), 2004, *The Rise of Fashion* (Minneapolis: University of Minnesota Press)

R

Ragg, Laura M., 1972, *Jane Austen in Bath* (Folcroft, Pa.: Folcroft Library Editions)

Rajan, Rajeswari Sunder, 2000, 'Austen in the World: Postcolonial Mappings', in *The Postcolonial Jane Austen*, You-me Park and Rajeswari Sunder Rajan (eds) (London, New York: Routledge), pp. 3–25

Rauser, Amelia, 2015, 'Living Statues and Neoclassical Dress in Late Eighteenth-Century Naples', *Art History*, vol. 38, pp. 462–87

Rauser, Amelia, 2017, 'Vitalist Statues and the Belly Pad of 1793', *Journal18: A Journal of Eighteenth-Century Art and Culture*, no. 3, <www.journal18.org/issue3/vitalist-statues-and-the-belly-pad-of-1793/> (accessed 13 April 2017)

Ray, Joan Klingel, and Richard James Wheeler, 2005, 'James Stanier Clarke's Portrait of Jane Austen', *Persuasions*, vol. 27, pp. 112–18

Rendell, Jane, 2002, *The Pursuit of Pleasure: Gender, Space & Architecture in Regency London* (New Brunswick, NJ: Rutgers University Press)

Ribeiro, Aileen, 1983, *A Visual History of Costume: The Eighteenth Century* (London, New York: B. T. Batsford)

Ribeiro, Aileen, 1986, *Dress and Morality* (New York: Holmes & Meier)

Ribeiro, Aileen, 1988, *Fashion in the French Revolution* (New York: Holmes & Meier)

Ribeiro, Aileen, 1991, 'Fashion in the Eighteenth Century: Some Anglo-French Comparisons', *Textile History*, vol. 22, pp. 329–45

Ribeiro, Aileen, 1995, *The Art of Dress: Fashion in England and France, 1750 to 1820* (London, New Haven: Yale University Press)

Ribeiro, Aileen, 1999, *Ingres in Fashion: Representations of Dress and Appearance in Ingres's Images of Women* (London, New Haven: Yale University Press)

Ribeiro, Aileen, 2008, 'Fashion à l'Antique: Thomas Hope and Regency Dress', in *Thomas Hope: Regency Designer*, David Watkin and Philip Hewat-Jaboor (eds) (London, New Haven: Yale University Press [for] the Bard Graduate Center for Studies in the Decorative Arts, Design, and Culture, New York), pp. 77–89

Ribeiro, Aileen, 2011, *Facing Beauty: Painted Women & Cosmetic Art* (London, New Haven: Yale University Press)

Richardson, Catherine, Graeme Murdock and Mark Merry, 2003, 'Clothing, Culture and Identity in Early Modern England: Creating a New Tool for Research', *Textile History*, vol. 34, pp. 229–34

Richmond, Vivienne, 2009, '"Indiscriminate liberality subverts the morals and depraves the habits of the poor": A Contribution to the Debate on the Poor Law, Parish Clothing Relief and Clothing Societies in Early Nineteenth-Century England', *Textile History*, vol. 40, pp. 51–69

Richmond, Vivienne, 2013, *Clothing the Poor in Nineteenth-Century England* (Cambridge: Cambridge University Press)

Riello, Giorgio, 2006, *A Foot in the Past: Consumers, Producers, and Footwear in the Long Eighteenth Century* (Oxford: Pasold Research Fund, Oxford University Press)

Riello, Giorgio, 2009, 'The Globalisation of Cotton Textiles: Indian Cottons, Europe, and the Atlantic World, 1600–1850', in *The Spinning World: A Global History of Cotton Textiles, 1200–1850*, Giorgio Riello and Prasannan Parthasarathi (eds) (Oxford: Oxford University Press, Pasold Research Fund), pp. 261–87

Riello, Giorgio, 2011, 'The Object of Fashion: Methodological Approaches to the History of Fashion', *Journal of Aesthetics and Culture*, vol. 3

Riello, Giorgio, 2013, *Cotton: The Fabric that Made the Modern World* (Cambridge, New York: Cambridge University Press)

Riello, Giorgio, and Prasannan Parthasarathi (eds), 2009, *The Spinning World: A Global History of Cotton Textiles, 1200–1850* (Oxford: Oxford University Press, Pasold Research Fund)

Riello, Giorgio, and Tirthankar Roy, 2009, *How India Clothed the World: The World of South Asian Textiles, 1500–1850* (Leiden, Boston: Brill)

Riley, Margot, 2005, 'Cast-Offs: Civilization, Charity or Commerce? Aspects of Second Hand Clothing Use in Australia, 1788–1900', in *Old Clothes, New Looks: Second Hand Fashion*, Alexandra Palmer and Hazel Clark (eds) (Oxford: Berg), pp. 49–66

Rizvi, Janet, Monisha Ahmed (India), 2009, *Pashmina: The Kashmir Shawl and Beyond* (Mumbai: Marg Publications)

Roberts, Charlotte, and Margaret Cox, 2003, *Health and Disease in Britain: From Prehistory to the Present Day* (Gloucester: Sutton Publishing)

Roberts, Warren, 1980, *Jane Austen and the French Revolution* (New York: St. Martin's Press)

Robinson Walker, Linda, 2013, 'Jane Austen, the Second Anglo-Mysore War, and Colonel Brandon's Forcible Circumcision: A Rereading of *Sense and Sensibility*', *Persuasions On-Line*, vol. 34 <www.jasna.org/persuasions/on-line/vol34no1/walker.html> (accessed 20 February 2014)

Roche, Daniel, 1994, *The Culture of Clothing: Dress and Fashion in the Ancien Régime* (Cambridge: Cambridge University Press)

Rodgers, Lise, 2011, 'Getting Dressed with Jane', *Sensibilities*, vol. 42, pp. 45–62

Rodi, Robert, 2012, *Bitch in a Bonnet: Reclaiming Jane Austen from the Stiffs, the Snobs, the Simps and the Saps* (Lexington, Ky.: n.pub.)

Rothstein, Natalie (ed.), 1984, *Four Hundred Years of Fashion* (London: Victoria and Albert Museum in association with William Collins)

Rothstein, Natalie, 1994, *The Victoria & Albert Museum's Textile Collection: Woven Textile Design in Britain from 1750 to 1850* (London: Victoria and Albert Publications)

S

Saïd, Edward, 1994, *Culture and Imperialism* (London: Vintage Press)

Sales, Roger, 1994, *Jane Austen and Representations of Regency England* (London, New York: Routledge)

Sanderson, Elizabeth, 1986, 'The Edinburgh Milliners 1720–1820', *Costume*, vol. 20, pp. 18–28

Sanderson, Elizabeth, 1997, 'Nearly New: The Second-Hand Clothing Trade in Eighteenth-Century Edinburgh', *Costume*, vol. 31, pp. 38–48

Sanderson, Elizabeth, 2001, '"The New Dresses": A Look at How Mantuamaking Became Established in Scotland', *Costume*, vol. 35, pp. 14–23

Schoeser, Mary, 2007, 'A Secret Trade: Plate-Printed Textiles and Dress Accessories, c.1620–1820', *Dress*, vol. 34, pp. 49–59

Scott, Anne M., 1976, 'Women's Working Dress on the Farms of the East Borders', *Costume*, vol. 10, pp. 41–8

Selwyn, David, 1999, *Jane Austen and Leisure* (London, Rio Grande, Ohio: Hambledon Press)

Selwyn, David (ed.), 2003, *Jane Austen and Lyme Regis* (Chawton: Jane Austen Society)

Sewell, William H., 2010, 'The Empire of Fashion and the Rise of Capitalism in Eighteenth-Century France', *Past & Present*, vol. 206, pp. 81–120

Shawcross, Rebecca, 2014, *Shoes: An Illustrated History* (London: Bloomsbury)

Simons, Judy, 2009, 'Jane Austen and Popular Culture', in *A Companion to Jane Austen*, Claudia L. Johnson and Clara Tuite (eds), Blackwell Companions to Literature and Culture, 57 (Oxford: Wiley-Blackwell), pp. 467–77

Skillen, Katharine, 2012, 'Travel in the Time of Jane Austen', *Austentations*, no. 12, pp. 6–10

Sleeper-Smith, Susan (ed.), 2009, *Rethinking the Fur Trade: Cultures of Exchange in an Atlantic World* (Lincoln: University of Nebraska Press)

Smiles, Sam, 2002, 'Defying Comprehension: Resistance to Uniform Appearance in Depicting the Poor, 1770s to 1830s', *Textile History*, vol. 33, pp. 22–36

Smith, Chloe Wigston, 2009, 'Dressing the British: Clothes, Customs, and Nation in W. H. Pyne's "The Costume of Great Britain"', *Studies in Eighteenth-Century Culture*, vol. 38, pp. 143–71

Smith, Chloe Wigston, 2010, 'Clothes without Bodies: Objects, Humans, and the Marketplace in Eighteenth-Century It-Narratives and Trade Cards', *Eighteenth-Century Fiction*, vol. 23, pp. 347–80

Smith, Chloe Wigston, 2013, *Women, Work and Clothes in the Eighteenth-Century Novel* (Cambridge: Cambridge University Press)

Smith, D. J., 1983, 'Army Clothing Contractors and the Textile Industries in the 18th Century', *Textile History*, vol. 14, pp. 153–64

Smith, Erin, 2010, 'Dancing in a New Direction: Jane Austen and the Regency Waltz', *Persuasions On-Line*, vol. 30 <http://www.jasna.org/persuasions/on-line/vol30no2/smith.html> (accessed 20 February 2014)

Smith, Kate, 2012, 'Sensing Design and Workmanship: The Haptic Skills of Shoppers in Eighteenth-Century London', *Journal of Design History*, vol. 25, pp. 1–10

Solinger, Jason D., 2012, *Becoming the Gentleman: British Literature and the Invention of Modern Masculinity, 1660–1815* (New York: Palgrave Macmillan)

Sorge, Lynn, 1998, 'Eighteenth-Century Stays: Their Origins and Creators', *Costume*, vol. 32, pp. 18–32

Sorge-English, Lynn, 2011, *Stays and Body Image in London: The Staymaking Trade, 1680–1810* (London: Pickering & Chatto)

Southam, Brian (ed.), 1987, *Jane Austen: The Critical Heritage*, vol. 2: *1870–1940* (London: Routledge & Kegan Paul)

Southam, Brian, 1999, 'Portraits of Jane and Cassandra Austen?', letter, *Times Literary Supplement*, 15 October, p. 19

Southam, Brian, 2000, *Jane Austen and the Navy* (London: National Maritime Museum)

Southam, Brian, 2003, 'Jane Austen's Sailor Brothers: Francis and Charles in Life and Art', *Persuasions*, vol. 25, pp. 33–45

Southam, Brian, 2006, *Jane Austen's Literary Manuscripts: A Study of the Novelist's Development through the Surviving Papers*, rev. edn (London: A. and C. Black)

Spufford, Margaret, 1984, *The Great Reclothing of Rural England* (London: Hambledon Press)

Squire, Geoffrey, 1970, 'Liberty, Equality and Antiquity: Dress, 1785–1820',

Costume, vol. 4, Supplement no. 1, pp. 4–16

Staniland, Kay, 1997, *In Royal Fashion: The Clothes of Princess Charlotte of Wales & Queen Victoria, 1796–1901* (London: Museum of London)

Staniland, Kay, 2000, 'Princess Charlotte's Wedding Dress', *Costume*, vol. 34, pp. 70–80

Starobinski, Jean (ed.), 1989, *Revolution in Fashion: European Clothing, 1715–1815* (New York: Abbeville Press)

Steedman, Carolyn, 2009, *Labours Lost: Domestic Service and the Making of Modern England* (Cambridge: Cambridge University Press)

Steele, Valerie, 2010, *The Berg Companion to Fashion* (Oxford, New York: Berg)

Stevens, Christine, 2002, 'Welsh Peasant Dress – Workwear or National Costume?', *Textile History*, vol. 33, pp. 63–78

Stobart, Jon, 2011, 'Gentlemen and Shopkeepers: Supplying the Country House in Eighteenth-Century England', *Economic History Review*, vol. 64, pp. 885–904

Styles, John, 1994, 'Clothing the North: The Supply of Non-Élite Clothing in the Eighteenth-Century North of England', *Textile History*, vol. 25, pp. 139–66

Styles, John, 2002, 'Involuntary Consumers? Servants and Their Clothes in Eighteenth-Century England', *Textile History*, vol. 33, pp. 9–21

Styles, John, 2007, *The Dress of the People: Everyday Fashion in Eighteenth-Century England* (London, New Haven: Yale University Press)

Styles, John, 2009, 'What Were Cottons for in the Early Industrial Revolution?' in The *Spinning World: A Global History of Cotton Textiles, 1200–1850*, Giorgio Riello and Prasannan Parthasarathi (eds) (Oxford: Oxford University Press, Pasold Research Fund), pp. 307–26

Styles, John, 2010, 'Custom or Consumption: Plebeian Fashion in Eighteenth-Century England', in *The Fashion History Reader: Global Perspectives*, Peter McNeil and Giorgio Riello (eds) (Abingdon, New York: Routledge), pp. 179–90

Sulloway, Alison G., 1989, *Jane Austen and the Province of Womanhood* (Philadelphia: University of Pennsylvania Press)

Summers, Leigh, 2002, 'Yes, They Did Wear Them: Working-Class Women and Corsetry in the Nineteenth Century', *Costume*, vol. 36, pp. 65–74

Sutherland, Kathryn, 2002, 'The Hampshire Sphinx: Bonnets, Portraits, and Family Stories: Jane Austen and Her Biographers', *Times Literary Supplement*, 6 December, pp. 15–16

Sutherland, Kathryn, 2005, *Jane Austen's Textual Lives: From Aeschylus to Bollywood* (Oxford: Oxford University Press)

Sutherland, Kathryn, 2014, 'Jane Austen and Social Judgement', *Discovering Literature: Romantics and Victorians* <www.bl.uk/romantics-and-victorians/articles/jane-austen-and-social-judgement> (accessed 13 March 2016)

Sutherland, Kathryn (ed.), 2017, *Jane Austen: Writer in the World* (Oxford: Bodleian Library)

Svelte, Dita, 2017, '"Do you call this thing a coat?": Wit, the Epigram and the Detail in the Figure of the Ultimate Dandy, Beau Brummell', *Fashion Theory*, vol. 22, pp. 1–28

Swain, Margaret, 1972a, 'Men's Nightgowns of the Eighteenth Century', *Zeitschrift für Waffen- und Kostümkunde*, vol. 14, pp. 105–16

Swain, Margaret H., 1972b, 'Nightgown into Dressing Gown: A Study of Mens' [sic] Nightgowns, Eighteenth Century', *Costume*, vol. 6, pp. 10–21

Swallow, Kelly Anne, 2015, *Regency Fashion: Taking a Turn through Time*, vol. 1: *Gowns*; vol. 2: *Ladies' Outerwear, Gentlemen's and Children's Clothing*; vol. 3: *Ladies' Accessories* <http://www.blurb.co.uk/b/6495924-regency-fashion-taking-a-turn-through-time> (accessed 9 July 2017)

Sykas, Philip, 1999. 'Calico Catalogues: Nineteenth-Century Printed Dress Fabrics from Pattern Books', *Costume*, vol. 33, pp. 57–67

Sykas, Philip A., 2001, 'The North West Pattern Book Survey', *Textile History*, vol. 32, pp. 156–74

Sykas, Philip A., 2009, 'Fustians in Englishmen's Dress: From Cloth to Emblem', *Costume*, vol. 43, pp. 1–18

T

Takeda, Sharon Sadako, and Kaye Durland Spilker, 2010, *Fashioning Fashion: European Dress in Detail, 1700–1915* (Los Angeles: Los Angeles County Museum of Art)

Tarrant, Naomi E. A., 1994, *The Development of Costume* (Edinburgh: National Museums of Scotland in conjunction with Routledge)

Tarrant, Naomi E. A., 1999, 'The Real Thing: The Study of Original Garments in Britain since 1947', *Costume*, vol. 33, pp. 12–22

Tarrant, Naomi E. A., 2010, 'The Arrival of the Country Relations: Alexander Carse's Painting of 1812', *Costume*, vol. 44, pp. 75–80

Tarrant, Naomi E. A., 2015, 'Mirrors and Sight: or How do I look in this?' *Costume*, vol. 49, pp. 158–67

Taylor, Lou, 1983, *Mourning Dress: A Costume and Social History* (London: G. Allen and Unwin)

Tebbutt, Melanie, 1984, *Making Ends Meet: Pawnbroking and Working-Class Credit* (London: Methuen)

Thompson, Allison, 2000, 'The Felicities of Rapid Motion: Jane Austen in the Ballroom', *Persuasions On-Line*, vol. 21 <www.jasna.org/persuasions/on-line/vol21no1/thompson.html> (accessed 20 February 2014)

Thompson, Allison, 2010, 'The Rules of the Assembly: Dancing at Bath and Other Spas in the Eighteenth Century', *Persuasions On-Line*, vol. 31<www.jasna.org/persuasions/on-line/vol31no1/thompson.html> (accessed 20 February 2014)

Thompson, James, and Suzanne R. Pucci (eds), 2003, *Jane Austen and Co.: Remaking the Past in Contemporary Culture* (Albany: State University of New York Press)

Thorburn, W. A., 1976, 'Military Origins of Scottish National Dress', *Costume*, vol. 10, pp. 29–40

Thornton, Nicholas, 1997, 'Enigmatic Variations: The Features of British Smocks', *Textile History*, vol. 28, pp. 176–84

Tobin, Shelley, 1999, *Marriage a La Mode: Three Centuries of Wedding Dress* (London: National Trust)

Todd, Janet (ed.), 2005, *Jane Austen in Context*, Cambridge Edition of the Works of Jane Austen (Cambridge: Cambridge University Press)

Tomalin, Claire, 2007, *Jane Austen: A Life*, rev. and updated edn (London: Penguin)

Toomer, Heather, and Elspeth Reed, 2013, *White-Embroidered Costume Accessories: The 1790s to 1840s* (Great Britain: Heather Toomer Antique Lace, 2008)

Toplis, Alison, 2011, *The Clothing Trade in Provincial England, 1800–1850* (London: Pickering & Chatto)

Tozer, Jane, and Sarah Levitt, 1983, *Fabric of Society: A Century of People and Their Clothes, 1770–1870. Essays Inspired by the Collections at Platt Hall, the Gallery of English Costume, Manchester* (Carno, Powys: Laura Ashley)

Tuite, Clara, 2000, 'Domestic Retrenchment and Imperial Expansion: The Property Plot of *Mansfield Park*', in *The Postcolonial Jane Austen*, You-me Park and Rajeswari Sunder Rajan (eds) (London, New York: Routledge), pp. 93–115

V

Vallone, Lynne, 1995, *Disciplines of Virtue: Girls' Culture in the Eighteenth and Nineteenth Centuries* (London, New Haven: Yale University Press)

Vickery, Amanda, 1993, 'Women and the World of Goods: A Lancashire Consumer and Her Possessions, 1751–1781', in *Consumption and the World of Goods*, Roy Porter and John Brewer (eds) (London: Routledge), pp. 274–304

Vickery, Amanda, 1998, *The Gentleman's Daughter: Women's Lives in Georgian England* (London: Yale University Press)

Vickery, Amanda, 2009a, *Behind Closed Doors: At Home in Georgian England* (New Haven: Yale University Press)

Vickery, Amanda, 2009b, 'The Theory & Practice of Female Accomplishment', in *Mrs. Delany & Her Circle*, Mark Laird and Alicia Weisberg-Roberts (eds) (London, New Haven: Yale Center for British Art, Sir John Soane's Museum in association with Yale University Press), pp. 94–109

Vickery, Amanda, 2013, 'Mutton Dressed as Lamb? Fashioning Age in Georgian England', *Journal of British Studies*, vol. 52, pp. 858–86

Vigeon, Evelyn, 1977, 'Clogs or Wooden Soled Shoes', *Costume*, vol. 11, pp. 1–27

Vincent, Susan J., 2009, *The Anatomy of Fashion: Dressing the Body from the Renaissance to Today* (Oxford, New York: Berg)

Vincent, Susan J., 2018a, *Hair: An Illustrated History* (London: Bloomsbury Visual Arts)

Vincent, Susan J., 2018b, 'Ogling and Quizzing: The Eyeglass in the Long Eighteenth Century', *Fashion Studies*, vol. 1 <www.fashionstudies.ca/ogling-quizzing-and-spyingoqs1>

W

Wagner, Tamara S., 2012, '"Would you have us laughed out of Bath?" Shopping Around for Fashion and Fashionable Fiction in Jane Austen Adaptations', in *Women, Popular Culture, and the Eighteenth Century*, Tiffany Potter (ed.) (Toronto: University of Toronto), pp. 257–73

Walker, Richard, 1985, *Regency Portraits*, 2 vols (London: National Portrait Gallery)

Walker, Richard, 1989, *Savile Row: An Illustrated History* (New York: Rizzoli)

Walsh, Claire, 2006, 'Shops, Shopping and the Art of Decision Making in Eighteenth-Century England', in John Styles and Amanda Vickery (eds), *Gender, Taste, and Material Culture in Britain and North America, 1700–1830* (New Haven: Yale Center for British Art, Paul Mellon Centre for Studies in British Art), pp. 13–26

Walsh, Claire, 2008, 'Shopping at First Hand? Mistresses, Servants and Shopping for the Household in Early Modern England', in *Buying for the Home: Shopping for the Domestic from the Seventeenth Century to the Present*, D. E. Hussey and Margaret Ponsonby (eds) (Aldershot: Ashgate), pp. 13–26

Waterhouse, Harriet, 2007, 'A Fashionable Confinement: Whaleboned Stays and the Pregnant Woman', *Costume*, vol. 41, pp. 53–65

Watkin, David, and Philip Hewat-Jaboor (eds), 2008, *Thomas Hope: Regency Designer* (London, New Haven: Yale University Press [for] the Bard Graduate Center for Studies in the Decorative Arts, Design, and Culture, New York)

Waugh, Norah, 1954, *Corsets and Crinolines* (London: B. T. Batsford; repr. New York: Theatre Arts Books, 1995)

Waugh, Norah, 1964, *The Cut of Men's Clothes: 1600–1900* (London: Faber and Faber; repr. 1994)

Waugh, Norah, 1968, *The Cut of Women's Clothes: 1600–1900* (London: Faber and Faber; repr. 1994)

Wells, Juliette, 2011, *Everybody's Jane: Austen in the Popular Imagination* (London, New York: Continuum)

Wheeler, David, 2004, 'Jane Austen and 18th-Century English Spa Culture', *English Studies*, vol. 85, pp. 120–133

Wheeler, Richard James, 1998, *James Stanier Clarke: His Watercolour Portrait of Jane Austen Painted 13th November 1815 in His 'Friendship Book'* (Sevenoaks: Codex)

Wheeler, Richard James, 1999, 'William Legg and the Rice Portrait', letter, *Times Literary Supplement*, 8 January, p. 15

White, Cynthia L., 1970, *Women's Magazines, 1693–1968* (London: Michael Joseph)

Whyte, Dorothy, 1970, 'Paisley Shawls, and Others', *Costume*, vol. 4, pp. 32–6

Whyte, Dorothy, 1976, 'Edinburgh Shawls and Their Makers', *Costume*, vol. 10, pp. 16–28

Wilcox, David, 2012, 'The Clothing of a Georgian Banker, Thomas Coutts: A Story of Museum Dispersal', *Costume*, vol. 46, pp. 17–54

Wild, Dawn, 2002, 'The Rice Portrait', *Times Literary Supplement*, 24 May, p. 17

Wilson, Cheryl A., 2009, *Literature and Dance in Nineteenth-Century Britain: Jane Austen to the New Woman* (Cambridge: Cambridge University Press)

Wilson, Elizabeth, 2007, 'A Note on Glamour', *Fashion Theory*, vol. 11, pp. 95–108

Wiltshire, John, 1992, *Jane Austen and the Body: 'The Picture of Health'* (Cambridge: Cambridge University Press)

Wiltshire, John, 2001, *Recreating Jane Austen* (Cambridge: Cambridge University Press)

Wiltshire, John, 2009, 'By Candlelight: Jane Austen, Technology and the Heritage Film', in *The Cinematic Jane Austen: Essays on the Filmic Sensibility of the Novels*, David Monaghan, Ariane Hudelet and John Wiltshire (eds) (Jefferson, NC: McFarland), pp. 38–56

Womick, Stephanie Robinson, 2011, 'Fashioning Femininities: Sartorial Literacy in English Domestic Fiction, 1740–1853' (unpublished PhD thesis, University of North Carolina at Greensboro)

Woods, R. I., 1996, 'The Population of Britain in the Nineteenth Century', in *British Population History: From the Black Death to the Present Day*, Michael Anderson (ed.) (Cambridge: Cambridge University Press), pp. 281–358

Wylie, Judith, 2007, '"Do you understand muslins, Sir?": Fashioning Gender in *Northanger Abbey*', in *Styling Texts: Dress and Fashion in Literature*, Cynthia G. Kuhn and Cindy L. Carlson (eds) (Youngstown, NY: Cambria Press), pp. 129–48

Y

Yaffe, Deborah, 2013, *Among the Janeites: A Journey through the World of Jane Austen Fandom* (Boston: Mariner Books / Houghton Mifflin Harcourt)

Yale Center for British Art, 1975, *The Kashmir Shawl* (New Haven: Yale University Art Gallery)

Yates, Bridget, 1973, 'Rural Dress in Norfolk', *Costume*, vol. 7, pp. 6–9

Young, Peter, 2013, *Oak* (London: Reaktion Books)

Picture credits

Index

Numbers in italics refer to image captions.